OUR THEATRES IN THE NINETIES BY BERNARD SHAW

IN THREE VOLUMES

VOLUME III

LONDON

CONSTABLE AND COMPANY

LIMITED

Revised and reprinted for this Standard Edition 1932
Reprinted 1948

PRINTED IN GREAT BRITAIN
BY R. & R. CLARK, LIMITED, EDINBURGH

OUR THEATRES IN THE NINETIES

LONDON

PUBLISHED BY

Constable and Company Ltd.

10—12 ORANGE STREET W.C.2

•

INDIA

Longmans, Green and Company Ltd.

BOMBAY. CALCUTTA MADRAS

•

CANADA

Longmans, Green and Company Ltd.

TORONTO

These criticisms were contributed week
by week to THE SATURDAY REVIEW from
January 1895 to May 1898

OUR THEATRES IN THE NINETIES

BETTER THAN SHAKESPEAR

THE PILGRIM'S PROGRESS. A mystery play, with music, in four acts, by G. G. Collingham; founded on John Bunyan's immortal allegory. Olympic Theatre, 24 December 1896.

BLACK-EY'D SUSAN; OR, ALL IN THE DOWNS. Douglas Jerrold's famous nautical drama, in two acts. Preceded by J. Maddison Morton's domestic comedy, in two acts, ALL THAT GLITTERS IS NOT GOLD. Adelphi Theatre, 23 December 1896.

THE EIDER DOWN QUILT. Farcical comedy, in three acts, by Tom S. Wotton. Terry's Theatre, 21 December 1896.

BETSY. The celebrated comedy, in three acts, by F. C. Burnand. Revival. Criterion Theatre, 29 December 1896.

HOLLY TREE INN. Adapted by Mrs Oscar Beringer from Charles Dickens's story. In one act. Terry's Theatre, 28 December 1896. [2 *January* 1897]

WHEN I saw a stage version of The Pilgrim's Progress announced for production, I shook my head, knowing that Bunyan is far too great a dramatist for our theatre, which has never been resolute enough even in its lewdness and venality to win the respect and interest which positive, powerful wickedness always engages, much less the services of men of heroic conviction. Its greatest catch, Shakespear, wrote for the theatre because, with extraordinary artistic powers, he understood nothing and believed nothing. Thirty-six big plays in five blank verse acts, and (as Mr Ruskin, I think, once pointed out) not a single hero! Only one man in them all who believes in life, enjoys life, thinks life worth living, and has a sincere, unrhetorical tear dropped over his death-bed; and that man—Falstaff! What a crew they are— these Saturday to Monday athletic stockbroker Orlandos, these villains, fools, clowns, drunkards, cowards, intriguers, fighters, lovers, patriots, hypochondriacs who mistake themselves (and are mistaken by the author) for philosophers, princes without any sense of public duty, futile pessimists who imagine they are confronting a barren and unmeaning world when they are only contemplating their own worthlessness, self-seekers of all kinds, keenly observed and masterfully drawn from the romantic-commercial point of view. Once or twice we scent among them an anticipation of the crudest side of Ibsen's polemics on the Woman Question, as in All's Well that Ends Well, where the man cuts as meanly selfish a figure beside his enlightened lady doctor wife as Helmer beside Nora; or in Cymbeline, where Posthumus, having, as he believes, killed his wife for inconstancy, speculates for a moment on what his life would have been worth if the same standard of continence had been applied to himself. And certainly no modern study of the voluptuous temperament, and the spurious heroism and heroinism which its ecstasies produce, can add much to Antony and Cleopatra, unless it were some sense of the spuriousness on the author's part. But search for statesmanship, or even citizenship, or any sense of the commonwealth, material or spiritual, and you will not find the making of a decent vestryman or curate in the whole horde. As to faith, hope, courage, conviction, or any of the true heroic qualities, you find nothing but death made sensational, despair made stage-sublime, sex made romantic, and barrenness covered up by sentimentality and the mechanical lilt of blank verse.

All that you miss in Shakespear you find in Bunyan, to whom the true heroic came quite obviously and naturally. The world was to him a more terrible place than it was to Shakespear; but he saw through it a path at the end of which a man might look not only forward to the Celestial City, but back on his life and say:—"Tho' with great difficulty I am got hither, yet now I do not repent me of all the trouble I have been at to arrive where I am. My sword I give to him that shall succeed me in my pilgrimage, and my courage and skill to him that can get them." The heart vibrates like a bell to such an utterance as this: to turn from it to "Out, out, brief candle," and "The rest is silence," and "We are such stuff as dreams are made of; and our little life is rounded by a sleep" is to turn from life, strength, resolution, morning air and eternal youth, to the terrors of a drunken nightmare.

Let us descend now to the lower ground where Shakespear is not disabled by his inferiority in energy and elevation of spirit. Take one of his big fighting scenes, and compare its blank verse, in point of mere rhetorical strenuousness, with Bunyan's prose. Macbeth's famous cue for the fight with Macduff runs thus:—

> Yet I will try the last: before my body
> I throw my warlike shield. Lay on, Macduff,
> And damned be him that first cries Hold, enough!

Turn from this jingle, dramatically right in feeling, but silly and resourceless in thought and expression, to Apollyon's cue for the fight in the Valley of Humiliation: "I am void of fear in this matter. Prepare thyself to die; for I swear by my infernal den that thou shalt go no farther: here will I spill thy soul." This is the same thing done masterly. Apart from its superior grandeur, force, and appropriateness, it is better claptrap and infinitely better word-music.

Shakespear, fond as he is of describing fights, has hardly ever sufficient energy or reality of imagination to finish without betraying the paper origin of his fancies by dragging in something classical in the style of the Cyclops' hammer falling "on Mars's armor, forged for proof eterne." Hear how Bunyan does it: "I fought till my sword did cleave to my hand; and when they were joined together as if the sword grew out of my arm; and when the blood run thorow my fingers, then I fought with most courage." Nowhere in all Shakespear is there a touch like that of the blood running down through the man's fingers, and his courage rising to passion at it. Even in mere technical adaptation to the art of the actor, Bunyan's dramatic speeches are as good as Shakespear's tirades. Only a trained dramatic speaker can appreciate the terse manageableness and effectiveness of such a speech as this, with its grandiose exordium, followed up by its pointed question and its stern threat: "By this I perceive thou art one of my subjects; for all that country is mine, and I am the Prince and the God of it. How is it then that thou hast ran away from thy

3

King? Were it not that I hope thou mayst do me more service, I would strike thee now at one blow to the ground." Here there is no raving and swearing and rhyming and classical allusion. The sentences go straight to their mark; and their concluding phrases soar like the sunrise, or swing and drop like a hammer, just as the actor wants them.

I might multiply these instances by the dozen; but I had rather leave dramatic students to compare the two authors at first-hand. In an article on Bunyan lately published in the Contemporary Review—the only article worth reading on the subject I ever saw (yes, thank you: I am quite familiar with Macaulay's patronizing prattle about The Pilgrim's Progress)—Mr Richard Heath, the historian of the Anabaptists, shews how Bunyan learnt his lesson, not only from his own rough pilgrimage through life, but from the tradition of many an actual journey from real Cities of Destruction (under Alva), with Interpreters' houses and convoy of Greathearts all complete. Against such a man what chance had our poor immortal William, with his "little Latin" (would it had been less, like his Greek!), his heathen mythology, his Plutarch, his Boccaccio, his Holinshed, his circle of London literary wits, soddening their minds with books and their nerves with alcohol (quite like us), and all the rest of his Strand and Fleet Street surroundings, activities, and interests, social and professional, mentionable and unmentionable? Let us applaud him, in due measure, in that he came out of it no blackguardly Bohemian, but a thoroughly respectable snob; raised the desperation and cynicism of its outlook to something like sublimity in his tragedies; dramatized its morbid, self-centred passions and its feeble and shallow speculations with all the force that was in them; disinfected it by copious doses of romantic poetry, fun, and common sense; and gave to its perpetual sex-obsession the relief of individual character and feminine winsomeness. Also—if you are a sufficiently good Whig—that after incarnating the spirit of the whole epoch which began with the sixteenth century and is ending (I hope) with the nineteenth, he is still the idol of all well-read children. But as he never thought a noble life worth living or a great work worth doing, because the commercial profit-and-loss sheet shewed that the one did not bring happiness nor the other money, he never struck the great vein—the vein in which Bunyan told of that "man of a very stout countenance" who went up to the keeper of the book of life and said, not "Out, out, brief candle," but "Set down my name, sir," and immediately fell on the armed men and cut his way into heaven after receiving and giving many wounds.

Let me not, however, be misunderstood by the Anglo-American Theatrical Syndicate, Limited, which has introduced the entertainment at the Olympic described as The Pilgrim's Progress, a mystery play, by G. G. Collingham, founded on John Bunyan's Immortal Allegory. That syndicate has listened to the voice of Demas; and I wish it joy of the silver mines to which he has led it. As to Mr Collingham, he does not take my view of the excellence of Bunyan's language or ideas. It is true that his hero is called Christian, and the villain Apollion, on the analogy of Rapscallion, Scullion, and the like, instead of Appol Lyon, which is what Bunyan called him. Also, three of the scenes are called Vanity Fair, The Valley of the Shadow of Death, and Doubting Castle, from which Christian escapes with the key called Promise. I fancied, too, I detected a paraphrase of a Bunyan passage in the following couplet:

> Heed not this king: he never gives reward,
> But always leaves his followers in the lurch.

But, these points apart, it would not have occurred to me that Mr Collingham or anyone else connected with the Olympic production had ever read or heard of Bunyan. It has been stated publicly that "Mr Collingham" is a lady who has been encouraged to venture a good deal of her private means on the production of a work which is perilously deficient in the stage qualities needed to justify such encouragement. If this is true, I need not say what I think of the enterprise. If not, I desire to treat it with respect because it has attracted capital; for the other day, when subscriptions were invited to produce Little Eyolf, several of those colleagues of mine who still devotedly keep knocking their heads against the Norwegian stone wall laid great stress on this failure on Ibsen's part to attract capital from the ordinary theatrical sources. I sardonically invite them to go and revel in The Pilgrim's Progress as a play which has attracted capital enough to produce Little Eyolf six times over.

The new bill at the Adelphi should not be missed by anyone who wishes to qualify as an experienced playgoer. All that Glitters is not Gold is a most fearful specimen of obsolete pinchbeck, in spite of the pleasant qualities of the author of Box and Cox. But, of course, what one goes for is Black-Ey'd Susan, not Wills's genteel edition, with which Mrs Kendal made us cry so at the St James's, but the real original, with San Domingo Billy, hornpipe, song about My sweet Willy-yum, and nautical lingo all complete. Mr Terriss makes brilliant play with his diamond shoe-buckles in the hornpipe, justifies his ear in his song, and delivers the jargon of the first two scenes like a conjurer producing miles of ribbon from his mouth. Miss Millward, when rudely accosted by Mr Fulton as Captain Crosstree, says, "He is intoxicated. I must hence," as if that were the most natural observation possible for the wife of an able seaman. But Black-Ey'd Susan, when it once gets to business, is an excellent play. It is the second act that tries the actor; and here Mr Terriss plays with perfect judgment, producing just the right effect of humble but manly sincerity and naturalness in great distress by the most straightforward methods. Is it not odd that the Adelphi is the only theatre in London devoted to sentimental modern drama where the acting is not vulgar? In other houses the actors' subordination of drama to "good taste," their consciousness of the stalls, their restrained drawing room voices, made resonant enough for the theatre by clarionet effects from the nose, their perpetual thinking of their manners and appearance when they ought to be thinking of their work, all produce a detestable atmosphere of candidature for social promotion which makes me wish sometimes that the stage were closed to all classes except only those accustomed to take their position for granted and their own ways as the standard

6

ways, or those who frankly make no social pretension at all. At the Adelphi the actors provide for their appearance in their dressing rooms, and when they come on the stage go straight for the play with all their force, as if their point of honor lay in their skill, and not in persuading smart parties in the boxes that it would be quite safe to send them cards for an "At Home" in spite of their profession. The result is that they look better, dress better, and behave better than their competitors at the intentionally fashionable theatres. Instead of having caught the "form" of South Kensington (and what an appalling complaint that is for anyone to catch!), they have universal good manners, the proof being that Mr Terriss, without the slightest self-disguise or "character-acting" trickery of any sort, is equally engaging and equally natural as the officer in One of the Best and as the common sailor in Black-Ey'd Susan. Miss Millward, though she is, I am told, always so scrupulously in fashion that women's hearts sink if they see her sleeves vary by an inch from their latest frocks, is always in her part, and always fits it if there is any sort of possible humanity and charm in it. Mr Fulton, too, is a courageous and self-respecting actor who is at home everywhere on the stage. Even Mr Harry Nicholls, badly spoiled funny man as he is, has serious qualities as an actor, and can make real bricks when the author provides any straw. In short, the secret of the Adelphi is not, as is generally assumed, bad drama, but simply good acting and plenty of it. And, unlike most critics, I am fond of acting.

The Eider Down Quilt, at Terry's, a somewhat artlessly amusing piece, owes a good deal to the genius of Miss Fanny Brough as a lady who has, as she believes, sat on a man and smothered him, and to Mr de Lange, who tries the very dangerous experiment of taking a purely farcical figure (an Italian waiter disguised as a prince), and making a realistic character study of him. However, the result justifies the attempt; and Alberto da Bologna is another of Mr de Lange's successes.

Betsy has been revived at the Criterion to give Mr Wyndham a holiday. I hope he will enjoy it at least as much as I enjoyed Betsy, which, though funny, is somewhat too pre-Ibsenite for

7

my taste.

The afternoon performances of Love in Idleness at Terry's now begin with Mrs Oscar Beringer's adaptation of Boots at the Holly Tree Inn, in which Master Stewart Dawson, late of Little Eyolf, and Miss Valli Valli play the tiny elopers. It is very prettily done, and just the sort of piece that old people like.

A MUSICAL FARCE

A MAN ABOUT TOWN. A new musical farce by Huan Mee. Music by Alfred Carpenter. Avenue Theatre, 2 January 1897.

[9 *January* 1897]

I CANNOT pretend to be an expert in the criticism of musical farce. When I was a musical critic I always contended resolutely that musical farces were in the nature of dramatic entertainments, and were consequently the business of the dramatic critic. Now that I am a dramatic critic, I have come to the conclusion that I was mistaken, and that a musical farce is clearly the business of the musical critic. Unfortunately this view, however sound in logic, does not work in practice as well as the other. A dramatic critic is so familiar with brainless sentiment and vulgar tomfoolery that he can stand anything except a masterpiece: a musical critic is so familiar with masterpieces that he can hardly stand anything else. Let him loose on a musical farce, and all his critical faculty is swept away by an overwhelming sense of outrage at the triviality and indecency of the spectacle which the management has dared to offer as a treat to him—to *him*, the intimate of Beethoven and Wagner! He becomes indignant, intolerant, impossible, libellous. It is as if you asked the Astronomer Royal to review Zadkiel's predictions or Napoleon's Book of Fate. As a practical journalist, I cannot refuse to recognize this. I still maintain that, technically, the criticism of musical farce is the business of the musical critic; but in view of the almost inconceivable damages in which this journal would probably be mulcted if it were made the vehicle for the feelings with which my musical colleague, pampered on weekly banquets of great works, contemplates the sort of thing

8

that syndicates delight in, I do not mind taking his place occasionally when the post seems likely to be one of exceptional danger. I mention these facts, not only to assert my own dignity, which seldom comes away from a musical farce quite unwounded, but because they are in themselves a significant criticism of the contemporary theatre.

Such an entertainment as A Man about Town seems to me to require close commercial as well as artistic criticism. If I go to see As You Like It, or Little Eyolf, or Black-Ey'd Susan, or any other known dramatic masterpiece, popular or classical, I have nothing to consider but the degree of artistic success attained in the representation. The result cannot be measured in money: when Miss Julia Arthur and Mr Cooper Cliffe take the places of Miss Ellen Terry and Sir Henry Irving in the cast of Cymbeline, though nobody expects quite so interesting a performance, nobody dreams of paying lower prices at the doors on that account. But when we come to a variety entertainment, whether at the theatre, the Aquarium, or a music-hall, I confess I do not see how judgment can be delivered without reference to quantity, quality, and price. I remember losing myself once in Milan, and wandering into a big garden where a crowd of people were consuming the usual light refreshments at small tables before a Punch and Judy stage large enough to accommodate human actors. I sat down with the rest, and, at the cost of a bottle of the Milanese equivalent for Apollinaris, witnessed a musical farce. Now that farce filled me with appreciation and even gratitude. But if I had had to leave my fireside (or anybody else's) on a winter night in London, and pay half a guinea to witness three acts of it, I should have felt myself the most pitiable of gulls at the fall of the curtain. Even if I had paid only a shilling for a gallery seat, I should not have considered myself handsomely treated as shillingsworths of entertainment go in London. For at a music-hall I could have procured on the same terms a larger quantity of singing and dancing of rather better quality, as well as an exhibition of acrobatic work, juggling, and tableaux vivants, all three involving a degree of genuine trained professional skill far beyond anything that musical farce demands.

What, then, is the justification for the difference in price between A Man about Town and the animated Punch and Judy
show of Milan? First, there is scenery. But why is it so ugly? In
the first act, an attempt at a harmony in two shades of terra-cotta,
carried out in the wall-paper, curtains, and upholstery, is murdered by a ceiling, a carpet, and a conservatory, of such horribly
discordant colors that it is difficult to look at them without a
shriek of agony. Why not repaint the ceiling, change the carpet,
and fill the conservatory with a bank of flowers of the right color?
Are not these the details which differentiate the "style" of a West
End theatre from the conventions of the Milanese booth, and the
makeshifts of the provinces? In musical farce a special degree of
ingenuity is required in dealing with interiors, because the stage
has to be left free for dancing. Carelessness as to the color of the
carpet becomes a crime under such circumstances.

Then, as to the dancing! Dancing is a very highly skilled art.
Roughly speaking, there are two broad divisions of it. In the
higher, or classical division, the dancer dances with her (or his)
whole body. In the lower, or step-dancing division, all that is
necessary is very rapid and neat bravura with the feet alone. The
stage, however, is always liable to the incursions of beauteous
persons whose misfortune it is to be unable to dance at all, and
who suffer from a similar disability in respect of singing or acting.
Some excuse being necessary for the exhibition of their charms on
the boards, an unskilled accomplishment had to be invented for
them. And this was the origin of the skirt-dance, or dance which
is no dance, thanks to which we soon had young ladies, carefully
trained on an athletic diet of tea, soda-water, rashers, brandy, ice-
pudding, champagne, and sponge-cake, laboriously hopping and
flopping, twirling and staggering, as nuclei for a sort of bouquet
of petticoats of many colors, until finally, being quite unable to
perform the elementary feat, indispensable to a curtsey, of lowering and raising the body by flexing and straightening the knee,
they frankly sat down panting on their heels, and looked piteously at the audience, half begging for an encore, half wondering

how they would ever be able to get through one. The public on such occasions behaved with its usual weakness. It is the foible of the gallery to affect connoisseurship, and to pretend to like what it does not understand. Besides, it felt the charm of the petticoats, and was mean enough to ape a taste for the poor girls' pitiful sham dancing, when it was really gloating over their variegated underclothing. Who has not seen a musical farce or comic opera interrupted for five minutes whilst a young woman without muscle or practice enough to stand safely on one foot—one who, after a volley of wild kicks with her right leg, has, on turning to the other side of the stage, had to confess herself ignominiously unable to get beyond a stumble with her left, and, in short, could not, one would think, be mistaken by her most infatuated adorer for anything but an object-lesson in saltatory incompetence— clumsily waves the inevitable petticoats at the public as silken censers of that *odor di femmina* which is the real staple of five-sixths of our theatrical commerce? Now I am no Puritan; and I have reached the age which is universally admitted to be the most abandoned to the power of beauty; but for the life of me I cannot admire a duffer. I am not to be fascinated too cheaply. The young lady who can do no more than the first sufficiently brazen girl in the street could may shake all the silk in Marshall & Snelgrove's at me in vain. As a critic I tick her off remorselessly thus:—"No strength, no skill, no work, no brains, no use." And then, as a human being, I add, "Poor girl! where will she be five years hence?" I have no doubt whatever that melancholy questions of this sort drive the better class of playgoers away from the houses where they suggest themselves, although the delight of the respectable playgoer in comic opera is proved by the solid popularity of the Savoy, where one can have plenty of fun, music, brilliant dresses, artistic decoration, and pretty faces, without an uneasy sense of being an accomplice in the most questionable sort of exploitation.

Such, then, was the birth of skirt-dancing. Its worthlessness has been to some extent alleviated by competition; for what everybody can do, soon begins to be done better by some than by others. In the early days of the fashion a first-rate classical dancer at the Alhambra put on a skirt and a few petticoats, and shewed what a skilled artist was like in a costume which was really rather an improvement on the ridiculous conventional dress, half ostrich, half teetotum, of the *prima ballerina assoluta*. It cannot be said that the experiment succeeded in making either the managers or the public much more exacting; but it suggested to less eminent artists that the instruction which had failed to make them conspicuous as classical dancers might make them quite resplendent as skirt-dancers. Consequently the altogether incompetent professional beauty began to give way to the ambitious ballet-girl, and to the step-dancer from the music-halls, the result, up to date, being a dance which is a mixture of cheap *pas seul* with the sort of kick-up a music hall "serio-comic" ends her turn with. And if only our audiences would exercise any sort of discernment in watching these performances, they might eventually get something like value for their money. The formula for criticizing a dancer is simple enough. At the two extremes of the art are the step-dancer who dances with the feet alone, with spine rigid, shoulders pushed up to the top of it and nailed hard there, fists clinched, neck stiff as iron, and head held convulsively as if only the most violent effort of continence on the dancer's part could keep it from exploding. At the other you have the perfect dancer along whose limbs the rhythmic stream flows unbroken to the very tips of the fingers and roots of the hair, whose head moves beautifully, whose nape and wrists make the music visible, who can flex the spine at each vertebra more certainly than an ordinary person can flex his finger at each joint, and who is the personification of skill, grace, strength, and health. Between the two extremes come dancers who can use not only their feet but their legs—cancanist high-kickers and the like—and dancers who can not only step and kick, but use their hands in a stiff, conscious way, and twitch and nod their heads grotesquely. Some of these can keep up appearances fairly with their elbows; but their stiff shoulders and necks bewray them. The frequency of these cases of partial results, obviously arrived at by mere external imitation of good dancers, convinces me that the ordinary system of training is brutally wrong. I found out long ago from my observation of orchestral conducting that the physical difference between Carl Rosa's conducting and Richter's was that Rosa, having observed, no doubt, that good conductors had remarkable play at the wrist, kept his shoulder genteelly rigid, and raised his bâton from the wrist, with the result that it acted like the lid of a tin box, whereas Richter raises his arm from the shoulder, and leaves his wrist and arm free to dance on the waves of rhythm. Most of our dancers, like most of our conductors, are Carl Rosas, not Richters. They persist in trying to work from the extremities instead of from the centre—to effect the cause instead of causing the effect. Delsarte pointed out this long ago; and if he had not tried to found a quack religion on his observation, he might have gained some respectful attention for it.

Now if I apply all this to the dancing of Miss Alice Lethbridge in The Man about Town, what do I find? First, that I must not class Miss Lethbridge with the impostors for whose incompetent sakes skirt-dancing was invented. She is a sufficiently hard-working and conscientious practitioner of the art in its present phase. Second, that she has not the constitutional promptitude and rapidity of pedalling—the *prestissimo vivacissimo*—which make the step-dancer, and that therefore she can hope to excel only in the slower movements—the *andantes* of the dance—which were popularized by Miss Kate Vaughan. And I find that her grace in this department is marred by the fact that in her dutiful determination to keep her shoulders down—the stock cry of the dancing school—she holds her head wilfully aloft from the neck, and so puts it out of the dance. It seems to me, as a mere amateur, that shoulders might very well be left to the action of gravitation if only their proprietresses would let their spines alone and not hold them like pokers. At all events, it is in the carriage of her head that Miss Lethbridge clearly falls short in her dancing; and as there is no compensating brilliancy in the twinkling of her feet, I am reluctantly obliged to confess that I did not share the apparently entire and enthusiastic satisfaction of the gallery with

13

her performance.

There is nothing left to judge A Man about Town by except the players. In a silly sort of way, I found their odds and ends of fun amusing enough—better, at all events, than I expected. But then, I confess, I was prepared for the worst. Mr Lonnen sticks, as ever, unaffectedly to his work, and disarms the natives of this innocent country by his light-heartedly sympathetic blarney. Miss Alma Stanley raises musical farce to genial magnificence. Mr Sidney Howard's Frenchman is clever and most artistically executed—quite the best bit of work in the piece, technically. And Miss May Edouin worried her part so pluckily that it passed as quite a success.

The gallery was specially fractious, because matters have now come to a pass at which managers have to surround the first-nighters upstairs with a cordon of police. The gallery declares that this is an attack on its right to hoot and hiss. With due respect, the gallery has no right to hoot, nor to hiss, nor to indulge in any other offensive demonstration towards its fellow-citizens, whether authors or actors. If a play fails, the penalty to both author, manager, and company is quite severe enough without being aggravated by the infliction of the pillory. If it succeeds, the fact will become apparent at the pay-boxes without any uproar. My advice to the gallery is to do what the balcony does—behave itself.

SATAN SAVED AT LAST

THE SORROWS OF SATAN, a play in four acts. Adapted by Herbert Woodgate and Paul M. Berton from the famous novel of that name, by Marie Corelli. Shaftesbury Theatre, 9 January 1897.
[16 *January* 1897]

I WISH this invertebrate generation would make up its mind either to believe in the devil or disbelieve in him. The Norwegians, we learn from Ibsen's Brand, prefer an easygoing God, whom they can get round, and who does not mean half what he says when he is angry. I have always thought that there is a good deal to be said for this amiable theology; but when it comes to the devil, I claim, like Brand, "all or nothing." A snivelling, remorseful devil, with his heart in the right place, sneaking about the area railings of heaven in the hope that he will presently be let in and forgiven, is an abomination to me. The Lean Person in Peer Gynt, whose occupation was gone because men sinned so half-heartedly that nobody was worth damning, gained my sympathy at once. But a devil who is himself half-hearted—whose feud with heaven is the silliest sort of lovers' quarrel—who believes that he is in the wrong and God in the right—pah! He reminds me of those Sunday School teachers who cannot keep from drinking and gambling, though they believe in teetotalism and long to be the most respectable men in the parish. I cannot conceive how such a creature can charm the imagination of Miss Marie Corelli. It will be admitted that she is not easy to please when fashionable women and journalists are in question. Then why let the devil off so cheaply?

Let me not, however, dismiss The Sorrows of Satan too cavalierly; for I take Miss Marie Corelli to be one of the most sincere and independent writers at present before the public. Early in 1886, when she made her mark for the first time with A Romance of Two Worlds, she took her stand boldly as the apostle of romantic religion. "Believe," she said, "in anything or everything miraculous and glorious—the utmost reach of your faith can with difficulty grasp the majestic reality and perfection of everything you can see, desire, or imagine." Here we have that sure mark of romantic religion—the glorification of the miraculous. Again, "walking on the sea can be accomplished now by anyone who has cultivated sufficient inner force." Two years later, A Romance of Two Worlds was prefaced by a list of testimonials from persons who had found salvation in the Electric Christianity of the novel. Lest anyone should suppose that Electric Christianity was a fictitious religion, Miss Corelli took the opportunity to say of it, "Its tenets are completely borne out by the New Testament, which sacred *little book* [italics mine], however, has much of its mystical and true meaning obscured nowadays through the indifference of those who read and the apathy of those who hear. . . . My creed has its foundation in Christ alone . . . only Christ, only the old old story of Divine love and sacrifice. . . . The proof of the theories set forth in the Romance is, as I have stated, easily to be found in the New Testament. . . . I merely endeavored to slightly shadow forth the miraculous powers which I *know* are bestowed on those who truly love and understand the teachings of Christ." The miraculous powers, I may mention, included making trips round the solar system, living for ever, seeming to improvise on the pianoforte by playing at the dictation of angels, knocking people down with electric shocks at will and without apparatus, painting pictures in luminous paint, and cognate marvels. When I say that Miss Corelli is sincere, I of course do not mean that she has ever acted on the assumption that her "religion" is real. But when she takes up her pen, she imagines it to be real, because she has a prodigiously copious and fluent imagination, without, as far as I have been able to ascertain, the knowledge, the training, the observation, the critical faculty, the humor, or any other of the acquirements and qualities which compel ordinary people to distinguish in some measure (and in some measure only; for the best of us is not wholly un-Corellian) between what they may sanely believe and what they would like to believe. Great works in fiction are the arduous victories of great minds over great imaginations: Miss Corelli's works are the cheap victories of a profuse imagination over an apparently commonplace and carelessly cultivated mind. The story of the Passion in the New Testament not being imaginative enough for her, and quite superfluously thoughtful and realistic, she rewrote it to her taste; and the huge circulation of her version shows that, to the minds of her readers, she considerably improved it. Having made this success with the hero of Barabbas, she next turned her attention to Satan, taking all the meaning out of him, but lavishing imagination on him until he shone all over with stage fire. I do not complain of the process: I neither grudge Miss Corelli to her disciples nor her disciples to Miss Corelli; but I must warn my readers that nothing that I have to say about the play must be taken as implying that it is possible, real, or philosophically coherent.

Let me now come down from my high horse, and take the play on its own ground. The romantic imagination is the most un-originative, uncreative faculty in the world, an original romance being simply an old situation shewn from a new point of view. As John Gabriel Borkman says, "the eye, born anew, transforms the old action." Miss Corelli's eye, not having been born anew, transforms nothing. Only, it was born recently enough to have fallen on the music dramas of Wagner; and just as she gave us, in Thelma, a version of the scene in Die Walküre where Brynhild warns Siegmund of his approaching death, so in The Sorrows of Satan she reproduces Vanderdecken, the man whose sentence of damnation will be cancelled if he can find one soul faithful to the death. Wagner's Vanderdecken is redeemed by a woman; but Miss Corelli, belonging to that sex herself, knows better, and makes the redeemer a man. I am bound to say that after the most attentive study of the performance, I am unable to report the logical connection between the drowning of Geoffrey Tempest in the shipwreck of Satan-Vanderdecken Rimanez' yacht in the Antarctic circle, and the immediate ascension to heaven of Satan in a suit of armor; but I have no doubt it is explained in the novel: at all events, the situation at the end of the Flying Dutchman, with the ship sinking, and the redeemed man rising from the sea in glory, is quite recognizable. It seems hard that Geoffrey Tem-pest should be left in the cold water; but the spectacle of Satan ascending in fifteenth-century splendor, with his arm round a gentleman in shirt and trousers, evidently would not do; so poetic justice has to be sacrificed to stage effect.

The most forcible scene in the play is that in the fourth act, where the villain of the piece, Lady Sybil, plays false to her trust-ing husband by trying to seduce the virtuous demon. In an ordinary man-made play the villain would be a man and the sym-pathetic personages women; but as The Sorrows of Satan are woman-made, the sexes are reversed. This novelty is heightened by the operatic culture of the author, which enables her to blend the extremity of modern fashionableness with the extremity of medieval superstition, in the assured foreknowledge that the public will not only stand it but like it. All the essentials of the church scene from Gounod's Faust are in that fourth act, with even some of the accessories—the organ, for instance. The scene succeeds, as certain other scraps of the play succeed, because Miss Corelli has the courage and intensity of her imagination. This does not, of course, save her from absurdity—indeed it rather tends to involve her in it—but absurdity is the one thing that does not matter on the stage, provided it is not psychological absurdity. Still, a dramatist had better not abuse his immunity from common sense. It is true that if a man goes into the National Gallery, and raises the objection that all these pretended figures and landscapes and interiors are nothing but canvas and colored clay, there is nothing for it but to conduct him to the entrance and shoot him gently over the balustrade into the prosaic street. All the same, the more completely a painter can make us overlook that objection the better. Miss Corelli is apt to forget this. The introduction of a devil in footman's livery passed off excellently; but when he subsequently turned his hand to steering the yacht, and adopted a cardinal's costume as the most convenient for that duty, I confess I began to realize what a chance the management lost in not securing Mr Harry Nicholls for the part. The young nobleman who played baccarat so prodigally did not shatter my illusions until he suddenly staked his soul, at which point I missed Meyerbeer's Robert le Diable music rather badly. On the other hand, I have no objection whatever to Satan, after elaborately disguising himself as a modern *chevalier d'industrie*, giving himself away by occasional flashes of lightning. Without them the audience would not know that he was the devil: besides, it reminds one of Edmund Kean.

These, however, are trifles: any play can be ridiculed by simply refusing to accept its descriptive conventions. But, as I have said, a play need not be morally absurd. Real life, in spite of the efforts of States, Churches, and individuals to reduce its haphazards to order, *is* morally absurd for the most part: Prometheus gains but little on Jupiter; and his defeats are the staple of tragedy. It is the

privilege of the drama to make life intelligible, at least hypothetic-
ally, by introducing moral design into it, even if that design be
only to shew that moral design is an illusion, a demonstration
which cannot be made without some counter-demonstration of
the laws of life with which it clashes. If the dramatist repudiates
moral interest, and elects to depend on humor, sensuousness, and
romance, all the more must he accept the moral conventions
which have become normal on the stage. Now Miss Corelli has
flatly no humor—positively none at all. She is, in a very bookish
way, abundantly sensuous and romantic; but she vehemently
repudiates the conventional moral basis, professing, for instance,
a loathing for the normal course of fashionable society, with its
marriage market, its spiritual callousness, and its hunt for pleasure
and money. But if Miss Corelli did not herself live in the idlest of
all worlds, the world of dreams and books (so idle that people do
not even learn to ride and shoot and sin in it), she would know
that it is vain to protest against a necessary institution, however
corrupt, until you have an efficient and convincing substitute
ready. "Electric Christianity" (symbolized in the play by Satan's
flashes of lightning) will not convince anybody with a reasonably hard head on his or her shoulders that it is an efficient substitute even for the morals of Mayfair. The play is morally absurd
from beginning to end. Satan is represented, not as the enemy of
God, but as his victim and moral superior: nevertheless he wor-
ships God and is rewarded by reconciliation with him. He is
neither Lucifer nor Prometheus, but a sham revolutionist bidding
for a seat in the Cabinet. Lady Sybil is stigmatized as a "wanton"
because she marries for money; but the man who buys her in the
marriage market quite openly by offering to take "The Hall,
Willowsmere," if she will marry him, as a set-off to the disagree-
ableness of living with a man she does not care for, not only
passes without reproach, and is permitted to strike virtuous attitudes at her expense, but actually has his death accepted as a
sufficient atonement to redeem the devil. Please observe that he
is thereby placed above Christ, whose atonement and resistance
to the temptation in the desert were ineffectual as far as Satan was

concerned. At the same time we are permitted to take to our bosoms an American girl, because, to gratify her Poppa's love of a title without forfeiting her own self-respect, she has heroically refused a silly young Duke and married a venal old Earl. Further, the parade of contempt for wealth and fashion is accompanied by the rigid exclusion of all second-class, poor or lowly persons from the play except in the capacity of servants. The male characters are a Prince, a millionaire, an Earl, a Viscount, a Duke, and a Baronet, with their servants, two caricatured solicitors and a publisher being introduced for a moment to be laughed at for their vulgarity. The feminine side is supplied by Lady Sybil, Lady Mary, Miss Charlotte Fitzroy (who, lest her name should fail to inspire awe, is carefully introduced as "Lord Elton's sister-in-law"), a millionairess, a Duchess, one vulgar but only momentary landlady, and Mavis Clare. Mavis Clare might be Miss Corelli herself, so haughtily does she scorn the minions of fashion and worms of the hour (as Silas Wegg put it) who provide her with the only society she seems to care for.

The adaptation from Miss Corelli's novel has been made by Messrs Herbert Woodgate and Paul Berton. I nevertheless hold Miss Corelli responsible for it. She is quite as capable of dramatizing her novels as anyone who is likely to save her the trouble; and a little work in this direction would do her no harm. A good deal of the dialogue is redundant, slovenly, and full of reach-me-down phrases which vulgarize every scene in which the author has not been stirred up by strong feeling. Most of the critics of whose hostility Miss Corelli complains so bitterly could teach her to double the distinction of her style in ten lessons. No doubt she could return the compliment by elevating their imaginations; so the lessons could be arranged on reciprocal terms.

The play has not called forth any great display of acting at the Shaftesbury. Mr Lewis Waller, by a touch or two on his eye-brows, makes himself passably like the famous devil on the roof of Notre Dame, and keeps up appearances so well that he appears to be talking impressively and cleverly even when he is observing at a garden party that "the man who pretends to understand women betrays the first symptoms of insanity." Mr Yorke Stephens, with unquenchable politeness and unassailable style, fulfils his obligations to Miss Corelli and the audience most scrupulously, but with the air of a man who has resolved to shoot himself the moment the curtain is down. He lacks that priceless gift of stupidity which prevents most leading men from knowing a bad part from a good one; and so, though he plays Geoffrey Tempest expertly, he cannot wallow in him as a worse actor might. His address never fails him; but as he is essentially a sceptical actor, his function of the Redeemer of Satan does not seem to impress him; and there is a remarkably reassuring ring in his "O Lucio, Lucio, my heart is broken!" Miss Granville would do very well as Lady Sybil if only she were trained hard enough to get the requisite force of execution and to maintain her grip firmly all through. As it is, she hardly gets beyond a string of creditable attempts to act. The other parts are of no great importance.

There is a play without words at the Prince of Wales' Theatre, entitled A Pierrot's Dream, about which I have more to say than there is room for this week. Meanwhile I may admit that I found it a very delectable entertainment, Mlle Litini's Pierrot having a quite peculiar charm in addition to the accomplishments which one expects as a matter of course from Pierrots. Rossi's Pochinet, in a rougher way, is also excellent.

AT THE PANTOMIME

ALADDIN. The Drury Lane Pantomime. Arranged by Mr Oscar Barrett. Scenario partly by the late Sir Augustus Harris. Written by Arthur Sturgess and Horace Lennard.

[23 *January* 1897]

WHEN the Superior Person—myself, for instance—takes it upon himself to disparage burlesque, opera bouffe, musical farce, and Christmas pantomime as the mere sillinesses and levities of the theatre, let him not forget that but for them our players would have no mimetic or plastic training, and the art of the stage

21

machinist, the costumier, the illusionist scene-painter would be extinct. The late Sir Augustus Harris's description of Wagner's Das Rheingold as "a damned pantomime" was, on its own plane, a thoroughly sound one. For suppose the theatre had been given over entirely throughout this century to plays of the Robertson and Pinero school, performed in the Hare-Bancroft style, in built-in stage drawing rooms, by actors tailored and millinered as they would be for a fashionable At-home. Das Rheingold would in that case have been impossible: nobody would have known how to work the changes, to suspend the Rhine maidens, to transform Alberich into a dragon, to assemble the black clouds that are riven by Donner's thunderbolt, or to light up Froh's rainbow bridge. Under such circumstances, some of the most magnificent pages in the Rheingold score would not have come into existence; for your great man does not waste his work on the impracticable. And pray how was it that Wagner found the stage machinists ready for the series of landscape and seascape effects which we find in his most characteristic works? Nay, how did the much simpler stage illusions of Der Freischütz, Oberon, and Robert le Diable become possible before the Bayreuth epoch? The answer surely is that during all those years which are marked for us in theatrical annals only by events in the careers of great artists, there must have been a continual output of ballets, extravaganzas, and fairy plays of all sorts, in which the phantasmagoric properties of paint and pasteboard, traps and transformations, red fire and green glasses, were studied and cultivated much more practically and incessantly than the five species of counterpoint. To experts in this odd craft, Das Rheingold was no impossible dream, but simply "a damned pantomime." It is clear to me, then, that we owe the present enormously effective form of the Nibelung tetralogy, a work which towers among the masterpieces of the world's art, to the persistence of just such entertainments as Aladdin.

This relationship between Bayreuth and Drury Lane is by no means unconscious on the part of Drury Lane. The two are on borrowing terms. Twenty years ago it would have seemed the wildest extravagance to suggest that we should soon have Wagner figuring alongside the music-hall composers in a medley of popular music; but the thing has come to pass for all that. Aladdin's combat with the Slave of the Lamp is accompanied by the heroic strains of the famous Siegfried motifs; and the trombones blare out Alberich's curse on the Ring when mention is first made of Abanazar's greed for gold. Such quotations would once have produced the effect of a violently incongruous patch on the rest of the musical fabric, resembling it neither in harmony, melodic intervals, nor instrumental coloring. Today the Wagnerian technique has been so completely assimilated and popularized that the quotations are quite indistinguishable by anyone who does not know the originals. On the other hand, a bar from a minuet by Mozart, Schubert, or Beethoven stands out delicately and elegantly in very notable contrast to the modern style.

As it happens, being no great pantomime goer, I never saw one of Mr Oscar Barrett's pantomimes until I went to Aladdin; so I am perhaps unwittingly disparaging his former achievements when I say that it is the best modern Christmas pantomime I have seen. Not that it is by any means faultless. It is much too long, even for the iron nerves of childhood. The first part alone would be a very ample and handsome entertainment. But if thirteen changes and a transformation are *de rigueur*, the surfeit might be lightened by a little cutting; for one or two of the scenes, especially the laundry scene in the first part, are dragged out to a tediousness that defies even Mr Dan Leno's genius. The instrumentation of the ballet in the second part, too, unaccountably discredits the musical taste and knowledge which are so conspicuous in the first part. For here, just at the point when about two and a half hours of orchestration have made one's nerves a little irritable, this big, glittering ballet begins with a reinforcement of two military bands, coarse in tone, and with all the infirmities of intonation produced by valves in brass instruments. The result is a pandemonium which destroys the hitherto admirable balance of sound, and sets up just that perilous worry—the bane of spectacular ballets—which Mr Barrett up to that moment triumphantly avoids. This is the more unexpected because the ballet scene in the first part is a conspicuous example of just the kind of musical judgment that fails him afterwards. In it Mr Barrett fills the back of the stage with trumpets, and overwhelms the house with their ringing clangor, the effect, though of the fiercest kind within the limits of music, being magnificent. But this clarion outbreak is the climax of a long series of effects beginning quietly with a unison movement for the bass strings, and gradually leading up to the *coup de cuivre*. It is astonishing that the same hand that planned the music of this scene should afterwards begin a similar one by flinging those two horrible extra bands at our heads.

Let me add, so as to get my faultfinding all together, that I do not see why the traditional privileges of vulgarity in a pantomime should be so scrupulously respected by a manager whose reputation has been made by the comparative refinement of his taste and the superiority of his culture in spectacular and musical matters. Why, for instance, is the "principal boy" expected to be more vulgar than the principal girl, when she does not want to, and when there is not the slightest reason to suppose that anyone else wants her to? I cannot for the life of me see why Miss Ada Blanche, who at certain moments sings with a good deal of feeling and speaks with propriety, should not be as refined throughout as Miss Decima Moore. But as that would not be customary, Miss Blanche takes considerable trouble, which is probably quite uncongenial to her, to be rowdy and knowing. Again, Mr Herbert Campbell, though he is incapable of the delicate *nuances* of Mr Leno, is an effectively robust comedian, whose power of singing like a powerful accordion, which some miracle-worker has got into perfect tune, is not unacceptable. But why should it be a point of honor with him to carry the slangy tone and street-corner pronunciation of his music-hall patter into those lines of his part in which he is supposed for the moment to be, not the popular funny man, but the magician of the fairy tale. Mr Campbell can say "face" instead of "fice," "slave" instead of "slive," "brain" instead of "brine," if he likes; and yet he takes the greatest possible pains to avoid doing so lest his occupation as a comically vulgar person should be gone. Naturally, when this occurs in a classic passage, it destroys the effect by suggesting that he mispronounces, not as a comic artist, but because he cannot help it, which I have no doubt is the last impression Mr Campbell would desire to convey. There are passages in his part which should either be spoken as carefully as the speech of the Ghost in Hamlet or else not spoken at all. Pray understand that I do not want the pantomime artists to be "funny without being vulgar." That is the mere snobbery of criticism. Every comedian should have vulgarity at his fingers' ends for use when required. It is the business of old Eccles and Perkyn Middlewick to be vulgar as much as it is the business of Parolles and Bobadil to be cowardly or Coriolanus to be haughty. But vulgarity in the wrong place, or slovenliness of speech in any place as a matter of personal habit instead of artistic assumption, is not to be tolerated from any actor or in any entertainment. Especially in a pantomime, where fun, horseplay, and the most outrageous silliness and lawlessness are of the essence of the show, it is important that nothing should be done otherwise than artistically.

Fortunately the Drury Lane pantomime offers more positive than negative evidence under this head. The knockabout business is not overdone; and what there is of it—mostly in the hands of Mr Fred Griffiths as a Chinese policeman—is funny. Mr Leno only falls twice; and on both occasions the gravest critics must shriek with merriment. Mr Cinquevalli's juggling need not be described. It is as well known in London as Sarasate's fiddling; and it fits very happily into the pantomime: indeed, it would be hard to contrive a better pantomime scene of its kind than that in which Cinquevalli, as Slave of the Lamp, appears in the Aladdin household and begins to do impossible things with the plates and tubs. His wonderful address and perfect physical training make him effective even when he is not juggling, as when he is flinging two plates right and left all over the stage, and fielding them (in the cricketing sense) with a success which, though highly diverting, is, no doubt, contemptibly cheap to him. Madame Grigolati's aerial dancing is also, of course, familiar; but it, too, fits perfectly into the pantomime, and is the first exhibition of the kind in which I have seen the aerial device used to much artistic purpose, or maintain its interest after the first novelty of seeing the laws of gravitation suspended in favor of a dancer had worn off. In short, nobody is allowed to take a prominent and independent part in the pantomime without solid qualifications. The second-rate people are not allowed to stand in the corner improvising second-rate tomfooleries. The rank and file are well disciplined; and there is not only order on the stage, but a considerable degree of atmosphere and illusion—qualities which the only Harrisian pantomime I ever saw signally failed to attain. The comedians do not pester you with topical songs, nor the fairy queen (who is only present in a rudimentary form) with sentimental ones. Indeed, the music shews the modern tendency to integrate into a continuous score, and avoid set "numbers." The point reached in this respect is not Wagnerian; but it is fairly level with Gounod, who, by the way, is profusely, and sometimes amusingly, quoted. Mr Barrett is catholic in his tastes, and takes his goods where he can find them, Wagner and Bellini being equally at his command. Thus, Abanazar's exhortation to Aladdin to take the magic ring leads to an outburst of "Prendi l' anell' ti dono" from La Sonnambula (not recognized, I fear, by the present generation, but very familiar to fogies of my epoch); and a capital schoolboy chorus in the second scene is provided by a combination of the opening strains of the Kermesse in Gounod's Faust with a tune which flourished in my tenderest youth as Tidd yiddy ido, Chin-Chon-Chino, and which was used freely by Mr Glover in last year's pantomime.

The best scenic effect is that achieved in the last scene of the first part, where the stage picture, at the moment when the procession of bearded patriarchs is passing down from the sun, is very fine. In some of the other scenes, especially those in which a front scene opens to reveal a very luminous distance, the effect is generally to make the foreground dingy and destroy its illusion. No doubt people seldom attend to the foreground under

26

such circumstances: all the same, the effect on them would be greater if the foreground would bear attention; and it seems to me that this could be managed at least as well on the stage as in the pictures of Turner, who also had to struggle with a tradition of dingy foregrounds.

Mr Barrett does not consider the transformation scene and harlequinade out of date. His transformation scene is very pretty; and the harlequinade is of the kind I can remember when the institution was in full decay about twenty-five years ago: that is, the old woman and the swell have disappeared; the policeman has no part; the old window-trap, through which everybody jumped head foremost except the pantaloon (who muffed it), is not used; the harlequin and columbine do not dance; and the clown neither burns people with a red-hot poker nor knocks at the baker's door and then lies down across the threshold to trip him up as he comes out. But there *is* a clown, who acts extensively as an advertisement agent, and plays the pilgrims' march from Tannhauser on the trombone until a hundred-ton weight is dropped on his head. His jokes, you see, are faithful to the old clowny tradition in being twenty years out of date. His name is Huline; and he is exactly like "the Great Little Huline" of my schooldays. And there is a pantaloon, another Huline, whose sufferings and humiliations are luxuries and dignities compared to those which pantaloons once had to undergo.

Let me add, as a touching example of the maternal instinct in Woman (bless her!), that the performance I witnessed was an afternoon one, and that though the house was packed with boys and girls trying to get a good peep at the stage, I never saw the *matinée* hat in grosser feather and foliage. The men, on the other hand, took their hats off, and sacrificed themselves to the children as far as they could. Brutes!

THE NEW IBSEN PLAY

John Gabriel Borkman. A play in four acts. By Henrik Ibsen. Translated by William Archer. London: Heinemann. 1897.

[30 *January* 1897]

The appearance some weeks ago in these columns of a review of the original Norwegian edition of Ibsen's new play, John Gabriel Borkman, relieves me from repeating here what I have said elsewhere concerning Mr William Archer's English version. In fact, the time for reviewing it has gone by: all who care about Ibsen have by this time pounced on the new volume, and ascertained for themselves what it is like. The only point worth discussing now is the play's chances of performance.

Everybody knows what happened to Little Eyolf. None of our managers would touch it; and it was not until the situation was made very pressing indeed by the advent of the proof-sheets of its successor that it was produced. As it happened, a certain section of the public—much the same section, I take it, as that which supplies the audiences for our orchestral concerts—jumped at the opportunity; and the experiment, in its original modesty, proved handsomely remunerative. Then commercial enterprise, always dreaming of "catches-on," long runs, and "silver mines," attempted to exploit the occasion in the usual way, and of course made an inglorious mess of it. A fashionable run of one of Ibsen's dramatic studies of modern society is about as feasible as a fashionable run of Beethoven's posthumous quartets. A late Ibsen play will not bring in twenty thousand pounds: it will only bring in fifteen hundred or two thousand. On the other hand, the play which *may* bring in twenty thousand pounds also may, and in nine cases out of ten does, bring in less than half its very heavy expenses; whereas the expenses of an Ibsen play, including a rate of profit for the entrepreneur which would be considered handsome in any ordinary non-speculative business, can be kept well within its practically certain returns, not to mention a high degree of artistic credit and satisfaction to all concerned. Under

28

these circumstances, it can hardly be contended that Ibsen's plays are not worth producing. In legitimate theatrical business Ibsen is as safe and profitable as Beethoven and Wagner in legitimate musical business.

Then, it will be asked, why do not the syndicates and managers take up Ibsen? As to the syndicates, the answer is simple. Enterprises with prospects limited to a profit of a few hundred pounds on a capital of a thousand do not require syndicates to finance them. An energetic individual enthusiast and a subscription can get over the business difficulties. The formation of a wealthy syndicate to produce a Little Eyolf would be like the promotion of a joint-stock company to sweep a crossing. As to the managers, there are various reasons. First, there is the inevitable snobbery of the fashionable actor-manager's position, which makes him ashamed to produce a play without spending more on the stage mounting alone than an Ibsen play will bring in. Second, our managers, having for the most part only a dealer's knowledge of art, cannot appreciate a new line of goods.

It is clear that the first objection will have to be got over somehow. If every manager considers it due to himself to produce nothing cheaper than The Prisoner of Zenda, not to mention the splendors of the Lyceum, then goodbye to high dramatic art. The managers will, perhaps, retort that if high dramatic art means Ibsen, then they ask for nothing better than to get rid of it. I am too polite to reply, bluntly, that high dramatic art *does* mean Ibsen; that Ibsen's plays are at this moment the head of the dramatic body; and that though an actor-manager can, and often does, do without a head, dramatic art cannot. Already Ibsen is a European power: this new play has been awaited for two years, and is now being discussed and assimilated into the consciousness of the age with an interest which no political or pontifical utterance can command. Wagner himself did not attain such a position during his lifetime, because he was regarded merely as a musician —much the same thing as regarding Shakespear merely as a grammarian. Ibsen is translated promptly enough nowadays; yet no matter how rapidly the translation comes on the heel of the original, newspapers cannot wait for it: detailed accounts based on the Norwegian text, and even on stolen glimpses of the proof-sheets, fly through the world from column to column as if the play were an Anglo-American arbitration treaty. Sometimes a foolish actor informs the public that Ibsen is a noisome nuisance. The public instantly loses whatever respect it may previously have had, not only for that foolish actor's critical opinion, but for his good sense. But if Ibsen were to visit London, and express his opinion of our English theatre—as Wagner expressed his opinion of the Philharmonic Society, for example—our actors and managers would go down to posterity as exactly such persons as Ibsen described them. He is master of the situation, this man of genius; and when we complain that he does not share our trumpery little notions of life and society; that the themes that make us whine and wince have no terrors for him, but infinite interest; and that he is far above the barmaid's and shop superintendent's obligation to be agreeable to Tom, Dick, and Harry (which naturally convinces Tom, Dick, and Harry that he is no gentleman), we are not making out a case against him, but simply stating the grounds of his eminence. When any person objects to an Ibsen play because it does not hold the mirror up to his own mind, I can only remind him that a horse might make exactly the same objection. For my own part, I do not endorse all Ibsen's views: I even prefer my own plays to his in some respects; but I hope I know a great man from a little one as far as my comprehension of such things go. Criticism may be pardoned for every mistake except that of not knowing a man of rank in literature when it meets one.

It is quite evident, then, that Ibsen can do without the managers. There remains the question: Can they do without Ibsen? And it is certainly astounding how long English stupidity can stave off foreign genius. It took Mozart's Don Giovanni, the greatest opera in the world, guaranteed by contemporary critics to be void of melody and overwhelmed with noisy orchestration, thirty years to reach London; and Wagner's Tristan und Isolde made its way last year into the repertory of our Royal Italian

Opera thirty-eight years after its composition. But even at this moderate rate of progress Ibsen may be regarded as fairly due by this time. The play which stands out among his works as an ideal Lyceum piece, The Pretenders, was his tenth play; and yet it was written thirty-four years ago. Peer Gynt is over thirty. Why, even A Doll's House is eighteen years old. These figures are significant, because there is an enormous difference between the effect of Ibsen's ideas on his own contemporaries and on those who might be his sons and grandsons. Take my own case. I am a middle-aged, old-fashioned person. But I was only two years old when The Vikings at Helgeland was written. Now, considering that Little Eyolf, written only a couple of years ago, already attracts an audience sufficiently numerous to pay for its production with a handsome little profit, is it to be believed that playgoers from ten to twenty years younger than I am are not yet ready for at least the great spectacular dramas, charged with romantic grandeur and religious sentiment, which Ibsen wrote between 1855 (the date of Lady Inger) and 1866 (the date of Peer Gynt)?

But alas! our managers are older in their ideas than Ibsen's grandmother. It is Sir Henry Irving's business, as the official head of his profession—*tu t'as voulu, Georges Dandin*—to keep before us the noble side of that movement in dramatic art of which The Sign of the Cross and The Sorrows of Satan are the cheap and popular manifestations. But how can he bring his transfigurations and fantasies to bear on the realities of the modern school? They have no more to do with Ibsen than with Shakespear or any other author save only Henry Irving himself. His theatre is not really a theatre at all: an accident has just demonstrated that nobody will go there to see a play, especially a play by Shakespear! They go only to see Sir Henry Irving or Miss Ellen Terry. When he sprains his knee and Miss Terry flies south leaving only Shakespear and the Lyceum company—O that company!—in possession, the theatre becomes a desert: Shakespear will not pay for gas enough to see him by. Back comes Miss Terry; up goes Shakespear, Wills, Sardou, anybody; the public rallies; and by the time the sprain is cured, all will be well. No: the Lyceum is incorrigible: its debt to modern dramatic art is now too far in arrear ever to be paid. After all, why, after inventing a distinct *genre* of art, and an undeniably fascinating one at that, should Sir Henry Irving now place himself at the disposition of Ibsen, and become the Exponent of Another on the stage which he has hitherto trodden as the Self-Expounded? Why should Miss Terry, whom we have adored under all sorts of delicious, nonsensical disguises, loving especially those which made her most herself, turn mere actress, and be transformed by Norwegian enchantments into an embodiment of those inmost reproaches of conscience which we now go to the Lyceum to forget? It is all very well for Mr Walkley to point out that Sir Henry Irving, Miss Ellen Terry and Miss Geneviève Ward would exactly suit the parts of Borkman, Ella and Gunhild in the new play; but what Sir Henry Irving wants to know is not whether he would suit the part, since he has good reason to consider himself actor enough to be able to suit many parts not worth his playing, but whether the part would suit him, which is quite another affair. That is the true centripetal force that keeps Ibsen off the stage.

Unfortunately when we give up the Lyceum, we give up the only theatre of classic pretensions, officially recognized as such, in London. Mr Oscar Barrett, when the details of his next pantomime are disposed of, might conceivably try one of the big spectacular Ibsen plays at Drury Lane; but the experiment would be more of a new departure for him and for the theatre than for Sir Henry Irving and the Lyceum. Mr Wyndham acts better than anybody else; he makes his company act better than any other company—so well that they occasionally act him off his own stage for months together; and he has not only the cleverness of the successful actor-manager, which is seldom more than the craft of an ordinary brain stimulated to the utmost by an overwhelming professional instinct, but the genuine ability of a good head, available for all purposes. But the pre-Ibsenite drama, played as he plays it, will last Mr Wyndham's time; and the public mind still copes with the Ibsenite view of life too slowly and clumsily for the Criterion. The most humorous passages of

Ibsen's work—three-fourths of The Wild Duck, for instance—still seem to the public as puzzling, humiliating, and disconcerting as a joke always does to people who cannot see it. Comedy must be instantly and vividly intelligible or it is lost: it must therefore proceed on a thoroughly established intellectual understanding between the author and the audience—an understanding which does not yet exist between Ibsen and our playgoing public. But tragedy, like Handel's "darkness that might be felt," is none the worse theatrically for being intellectually obscure and oppressive. The pathos of Hedwig Ekdal's suicide or Little Eyolf's death is quite independent of any "explanation" of the play; but most of the fun of Hjalmar Ekdal, Gregers Werle, Relling, Molvik and Gina, to an audience still dominated by conventional ideals, must be as imperceptible, except when it hurts, as it is to Hjalmar himself. This puts the comedy houses out of the question, and leaves us with only Mr Alexander and Mr Tree to look to. Both of them have been more enterprising than the public had any right to expect them to be. Mr Tree actually produced An Enemy of The People; but I doubt if he has ever realized that his Stockman, though humorous and entertaining in its way, was, as a character creation, the polar opposite of Ibsen's Stockman. None the less, Mr Tree's notion of feeding the popular drama with ideas, and gradually educating the public, by classical matinées, financed by the spoils of the popular plays in the evening bill, seems to have been the right one. Mr Alexander's attempts to run Guy Domville and The Divided Way fairly proved that such plays should not be substituted for The Prisoner of Zenda and Shakespear; for I submit that we do not want to suppress either Rose-Hope or Shakespear, and that we can spare Sudermann, Ibsen, and Mr Henry James from the footlights better than we could spare the entertainments which please everybody. But why not have both? If Mr Alexander, instead of handing over Magda to fail in the evening bill at another theatre, had produced it and Sodom's Ende and so forth at a series of matinées of the Saturday Pop class, financing them from the exchequer of the kingdom of Ruritania, and aiming solely at the nourishment of the drama and the prevention of stagnation in public taste, he might have laid the foundations of a genuine classic theatre, in which the cultivated people who never dream of going to the theatre now would take their boxes and stalls by the season, and the hundred thousand people who go to the St James's twice a year would be represented financially by four thousand going once a week.

At all events, the time for forlorn hopes has gone by. I observe by the publishers' columns that Mr Charles Charrington, the only stage-manager of genius the new movement has produced, and quite its farthest-seeing pioneer, has taken to literature. Miss Janet Achurch has relapsed into Shakespear, and is going to play Cleopatra at the forthcoming Calvertian revival in Manchester, after which I invite her to look Ibsen in the face again if she can. Miss Robins is devoting the spoils of Little Eyolf to Echegaray's Mariana, which must, for business reasons, be produced very soon. There are no signs of a fresh campaign on Miss Farr's part. The only other Ibsenite enthusiast is Mrs Patrick Campbell, who is busy studying Emma Hamilton, the heroine of "the celestial bed," which will, I trust, figure duly in the forthcoming Nelson drama at the Avenue.

Altogether, the prospects of a speedy performance of John Gabriel Borkman are not too promising.

OLIVIA

OLIVIA. A play in four acts. By the late W. G. Wills. Founded on an episode in The Vicar of Wakefield. Revival. Lyceum Theatre, 30 January 1897.

THE FREE PARDON. An original domestic drama in four acts. By F. C. Philips and Leonard Meyrick. Olympic Theatre, 28 January 1897.

THE PRODIGAL FATHER. An extravagant farce in three acts. By Glen Macdonough. Strand Theatre, 1 February 1897.

[6 *February* 1897]

THE world changes so rapidly nowadays that I hardly dare speak to my juniors of the things that won my affections when I was a sceptical, imperturbable, hard-headed young man of twenty-three or thereabouts. Now that I am an impressionable, excitable, sentimental—if I were a woman everybody would say hysterical—party on the wrong side of forty, I am conscious of being in danger of making myself ridiculous unless I confine my public expressions of enthusiasm to great works which are still before their time. That is why, when Olivia was revived at the Lyceum last Saturday, I blessed the modern custom of darkening the auditorium during the performance, since it enabled me to cry secretly. I wonder what our playgoing freshmen think of Olivia. I do not, of course, mean what they think of its opening by the descent of two persons to the footlights to carry on an expository conversation beginning, "It is now twenty-five years since, etc.," nor the antediluvian asides of the "I do but dissemble" order in Thornhill's part, at which the gallery burst out laughing. These things are the mere fashions of the play, not the life of it. And it is concerning the life of it that I ask how the young people who see it today for the first time as I saw it nearly twenty years ago at the old Court Theatre feel about it.

I must reply that I have not the least idea. For what has this generation in common with me, or with Olivia, or with Goldsmith? The first book I ever possessed was a Bible bound in black leather with gilt metal rims and a clasp, slightly larger than my sisters' Bibles because I was a boy, and was therefore fitted with a bigger Bible, precisely as I was fitted with bigger boots. In spite of the trouble taken to impress me with the duty of reading it (with the natural result of filling me with a conviction that such an occupation must be almost as disagreeable as going to church), I acquired a considerable familiarity with it, and indeed once read the Old Testament and the four Gospels straight through, from a vainglorious desire to do what nobody else had done. A sense of the sanctity of clergymen, and the holiness of Sunday, Easter, and Christmas—sanctity and holiness meaning to me a sort of reasonlessly inhibitory condition in which it was wrong to do what I liked and especially meritorious to make myself miserable—was imbibed by me, not from what is called a strict bringing-up (which, as may be guessed by my readers, I happily escaped), but straight from the social atmosphere. And as that atmosphere was much like the atmosphere of Olivia, I breathe it as one to the manner born.

The question is, then, has that atmosphere changed so much that the play is only half comprehensible to the younger spectators? That there is a considerable change I cannot doubt; for I find that if I mention Adam and Eve, or Cain and Abel, to people of adequate modern equipment under thirty, they do not know what I am talking about. The Scriptural literary style which fascinated Wills as it fascinated Scott is to them quaint and artificial. Think of the difference between the present Bishop of London's History of the Popes and anything that the Vicar of Wakefield could have conceived or written! Think of the eldest daughters of our two-horse-carriage vicars going out, as female dons with Newnham degrees, to teach the granddaughters of ladies shamefacedly conscious of having been educated much as Mrs Primrose was; and ponder well whether such domestic incidents can give any clue to poor Olivia going off by coach to be "companion" to "some old tabby" in Yorkshire, and—most monstrous of all—previously presenting her brothers with her Prayer-book and her Pilgrim's Progress, and making them promise to pray for her every night at their mother's knee. Read The Woman Who Did, bearing in mind its large circulation and the total failure of the attempt to work up the slightest public feeling against it; and then consider how obsolescent must be that part of the interest of Olivia which depends on her sense of a frightful gulf between her moral position as a legally married woman and that in which she feels herself when she is told that the legal part of the ceremony was not valid. Take, too, that old notion of the home as a sort of prison in which the parents kept their children locked up under their authority, and from which, therefore, a daughter who wished to marry without their leave had to escape through the window as from the Bastille! Must not this conception, which alone can give any reality to the elopement of Olivia, be very historical and abstract to the class of people to whom a leading London theatre might be expected to appeal? It is easy for me, taught my letters as I was by a governess who might have been Mrs Primrose herself, to understand the Wakefield vicarage; but what I want to know is, can it carry any conviction to people who are a generation ahead of me in years, and a century in nursery civilization?

If I, drowning the Lyceum carpet with tears, may be taken as one extreme of the playgoing body, and a modern lady who, when I mentioned the play the other day, dismissed it with entire conviction as "beneath contempt," as the other, I am curious to see whether the majority of those between us are sufficiently near my end to produce a renewal of the old success. If not, the fault must lie with the rate of social progress; for Olivia is by a very great deal the best nineteenth-century play in the Lyceum repertory; and it has never been better acted. The Ellen Terry of 1897 is beyond all comparison a better Olivia than the Ellen Terry of 1885. The enchanting delicacy and charm with which she first stooped to folly at the old Court Theatre was obscured at the Lyceum, partly, perhaps, by a certain wrathful energy of developed physical power, pride, strength, and success in the actress, but certainly, as I shall presently shew, by the Lyceum conditions. Today the conditions are altered; the vanities have passed away with the water under the bridges; and the delicacy and charm have returned. We have the original Olivia again, in appearance not discoverably a week older, and much idealized and softened by the disuse of the mere brute force of tears and grief, which Miss Terry formerly employed so unscrupulously in the scene of the presents and of the elopement that she made the audience positively howl with anguish. She now plays these scenes with infinite mercy and art, the effect, though less hysterical, being deeper, whilst the balance of the second act is for the first time properly adjusted. The third act should be seen by all those who know Ellen Terry only by her efforts to extract a precarious sustenance for her reputation from Shakespear: it will teach them what an artist we have thrown to our national theatrical Minotaur. When I think of the originality and modernity of the

37

talent she revealed twenty years ago, and of its remorseless waste ever since in "supporting" an actor who prefers The Iron Chest to Ibsen, my regard for Sir Henry Irving cannot blind me to the fact that it would have been better for us twenty-five years ago to have tied him up in a sack with every existing copy of the works of Shakespear, and dropped him into the crater of the nearest volcano. It really serves him right that his Vicar is far surpassed by Mr Hermann Vezin's. I do not forget that there never was a more beautiful, a more dignified, a more polished, a more cultivated, a more perfectly mannered Vicar than Sir Henry Irving's. He annihilated Thornhill, and scored off everybody else, by sheer force of behavior. When, on receiving that letter that looked like a notice of distraint for rent, he said, with memorable charm of diction, "The law never enters the poor man's house save as an oppressor," it was difficult to refrain from jumping on the stage and saying, "Heaven bless you, sir, why dont you go to London and start a proprietary chapel? You would be an enormous success there." There is nothing of this about the Vezin Vicar. To Farmer Flamborough he may be a fine gentleman; but to Thornhill he is a very simple one. To the innkeeper he is a prodigy of learning; but out in the world, looking for his daughter, his strength lies only in the pathos of his anxious perseverance. He scores off nobody except in his quaint theological disputation with the Presbyterian; but he makes Thornhill ashamed by not scoring off him. It is the appeal of his humanity and not the beauty of his style that carries him through; and his idolatry of his daughter is unselfish and fatherly, just as her affection for him is at last touched with a motherly instinct which his unworldly helplessness rouses in her. Handling the part skilfully and sincerely from this point of view, Mr Hermann Vezin brings the play back to life on the boards where Sir Henry Irving, by making it the occasion of an exhibition of extraordinary refinement of execution and personality, very nearly killed it as a drama. In the third act, by appealing to our admiration and artistic appreciation instead of to our belief and human sympathy, Sir Henry Irving made Olivia an orphan. In the famous passage where the Vicar tries to reprove his daughter, and is choked by the surge of his affection for her, he reproved Olivia like a saint and then embraced her like a lover. With Mr Vezin the reproof is a pitiful stammering failure: its break-down is neither an "effect" nor a surprise: it is foreseen as inevitable from the first, and comes as Nature's ordained relief when the sympathy is strained to bursting point. Mr Vezin's entry in this scene is very pathetic. His face is the face of a man who has been disappointed to the very heart every day for months; and his hungry look round, half longing, half anticipating another disappointment, gives just the right cue for his attitude towards Thornhill, to whom he says, "I forget you," not in conscious dignity and judgment, but as if he meant, "Have I, who forget *myself*, any heart to remember *you* whilst my daughter is missing?" When a good scene is taken in this way, the very accessories become eloquent, like the decent poverty of Mr Vezin's brown overcoat. Sir Henry Irving, not satisfied to be so plain a person as the Vicar of Wakefield, gave us something much finer and more distinguished, the beauty of which had to stand as a substitute for the pathos of those parts of the play which it destroyed. Mr Vezin takes his part for better for worse, and fits himself faithfully into it. The result can only be appreciated by those whose memory is good enough to compare the effect of the third act in 1885 and today. Also, to weigh Olivia with the Vicar right against Olivia with the Vicar wrong. I purposely force the comparison between the two treatments because it is a typical one. The history of the Lyceum, with its twenty years' steady cultivation of the actor as a personal force, and its utter neglect of the drama, is the history of the English stage during that period. Those twenty years have raised the social status of the theatrical profession, and culminated in the official recognition of our chief actor as the peer of the President of the Royal Academy, and the figure-heads of the other arts. And now I, being a dramatist and not an actor, want to know when the drama is to have its turn. I do not suggest that G.B.S. should condescend to become K.C.B.; but I do confidently affirm that if the actors think they can do without the drama, they are most prodigiously mistaken. The huge relief with which I found myself turning from Olivia as an effective exhibition of the extraordinary accomplishments of Sir Henry Irving to Olivia as a naturally acted story has opened my eyes to the extent to which I have been sinking the true dramatic critic in the connoisseur in virtuosity, and forgetting what they were doing at the Lyceum in the contemplation of how they were doing it. Henceforth I shall harden my heart as Wagner hardened his heart against Italian singing, and hold diction, deportment, sentiment, personality, and character as dust in the balance against the play and the credibility of its representation.

The rest of the company, not supporting, but supported *by* Mr Vezin and Miss Terry—thereby reverting to the true artistic relation between the principal parts and the minor ones—appear to great advantage. Only, one misses Mr Terriss as Thornhill, since Mr Cooper cannot remake himself so completely as to give much point to Olivia's line, once so effective, "As you stand there flicking your boot, you look the very picture of vain indifference." Mr Norman Forbes does not resume his old part of Moses, which is now played by Mr Martin Harvey. Mr Macklin as Burchell and Mr Sam Johnson as Farmer Flamborough, Master Stewart Dawson and Miss Valli Valli as Dick and Bill, and Miss Julia Arthur as Sophia, all fall admirably into their places. Miss Maud Milton is a notably good Mrs Primrose: her share in the scene of the pistols, which attains a most moving effect, could not have been better. Miss Edith Craig makes a resplendent Bohemian Girl of the gipsy, the effect being very nearly operatic. Miss Craig may have studied her part from the life; but if so, I should be glad to know where, so that I may instantly ride off to have my fortune told by the original.

The new play at the Olympic is one of those melodramas which produce no illusion, but which, played with well-known incidents and situations according to certain rules, are now watched by adept playgoers with the same interest that a football match creates. The game is rather exciting in the third act, and tolerable in the others. Its success, if it does succeed, will be due mainly to the acting of Miss Cicely Richards, who pulls it through with great ability, seconded effectively by Mr Cockburn. Miss Esme Beringer's impersonation of the heroine, though altogether artificial, is clever; and Mr Courtenay Thorpe manages to play with some distinction as the father. Mr Abingdon is a comic American interviewer; but the part is beneath criticism. Besides, Mr Abingdon has no command of the American language. The manageress, Mrs Charles Sugden, is competent and intelligent as the lady villain.

The Prodigal Father, at the Strand, is a lively piece, without any other particular merit. It restores Miss Florence Gerard to the London stage after a long absence. She was, I think, unwise to begin with such a piece as the curtain-raiser entitled A Merry Christmas, which depends on that fastidious elegance of style which is so soon unlearnt in America and the Colonies; but in The Prodigal Father she was more than equal to the occasion. In fact, the whole cast, which included Miss May Palfrey, Miss Lulu Valli, Messrs Harry Paulton, Charles Collette, and Charles Weir —a strong combination—is more or less underparted.

MR WILSON BARRETT AS THE MESSIAH

THE DAUGHTERS OF BABYLON. A play in four acts, by Wilson Barrett. Lyric Theatre, 6 February 1897.

[13 *February* 1897]

MR WILSON BARRETT, responding to the editor of the Academy, has just declared that his favorite books in 1896 were the Bible and Shakespear. No less might have been expected from a manager who has combined piety with business so successfully as the author of The Sign of the Cross. Isaiah has especially taken hold of his imagination. No doubt when he read, "Yea, they are greedy dogs which can never have enough; and they are shepherds that cannot understand: they all look to their own way, every one for his gain, from his quarter," he recognized in Isaiah the makings of a first-rate dramatic critic. But what touched him most was the familiar "He shall feed his flock like a shepherd: he shall gather the lambs with his arm, and carry them in his bosom, and shall gently lead those that are with young." If Mr Barrett had been a musician, like Handel, he would have wanted to set that text to music. Being an actor, he "saw himself in the part," and could not rest until he had gathered a lamb with his arm and carried it on to the stage in The Daughters of Babylon. The imagined effect was not quite realized on the first night, partly, no doubt, because Mr Edward Jones, the conductor of the band, omitted to accompany the entry with the obvious Handelian theme, and perhaps partly because the lamb proved unworthy of the confidence placed by Mr Barrett in its good manners. But the strongest reason was that metaphor is not drama, nor *tableau vivant* acting. I hold Mr Wilson Barrett in high esteem as a stage manager and actor; and I have no doubt that Mr Wilson Barrett would allow that I am a fairly competent workman with my pen. But when he takes up the tools of my craft and tries his hand at dramatic literature, he produces exactly the same effect on me as I should produce on him if I were to try my hand at playing Othello. A man cannot be everything. To write in any style at all requires a good many years practice: to write in the Scriptural style well enough to be able to incorporate actual passages from the Authorized Version of the Bible without producing the effect of patching a shabby pair of trousers with snippets of fifteenth-century Venetian brocade, requires not only literary skill of the most expert kind, but a special technical gift, such as Stevenson had, for imitating the turn of classical styles.

Mr Wilson Barrett is here fairly entitled to interrupt me by saying, "Do not waste your time in telling me what I know already. I grant it all. But I have reverently submitted my qualifications to expert opinion. Miss Marie Corelli, the most famous writer of the day, whose prodigious success has earned her the envious hate of the poor journeymen of literature to whom she will not even deign to send review copies of her books, tells me that I have 'the unpurchasable gift of genius'; that my language is 'choice and scholarly'; that I 'could win the laurels of the poet had I not opted for those of the dramatist'; that I have power and passion, orchidacity and flamboyancy; and that my Babylon is better than The Sign of the Cross, which was not only enormously successful, but was approved by the clerical profession, to whom Greek and Hebrew are as mother tongues. Who are you, pray, Mr Saturday Reviewer, that I should set this mass of disinterested authority beneath your possibly envious disparagements?"

This is altogether unanswerable as far as the weight of authority is concerned. I confess that I am in an infinitesimal minority, and that my motives are by no means above suspicion. Therefore I must either hold my tongue or else re-write the play to shew how it ought to be done. Such a demonstration is beyond my means, unless a public subscription be raised to remunerate my toil; but I do not mind giving a sample or two. Suppose I were to tell Mr Wilson Barrett that among the many judicial utterances in the Bible, by Solomon, Festus, Felix, Pilate, and others, I had found such a remark as "The evidence against thee is but slight," would he not burst out laughing at me for my ridiculous mixture of modern Old Bailey English with the obsolete fashion of using the second person singular? Yet he has used that very phrase in The Daughters of Babylon. Pray observe that I should not at all object to the wording of the whole drama in the most modern vernacular, even if it were carried to the extent of making the Babylonian idol seller talk like a coster. But modern vernacular seasoned with thees and thous and haths and whithers to make it sound peradventurously archaic is another matter. Let us have "There is not sufficient evidence against you," or else let us talk loftily of accusation and testimony, not of cases and evidence. Again, there is not, as far as I can remember, any account of an auction in the Bible; but if there were I should unhesitatingly reject it as apocryphal if one of the parties, instead of saying "Who is he that biddeth against me for this woman?" were to exclaim, "I demand to know the name of my opponent," which is Mr Barrett's authorized version. If he had made Jediah say, "May I ask who the gentleman is?" that would have been perfectly allowable; but the phrase as it stands belongs neither to Christy's nor

43

to the literary convention of the ideal Babylon: it is the ineptitude of an amateur. And would it not have been easier to write, "The nether milestone is not so hard," than "The nether milestone is *tender in comparison*"? As to "We have wandered from the object of our visit, my lord," I really give it up in despair, and intemperately affirm that the man who, with a dozen tolerably congruous locutions ready to his hand, could select that absurdly incongruous one, does not know the Bible from Bow Bells.

Miss Marie Corelli, who finds Mr Barrett's phrases "choice and scholarly," gets over the difficulty of describing Ishtar in the blunt language of Scripture, by calling her, very choicely, "the Queen of the Half World of Babylon"—five words for one. Ishtar is very bitter throughout the play concerning the ferocity of the Jewish law to women. Yet we find Lemuel, in the true spirit of a British tar, saying, "I will not harm thee, who art—whate'er thy sins—a Woman." I could not give a better example of the way in which the actor-dramatist will forget everything else, drama, common-sense, and all, the moment an opening for some hackneyed stage effect, chivalrous pose or sympathy-catching platitude occurs to him.

The Daughters of Babylon, then, is not likely to please critics who can write; for nothing antagonizes a good workman so much as bad workmanship in his own craft. It will encounter also a prejudice against his exploitation of the conception of religious art held by the average English citizen. Against that prejudice, however, I am prepared to defend it warmly. I cannot for the life of me understand why Mr Wilson Barrett should not do what Ary Scheffer and Müller, Sir Noel Paton and Mr Goodall, Mr Herbert Schmalz and the publishers of the Doré Bible, not to mention Miss Corelli herself, are doing, or have been doing, all through the century without protest. For my part, whilst, as a Superior Person, I reserve the right to look down on such conceptions of religion as Cæsar might have looked down at a toy soldier, yet the advance from the exploitation of illiterate and foolish melodramatic conventions in which nobody believes, to that of a sentiment which is a living contemporary reality, and which identifies

44

the stage at last with popular artistic, literary and musical culture (such as it is), is to me more momentous than the production of John Gabriel Borkman at the Lyceum would be. Mr Wilson Barrett has found that he can always bring down the house with a hymn: the first act of The Daughters of Babylon, after driving the audience nearly to melancholy madness by its dulness, is triumphantly saved in that way. Well, any one who takes a walk round London on Sunday evening will find, at innumerable street corners, little bands of thoroughly respectable citizens, with their wives and daughters, standing in a circle and singing hymns. It is not a fashionable thing to do—not even a conventional thing to do: they do it because they believe in it. And pray why is that part of their lives not to find expression in dramatic art as it finds expression, unchallenged, in all the other fine arts? Are we to drive Mr Wilson Barrett back from his texts, his plagal cadences, and his stage pictures from the Illustrated Bible, to "Arrest that man: he is a murderer," or "Release that man: he is in-know-scent," or "Richard Dastardson: you shall rre-pent-er that-er b-er-low"? The pity is that Mr Wilson Barrett does not go further and gratify his very evident desire to impersonate the Messiah without any sort of circumlocution or disguise. That we shall have Passion Plays in the London theatres as surely as we shall some day have Parsifal has for a long time past been as certain as any development under the sun can be; and the sooner the better. I have travelled all the way to Ober Ammergau to see a Passion Play which was financed in the usual manner by a syndicate of Viennese Jews. Why should not the people who cannot go so far have a Passion Play performed for them in Shaftesbury Avenue? The fact that they want it is proved, I take it, by the success of Barabbas. Depend on it, we shall see Mr Wilson Barrett crucified yet; and the effect will be, not to debase religion, but to elevate the theatre, which has hitherto been allowed to ridicule religion but not to celebrate it, just as it has been allowed to jest indecently with sex questions but not to treat them seriously.

As it is, The Daughters of Babylon suffers a good deal from

our religious prudery. Mr Wilson Barrett underplays his part to an extent quite unaccountable on the face of it, the fact being that he plays, not Lemuel, but the Messiah disguised as Lemuel, and therefore excludes all fear, passion, and perplexity from his conception, retaining only moral indignation for strong effects, and falling back at other times on superhuman serenity, indulgence, pity, and prophetic sadness. In short, he is playing a part which he did not venture to write; and the result is that the part he did write is sacrificed without any apparent compensation. It is dangerous for an actor to mean one part whilst playing another, unless the audience is thoroughly in the secret; and it is quite fatal for an author to mean one play and write another. There was no such want of directness in The Sign of the Cross. In it the Christian scenes were as straightforward as the Roman ones; and Marcus Superbus was meant for Marcus Superbus and nobody else. In The Daughters of Babylon the Jewish scenes are symbolic; and though the Babylonian scenes are straightforward enough (and therefore much more effective), they are pervaded by the symbolic Lemuel, who lets them down dramatically every time he enters. With this doubleness of purpose at the heart of it, the play may succeed as a spectacle and a rite; but it will not succeed as a melodrama.

Like all plays under Mr Barrett's management, The Daughters of Babylon is excellently produced. The scene painters are the heroes of the occasion. Mr Telbin's grove standing among the cornfields on a hilly plain, and Mr Hann's view of Babylon by night, in the Doré style, are specially effective; and the tents of Israel on the hillside make a pretty bit of landscape in Mr Ryan's Judgment Seat by the City of Zoar, in which, however, the necessity for making the judgment seat "practicable" left it impossible for the artist to do quite as much as Mr Telbin. The cast, consisting of thirty-three persons, all of them encouraged and worked up as if they were principals—a feature for which Mr Wilson Barrett, as manager, can hardly have too much credit—must be content for the most part with a general compliment, the names being too many for mention. Mr Franklin McLeay's Jediah bears

46

traces of the epilepsy of Nero, an inevitable consequence of a whole year's run of convulsions; but he again makes his mark as an actor of exceptional interest and promise, who should be seen in a part sufficiently like himself to be played without the somewhat violent disguises he assumes at the Lyric. Mr Ambrose Manning, as Alorus the Affable, has the only one of the long parts which is not occasionally tedious, a result largely due to his judgment in completely throwing over the stagey style which all the rest frankly adopt. Mr Charles Hudson also contrives to emerge into some sort of particularity; but the other sixteen gentlemen defy distinction, except, perhaps, the fat Babylonian executioner, Mr George Bernage, whose comfortable appearance is so little suited to his occupation as chief baker at the Nebuchadnezzaresque fiery furnace that his fearsomest utterances provoke roars of laughter. Miss Maud Jeffries appears to much advantage in rational dress in the Babylonian scenes. She makes Elna much more interesting than that whited wall the Christian Martyr in The Sign of the Cross, and seems to have the American intelligence, character and humor, without the American lack of vitality. Indeed, her appearance in the first scene of the second act is the beginning of the play, as far as any dramatic thrill is concerned. Miss Lily Hanbury, specially engaged to be orchidaceous and flamboyant as the Improper Person of Babylon, and wholly guiltless of the least aptitude for the part, honestly gives as much physical energy to the delivery of the lines as she can, and is very like a pet lamb pretending to be a lioness. When Lemuel decided to let his sweetheart, himself, and all his faithful confederates be baked in the fiery furnace sooner than accept her proffered affection, the sympathy of the audience departed from him for ever. So did mine; but, all the same, I beg Miss Hanbury not to imagine, whatever the gallery may think, that she has learnt to act heavy parts merely because she has picked up the mere mechanics of ranting. And I implore her not to talk about "the lor of Babylon." The quarter-century during which Sir Henry Irving has been attacking his initial vowels with a more than German scrupulousness should surely by this time have made it possible for a leading actress to pronounce two consecutive vowels without putting an "r" between them.

The musical arrangements are so lavish as to include a performance of Max Bruch's Kol Nidrei (familiar as a violoncello piece) between the first and second acts, by a Dutch solo violinist of distinction, M. Henri Seiffert.

FOR ENGLAND, HOME, AND BEAUTY

NELSON'S ENCHANTRESS. A new play in four acts. By Risden Home. Avenue Theatre, 11 February 1897.

MY FRIEND THE PRINCE. A new play in three acts, suggested by the American farce My Friend from India. By Justin Huntly McCarthy. Garrick Theatre, 13 February 1897.

SWEET NANCY. A comedy in three acts, adapted from Miss Rhoda Broughton's novel Nancy, by Robert Buchanan. Also A BIT OF OLD CHELSEA, in one act, by Mrs Oscar Beringer. Court Theatre, 8 February 1897.   [20 *February* 1897]

I AM beginning seriously to believe that Woman is going to regenerate the world after all. Here is a dramatist, the daughter of an admiral who was midshipman to Hardy, who was captain to Nelson, who committed adultery with Lady Hamilton, who was notoriously a polyandrist. And what is her verdict on Lady Hamilton? Simply that what the conventional male dramatist would call her "impurity" was an entirely respectable, lovable, natural feature of her character, inseparably bound up with the qualities which made her the favorite friend of England's favorite hero. There is no apology made for this view, no consciousness betrayed at any point that there is, or ever was, a general assumption that it is an improper view. There you have your Emma Hart, in the first act the mistress of Greville, in the second repudiated by Greville and promptly transferring her affection to his uncle, in the third married to the uncle and falling in love with another man (a married man), and in the fourth living with this man during his wife's lifetime, and parting from him at his death with all the honors of a wife. There is no more question raised as to the propriety of it all than as to Imogen's virtue in repulsing Iachimo. An American poetess, Mrs Charlotte Stetson Perkins, has described, in biting little verses, how she met a Prejudice; reasoned with it, remonstrated with it, satirized it, ridiculed it, appealed to its feelings, exhausted every argument and every blandishment on it without moving it an inch; and finally "just walked through it." A better practical instance of this could hardly be found than Nelson's Enchantress. Ibsen argues with our prejudices—makes them, in fact, the subject of his plays. Result: we almost tear him to pieces, and shut our theatre doors as tight as we can against him. Risden Home walks through our prejudices straight on to the stage; and nobody dares even whisper that Emma is not an edifying example for the young girl of fifteen. Only, in the House of Commons a solitary Admiral wants the licence of the theatre withdrawn for its presumption in touching on the morals of the quarter-deck. What does this simple salt suppose would have happened to the theatre if it had told the whole truth on the subject?

In order to realize what a terrible person the New Woman is, it is necessary to compare Nelson's Enchantress with that ruthlessly orthodox book, The Heavenly Twins. It is true that Madame Sarah Grand, though a New Woman, will connive at no triflings with "purity" in its sense of monogamy. But mark the consequence. She will tolerate no Emma Harts; but she will tolerate no Nelsons either. She says, in effect, "Granted, gentlemen, that we are to come to you untouched and unspotted, to whom, pray, are we to bring our purity? To what the streets have left of *your* purity, perhaps? No, thank you: if we are to be certified pure, you shall be so certified too: wholesome husbands are as important to us as wholesome wives are to you." We all remember the frantic fury of the men, their savage denunciations of Madame Sarah Grand, and the instant and huge success of her book. There was only one possible defence against it; and that was to deny boldly that there was anything unwholesome in the incontinences of men—nay, to appeal to the popular instinct in defence of the virility, the good-heartedness, and the lovable humanity of Tom Jones. Alas for male hypocrisy! No sooner has the expected popular response come than another New Woman promptly assumes that what is lovable in Tom Jones is lovable in Sophia Western also, and presents us with an ultra-sympathetic Enchantress heroine who is an arrant libertine. The dilemma is a pretty one. For my part, I am a man; and Madame Grand's solution fills me with dismay. What I should like, of course, would be the maintenance of two distinct classes of women, the one polyandrous and disreputable and the other monogamous and reputable. I could then have my fill of poly-gamy among the polyandrous ones with the certainty that I could hand them over to the police if they annoyed me after I had be-come tired of them, at which date I could marry one of the mono-gamous ones and live happily ever afterwards. But if a woman were to say such a thing as this about men I should be shocked; and of late years it has begun to dawn on me that perhaps when men say it (or worse still, act on it without confessing to it) women may be disgusted. Now it is a very serious thing for Man to be an object of disgust to Woman, on whom from his cradle to his grave he is as dependent as a child on its nurse. I would cheerfully accept the unpopularity of Guy Fawkes if the only alternative were to be generally suspected by women of nasty ideas about them: consequently I am forced to reconsider my position. If I must choose between accepting for myself the asceticism which I have hitherto light-heartedly demanded from all respectable women, and extending my full respect and toler-ance to women who live as freely as Nelson's Enchantress, why then—but space presses, and this is not dramatic criticism. To business!

It is a pity that the Nelson of the play is a mere waxwork Nelson. The real man would have been an extraordinarily in-teresting hero. Nelson was no nice, cultured gentleman. He started sailoring and living on a scorbutic diet of "salt horse" at twelve; was senior officer of an expedition and captain of a 44-gun ship when he was twenty-two; and was admiral in com-mand of a fleet in one of the greatest naval engagements of modern times when he was forty. Could any character actor hit off the amphibiousness of such a person, and yet present to us also the inveterately theatrical hero who ordered his engagements like an actor-manager, made his signals to the whole British public, and wrote prayers for publication in the style of The Sign of the Cross instead of offering them up to the god of battles. With consummate professional skill founded on an apprenticeship that began in his childhood, having officers to match and hardy and able crews, and fighting against comparative amateurs at a time when the average French physique had been driven far below the average English one by the age of starvation that led to the burning of the châteaux and the Revolution, he solemnly devoted himself to destruction in every engagement as if he were leading a forlorn hope, and won not only on the odds, but on the boldest presumption on the odds. When he was victorious, he insisted on the fullest measure of glory, and would bear malice if the paltriest detail of his honors—the Mansion House dinner, for example—were omitted. When he was beaten, which usually happened promptly enough when he made a shore attack, he denied it and raged like a schoolboy, vowing what he would do to his adversary the next time he caught him. He always played even his most heroic antagonists off the stage. At the battle of the Nile, Brueys, the French admiral, hopelessly out-manœuvred and outfought, refused to strike his colors and fought until the sea swallowed him and his defeat. Nothing could be more heroic. Nelson, on the other hand, was knocked silly, and remained more or less so for about three years, disobeying orders and luxuriating with Lady Hamilton, to the scandal of all Europe. And yet who in England ever mentions the brave Brueys or that nasty knock on the head? As to Nelson's private conduct, he, sailor-like, married a widow on a foreign station; pensioned her off handsomely when she objected to his putting another woman in her place; and finally set up a *ménage à trois* with Sir William and Lady Hamilton, the two men being deeply attached to one another and to the lady, and the lady polyandrously attached to both of them. The only child of this "group marriage" was Nelson's, and not the lawful husband's. Pray what would you say, pious reader, if this were the story of the hero of an Ibsen play instead of the perfectly well known, and carefully never told, story of England's pet hero?

Risden Home, I regret to say, does not rise to the occasion. Though she deals with Lady Hamilton like a New Woman, she deals with Nelson like a Married one, taking good care that he shall not set a bad example to husbands. She first gives us a momentary glimpse of Captain Horatio Nelson as an interesting and elegant young man, who could not possibly have ever suffered from scurvy. She introduces him again as Admiral Nelson immediately after the battle of the Nile, with two eyes and an undamaged scalp. Lady Hamilton does not make a scene by crying "O my God!" and fainting on his breast. On the contrary, in a recklessly unhistorical conversation, they both confess their love and part for ever, to the entire satisfaction of the moral instincts of the British public. Everything having thus been done in proper form, Nelson is made Duke of Bronté for the Nile victory instead of for hanging Carracciolo; the remainder of Sir William Hamilton's lifetime is tactfully passed over; the existence of Lady Nelson and little Horatia is politely ignored; and Nelson is not reintroduced until his brief stay at Merton on the eve of Trafalgar. The fact that he has only just returned from spending two years very contentedly on board ship away from his Enchantress is not insisted on. He recites his Wilson-Barrettian prayer; parts from the heartbroken Emma; and is presently seen by her in a vision, dying in the cockpit of the Victory, and—considerate to the last of the interests of morality in the theatre—discreetly omitting his recommendation of his illegitimate daughter to his country's care.

Need I add, as to Emma herself, that we are spared all evidence of the fact that Greville only allowed her £20 a year to dress on and pay her personal expenses; of her change from a sylph to a Fat Lady before the Nile episode; and of the incorrigible cabotinage which inspired her first meeting with Nelson, her poses plastiques, and her habit, after Nelson's death, of going to concerts and fainting publicly whenever Braham was announced to sing 'Twas in Trafalgar's Bay. In short, the Emma of the play is an altogether imaginary person historically, but a real person humanly; whereas the Nelson, equally remote from history, is a pure heroic convention. It still remains true that the British public is incapable of admiring a real great man, and insists on having in his place the foolish image they suppose a great man to be.

Under such restrictions no author can be genuinely dramatic. Risden Home has had no chance except in the Greville episode of the first act; and this is of quite extraordinary merit as plays go nowadays. Greville is drawn as only a woman could draw him. Although the character sketches certainly lack the vividness, and the dialogue lacks the force and the independence of literary forms and conventions which a more practised hand could have given them, yet they are several knots ahead of average contemporary dramatic fiction. The literary power displayed is, after Mr Wilson Barrett and Miss Corelli, positively classical; and the author has plenty of scenic instinct. We have probably not heard the last of Risden Home.

Mrs Patrick Campbell, in a wig so carefully modelled on that head of hair which is one of Miss Elizabeth Robins's most notable graces that for a moment I could hardly decide whether I was looking at Miss Robins made up like Mrs Campbell or Mrs Campbell made up like Miss Robins, is a charming Lady Hamilton. She even acts occasionally, and that by no means badly. In the first scene, her delivery of the long speech to Greville—an excellently written speech for stage use—is delivered as a schoolgirl repeats her catechism: its happy indifference of manner and glib utterance almost unhinged my reason. But in the scene of the breach with Greville she played excellently; and the rest of her part, though often underdone, was not ill done—sometimes very much the reverse—and always gracefully and happily done. Mr Forbes Robertson, as the waxwork Nelson, has no difficulty in producing the necessary effect, and giving it more interest than it has any right to expect. Mr Nutcombe Gould plays Sir

William Hamilton; Mr Ben Greet, Romney; and Mr Sydney Brough, Sir John Trevor. The mounting is all that can be desired, except that the studies in Romney's studio are absurdly made to resemble the well-known portraits of the real Lady Hamilton instead of Mrs Campbell.

My Friend the Prince, at the Garrick, is a farce in three acts— just two acts too long for a farce. The utter levity with which Mr McCarthy wastes his talent is unpardonable: that handsome princess might easily have made a play of My Friend the Prince if the author had been in the least in earnest. Mr Welch makes a poor part funny by the most abandoned clowning; Mr Kaye, in spite of his mannerism, makes a genuine character of the *parvenu*; Miss Juliet Nesville is perfect as Gilberte; and Mr Aubrey Bouci- cault, though he forgets sometimes that the grimacing style for which we readily enough forgive an older actor like Mr Blakeley is out of the question for the rising generation of comedians, is sufficiently ludicrous as Pink Jannaway. For the rest, the ladies might be worse; and the gentlemen might be better.

I wish, for Miss Hughes's sake, I could confidently predict a long run for Sweet Nancy at the Court. When Nancy was pub- lished I was one of Miss Rhoda Broughton's admirers; for she was the first novelist who went straight to life for her pictures, taken from the children's point of view, of the household life of the genteel, impecunious, modern middle-class family, held to- gether only by economic pressure, the family habit, and the common struggle to keep up appearances and conform to con- ventions. Such children (I was one myself) knew the nobler human relations and wider social duties by name only as appetiz- ing subjects of derision. Miss Broughton distilled the irreverent fun of this into fiction with great humor; but when she wanted to be serious, she had no idea of the tragic scope of her theme, and had to fall back on romance and idealism, with its lumps in the throat, self-pity, separations, misunderstandings, griefs, deaths, and so on. At least it was so in the Nancy days: since then I have read no novels of Miss Broughton's, and hardly half a dozen of anyone else's.

In the play which Mr Robert Buchanan has extracted from Nancy, the merriment of the nursery scenes is effectively reproduced—a job well inside Mr Buchanan's powers—but the false sentiment does not stand the strain of the stage so well. However much quadrigenarian critics may relish the successful courtship of Sir Roger Tempest, aged forty-seven, with Nancy, aged eighteen, it is impossible for any considerate person to forget that Sir Roger is taking a revolting advantage of the girl's utter inability to realize what it will be like, at thirty-nine, to have a husband of sixty-eight. The marriage is half a purchase and half a seduction; and nothing can make the sentiment of a play founded on a sympathetic view of such a marriage quite wholesome. The fun supplied by the children operates as an antidote during the first two acts; but in the third their subsidence leaves the conclusion obvious, flimsy and mushy.

Sweet Nancy is well cast and played up to a certain point. Miss Hughes is as pretty, lively, clever, and amusing as she can be; Mr Maurice just suits Sir Roger; Miss Cowen and Miss Faber as the mother and daughter are excellent—indeed Miss Faber is almost painfully good as Barbara; and the children, impersonated by Messrs Martin Harvey, Hubert Short, Trebel, and the irrepressible Miss Beatrice Ferrar, are immense. But Miss Hughes, too true a comedian to be able to give any plausibility to false pathos, betrays weak spots in the play which a worse actress would cover up; and the part of Mrs Huntly, small in bulk, but of great dramatic importance, is underrated by Miss Helen Ferrers, who plays it confidently and offhandedly in a style which makes it impossible to sympathize with Nancy's jealousy, or to understand the disadvantage at which she feels placed by the experience and faultless finish of Zephine as drawn by Miss Broughton. However, a good deal of Sweet Nancy is highly diverting; Miss Hughes's personal success is unquestionable; and the little play by Mrs Oscar Beringer, called A Bit of Old Chelsea, must be well worth seeing if it is all as good as the last five minutes of it. I arrived too late to be able to answer for the earlier passages.

Next week, at the Court Theatre, Miss Robins takes the second step in the enterprise inaugurated by Little Eyolf with five *matinées* of Echegaray's Mariana.

THE ECHEGARAY MATINÉES

MARIANA. By José Echegaray. Translated by James Graham. Court Theatre, 22 February 1897.　　　[27 *February* 1897]

IT is now nearly two years since I pointed out, on the publication of Mr James Graham's translations of Echegaray, that Mariana was pre-eminently a play for an actress-manageress to snap up. The only person who appreciated the opportunity in this country was Miss Elizabeth Robins. Mr Daly, on the other side of the Atlantic, tried to secure the play for Miss Ada Rehan; but early as Mr Daly gets up in the morning, Miss Robins gets up earlier: otherwise we might have had Mariana, touched up in Mr Daly's best Shakespearean style, at the Comedy last season instead of Countess Gucki.

The weakness of Mariana lies in the unconvincing effect of the disclosure which brings about the catastrophe. When a circumstance that matters very little to us is magnified for stage purposes into an affair of life and death, the resultant drama must needs be purely sensational: it cannot touch our consciences as they are touched by plays in which the motives are as real to us as the actions. If the atmosphere of Mariana were thoroughly conventional and old-fashioned, or if Mariana were presented at first as a fanatical idealist on the subject of "honor," like Ruy Gomez in Hernani, or Don Pablo, we might feel with her that all was lost when she discovered in her chosen Daniel the son of the man with whom her mother had eloped, even though that circumstance does not involve the remotest consanguinity between them. But since she is introduced as the most wayward and wilful of modern women, moving in a by no means serious set, the fanatical action she takes is to a Londoner neither inevitable nor natural. For us there are only two objections to Daniel. The first —that it would be very embarrassing to meet his father—is

56

trivial, and might be got over simply by refusing to meet him. The other—the repulsion created by the idea of Daniel's close relationship to the man she loathes—is credible and sufficient enough; but it is quite incompatible with the persistence of such an ardent affection for him that she can only fortify herself against his fascination by marrying a murderously jealous and strait-laced man for whom she does not care. In short, the discovery either produces a revulsion of feeling against Daniel or it does not. If it does, the monstrous step of marrying Pablo is unnecessary; if not, Mariana is hardly the woman to allow a convention to stand between her and her lover. At all events, it seems to me that the motive of the catastrophe, however plausible it may be in Spain, is forced and theatrical in London; that the situation at the end of the third act is unconvincing; and that Englishwomen will never be able to look at Mariana and say, "But for the grace of God, there go I," as they do at Ibsen's plays. But with this reservation, the play is a masterly one. Not only have we in it an eminent degree of dramatic wit, imagination, sense of idiosyncrasy, and power over words (these qualifications are perhaps still expected from dramatists in Spain), but we have the drawing room presented from the point of view of a man of the world in the largest sense. The average British play purveyor, who knows what a greengrocer is like, and knows what a stockbroker or editor is like, and can imagine what a duke is like, and cannot imagine what a Cabinet Minister is like; who has been once to the private view at the Academy in the year when his own portrait was exhibited there, and once to the Albert Hall to hear Albani in Elijah, and once to the Opera to hear Carmen, and has cultivated himself into a perfect museum of chatty ignorances of big subjects, is beside Echegaray what a beadle is beside an ambassador. Echegaray was a Cabinet Minister himself before the vicissitudes to which that position generally leads in Spain drove him, at forty-two, to turn his hand in exile to dramatic authorship. When you consider what a parochially insular person even Thackeray was, and how immeasurably most of our dramatists fall short of Thackeray in width of social horizon, you will be prepared for the effect of superiority Echegaray produces as a man who comprehends his world, and knows society not as any diner-out or Mayfair butler knows it, but as a capable statesman knows it.

The performance on Monday last began unhappily. In the first act everybody seemed afraid to do more than hurry half-heartedly over an exposition which required ease, leisure, confidence, and brightness of comedy style to make it acceptable. In the preliminary conversation between Clara and Trinidad, Miss Sitgreaves and Miss Mary Keegan, though neither of them is a novice, were so ill at ease that we hardly dared look at them; and their relief when Mr Hermann Vezin and Mr Martin Harvey came to keep them in countenance was obvious and heartfelt. Yet, later on, Miss Sitgreaves, who is unmistakeably a clever actress, made quite a hit; and Miss Keegan walked in beauty like the night with more than her customary aplomb. Even Miss Robins had to force her way in grey desperation through the first act until quite near the end, when Mr Irving's fervour and a few lucky signs from the audience that the play was fastening upon them got the performance under way at last. Thereafter all went well. Miss Robins and Mr Hermann Vezin carried the representation in the second act to a point at which even the picked part of the audience were reassured and satisfied, and the ordinary part became ruefully respectful, and perhaps even wondered whether it might not be the right thing, after all, to enjoy this sort of play more than looking at a tailor's advertisement making sentimental remarks to a milliner's advertisement in the middle of an upholsterer's and decorator's advertisement. However, much as I enjoyed Mr Hermann Vezin's performance as Don Felipe, I must tell him in a friendly way that his style of acting will not do for the stage of today. He makes two cardinal mistakes. The first is that he accepts as the first condition of an impersonation that it should be credibly verisimilar. He is wrong: he should first make himself totally incredible and impossible, and then, having fascinated the audience by an effect of singularity and monstrosity, heighten that effect by such appropriate proceedings as the part will lend itself to without absolute disaster. Second, he should remember that acting will no more go down without plenty of sentiment smeared all over it than a picture will without plenty of varnish. His matter-of-fact sensible ways in matter-of-fact sensible passages will not do: he should, either by thinking of his own greatness for half an hour in his dressing room, or, if he has neither patience nor vanity enough for that, by a simple internal application of alcohol, work himself into a somnambulistic, hysterical, maudlin condition in which the most commonplace remark will seem fraught with emotions from the very ocean-bed of solemnity and pathos. That is the way to convince our Partridges that you are a real actor. However, it is an ill wind which blows nobody any good; and as I happen to appreciate Mr Vezin's rational style of acting, and to have a quite unspeakable contempt for the sleepwalking, drunken style, I hail Mr Vezin's rare appearances with great enjoyment and relief. I wonder, by the way, why the possession of skill and good sense should be so fatal to an actor or actress as it is at present. Why do we never see Mr Vezin or Mr William Farren except when a revival of The School for Scandal or Olivia makes them absolutely indispensable? Why is it morally certain that if Mr Hare had not gone into management, we should for years past have heard of him, without ever seeing him, as everybody's dearest friend, only so "dry," so "unlucky," so any-excuse-for-engaging-some-third-rate-nonentity-in-his-place, that he would be only a name to young playgoers? Why should Sir Henry Irving and Mr Wyndham vanish instantly from the stage if they did not hold their places by the strong hand as managers? I said I wondered at these things; but that was only a manner of speaking, for I think I know the reasons well enough. They will be found in my autobiography, which will be published fifty years after my death.

Well, as I have intimated, Mr Vezin was an excellent Felipe, and in fact secured the success of the play by his support to Mariana in the critical second act. But Miss Robins would, I think, have succeeded at this point triumphantly, support or no support; for the scene is not only a most penetrating one, but it demands exactly those qualities in which her strength lies, notably an intensity in sympathizing with herself which reminds one of David Copperfield. The parallel will bear pursuing by those who are interested in arriving at a clear estimate of Miss Robins's peculiar assortment of efficiencies and deficiencies—an assortment commoner off the stage than on it. For instance, she fails as Mariana just where Dickens would have failed if he had attempted to draw such a character: that is, in conveying the least impression of her impulsive rapture of love for Daniel. Almost any woman on the stage, from the most naïve little animal in our musical farces up to the heartwise Miss Ellen Terry, could have played better to Daniel than Miss Robins did. Her love scenes have some scanty flashes of mischievous humor in them, of vanity, of curiosity of a vivisectionist kind—in short, of the egotistical, cruel side of the romantic instinct; but of its altruistic, affectionate side they have not a ray or beam. Only once did a genuine sympathetic impulse shew itself; and that was not to Daniel, but to the foster-father Felipe. Yet Miss Robins played the lover very industriously. She rose, and turned away, and changed chairs, and was troubled and tranquil, grave and gay, by turns, and gave flowers from her bosom, all most painstakingly. Being unable to put her heart into the work and let it direct her eyes, she laid muscular hold of the eyes at first hand and worked them from the outside for all they were worth. But she only drew blood once; and that was when she looked at Daniel and said something to the effect that "Nobody can look so ridiculous as a lover." There was no mistake about the sincerity of that, or of the instant response from the audience, which had contemplated Miss Robins's elaborately acted and scrupulously gentlemanlike gallantries with oppressed and doubting hearts.

I must say I cannot bring myself to declare this a short-coming on Miss Robins's part, especially since her success as the sympathetic Asta Allmers proves that it cannot have been the affection that eluded her, but only the romance. Among the Russian peasantry young people when they fall romantically in love are put under restraint and treated medically as lunatics. In this country they are privileged as inspired persons, like ordinary lunatics in ignorant communities; and if they are crossed, they may (and often do) commit murder and suicide with the deepest public sympathy. In John Gabriel Borkman (a performance of which is promised by Miss Robins immediately after Easter) a lady, Mrs Wilton, elopes with a young man. Being a woman of some experience, thoroughly alive to the possibility that she will get tired of the young man, or the young man of her, not to mention the certainty of their boring one another if they are left alone together too much with no resource but lovemaking, she takes the precaution of bringing another woman along with her. This incident has provoked a poignant squeal of indignation from the English Press. Much as we journalists are now afraid of Ibsen after the way in which we burnt our fingers in our first handling of him, we could not stand Mrs Wilton's forethought. It was declared on all hands an unaccountable, hideous, and gratuitously nasty blemish on a work to which, otherwise, we dared not be uncomplimentary. But please observe that if Ibsen had represented Mrs Wilton as finding a love letter addressed by Borkman Junior to Frida Feldal, and as having thereupon murdered them both and then slain herself in despair on their corpses, everybody would have agreed that a lady could do no less, and that Ibsen had shewn the instinct of a true tragic poet in inventing the incident. In this very play of Echegaray's, a man who has already murdered one wife out of jealousy shoots Mariana before the eyes of the audience on the same provocation, as a preliminary to killing her lover in a duel. This atrocious scoundrel is regarded as shewing a high sense of honor, although if, like the heroes of some of our divorce cases, he had merely threatened to kill his wife's pet dog out of jealousy of her attachment to it, public sympathy would have abandoned him at once. Under such circumstances, and with the newspapers containing at least three romantic murders a fortnight as symptoms of the insane condition of the public mind in sex matters, I hail the evidences of the Russian view in Miss Robins with relief and respect; and I sincerely hope that on this point she will not try to adapt her acting to the drama, but will insist on the drama being adapted to her acting.

This does not alter the fact that until we have a Mariana who can convince us that she is as great a fool about Daniel as Daniel is about her, we shall not have the Mariana of Echegaray. And when we get the right Mariana in that respect, she will probably fall short of Miss Robins in that side of the part which is motived by Mariana's intense revulsion from the brutality, selfishness, and madness which underlie the romantic side of life as exemplified by her mother's elopement with Alvarado. Here Miss Robins carries all before her; and if only her part as the modern woman cured of romance, and fully alive to the fact that the romantic view of her sex is the whole secret of its degradation, were not manacled to another part—that of the passionately romantic old-fashioned woman—her triumph in it would be complete. As it is, the performance must needs produce an effect of inequality; and those who, not being trained critical analysts, cannot discover the clue to its variations must be a good deal puzzled by the artificiality of Miss Robins's treatment of the love theme, which repeatedly mars the effect of her genuine power over the apparently more difficult theme of the lesson she has learnt from Alvarado, and of her impulse to place herself under the grim discipline of Pablo. The main fault really lies, as I have shewn, with the dramatist, who has planned his play on the romantic lines of Schiller and Victor Hugo, and filled it in with a good deal of modern realist matter.

Mr H. B. Irving, as Daniel, is untroubled by Russian scruples, and raves his way through the transports of the Spanish lover in a style which will not bear criticism, but nevertheless disarms it, partly by its courage and thoroughness, partly because it is the only possible style for him at the present stage of his trying but not unpromising development as an actor. Mr Welch's Castulo is a masterpiece of manner and make-up. Mr O'Neill is not quite fitted as Pablo: he looks more likely to get shot by

Miss Robins than to shoot her. Mr Martin Harvey, Mr George Bancroft, and Miss Mabel Hackney take care of the minor parts. As matters of detail I may suggest that the first act might have been improved by a little more ingenuity of management, and by a slight effort on the part of the company to conceal their hurry to get through it. Also that Mr Irving will certainly be cut off with a shilling if his father ever hears him speak of "the Marianer of my dreams," and that Miss Robins's diction, once very pleasant, and distinguished by a certain charming New England freshness, is getting stained and pinched with the tricks of genteel Bayswater cockneydom—a thing not to be suffered without vehement protest.

GALLERY ROWDYISM

The Mac Haggis. A farce in three acts. By Jerome K. Jerome and Eden Phillpotts. Globe Theatre, 25 February 1897.

[6 *March* 1897]

The Mac Haggis, at the Globe Theatre, is a wild tale of a prim young London gentleman who suddenly succeeds to the chieftainship of a Highland clan—such a clan as Mr Jerome K. Jerome might have conceived in a nightmare after reading Rob Roy. It is an intentionally and impenitently outrageous play: in fact its main assumptions are almost as nonsensical as those of an average serious drama; but its absurdity is kept within the limits of human endurance by the Jeromian shrewdness and humanity of its small change. Nevertheless it is not good enough for Mr Weedon Grossmith, being only the latest of a long string of farces written for him on the assumption that he is a funny man and nothing more. The truth is that he is the only first-rate comedian under fifty on the London stage. Later on he may find a worthy rival in Mr Welch; but at present his superiority in comedy is incontestable. In this Mac Haggis business, silly as much of it is, there is not a touch of caricature or a taint of clowning. Take for example the farcical duel with Black Hamish in the last act, which might have been designed as a bit of business for a circus clown. Mr

Grossmith lifts it to the comedy plane by acting that fight as if he were on Bosworth Field. His gleam of self-satisfaction when he actually succeeds in hitting his adversary's shield a very respectable thwack, and the blight that withers up that perky little smile as the terrible Hamish comes on undaunted, are finer strokes of comedy than our other comedians can get into the most delicate passages of parts written by Jones and Pinero. He never caricatures, never grimaces, never holds on to a laugh like a provincial tenor holding on to his high B flat, never comes out of his part for an instant, never relaxes the most anxious seriousness about the affairs of the character he is impersonating, never laughs at himself or with the audience, and is, in consequence, more continuously and keenly amusing in farce than any other actor I ever saw except Jefferson. The very naturalness of his work leads the public into taking its finest qualities as a matter of course; so that whilst the most inane posing exhibitions by our tailor-made leading men are gravely discussed as brilliant conceptions and masterly feats of execution, Mr Grossmith's creations, exemplifying all the artistic qualities which the others lack, pass as nothing more than the facetiousnesses of a popular entertainer.

The Mac Haggis is happily cast and well played all round, Miss Laura Johnson giving an appalling intensity to the restless audacities of Eweretta. Miss Johnson will probably be able to do justice to a moderately quiet part when she is eighty-five or thereabouts: at present she seems to have every qualification of a modern actress except civilization. This was the secret of her success as Wallaroo in The Duchess of Coolgardie. In all her parts she "goes Fantee" more or less.

Although there were no dissentients to the applause at the end of The Mac Haggis, the authors did not appear to make the customary acknowledgments. For some time past the gods have been making themselves a more and more insufferable nuisance. The worry of attending first nights has been mercilessly intensified by the horrible noises they offer to their idols as British cheers. I do not object to a cheer that has the unmistakeable depth and solidity of tone that come only from a genuine ebullition of enthusiasm; but this underbred, heartless, incontinent, wide-mouthed, slack-fibred, brainless bawling is wearisome and disgusting beyond endurance. Naturally it provokes furious opposition; and of late an attempt has been made to countermine the people who bawl indiscriminately at everything and everybody by forming an opposition which resolutely boos at everybody and everything. This of course only makes two uproars, each stimulating the other to redoubled obstreperousness, where formerly there was but one. Both the managers and the authors have been forced at last to take action in the matter. Mr Henry Arthur Jones left the gods at the Garrick to howl vainly for the author for twenty-five minutes after the fall of the curtain; and Mr Jerome K. Jerome has followed his example both at the Prince of Wales and Globe Theatres. The managers held back until the first-nighters, getting bolder in their misconduct, began to interrupt the actors just as political speakers are interrupted at stormy election meetings. Then they called in the police.

Thereupon much soreness of feeling broke out. The first-nighters, quite unconscious that their silliness and rowdiness had long ago revolted the most indulgent of their friends, and still believing themselves to be a popular institution instead of an exasperating public nuisance, were deeply hurt at the unkindness of the managers, the injustice of the police (who are apt to propitiate public order with vicarious sacrifices on such occasions), and the attack on their privilege of clamor. Finally an understanding was arrived at. The right of the gallery to hiss and hoot and bawl to its heart's content was fully admitted as a principle of the British Constitution, the least infringement of which would be equivalent to the tearing up of Magna Charta; but it was agreed that the right should not be exercised until the fall of the curtain.

The result of this was of course that the gallery now began to hoot as an affirmation of its right to hoot, without reference to the merits of the performance. The gentlemen who had formerly lain in wait for such lines as "Let me tell you that you are acting detestably," or "Would that the end were come!" to disconcert the speaker with a sarcastic "Hear, hear!" felt that since they had exchanged this amusement for leave to hiss as much as they liked at the end of the play, the permission must not lie unused. The Daughters of Babylon was the first great occasion on which the treaty came into operation; and the gallery seized the opportunity to outdo itself in folly. In the first act every popular favorite in the cast was greeted by an outbreak of the old forced, artificial, unmanly, undignified, base-toned, meaningless howling which degrades the gallery to the level of a menagerie. At the end the hooting—the constitutional hooting—began, and immediately a trial of endurance set in between the hooters and those who wished to give Mr Wilson Barrett an ovation. After a prolonged and dismal riot, Mr Barrett turned the laugh against the hooters, shouted them down with half a dozen stentorian words, and finally got the audience out of the house. At Nelson's Enchantress the same medley of applause and hooting arose; and Mr Forbes Robertson, not caring, doubtless, to ask Risden Home to make her first public appearance by exposing herself to a half silly, half blackguardly mob demonstration, made her acknowledgments for her. But the moment he said—what else could he say?—that he would convey to her the favorable reception of her piece, the hooters felt that their constitutional rights would be ignored unless Mr Robertson conveyed the hoots as well as the plaudits. He very pointedly declined to do anything of the kind, and rebuked the constitutional party, which retired abashed but grumbling.

These little scenes before the curtain are so obviously mischievous and disgraceful, that the malcontents and the constitutionalists are now reinforced by a section of demonstrators whose object it is to put a stop to the speech-making, author-calling system altogether. It will be remembered that on the first night of The Notorious Mrs Ebbsmith Mr Hare was about to respond to the demand for a speech. Just as he opened his mouth to begin somebody called out "No speech." Mr Hare, with great presence of mind, immediately bowed and withdrew. Nobody has since been so successful in helping a manager out of a senseless ceremony; but the objection on principle to speech-making still struggles for expression in the tumult.

Here, then, we have so many elements of disorder that it is necessary to give the situation some serious consideration. Let us see, to begin with, whether the alleged constitutional right to hoot and hiss can be defended. I suppose it will not be denied that it is on the face of it so offensive and unmannerly a thing for one man to hiss and hoot at another that such conduct must stand condemned unless it can be justified as a criminal sentence is justified. I know that there are gallery-goers who contend that if the people who like the play applaud it, the people who dislike it should in justice shew, by expressing their dissatisfaction, that the approval is not unanimous. They might as well contend that if a gentleman who admires a lady tells her that she has pretty hands, any bystander who does not admire her should immediately in justice tell her that she has a red nose, or that because foolish admirers of actresses throw bouquets to them, those who think the compliment undeserved should throw bad eggs and dead cats. No: hooting must stand or fall by its pretension to be a salutary and necessary department of lynch law. Now in punishing criminals we treat them with atrocious cruelty—so much so that a good deal of crime goes unpunished at present because humane people will not call in the police or prosecute except in extreme cases. But cruel as our punishments are, we do not now make a sport of them as our forefathers did. Though we deal out sentences of hard labor and of penal servitude which some of the victims would willingly exchange, if they could, for the stocks, the pillory, or a reasonable degree of branding, flogging, or ear-clipping, it cannot be said of our methods that they are hypocritical devices for gratifying our own vilest lusts under the cloak of justice. We did not stop flogging women at the cart's tail through the streets because the women disliked it—we condemn women to much more dreadful penalties at every sessions—but because the public liked it. Solitary confinement is a diabolical punishment; but at least nobody gets any gratification out of it; and the fun of seeing a black flag go up on a prison flagstaff must be very poor compared to the bygone Tyburnian joys of seeing the culprit hanged. Hence I submit that if an author or actor is to be punished for a bad play or a bad performance, his punishment should not be made a popular sport. The punishment of setting him before the curtain to be hooted at is nothing but a survival of the pillory. Why should the theatre lag behind the police court in this respect? Why is the lust of the rabble to mock, jeer, insult, deride, and yell bestially at their unfortunate fellow-creatures recognized as sacred in the gallery when it is suppressed by the police everywhere else? I use the word rabble because it was invented to describe a crowd which has thrown away all decency of behavior and is conducting itself just as savagely and uproariously as it dares. The people in the stalls and balcony and amphitheatre are superior to the rabble, not because they pay more for admission, but because they do not yell, are content with clapping when they are pleased, and go home quietly when they are disappointed. The people in the pit and gallery who do yell, either approvingly or maliciously, and who remain making a disturbance until somebody comes out to confront them, are a rabble and nothing else. What right have they to behave in such a way? They dont do it at concerts; they dont do it in church; even in International Socialist Congresses and in the House of Commons, both notoriously disorderly places, such scenes are the exception and not the rule. As to the notion that such disorder has any beneficial effect as an informal censorship of the drama, I really cannot condescend to discuss so grotesque a pretension. If there is a case in which lynch law might be supposed to have some use in the theatre, it is that of the low comedian who deliberately interpolates obscene gags into musical farces, and implicates in them the performer to whom he is speaking. A single vigorous hiss from the gallery would cure any actor for ever of such black-guardism. When has that hiss ever been forthcoming? On the other hand, the gallery will trample furiously on delicate work like Mr Henry James's, and keep refined and sensitive artists who attempt original and thoughtful work in dread all through the first night lest some untheatrical line should provoke a jeer or some stroke of genuine pathos a coarse laugh. There would be

68

nothing to fear if playgoers were not demoralized by the low standard of manners and conduct prevailing in the gallery. What possibility is there of fine art flourishing where full licence to yell —the licence of the cockpit and prize-ring—is insisted on by men who never dream of misbehaving themselves elsewhere?

If I were starting in theatrical management tomorrow, I should probably abolish the shilling gallery on first nights, and make the lowest price of admission either half a crown or threepence, according to the district. A threepenny gallery is humble and decent, a half-crown one snobbish and continent. A shilling gallery has the vices of both and the virtues of neither. But if the shilling gallery is to continue, let it behave as the stalls behave: that is, applaud, when it wants to applaud, with its hands and not with its voice, and go home promptly and quietly when it does not want to applaud. If there is anything wrong with the performance, the management and the author will expiate it quite severely enough by heavy loss and disappointment. I may add that clapping as a method of applause has the great advantage of being far more expressive than shouting. The compass of vigor and speed of repercussion through which it varies is so great that its *nuances* are practically infinite: you can tell, if your ear is worth anything, whether it means a perfunctory "Thanks awf'ly," or a cool "Good evening: sorry I shant be able to come again," or an eager "Thank you *ever* so much: it was splendid," or any gradation between. Shouting can convey nothing but "Booh!" or "Hooray!" except, as I have said, in moments of real enthusiasm, quite foreign to the demonstrativeness of our theatre fanciers and greenroom gossip swallowers. Best of all would be no applause; but that will come later on. For the present, since we cannot contain ourselves wholly, let us at least express ourselves humanly and sensibly.

MADOX BROWN, WATTS, AND IBSEN

THE MARINERS OF ENGLAND. A new and original romantic
drama in four acts. By Robert Buchanan and Charles Marlowe.
Olympic Theatre, 9 March 1897.
SAUCY SALLY. A farce in three acts, by F. C. Burnand. Adapted
from La Flamboyante. Comedy Theatre, 10 March 1897.

[13 *March* 1897]

IT has not yet been noticed, I think, that the picture galleries in
London are more than usually interesting just now to those lovers
of the theatre who fully understand the saying "There is only
one art." At the Grafton Gallery we have the life-work of the
most dramatic of all painters, Ford Madox Brown, who was a
realist; at the New Gallery that of Mr G. F. Watts, who is an
idealist; and at the Academy that of Leighton, who was a mere
gentleman draughtsman.

I call Madox Brown a realist because he had vitality enough to
find intense enjoyment and inexhaustible interest in the world as
it really is, unbeautified, unidealized, untitivated in any way for
artistic consumption. This love of life and knowledge of its worth
is a rare thing—whole Alps and Andes above the common
market demand for prettiness, fashionableness, refinement, elegance of style, delicacy of sentiment, charm of character, sympathetic philosophy (the philosophy of the happy ending), decorative moral systems contrasting roseate and rapturous vice
with lilied and languorous virtue, and making "Love" face both
ways as the universal softener and redeemer, the whole being
worshipped as beauty or virtue, and set in the place of life to
narrow and condition it instead of enlarging and fulfilling it. To
such self-indulgence most artists are mere pandars; for the sense
of beauty needed to make a man an artist is so strong that the
sense of life in him must needs be quite prodigious to overpower
it. It must always be a mystery to the ordinary beauty-fancying,
life-shirking amateur how the realist in art can bring his unbeautified, remorseless celebrations of common life in among so

70

many pretty, pleasant, sweet, noble, touching fictions, and yet take his place there among the highest, although the railing, the derision, the protest, the positive disgust, are almost universal at first. Among painters the examples most familiar to us are Madox Brown and Rembrandt. But Madox Brown is more of a realist than Rembrandt; for Rembrandt idealized his color; he would draw life with perfect integrity, but would paint it always in a golden glow—as if he cared less for the direct light of the sun than for its reflection in a pot of treacle—and would sacrifice real color to that stage glow without remorse. Not so Madox Brown. You can all but breathe his open air, warm yourself in his sun, and smell "the green mantle of the standing pool" in his Dalton picture. Again, Rembrandt would have died rather than paint a cabbage unconditionally green, or meddle with those piercing aniline discords of color which modern ingenuity has extracted from soot and other unpromising materials. Madox Brown took to Paisley shawls and magenta ribbons and genuine greengrocer's cabbages as kindly as Wagner took to "false relations" in harmony. But turn over a collection of Rembrandt's etchings, especially those innumerable little studies which are free from the hobby of the chiaroscurist; and at once you see the uncompromising realist. Examine him at the most vulnerable point of the ordinary male painter—his studies of women. Women begin to be socially tolerable at thirty, and improve until the deepening of their consciousness is checked by the decay of their faculties. But they begin to be pretty much earlier than thirty, and are indeed sometimes at their best in that respect long before their chattering is, apart from the illusions of sex, to be preferred in serious moments to the silent sympathy of an intelligent pet animal. Take the young lady painted by Ingres as La Source, for example. Imagine having to make conversation for her for a couple of hours. Ingres is not merely indifferent to this: he is determined to make you understand that he values her solely for her grace of form, and is too much the classic to be affected by any more cordial consideration. Among Rembrandt's etchings, on the other hand, you will find plenty of women of all sorts; and you will be astonished and even scandalized at the catholicity of his interest and tolerance. He makes no conditions, classical or moral, with his heroines: Venus may be seventy, and Chloe in her least presentable predicament: no matter: he draws her for her own sake with enormous interest, neither as a joke, nor a moral lesson, nor a model of grace, but simply because he thinks her worth drawing as she is. You find the same thing in Madox Brown. Nature itself is not more unbiassed as between a pretty woman and a plain one, a young woman and an old one, than he. Compare the comely wife of John of Gaunt in the Wycliffe picture with the wife of Foscari, who has no shop-window good looks to give an agreeable turn to the pitifulness of her action as she lifts the elbow of the broken wretch whose maimed hands cannot embrace her without help. A *bonne bouche* of prettiness here would be an insult to our humanity; but in the case of Mrs John of Gaunt, the good looks of the wife as she leans over and grabs at the mantle of John, who, in the capacity of the politically excited Englishman, is duly making a fool of himself in public, give the final touch to the humor and reality of the situation. Nowhere do you catch the mature Madox Brown at false pathos or picturesque attitudinizing. Think of all the attitudes in which we have seen Francesca da Rimini and her lover; and then look at the Grafton Gallery picture of that deplorable, ridiculous pair, sprawling in a death agony of piteous surprise and discomfiture where the brutish husband has just struck them down with his uncouthly murderous weapon. You ask disgustedly where is the noble lover, the beautiful woman, the Cain-like avenger? You exclaim at the ineptitude of the man who could omit all this, and simply make you feel as if the incident had really happened and you had seen it— giving you, not your notion of the beauty and poetry of it, but the life and death of it. I remember once, when I was an "art critic," and when Madox Brown's work was only known to me by a few drawings, treating Mr Frederick Shields to a critical demonstration of Madox Brown's deficiencies, pointing out in one of the drawings the lack of "beauty" in some pair of elbows that had more of the wash tub than of The Toilet of Venus about them. Mr Shields contrived without any breach of good manners to make it quite clear to me that he considered Madox Brown a great painter and me a fool. I respected both convictions at the time; and now I share them. Only, I plead in extenuation of my folly that I had become so accustomed to take it for granted that what every English painter was driving at was the sexual beautification and moral idealization of life into something as unlike itself as possible, that it did not at first occur to me that a painter could draw a plain woman for any other reason than that he could not draw a pretty one.

Now turn to Mr Watts, and you are instantly in a visionary world, in which life fades into mist, and the imaginings of nobility and beauty with which we invest life become embodied and visible. The gallery is one great transfiguration: life, death, love and mankind are no longer themselves: they are glorified, sublimified, lovelified: the very draperies are either rippling lakes of color harmony, or splendid banners like the flying cloak of Titian's Bacchus in the National Gallery. To pretend that the world is like this is to live the heavenly life. It is to lose the whole world and gain one's own soul. Until you have reached the point of realizing what an astonishingly bad bargain that is you cannot doubt the sufficiency of Mr Watts's art, provided only your eyes are fine enough to understand its language of line and color.

Now if you want to emulate my asinine achievements as a critic on the occasion mentioned above in connection with Mr Shields, you cannot do better than criticize either painter on the assumption that the other's art is the right art. This will lead you by the shortest cut to the conclusion either that Mr Watts's big picture of the drayman and his horses is the only great work he ever achieved, or that there is nothing endurable in Madox Brown's work except the embroidery and furniture, a few passages of open-air painting, and such technical *tours de force* as his combination of the virtuosities of the portrait styles of Holbein, Antonio Moro, and Rembrandt in the imaginary portrait of Shakespear. In which event I can only wish you sense enough to see that your conclusion is not a proof of the futility of Watts or

Madox Brown but a *reductio ad absurdum* of your own critical method.

And now, what has all this to do with the drama? Even if it had nothing to do with it, reader, the question would be but a poor return for the pains I am taking to improve your mind; but let that pass. Have you never been struck with the similarity between the familiar paroxysms of Anti-Ibsenism and the abuse, the derision, the angry distaste, the invincible misunderstanding provoked by Madox Brown? Does it not occur to you that the same effect has been produced by the same cause—that what Ibsen has done is to take for his theme, not youth, beauty, morality, gentility, and propriety as conceived by Mr Smith of Brixton and Bayswater, but real life taken as it is, with no more regard for poor Smith's dreams and hypocrisies than the weather has for his shiny silk hat when he forgets his umbrella? Have you forgotten that Ibsen was once an Idealist like Mr Watts, and that you can read The Vikings, or The Pretenders, or Brand, or Emperor and Galilean in the New Gallery as suitably as you can hang Madox Brown's Parisina or Death of Harold in the Diploma Gallery at the Royal Academy? Or have you not noticed how the idealists who are full of loathing for Ibsen's realistic plays will declare that these idealistic ones are beautiful, and that the man who drew Solveig the Sweet could never have descended to Hedda Gabler unless his mind had given way.

I had intended to pursue this matter much further; but I am checked, partly by want of space, partly because I simply dare not go on to Leighton, and make the application of his case to the theatre. Madox Brown was a man; Watts is at least an artist and poet; Leighton was only a gentleman. I doubt if it was ever worth while being a gentleman, even before the thing had become the pet fashion of the lower-middle class; but today, happily, it is no longer tolerated among capable people, except from a few old Palmerstonians who do not take it too seriously. And yet you cannot cure the younger actor-managers of it. Sir Henry Irving stands on the Watts plane as an artist and idealist, cut off from Ibsen and reality by the deplorable limitations of that state, but at least not a snob, and only a knight on public grounds and by his own peremptory demand, which no mere gentleman would have dared to make lest he should have offended the court and made himself ridiculous. But the others!—the knights expectant. Well, let me not be too highminded at their expense. If they are Leightonian, they might easily be worse. There are less handsome things in the world than that collection of pictures at the Academy, with its leading men who are all gentlemen, its extra ladies whose Liberty silk robes follow in their flow the Callipygean curves beneath without a suggestion of coarseness, its refined resolution to take the smooth without the rough, Mayfair without Hoxton, Melbury Road without Saffron Hill. All very nice, gentlemen and ladies; but much too negative for a principle of dramatic art. To suppress instead of to express, to avoid instead of to conquer, to ignore instead of to heal: all this, on the stage, ends in turning a man into a stick for fear of creasing his tailor's handiwork, and a woman into a hairdresser's window image lest she should be too actressy to be invited to a fashionable garden-party.

The Mariners of England, the new Nelson play at the Olympic, is a frankly cynical exploitation of cant, claptrap, and playgoers' folly by Mr Robert Buchanan, in collaboration with "Charles Marlowe." Mr Buchanan takes the same liberties with Nelson as with himself, making that hero play to the gallery by saying, not the authentic "They have done for me at last, Hardy: I am shot through the backbone," but "They have done for me at last, Hardy: one last broadside and the day is ours." The dialogue includes more "God bless you's" than I have ever heard in one evening on the stage even in recent years. No doubt the public richly deserves what it has got in this melodrama; but that does not justify the slight put by Mr Buchanan on his own capacity, which, if it does not clamor to do better things than The Mariners of England, must certainly be the very laziest and most unconscionable capacity of its rank in the world.

Saucy Sally, at the Comedy, is a farcical comedy of the well-worn kind, about a gentleman who keeps two establishments,

75

and explains his absences from both by pretending to be a marine explorer. It is always amusing to see Mr Hawtrey lying his way in and out of domestic complications. His cleverness, tact, and humor are in constant play, with uproarious results, throughout the farce; but he needs them all to play up to Mrs Charles Calvert, whose performance as the mother-in-law is a triumph from the first look to the last word. I had not the advantage of seeing Mrs Calvert's Cleopatra thirty years ago; but if she was as incomparably the first actress in her line then as she is now, I deeply regret my loss. Mr Hendrie is good as the grateful sailor; but as to the rest it is a case of Mrs Calvert first, Mr Hawtrey a very good sixteenth, and the rest nowhere.

SHAKESPEAR IN MANCHESTER

ANTONY AND CLEOPATRA. Shakespearean revival by Mr Louis Calvert at the Queen's Theatre, Manchester.

[20 *March* 1897]

SHAKESPEAR is so much the word-musician that mere practical intelligence, no matter how well prompted by dramatic instinct, cannot enable anybody to understand his works or arrive at a right execution of them without the guidance of a fine ear. At the great emotional climaxes we find passages which are Rossinian in their reliance on symmetry of melody and impressiveness of march to redeem poverty of meaning. In fact, we have got so far beyond Shakespear as a man of ideas that there is by this time hardly a famous passage in his works that is considered fine on any other ground than that it sounds beautifully, and awakens in us the emotion that originally expressed itself by its beauty. Strip it of that beauty of sound by prosaic paraphrase, and you have nothing left but a platitude that even an American professor of ethics would blush to offer to his disciples. Wreck that beauty by a harsh, jarring utterance, and you will make your audience wince as if you were singing Mozart out of tune. Ignore it by "avoiding sing-song"—that is, ingeniously breaking the verse up so as to make it sound like prose, as the professional elocutionist prides himself on doing—and you are landed in a stilted, monstrous jargon that has not even the prosaic merit of being intelligible. Let me give one example: Cleopatra's outburst at the death of Antony:

> Oh withered is the garland of the war,
> The soldier's pole is fallen: young boys and girls
> Are level now with men: the odds is gone,
> And there is nothing left remarkable
> Beneath the visiting moon.

This is not good sense—not even good grammar. If you ask what does it all mean, the reply must be that it means just what its utterer feels. The chaos of its thought is a reflection of her mind, in which one can vaguely discern a wild illusion that all human distinction perishes with the gigantic distinction between Antony and the rest of the world. Now it is only in music, verbal or other, that the feeling which plunges thought into confusion can be artistically expressed. Any attempt to deliver such music prosaically would be as absurd as an attempt to speak an oratorio of Handel's, repetitions and all. The right way to declaim Shakespear is the sing-song way. Mere metric accuracy is nothing. There must be beauty of tone, expressive inflection, and infinite variety of *nuance* to sustain the fascination of the infinite monotony of the chanting.

Miss Janet Achurch, now playing Cleopatra in Manchester, has a magnificent voice, and is as full of ideas as to vocal effects as to everything else on the stage. The march of the verse and the strenuousness of the rhetoric stimulate her great artistic susceptibility powerfully: she is determined that Cleopatra shall have rings on her fingers and bells on her toes, and that she shall have music wherever she goes. Of the hardihood of ear with which she carries out her original and often audacious conceptions of Shakespearean music I am too utterly unnerved to give any adequate description. The lacerating discord of her wailings is in my tormented ears as I write, reconciling me to the grave. It is as if she had been excited by the Hallelujah Chorus to dance on the keyboard of a great organ with all the stops pulled out. I cannot—dare not—dwell on it. I admit that when she is using the rich middle of her voice in a quite normal and unstudied way, intent only on the feeling of the passage, the effect leaves nothing to be desired; but the moment she raises the pitch to carry out some deeply planned vocal masterstroke, or is driven by Shakespear himself to attempt a purely musical execution of a passage for which no other sort of execution is possible, then—well then, hold on tightly to the elbows of your stall, and bear it like a man. And when the feat is accompanied, as it sometimes is, by bold experiments in facial expression which all the passions of Cleopatra, complicated by seventy-times-sevenfold demoniacal possession, could but faintly account for, the eye has to share the anguish of the ear instead of consoling it with Miss Achurch's beauty. I have only seen the performance once; and I would not unsee it again if I could; but none the less I am a broken man after it. I may retain always an impression that I have actually looked on Cleopatra enthroned dead in her regal robes, with her hand on Antony's, and her awful eyes inhibiting the victorious Cæsar. I grant that this "resolution" of the discord is grand and memorable; but oh! how infernal the discord was whilst it was still unresolved! That is the word that sums up the objection to Miss Achurch's Cleopatra in point of sound: it is discordant.

I need not say that at some striking points Miss Achurch's performance shews the same exceptional inventiveness and judgment in acting as her Ibsen achievements did, and that her energy is quite on the grand scale of the play. But even if we waive the whole musical question—and that means waiving the better half of Shakespear—she would still not be Cleopatra. Cleopatra says that the man who has seen her "hath seen some majesty, and should know." One conceives her as a trained professional queen, able to put on at will the deliberate artificial dignity which belongs to the technique of court life. She may keep it for state occasions, like the unaffected Catherine of Russia, or always retain it, like Louis XIV, in whom affectation was nature; but that she should have no command of it—that she should rely in

modern republican fashion on her personal force, with a frank
contempt for ceremony and artificiality, as Miss Achurch does,
is to spurn her own part. And then, her beauty is not the beauty
of Cleopatra. I do not mean merely that she is not "with Phœbus'
amorous pinches black," or brown, bean-eyed, and pickaxe-
faced. She is not even the English (or Anglo-Jewish) Cleopatra,
the serpent of old Thames. She is of the broad-browed, column-
necked, Germanic type—the Wagner heroine type—which in
England, where it must be considered as the true racial heroic
type, has given us two of our most remarkable histrionic geniuses
in Miss Achurch herself and our dramatic singer, Miss Marie
Brema, both distinguished by great voices, busy brains, commanding physical energy, and untameable impetuosity and
originality. Now this type has its limitations, one of them being
that it has not the genius of worthlessness, and so cannot present
it on the stage otherwise than as comic depravity or masterful
wickedness. Adversity makes it superhuman, not subhuman, as
it makes Cleopatra. When Miss Achurch comes on one of the
weak, treacherous, affected streaks in Cleopatra, she suddenly
drops from an Egyptian warrior queen into a naughty English
petite bourgeoise, who carries off a little greediness and a little
voluptuousness by a very unheroic sort of prettiness. That is,
she treats it as a stroke of comedy; and as she is not a comedian, the
stroke of comedy becomes in her hands a bit of fun. When the
bourgeoise turns into a wild cat, and literally snarls and growls
menacingly at the bearer of the news of Antony's marriage with
Octavia, she is at least more Cleopatra; but when she masters herself, as Miss Achurch does, not in gipsy fashion, but by a heroic-
grandiose act of self-mastery, quite foreign to the nature of the
"triple turned wanton" (as Mr Calvert bowdlerizes it) of Shakespear, she is presently perplexed by fresh strokes of comedy—

He's very knowing.
I do perceive 't: theres nothing in her yet:
The fellow has good judgment.

At which what can she do but relapse farcically into the bour-

geoise again, since it is not on the heroic side of her to feel elegantly self-satisfied whilst she is saying mean and silly things,
as the true Cleopatra does? Miss Achurch's finest feat in this
scene was the terrible look she gave the messenger when he said,
in dispraise of Octavia, "And I do think she's thirty"—Cleopatra
being of course much more. Only, as Miss Achurch had taken
good care not to look more, the point was a little lost on Manchester. Later on she is again quite in her heroic element (and out
of Cleopatra's) in making Antony fight by sea. Her "I have sixty
sails, Cæsar none better," and her overbearing of the counsels
of Enobarbus and Canidius to fight by land are effective, but
effective in the way of a Boadicea, worth ten guzzling Antonys.
There is no suggestion of the petulant folly of the spoiled beauty
who has not imagination enough to know that she will be
frightened when the fighting begins. Consequently when the
audience, already puzzled as to how to take Cleopatra, learns that
she has run away from the battle, and afterwards that she has sold
Antony to Cæsar, it does not know what to think. The fact is,
Miss Achurch steals Antony's thunder and Shakespear's thunder
and Ibsen's thunder and her own thunder so that she may ride
the whirlwind for the evening; and though this *Walkürenritt* is
intense and imposing, in spite of the discords, the lapses into
farce, and the failure in comedy and characterization—though
once or twice a really memorable effect is reached—yet there is
not a stroke of Cleopatra in it; and I submit that to bring an
ardent Shakespearean like myself all the way to Manchester to
see Antony and Cleopatra with Cleopatra left out, even with
Brynhild-cum-Nora Helmer substituted, is very different from
bringing down soft-hearted persons like Mr Clement Scott and
Mr William Archer, who have allowed Miss Achurch to make
Ibsen-and-Wagner pie of our poor Bard's historical masterpiece
without a word of protest.

And yet all that I have said about Miss Achurch's Cleopatra
cannot convey half the truth to those who have not seen Mr
Louis Calvert's Antony. It is on record that Antony's cooks put
a fresh boar on the spit every hour, so that he should never have

to wait long for his dinner. Mr Calvert looks as if he not only had the boars put on the spit, but ate them. He is inexcusably fat: Mr Bourchier is a sylph by comparison. You will conclude, perhaps, that his fulness of habit makes him ridiculous as a lover. But not at all. It is only your rhetorical tragedian whose effectiveness depends on the oblatitude of his waistcoat. Mr Calvert is a comedian—brimming over with genuine humane comedy. His one really fine tragic effect is the burst of laughter at the irony of fate with which, as he lies dying, he learns that the news of Cleopatra's death, on the receipt of which he mortally wounded himself, is only one of her theatrical, sympathy-catching lies. As a lover, he leaves his Cleopatra far behind. His features are so pleasant, his manner so easy, his humor so genial and tolerant, and his portliness so frank and unashamed, that no good-natured woman could resist him; and so the topsiturvitude of the performance culminates in the plainest evidence that Antony is the seducer of Cleopatra instead of Cleopatra of Antony. Only at one moment was Antony's girth awkward. When Eros, who was a slim and rather bony young man, fell on his sword, the audience applauded sympathetically. But when Antony in turn set about the Happy Despatch, the consequences suggested to the imagination were so awful that shrieks of horror arose in the pit; and it was a relief when Antony was borne off by four stalwart soldiers, whose sinews cracked audibly as they heaved him up from the floor.

Here, then, we have Cleopatra tragic in her comedy, and Antony comedic in his tragedy. We have Cleopatra heroically incapable of flattery or flirtation, and Antony with a wealth of blarney in every twinkle of his eye and every fold of his chin. We have, to boot, certain irrelevant but striking projections of Miss Achurch's genius, and a couple of very remarkable stage pictures invented by the late Charles Calvert. But in so far as we have Antony and Cleopatra, we have it partly through the genius of the author, who imposes his conception on us through the dialogue in spite of everything that can be done to contradict him, and partly through the efforts of the secondary performers.

Of these Mr George F. Black, who plays Octavius Cæsar, speaks blank verse rightly, if a little roughly, and can find his way to the feeling of the line by its cadence. Mr Mollison—who played Henry IV here to Mr Tree's Falstaff—is Enobarbus, and spouts the description of the barge with all the honors. The minor parts are handled with the spirit and intelligence that can always be had by a manager who really wants them. A few of the actors are certainly very bad; but they suffer rather from an insane excess of inspiration than from apathy. Charmian and Iras (Miss Ada Mellon and Miss Maria Fauvet) produce an effect out of all proportion to their scanty lines by the conviction and loyalty with which they support Miss Achurch; and I do not see why Cleopatra should ungratefully take Iras's miraculous death as a matter of course by omitting the lines beginning "Have I the aspic in my lips," nor why Charmian should be robbed of her fine reply to the Roman's "Charmian, is this well done?" "It is well done, and fitted for a princess descended of so many royal kings." No doubt the Cleopatras of the palmy days objected to anyone but themselves dying effectively, and so such cuts became customary; but the objection does not apply to the scene as arranged in Manchester. Modern managers should never forget that if they take care of the minor actors the leading ones will take care of themselves.

May I venture to suggest to Dr Henry Watson that his incidental music, otherwise irreproachable, is in a few places much too heavily scored to be effectively spoken through? Even in the *entr'actes* the brass might be spared in view of the brevity of the intervals and the almost continuous strain for three hours on the ears of the audience. If the music be revived later as a concert suite, the wind can easily be restored.

Considering that the performance requires an efficient orchestra and chorus, plenty of supernumeraries, ten or eleven distinct scenes, and a cast of twenty-four persons, including two leading parts of the first magnitude; that the highest price charged for admission is three shillings; and that the run is limited to eight weeks, the production must be counted a triumph of management.

There is not the slightest reason to suppose that any London manager could have made a revival of Antony and Cleopatra more interesting. Certainly none of them would have planned that unforgettable statue death for Cleopatra, for which, I suppose, all Miss Achurch's sins against Shakespear will be forgiven her. I begin to have hopes of a great metropolitan vogue for that lady now, since she has at last done something that is thoroughly wrong from beginning to end.

MEREDITH ON COMEDY

AN ESSAY ON COMEDY. By George Meredith. Westminster: Archibald Constable and Co. 1897.   [27 *March* 1897]

TWENTY years ago Mr George Meredith delivered a lecture at the London Institution on Comedy and the Uses of the Comic Spirit. It was afterwards published in the New Quarterly Magazine, and now reappears as a brown buckram book, obtainable at the inconsiderable price (considering the quality) of five shillings. It is an excellent, even superfine, essay, by perhaps the highest living English authority on its subject. And Mr Meredith is quite conscious of his eminence. Speaking of the masters of the comedic spirit (if I call it, as he does, the Comic Spirit, this darkened generation will suppose me to refer to the animal spirits of tomfools and merryandrews), he says, "Look there for your unchallengeable upper class." He should know; for he certainly belongs to it. At the first page I recognize the true connoisseur, and know that I have only to turn it to come to the great name of Molière, who has hardly been mentioned in London during the last twenty years by the dramatic critics, except as representing a quaint habit of the Comédie Française. That being so, why republish an essay on comedy now? Who cares for comedy today?—who knows what it is?—how many readers of Mr Meredith's perfectly straightforward and accurate account of the wisest and most exquisite of the arts will see anything in the book but a brilliant sally of table talk about old plays: to be enjoyed, without practical application, as one of the rockets in the grand firework display of contemporary *belles-lettres*?

However, since the thing is done, and the book out, I take leave to say that Mr Meredith knows more about plays than about playgoers. "The English public," he says, "have the basis of the comic in them: an esteem for common sense." This flattering illusion does not dupe Mr Meredith completely; for I notice that he adds "taking them generally." But if it were to be my last word on earth I must tell Mr Meredith to his face that whether you take them generally or particularly—whether in the lump, or sectionally as playgoers, churchgoers, voters, and what not—they are everywhere united and made strong by the bond of their common nonsense, their invincible determination to tell and be told lies about everything, and their power of dealing acquisitively and successfully with facts whilst keeping them, like disaffected slaves, rigidly in their proper place: that is, outside the moral consciousness. The Englishman is the most successful man in the world simply because he values success—meaning money and social precedence—more than anything else, especially more than fine art, his attitude towards which, culture-affectation apart, is one of half diffident, half contemptuous curiosity, and of course more than clear-headedness, spiritual insight, truth, justice, and so forth. It is precisely this unscrupulousness and singleness of purpose that constitutes the Englishman's pre-eminent "common sense"; and this sort of common sense, I submit to Mr Meredith, is not only not "the basis of the comic," but actually makes comedy impossible, because it would not seem like common sense at all if it were not self-satisfiedly unconscious of its moral and intellectual bluntness, whereas the function of comedy is to dispel such unconsciousness by turning the searchlight of the keenest moral and intellectual analysis right on to it. Now the Frenchman, the Irishman, the American, the ancient Greek, is disabled from this true British common sense by intellectual virtuosity, leading to a love of accurate and complete consciousness of things—of intellectual mastery of them. This produces a positive enjoyment of disillusion (the most dreaded and hated of calamities in England), and consequently a love of comedy (the fine art of disillusion) deep enough to make huge sacrifices of dearly idealized institutions to it. Thus, in France, Molière was allowed to destroy the Marquises. In England he could not have shaken even such titles as the accidental sheriff's knighthood of the late Sir Augustus Harris. And yet the Englishman thinks himself much more independent, level-headed, and genuinely republican than the Frenchman—not without good superficial reasons; for nations with the genius of comedy often carry all the snobbish ambitions and idealist enthusiasms of the Englishman to an extreme which the Englishman himself laughs at. But they sacrifice them to comedy, to which the Englishman sacrifices nothing; so that, in the upshot, aristocracies, thrones, and churches go by the board at the attack of comedy among our devotedly conventional, loyal, and fanatical next-door neighbors; whilst we, having absolutely no disinterested regard for such institutions, draw a few of their sharpest teeth, and then maintain them determinedly as part of the machinery of worldly success.

The Englishman prides himself on this anti-comedic common sense of his as at least eminently practical. As a matter of fact, it is just as often as not most pigheadedly unpractical. For example, electric telegraphy, telephony, and traction are invented, and establish themselves as necessities of civilized life. The unpractical foreigner recognizes the fact, and takes the obvious step of putting up poles in his streets to carry wires. This expedient never occurs to the Briton. He wastes leagues of wire and does unheard-of damage to property by tying his wires and posts to such chimney stacks as he can beguile householders into letting him have access to. Finally, when it comes to electric traction, and the housetops are out of the question, he suddenly comes out in the novel character of an amateur in urban picturesqueness, and declares that the necessary cable apparatus would spoil the appearance of our streets. The streets of Nuremberg, the heights of Fiesole, may not be perceptibly the worse for these contrivances; but the beauty of Tottenham Court Road is too sacred to be so profaned: to its loveliness the strained bus-horse and his offal are the only accessories endurable by the beauty-loving

Cockney eye. This is your common-sense Englishman. His help-lessness in the face of electricity is typical of his helplessness in the face of everything else that lies outside the set of habits he calls his opinions and capacities. In the theatre he is the same. It is not common sense to laugh at your own prejudices: it is common sense to feel insulted when anyone else laughs at them. Besides, the Englishman is a serious person: that is, he is firmly persuaded that his prejudices and stupidities are the vital material of civilization, and that it is only by holding on to their moral prestige with the stiffest resolution that the world is saved from flying back into savagery and gorilladom, which he always conceives, in spite of natural history, as a condition of lawlessness and promiscuity, instead of, as it actually is, the extremity, long since grown unbearable, of his own notions of law and order, morality, and conventional respectability. Thus he is a moralist, an ascetic, a Christian, a truth-teller and a plain dealer by profession and by conviction; and it is wholly against this conviction that, judged by his own canons, he finds himself in practice a great rogue, a liar, an unconscionable pirate, a grinder of the face of the poor, and a libertine. Mr Meredith points out daintily that the cure for this self-treasonable confusion and darkness is Comedy, whose spirit overhead will "look humanely malign and cast an oblique light on them, followed by volleys of silvery laughter." Yes, Mr Meredith; but suppose the patients have "common sense" enough not to want to be cured! Suppose they realize the immense commercial advantage of keeping their ideal life and their practical business life in two separate conscience-tight compartments, which nothing but "the Comic Spirit" can knock into one! Suppose, therefore, they dread the Comic Spirit more than anything else in the world, shrinking from its "illumination," and considering its "silvery laughter" in execrable taste! Surely in doing so they are only carrying out the common-sense view, in which an encouragement and enjoyment of comedy must appear as silly and suicidal and "unEnglish" as the conduct of the man who sets fire to his own house for the sake of seeing the flying sparks, the red glow in the sky, the fantastic shadows on the walls, the excitement of the crowd, the gleaming charge of the engines, and the dismay of the neighbors. No doubt the day will come when we shall deliberately burn a London street every day to keep our city up to date in health and handsomeness, with no more misgiving as to our common sense than we now have when sending our clothes to the laundry every week. When that day comes, perhaps comedy will be popular too; for, after all, the function of comedy, as Mr Meredith after twenty years' further consideration is perhaps by this time ripe to admit, is nothing less than the destruction of old-established morals. Unfortunately, today such iconoclasm can be tolerated by our playgoing citizens only as a counsel of despair and pessimism. They can find a dreadful joy in it when it is done seriously, or even grimly and terribly as they understand Ibsen to be doing it; but that it should be done with levity, with silvery laughter like the crackling of thorns under a pot, is too scandalously wicked, too cynical, too heartlessly shocking to be borne. Consequently our plays must either be exploitations of old-established morals or tragic challengings of the order of Nature. Reductions to absurdity, however logical; banterings, however kindly; irony, however delicate; merriment, however silvery, are out of the question in matters of morality, except among men with a natural appetite for comedy which must be satisfied at all costs and hazards: that is to say, *not* among the English playgoing public, which positively dislikes comedy.

No doubt it is patriotically indulgent of Mr Meredith to say that "Our English school has not clearly imagined society," and that "of the mind hovering above congregated men and women it has imagined nothing." But is he quite sure that the audiences of our English school do not know too much about society and "congregated men and women" to encourage any exposures from "the vigilant Comic," with its "thoughtful laughter," its "oblique illumination," and the rest of it? May it not occur to the purchasers of half-guinea stalls that it is bad enough to have to put up with the pryings of Factory Inspectors, Public Analysts, County Council Inspectors, Chartered Accountants and the like, without admitting this Comic Spirit to look into still more delicate matters? Is it clear that the Comic Spirit would break into silvery laughter if it saw all that the nineteenth century has to shew it beneath the veneer? There is Ibsen, for instance: he is not lacking, one judges, in the Comic Spirit; yet his laughter does not sound very silvery, does it? No: if this were an age for comedies, Mr Meredith would have been asked for one before this. How would a comedy from him be relished, I wonder, by the people who wanted to have the revisers of the Authorized Version of the Bible prosecuted for blasphemy because they corrected as many of its mistranslations as they dared, and who reviled Froude for not suppressing Carlyle's diary and writing a fictitious biography of him, instead of letting out the truth? Comedy, indeed! I drop the subject with a hollow laugh.

The recasting of A Pierrot's Life at the *matinées* at the Prince of Wales Theatre greatly increases and solidifies the attraction of the piece. Felicia Mallet now plays Pierrot; but we can still hang on the upturned nose of the irresistible Litini, who reappears as Fifine. Litini was certainly a charming Pierrot; but the delicate, subtle charm was an intensely feminine one, and only incorporated itself dreamily with the drama in the tender shyness of the first act and the pathos of the last. Litini as a vulgar drunkard and gambler was as fantastically impossible as an angel at a horse-race. Felicia Mallet is much more credible, much more realistic, and therefore much more intelligible—also much less slim, and not quite so youthful. Litini was like a dissolute La Sylphide: Miss Mallet is frankly and heartily like a scion of the very smallest bourgeoisie sowing his wild oats. She is a good observer, a smart executant, and a vigorous and sympathetic actress, apparently quite indifferent to romantic charm, and intent only on the dramatic interest, realistic illusion, and comic force of her work. And she avoids the conventional gesture-code of academic Italian pantomime, depending on popularly graphic methods throughout. The result is that the piece is now much fuller of incident, much more exciting in the second act (hitherto the weak point) and much more vivid than before. Other changes have helped to bring this about. Jacquinet, no longer ridiculously condemned to clothe a Parisian three-card-trick man in the attire of the fashionable lover in L'Enfant Prodigue, appears in his proper guise with such success that it is difficult to believe that he is the same person. Miss Ellas Dee is a much prettier Louisette, as prettiness is reckoned in London, than her predecessor, whom she also surpasses in grace and variety of expression. Litini is a brilliant Fifine—the brevity of the part is regretted for the first time; and Rossi, though he is no better than before, probably would be if he had left any room for improvement. The band is excellent, and the music clever and effective, though it has none of those topical allusions which are so popular here—strangely popular, considering that the public invariably misses nine out of ten of them (who, for instance, has noticed that *entr'acte* in Saucy Sally in which the bassoon plays all manner of rollicking nautical airs as florid counterpoints to Tom Bowling?). Altogether the "play without words" is now at its best. One must be a critic to understand the blessedness of going to the theatre without having to listen to slipshod dialogue and affectedly fashionable or nasally stagey voices. Merely to see plastic figures and expressive looks and gestures is a delicious novelty to me; but I believe some of the public rather resent having to pay full price for a play without words, exactly as they resent having to pay for a doctor's advice without getting a bottle of nasty medicine along with it. Some of these unhappy persons may be observed waiting all through the performance for the speaking to begin, and retiring at last with loud expressions of disappointment at having been sold by the management. For my part, I delight in these wordless plays, though I am conscious of the difficulty of making any but the most threadbare themes intelligible to the public without words. In my youth the difficulty could have been got over by taking some story that everyone knew; but nowadays nobody knows any stories. If you put the Sleeping Beauty on the stage in dumb show, the only thing you could depend on the whole house knowing about her would be her private name and address, her salary, her engagements for next year, her favorite pastimes, and the name of her pet dog.

MR PINERO ON TURNING FORTY

THE PHYSICIAN. A new play of modern life in four acts. By Henry Arthur Jones. Criterion Theatre, 25 March 1897.

THE PRINCESS AND THE BUTTERFLY, or THE FANTASTICS. An original comedy in five acts. By Arthur W. Pinero. St James's Theatre, 29 March 1897. [3 *April* 1897]

WHEN I was a fastidious youth, my elders, ever eager to confer bad advice on me and to word it with disgusting homeliness, used to tell me never to throw away dirty water until I got in clean. To which I would reply that as I had only one bucket, the thing was impossible. So until I grew middle-aged and sordid, I acted on the philosophy of Bunyan's couplet:

> A man there was, tho' some did count him mad,
> The more he cast away, the more he had.

Indeed, in the matter of ideals, faiths, convictions and the like, I was of opinion that Nature abhorred a vacuum, and that you might empty your bucket boldly with the fullest assurance that you would find it fuller than ever before you had time to set it down again. But herein I youthfully deceived myself. I grew up to find the genteel world full of persons with empty buckets. Now The Physician is a man with an empty bucket. "By God!" he says (he doesnt believe in God), "I dont believe theres in any London slum, or jail, or workhouse, a poor wretch with such a horrible despair in his heart as I have today. I tell you Ive caught the disease of our time, of our society, of our civilization—middle age, disillusionment. My youth's gone. My beliefs are gone. I enjoy nothing. I believe in nothing. Belief! Thats the placebo I want. That would cure me. My work means nothing to me. Success means nothing to me. I cure people with a grin and a sneer. I keep on asking myself, 'To what end? To what end?'"

O dear! Have we not had enough of this hypochondriasis from our immortal bard in verse which—we have it on his own authority—"not marble, nor the gilded monuments of princes, shall outlive"? It is curable by Mr Meredith's prescription—the tonic of comedy; and when I see a comedian of Mr Wyndham's skill and a dramatist of Mr Jones's mother-wit entering into a physicianly conspiracy to trade in the disease it is their business to treat, I abandon all remorse, flatly refuse to see any "sympathetic" drama in a mere shaking of the head at life, and vow that at least one of Dr Carey's audience shall tell him that there is nothing in the world more pitiably absurd than the man who goes about telling his friends that life is not worth living, when they know perfectly well that if he meant it he could stop living much more easily than go on eating. Even the incorrigible Hamlet admitted this, and made his excuse for not resorting to the bare bodkin; but Dr Carey, who says "I never saw a man's soul," has not Hamlet's excuse. His superstitions are much cruder: they do not rise above those of an African witch-finder or Sioux medicine-man. He pretends to "cure" diseases—Mother Carey is much like Mother Seigel in this respect—and holds up a test-tube, whispering, "I fancy I'm on the track of the cancer microbe: I'm not sure I havent got my gentleman here." At which abject depth of nineteenth-century magicianism he makes us esteem Dr Diafoirus and the Apothecary in Romeo and Juliet as, in comparison, dazzling lights of science.

And now, as if it were not bad enough to have Mr Jones in this state of mind, we have Mr Pinero, who was born, as I learn from a recent biographic work of reference, in 1855, quite unable to get away from the same tragic preoccupation with the horrors of middle age. He has launched at us a play in five acts—two and a half of them hideously superfluous—all about being over forty. The heroine is forty, and can talk about nothing else. The hero is over forty, and is blind to every other fact in the universe. Having this topic of conversation in common, they get engaged in order that they may save one another from being seduced by the attraction of youth into foolish marriages. They then fall in love, she with a fiery youth of twenty-eight, he with a meteoric girl of eighteen. Up to the last moment I confess I had sufficient confidence in Mr Pinero's saving sense of humor to believe that he would give the verdict against himself, and admit that the meteoric girl was too young for the hero (twenty-seven years' discrepancy) and the heroine too old for the fiery youth (thirteen years' discrepancy). But no: he gravely decided that the heart that loves never ages; and now perhaps he will write us another drama, limited strictly to three acts, with, as heroine, the meteoric girl at forty with her husband at sixty-seven, and, as hero, the fiery youth at forty-nine with his wife at sixty-two.

Mr Henry Arthur Jones is reconciled to his own fate, though he cannot bear to see it overtake a woman. Hear Lady Val in his play! "I smell autumn; I scent it from afar. I ask myself how many years shall I have a man for my devoted slave. . . . Oh, my God, Lewin [she is an Atheist], it never can be worth while for a woman to live one moment after she has ceased to be loved." This, I admit, is as bad as Mr Pinero: the speech is actually paraphrased by Mrs St Roche in the St James's play. But mark the next sentence: "And you men have the laugh of us. Age doesnt wither you or stale your insolent, victorious, self-satisfied, smirking, commonplace durability! Oh, you brutes, I hate you all, because youre warranted to wash and wear for fifty years." Observe, *fifty* years, not forty. I turn again to my book of reference, and find, as I expected, that Mr Jones was born in 1851. I discover also that I myself was born in 1856. And this is '97. Well, my own opinion is that sixty is the prime of life for a man. Cheer up, Mr Pinero: courage, Henry Arthur! "What though the grey do something mingle with our younger brown" (excuse my quoting Shakespear), the world is as young as ever. Go look at the people in Oxford Street: they are always the same age.

As regards any conscious philosophy of life, I am bound to say that there is not so much (if any) difference between Mr Jones and Mr Pinero as the very wide differences between them in other respects would lead us to suppose. The moment their dramatic inventiveness flags, and they reach the sentimentally reflective interval between genuine creation and the breaking off work until next day, they fall back on the two great Shakespearean grievances—namely, that we cannot live for ever and that life is not worth living. And then they strike up the old tunes—"Out, out, brief candle!" "Vanitas vanitatum," "To what end?" and so on. But in their fertile, live moments they are as unlike as two men can be in the same profession. At such time Mr Pinero has no views at all. Our novelists, especially those of the Thackeray-Trollope period, have created a fictitious world for him; and it is about this world that he makes up stage stories for us. If he observes life, he does so as a gentleman observes the picturesqueness of a gipsy. He presents his figures coolly, clearly, and just as the originals like to conceive themselves—for instance, his ladies and gentlemen are not real ladies and gentlemen, but ladies and gentlemen as they themselves (mostly modelling themselves on fiction) aim at being; and so Bayswater and Kensington have a sense of being understood by Mr Pinero. Mr Jones, on the other hand, works passionately from the real. By throwing himself sympathetically into his figures he gives them the stir of life; but he also often raises their energy to the intensity of his own, and confuses their feelings with the revolt of his own against them. Above all, by forcing to the utmost their aspect as they really are as against their pose, he makes their originals protest violently that he cannot draw them—a protest formerly made, on exactly the same grounds, against Dickens. For example, Lady Val in The Physician is a study of a sort of clever fashionable woman now current; but it is safe to say that no clever fashionable woman, nor any admirer of clever fashionable women, will ever admit the truth or good taste of the likeness. And yet she is very carefully studied from life, and only departs from it flatteringly in respect of a certain energy of vision and intensity of conscience that belong to Mr Jones and not in the least to herself.

Compare with Lady Val the Princess Pannonia in Mr Pinero's play. You will be struck instantly with the comparative gentlemanliness of Mr Pinero. He seems to say, "Dear lady, do not be alarmed: I will shew just enough of your weaknesses to make you interesting; but otherwise I shall take you at your own valuation and make the most of you. I shall not forget that you are a

93

Princess from the land of novels. My friend Jones, who would have made an excellent Dissenting clergyman, has a vulgar habit of bringing persons indiscriminately to the bar of his convictions as to what is needful for the life and welfare of the real world. You need apprehend no such liberties from me. I have no convictions, no views, no general ideas of any kind: I am simply a dramatic artist, only too glad to accept a point of view from which you are delightful. At the same time, I am not insensible to the great and tragic issues that meet us wherever we turn. For instance, it is hardly possible to reach the age of forty without etc. etc. etc." And accordingly you have a cool, tasteful, polished fancy picture which reflects the self-consciousness of Princesses and the illusions of their imitators much more accurately than if Mr Jones had painted it.

The two plays present an extraordinary contrast in point of dramatic craft. It is no exaggeration to say that within two minutes from the rising of the curtain Mr Jones has got tighter hold of his audience and further on with his play than Mr Pinero within two hours. During those two hours, The Princess marks time complacently on the interest, the pathos, the suggestiveness, the awful significance of turning forty. The Princess has done it; Sir George Lamorant has done it; Mrs St Roche has done it; so has her husband. Lady Chichele, Lady Ringstead, and Mrs Sabiston have all done it. And they have all to meditate on it like Hamlet meditating on suicide; only, since soliloquies are out of fashion, nearly twenty persons have to be introduced to listen to them. The resultant exhibition of High Life Above Stairs is no doubt delightful to the people who had rather read the fashionable intelligence than my articles. To me not even the delight of playing Peeping Tom whilst Princess Pannonia was getting out of bed and flattering me with a vain hope that the next item would be her bath could reconcile me to two hours of it. If the women had worn some tolerable cap-and-apron uniform I could have borne it better; but those dreadful dresses, mostly out of character and out of complexion—I counted nine failures to four successes—upset my temper, which was not restored by a witless caricature of Mr Max Beerbohm (would he had written it himself!), or by the spectacle of gilded youth playing with toys whilst Sir George Lamorant put on a fool's cap and warned them that they would all be forty-five presently, or even by the final tableau, unspeakably sad to the British mind, of the host and hostess retiring for the night to separate apartments instead of tucking themselves respectably and domestically into the same feather bed. Yet who shall say that there is no comedy in the spectacle of Mr Pinero moralizing, and the public taking his reflections seriously? He is much more depressing when he makes a gentleman throw a glass of water at another gentleman in a drawing room, thereby binding the other gentleman in honor to attack his assailant in the street with a walking stick, whereupon the twain go to France to fight a duel for all the world as if they were at the Surrey Theatre. However, when this is over the worst is over. Mr Pinero gets to business at about ten o'clock, and the play begins in the middle of the third act—a good, old-fashioned, well-seasoned bit of sentimental drawing room fiction, daintily put together, and brightening at the end into a really light-hearted and amusing act of artificial comedy. So, though it is true that the man who goes to the St James's Theatre now at 7.45 will wish he had never been born, none the less will the man who goes at 9.30 spend a very pleasant evening.

The two authors have not been equally fortunate in respect of casting. Half Mr Jones's play—the women's half—is obliterated in performance. His Edana is a sterling, convinced girl-enthusiast. "Her face," says the Doctor, "glowed like a live coal." This sort of characterization cannot be effected on the stage by dialogue. Enthusiasts are magnetic, not by what they say, or even what they do, but by how they say and do it. Mr Jones could write "yes" and "no"; but it rested with the actress whether the affirmation and denial should be that of an enthusiast or not. Edana at the Criterion is played by Miss Mary Moore. Now Miss Moore is a dainty light comedian; and her intelligence, and a certain power of expressing grief rather touchingly and prettily, enable her to take painful parts on occasion without making herself ridiculous.

95

But they do not enable her to play an enthusiast. Consequently her Edana is a simple substitution of what she can do for what she is required to do. The play is not only weakened by this— all plays get weakened somewhere when they are performed— it is dangerously confused, because Edana, instead of being a stronger character than Lady Val, and therefore conceivably able to draw the physician away from her, is just the sort of person who would stand no chance against her with such a man. To make matters worse, Lady Val is played by Miss Marion Terry, who is in every particular, from her heels to her hairpins, exactly what Lady Val could not be, her qualities being even more fatal to the part than her faults. A more hopeless pair of misfits has never befallen an author. On the other hand, Mr Jones has been exceptionally fortunate in his men. Mr Alfred Bishop's parson and Mr J. G. Taylor's Stephen Gurdon are perfect. Mr Thalberg does what is wanted to set the piece going on the rising of the curtain with marked ability. The easy parts—which include some racy village studies—are well played. Mr Leslie Kenyon, as Brooker, has the tact that is all the part requires; and the Physician is played with the greatest ease by Mr Wyndham himself, who will no doubt draw all Harley Street to learn what a consulting room manner can be in the hands of an artist. The performance as a whole is exceptionally fine, the size of the theatre admitting of a delicacy of handling without which Mr Jones's work loses half its sincerity.

In The Princess matters are better balanced. There is a fearful waste of power: out of twenty-nine performers, of whom half are accustomed to play important parts in London, hardly six have anything to do that could not be sufficiently well done by nobodies. Mr Pinero seems to affirm his supremacy by being extravagant in his demands for the sake of extravagance; and Mr Alexander plays up to him with an equally high hand by being no less extravagant in his compliances. So the piece is at all events not underplayed; and it has crowned the reputation of Miss Fay Davis, whose success, the most sensational achieved at the St James's Theatre since that of Mrs Patrick Campbell as

Paula Tanqueray, is a success of cultivated skill and self-mastery on the artist's part, and not one of the mere accidents of the stage. Miss Neilson, ever fair and fortunate, puts a pleasant face on a long and uninteresting part, all about the horrors of having reached forty without losing "the aroma of a stale girlhood." The Princess is ladylike and highly literary. When, in the familiar dilemma of the woman of forty with an inexperienced lover, she is forced to prevent his retiring in abashed despair by explaining to him that her terrifying fluster over his more personal advances only means that she likes them and wants some more, she choicely words it, "I would not have it otherwise." And his ardor is volcanic enough to survive even that. The lover's part falls to Mr H. B. Irving, who is gaining steadily in distinction of style and strength of feeling. Mr Alexander has little to do beyond what he has done often before—make himself interesting enough to conceal the emptiness of his part. He laments his forty-five years as mercifully as such a thing may be done; and he secures toleration for the silly episodes of the fool's cap and the quarrel with Maxime. Mr Esmond makes the most of a comic scrap of character; and Miss Rose Leclercq is duly exploited in the conventional manner as Lady Ringstead. Miss Patty Bell's Lady Chichele is not bad: the rest I must pass over from sheer exhaustion.

THE NEW CENTURY THEATRE

THE YASHMAK. A new musical play by Cecil Raleigh and Seymour Hicks. Music by Napoleon Lambelet. Shaftesbury Theatre, 1 April 1897.

SKIPPED BY THE LIGHT OF THE MOON. Musical comedy in two acts, by G. R. Sims. Music by Henry W. May and George Pack. Théâtre Métropole, Camberwell, 5 April 1897.

THE SPHINX AND THE CHIMNEY POT. A galanty show in five scenes. By W. L. Bruckman. Steinway Hall, 3 April 1897.

[10 *April* 1897]

THE New Century Theatre is the title of the latest combination of enthusiasts for the regeneration of the drama in this country.

It is the same group which lately achieved the performances of Little Eyolf and Mariana. Its prospectus is out; its program is announced; its conviction that "with the new century a new departure may be looked for in English theatrical life" is in print; and we are assured that "the sole endeavor of the Executive will be to further the cause of Dramatic Art, and, without bias or prejudice, to pave the way for the permanent institution, artistically administered, which is essential to the development of the drama and acting." Subscriptions are invited for four series of *matinées*, at which John Gabriel Borkman, Admiral Guinea (a Henley-Stevenson play), and perhaps Peer Gynt will be performed.

Meanwhile, another equally aspiring combination, The Independent Theatre, with precisely the same lofty aims, announces three series of Ibsen *matinées*, at which The Lady from the Sea, The Wild Duck, and the inevitable Doll's House will be produced.

The public at large will not care whether it gets its performances from the New Century Theatre, the Independent Theatre Company, or any ordinary commercial syndicate. It will subscribe for its seats at a reduction of 20 per cent or so, or pay at the doors at the usual rates. It is no more called upon to choose between the two societies than between Mr George Alexander and Mr Beerbohm Tree. But how about the public-spirited believer in the drama who wishes to endow the cause which these societies profess to represent? Such pious founders sometimes ask me which section best deserves a cash donation. On such occasions I can only suggest that half the donation should be given to one society and half to the other. This advice is invariably received with the contempt its feeblemindedness deserves; the donation is withheld; and the inquirer buys tickets for the performances as they are announced, leaving the *entrepreneurs* to fight their differences out between themselves. Now this state of things will clearly not result in the establishment of a great endowed theatre. If a small firm is speculating in "the New Drama," no doubt its enterprise will be quickened and its standard raised by the competition of a rival small firm; but both of them must remain far more dependent on immediate commercial success than, say, Sir Henry Irving, who, if he wished to "pave the way" for any future development, could pave it with gold for a month more easily than the New Century and the Independents together could pave it with good intentions for a single night. Mr Alexander has produced plays at the St James's Theatre for the sake of their literary distinction, with no sort of hope that the loss on them would be so moderate as the entire capital of the enthusiasts; and Mr Tree experimented in Ibsen, in Henley and Stevenson, and in Fulda at the Haymarket. Mr Hare produced Mrs Lessingham and a couple of "problem plays" by Mr Grundy at the Garrick. Mr Forbes Robertson and Mr Harrison tried Sudermann at the Lyceum. It is only in the case of the initial experiments—the true pioneer work—that the enthusiasts can claim to be indispensable. For it must not be forgotten that management on the west end scale is not the only practical alternative offered by commercialism to enthusiasm. When the Independent Theatre, a year or so ago, issued a pamphlet demonstrating that the west end system of costly productions and long runs is only practicable for plays childish enough to appeal to great multitudes of pleasure-seekers, all the Press applauded its conclusiveness. But if the Independent Theatre and the New Century Theatre are so poor that they can only maintain their existence by making their performances cover expenses, in what way are they better qualified to get over the difficulty than the numerous managers who do not venture on the splendors and hazards of west end management, and who do, in fact, deal from year's end to year's end in plays which run no longer, are no better mounted, and are much worse acted than Little Eyolf and Mariana? If money can be made in a small way in the theatre as well as in a large way, there are plenty of managers in a small way to make it when once the opening is discovered. The New Century Theatre, by declaring that its object is "to raise the standard of merit in plays, while very largely lowering the standard of receipts required to constitute an honorable success"—that is, to

99

recoup the loss on the merit of the play by the gain on the shabbiness of the performance—seems to me to give away its case, not perhaps as against the managers of Drury Lane, but certainly as against the hundreds of managers who are accustomed to cut their productions to the measure of a week's business.

If we are to accept this no longer glorious situation, the Independent Theatre can claim that it is constituted in due commercial form as a joint-stock company, under the control of its shareholders and regulated by law, whereas the New Century Theatre has frankly no constitution at all, and boldly declares that though it will constitute anybody an Associate for five shillings, the Associates will have no franchise, and the self-elected committee will do what it likes. In uncommercial matters these despotic ways generally work capitally when the despots enjoy the complete confidence of the public. In this instance the despots are Mr William Archer, Mr H. W. Massingham, Mr Alfred Sutro, and Miss Elizabeth Robins. Mr Archer was once accused before a Parliamentary Commission by the Queen's Examiner of Plays (Mr Redford's predecessor) of having written up Ibsen in order to make money by translating him; but this official explanation of the rise of the New Drama shook the credit of the Censorship, not of Mr Archer, whose name practically places the committee above suspicion. Mr Massingham, Bayreuth pilgrim and editor of the Daily Chronicle, is more effectually bound by his position to consider the public interest than any election could make him. Mr Sutro is a munificent patron of the theatre. Miss Robins, it is true, has personal interests which are as irreconcilable with the perfect artistic integrity of the New Century as any actor-manager's; for she is an actress, and practically the proprietress of several important rights of representation; but this does not give her any power on the committee which she could not exercise more irresponsibly off it; and her claims as a pioneer, an artist, and a trustworthy business manager are unquestionable. It therefore seems to me that the committee is strong enough to command the confidence it claims if it demands support for a real New Century Theatre.

But what on earth relation has its high character to the small business job of exploiting the little sets of *matinées*, spiritually precious, but materially cheap, which are just getting on their legs commercially?

The Independent Theatre has equal claims from the uncommercial point of view. Its shareholders are largely the same stage army which supports the newer enterprise; it has tumbled through a good deal of fruitful work under ludicrously difficult circumstances; and its little group of shareholders, indifferent to dividends, form, with the two managing directors, Miss Dorothy Leighton and Mr Charles Charrington, a committee to which no exception can be taken. And again I ask, what can this organization do for the next century? What is it going to do even for the nineteenth that, after Little Eyolf, does not seem feasible "in the ordinary way of theatrical business"? If it carries out its latest program—I hope it may—it will do just what all such enterprises, including the latest, vehemently protest that nothing would induce them to do: that is, compete with the ordinary *entrepreneurs* for the little plums of the Ibsen business.

The truth is, there are only two uncommercial factors required to keep the drama moving and to set and maintain a high standard of performance. One is the individual pioneer—the adventurer who explores the new territory at his own risk and is superseded by commercial enterprise the moment he is seen to pick up anything. The most thoroughgoing example of this type in the present movement is Mr Charles Charrington. The welter of ruinous experiments into which he plunged after his pioneer victory and tour round the world with A Doll's House seemed rash, inexcusable, and senseless at the time; and its disastrous pecuniary failure seemed a salutary check to an otherwise incorrigible desperado. But today everybody is doing what he did. His view that the only live English fiction is to be found today not in plays but in novels, and his attempt to drag it on to the stage no matter how little playgoers and actors were accustomed to its characteristic atmosphere, cost him several years' income, and would have cost him his reputation for common sense had he possessed one. But since then Trilby has justified her misunderstood predecessor Clever Alice; and the apparently idiotic "quintuple bill" of scenes from stories by Barrie, Conan Doyle, Thackeray, and so on, put up by Mr Charrington at Terry's Theatre, now seems like an epitome of what theatrical enterprise, with its rage for adaptations of novels, has since become. Other more cautious pioneers followed—Mr Grein, Miss Farr, Miss Robins; but nobody foresaw so much and nobody suffered so much as Mr Charrington.

Now the first condition upon which the New Century Theatre can obtain any public support is a conviction on the part of the public that it can be implicitly trusted not to imitate the unintelligible rashness of Mr Charrington. Mr Charrington took all the money he could get from the dreamers of a New Century Theatre, added all his own to it, and flung the whole away in order to get a handful of critics and playgoers into a theatre to shew them for a night or two an attempt at something which they did not understand. Mr Charrington will not do that with the Independent Theatre capital, because the shareholders would not let him, even if he were still young enough to want to sacrifice himself again. Mr Archer may be depended on to permit no such exploits on the part of the new society, even if Miss Robins's honorable insistence on the perfect solvency of all her undertakings should miraculously desert her. Imprudence, the first condition of pioneering, will be strictly barred in both societies. Therefore the first factor, the adventurer-pioneer, will not be supplied by them.

What is the second factor? Surely it is a theatre like the Bayreuth Festspielhaus, where standard performances of classic works, new and old, can be given, where a repertory can be formed, where actors can graduate in their profession, and where the public can be educated. An "ordinary" manager with the requisite artistic ambition, foresight, and pertinacity might possibly develop it out of a series of regular and carefully nursed weekly *matinées* addressed in the first instance to what may be called the Monday Popular and Richter public. But he would do it all the faster if he were subsidized by a body like the New Century Theatre, or the Independent Theatre, or a combination of both. The fashionable people used to go to Sir Augustus Harris and say, "We want an Italian opera: get it up for us and we will guarantee you to such and such a figure." Has it yet occurred to the enthusiasts to go to Mr Alexander or Mr Tree or Sir Henry Irving and say, "We want a series of masterpieces concurrently with The Prisoner of Zenda, Trilby, and Madame Sans-Gêne: what guarantee will induce you to start a series of one or two classical *matinées* per week?" After all, that is virtually what has been done up to the present time on a small scale. Money has been given to (and by) Mr Grein, Miss Robins, Miss Farr, and others, who have thereupon taken theatres and done the best they could at every possible disadvantage. But if a really considerable sum could be raised, and an influential and representative committee formed, the New Century Theatre might announce its first season at the Lyceum Theatre under the management of Sir Henry Irving, whose prejudices against Ibsen cannot possibly be stronger than those of Sir Augustus Harris against Wagner. It should then immediately demand a grant from Government under the same head as the grants to the National Gallery and British Museum. For more reasons than I have time to give here I believe that these are the only lines on which there is much prospect of success.

At all events, they are the only lines which can claim the interest of a new departure. With all respect to the New Century Theatre, there is nothing whatever new about its prospectus. The phrases about "plays of intrinsic merit" and the like are all nonsense; and the program is nothing but the continuation under a new name of the series of *matinées* which Miss Robins has given from time to time for years. I have always upheld the value of these *matinées*. I wish them the utmost success, and cordially recommend both them and the series announced by the Independents to the support of the public. But their success will leave us no nearer the foundation of a standard theatre; and that is the work that Mr Archer and Mr Massingham should set about forthwith.

The Yashmak is an exceedingly copious musical hotchpotch in two acts, lasting two hours each. It must have started, I think, as a serious Franco-Oriental opera, for there are survivals in it here and there of pretentious and by no means unsuccessful numbers in that *genre*. I have seen much worse entertainments at the height of Mr Arthur Roberts's operatic vogue at the Prince of Wales Theatre. Miss Kitty Loftus, reaping at last the reward of her astonishing industry, is becoming something of an artist, and will certainly end as a considerable one if she maintains her present rate of improvement. Like Mr Lionel Mackinder, who shares the chief honors of the piece with her, she seems to have a reserve of genuine dramatic talent behind the mere virtuosity in tomfoolery which this sort of piece requires. A Miss Aileen d'Orme had the happy idea of singing a song in French, which is evidently by no means her native tongue. The gallery, immensely flattered by the implied compliment to its high-class taste and linguistic attainments, applauded chivalrously. Miss Love, whose accomplishments have the quality of pathos rather than of aptitude, disarms criticism. The Yashmak rather amused me—I do not know why—so I shall not be surprised if it makes its way with less exacting playgoers.

I did not see all, or even very much, of Mr Sims's Skipped by the Light of the Moon at the Métropole; for the train on which I relied to deposit me at Camberwell shot me out in a lost condition at a place called South Tottenham—south, no doubt, of the Orkney Islands, but many degrees north of Camberwell. The audience laughed at the drolleries of Mr George Walton as I never heard a London audience laugh before; and two attractive young ladies played the intermezzo from Cavalleria as a mandoline duet, under which treatment the harmonic progressions in the prelude made me understand for the first time (through no fault of the players, let me add) what is meant by "getting the needle."

Mr Bruckman's galanty show at the reception given by the Dutch Club at Steinway Hall last Saturday was not dramatic. It is a series of historical illustrations accompanied by a mock rhetorical lecture, and is distinguished from the old galanty shows only by the decorative grace of the silhouettes, and not by any mechanical ingenuity, it being destitute even of an efficient contrivance for passing the profiles steadily across the screen. I confess I had a childish hope that the figures would "work" and perform a little play in the style of The Broken Bridge; but it was not to be; and pretty as some of the silhouettes were, I cannot deny that I had had enough of them by the time the curtain fell.

MADAME SANS-GÊNE

MADAME SANS-GÊNE. Comedy in a prologue and 3 acts. By MM.
  Sardou and Moreau. Translated by J. Comyns Carr. Lyceum
  Theatre, 10 April 1896.   [17 *April* 1897]

IT is rather a nice point whether Miss Ellen Terry should be forgiven for sailing the Lyceum ship into the shallows of Sardoodledom for the sake of Madame Sans-Gêne. But hardly any controversy has arisen on this point: everyone seems content to discuss how Miss Ellen Terry can bring herself to impersonate so vulgar a character. And the verdict is that she has surmounted the difficulty wonderfully. In that verdict I can take no part, because I do not admit the existence of the difficulty. Madame Sans-Gêne is *not* a vulgar person; and Miss Ellen Terry knows it. No doubt most people will not agree with Miss Ellen Terry. But if most people could see everything that Miss Ellen Terry sees, they would all be Ellen Terries instead of what they are.

I know that it will not be conceded to me without a struggle that a washerwoman who spits on her iron and tells her employees to "stir their stumps" is not vulgar. Let me, therefore, ask those persons of unquestioned fashion who have taken to bicycling, what they do when they find their pneumatic tyres collapsing ten miles from anywhere, and wish to ascertain, before undertaking the heavy labor of looking for a puncture, whether the valve is not leaking. The workman's way of doing this is no trade secret. He puts a film of moisture on the end of the valve, and watches whether that film is converted into a bubble by an escape of air. And he gets the moisture exactly where Madame Sans-Gêne gets the moisture for her flat iron. It may be that the washerwoman of the future, as soon as a trebling of her wages and a halving of her hours of labor enable her to indulge in a little fastidiousness, will hang a scent bottle with a spray diffuser at her chatelaine, though even then I doubt if the fashionable cyclist will prefer the resources of civilisation to those of nature when nobody is looking. But by that time the washerwoman will no doubt smoke cigarets, as to which habit of tobacco smoking, in what form soever it be practised, I will say nothing more than that the people who indulge in it, whether male or female, have clearly no right to complain of the manners of people who spit on flat irons. Indeed I will go further, and declare that a civilization which enjoins the deliberate stiffening of its shirts with white mud and the hotpressing thereof in order that men may look in the evening like silhouettes cut out of mourning paper, has more to learn than to teach in the way of good manners (that is, good sense) from Madame Sans-Gêne.

As to "stir your stumps," that is precisely what an ideal duchess would say if she had to bustle a laundry, and had tact and geniality enough to make a success of it. It is true that she might as easily say, "More diligence, ladies, please"; but she would not say it, because ideal duchesses do not deliberately say stupid and underbred things. Indeed our military officers, whose authority in matters of social propriety nobody will dispute, are apt to push the Sans-Gêne style to extremes in smartening the movements of Volunteers and others in reviews and inspections, to say nothing of the emergencies of actual warfare.

Concerning Madame Sans-Gêne's use of slang, which she carries to the extent of remarking, when there is a question of her husband being compelled by the Emperor to divorce her and marry a more aristocratic but slenderer woman, "You like em crumby, dont you?", I can only say that her practice is in accord with that of the finest masters of language. I have known and conversed with men whose command of English, and sense of beauty and fitness in the use of it, had made them famous. They all revelled in any sort of language that was genuinely vernacular, racy, and graphic. They were just as capable as Madame Sans-Gêne of calling a nose a snout or a certain sort of figure crumby; and between such literary solemnities as "magistrate" or "police-man" and the slang "beak" or the good English "copper" they would not have hesitated for a moment on familiar occasions. And they would have been outraged in the last degree had they been represented as talking of "bereavements," "melancholy occasions," or any of the scores of pretentious insincerities, affectations and literary flourishes of tombstone, rostrum, shop-catalogue, foreign-policy-leading-article English which Miss Terry could pass off without a word of remonstrance as high-class conversation.

It is further objected that Miss Terry drops into the dialect of Whitechapel, or rather a sort of generalized country dialect with some Whitechapel tricks picked up and grafted on to it. Here I am coming on dangerous ground; for it is plain that criticism must sooner or later speak out fiercely about that hideous vulgarity of stage speech from which the Lyceum has long been almost our only refuge. It seems to me that actors and actresses never dream nowadays of learning to speak. What they do is this. Since in their raw native state they are usually quite out of the question as plausible representatives of those galaxies of rank and fashion, the *dramatis personae* of our smart plays, and having no idea that the simple remedy is to learn the alphabet over again and learn it correctly, they take great pains to parrot a detestable convention of "smart" talking, supposed to represent refined speech by themselves and that huge majority of their audiences which knows no better, but actually a caricature of the affectations of the parvenu and the "outsider." Hence the common complaint among the better sort of gentlefolk that an evening at the theatre leaves an uncomfortable, almost outraged sensation of having been entrapped, like the Vicar of Wakefield, to a dinner-party at which the lords and ladies are really footmen and lady's maids "shewing off." The vulgarity of this convention is innocent compared to its unbearable monotony, fatal to that individuality without which no actor can interest an audience. All countries and districts send us parliamentary speakers who have cultivated the qualities of their native dialect and corrected its faults whilst aiming at something like a standard purity and clearness of speech. Take Mr Gladstone for instance. For his purposes as an orator he has studied his speech as carefully and with as great powers of application as any actor. But he has never lost, and never wanted to lose, certain features of his speech which stamp him as a North-countryman. When Mr T. P. O'Connor delivers a speech, he does not inflict on us the vulgarities of Beggar's Bush; but he preserves for us all the music of Galway, though he does not say "Yis" for "Yes" like a Galway peasant any more than he says "Now" (Nah-oo) for "No" like a would-be smart London actor. It is so with all good speakers off the stage. Among good speakers the Irishman speaks like an Irishman, the Scotsman like a Scotsman, the American like an American, and so on. It should be so on the stage also, both in classical plays and representations of modern society, though of course it is the actor's business to assume dialects and drop or change them at will in character parts, and to be something of a virtuoso in speech in all parts. A very moderate degree of accomplishment in this direction would make an end of stage smart speech, which, like the got-up Oxford mince and drawl of a foolish curate, is the mark of a snob. Indeed, the brutal truth is that the English theatre is at present suffering severely from an epidemic of second-rate snobbery. From that, at least, we are spared whilst Miss Ellen Terry and Sir Henry Irving are on the stage.

It is natural for those who think this snobbishness a really fine and genuine accomplishment to conclude that everybody must lust after it, and, consequently, that Madame Sans-Gêne's neglect to acquire it in spite of her opportunities as Duchess of Dantzig is incredible. Now far be it from me to deny that Sardou's assumption that the Duchess has not learnt to make a curtsey or to put on a low-necked dress must be taken frankly as an impossible pretext for a bit of clowning which may or may not be worth its cost in versimilitude. But, apart from this inessential episode, the idea that Catherine, being happily Madame Sans-Gêne, should deliberately manufacture herself into a commonplace Court lady—a person with about as much political influence or genuine intimacy with ministers and princes as an upper house-maid in Downing Street—is to assume that she would gain by the exchange, and that her ideals and ambitions are those of an average solicitor's wife.

Here, then, you have the secret of Madame Sans-Gêne and Miss Terry's apparent condescension to a "vulgar" part. There are a few people in the world with sufficient vitality and strength of character to get to close quarters with uncommon people quite independently of the drill which qualifies common people (what-ever their rank) to figure in the retinue which is indispensable to the state of kings and ministers. And there are a few actresses who are able to interpret such exceptional people because they are exceptional themselves. Miss Terry is such an exceptional actress; and there the whole wonder of the business begins and ends. Granted this one rare qualification, the mere execution is nothing. The part does not take Miss Terry anywhere near the limit of her powers: on the contrary, it embarrasses her occasionally by its crudity. Réjane was also well within her best as Catherine; so that a comparison of the two artists is like comparing two athletes throwing the hammer ten feet. Miss Terry's difficulties are greater, because she has to make shift with a translation in-stead of the original text, and because her support, especially in the scenes with Lefebvre, is not so helpful as that enjoyed by Réjane. Also she coaxed the clowning scene through better than Réjane; and her retort upon the Queen of Naples, though it was perfectly genial and simple and laundresslike, set me wondering why we have never heard her deliver Marie Stuart's retort upon Elizabeth in Schiller's play, a speculation which Réjane certainly never suggested to me, and which I admit is not to the point. But, if there is to be any comparison, it must, as I have said, take us outside Madame Sans-Gêne, into which both actresses put as much acting as it will hold.

Sardou's Napoleon is rather better than Madame Tussaud's, and that is all that can be said for it. It is easy to take any familiar stage figure, make him up as Napoleon, put into his mouth a few allusions to the time when he was a poor young artillery officer in Paris and to Friedland or Jena, place at his elbow a Sherlock Holmes called Fouché and so forth, just as in another dress, and with Friedland changed to Pharsalia, you would have a stage Julius Cæsar; but if at the end of the play the personage so dressed up has felt nothing and seen nothing and done nothing that might not have been as appropriately felt, seen, and done by his valet, then the fact that the hero is called Emperor is no more important than the fact that the theatre, in nine cases out of ten, is called the Theatre Royal. On the other hand, if you get as your hero a prince of whom nobody ever heard before—say Hamlet— and make him genuinely distinguished, then he becomes as well known to us as Marcus Aurelius. Sardou's Napoleon belongs to the first variety. He is nothing but the jealous husband of a thousand fashionable dramas, talking Buonapartiana. Sir Henry Irving seizes the opportunity to shew what can be done with an empty part by an old stage hand. The result is that he produces the illusion of the Emperor behind the part: one takes it for granted that his abstinence from any adequately Napoleonic deeds and utterances is a matter of pure forbearance on his part. It is an amusingly crafty bit of business, and reminds one pleasantly of the days before Shakespear was let loose on Sir Henry Irving's talent.

Mr Comyns Carr's translation is much too literary. Catherine does not speak like a woman of the people except when she is helping herself out with ready-made locutions in the manner of Sancho Panza. After a long speech consisting of a bundle of such locutions padded with forced mistakes in grammar, she will say, "That was my object," or some similarly impossible piece of Ciceronian eloquence. It is a pity; for there never was a play more in need of an unerring sense of the vernacular and plenty of humorous adroitness in its use.

NOT WORTH READING

[24 *April* 1897]

To those managers who so kindly invited me to spend Easter Saturday at the theatre in London I have nothing to offer but my apologies. I grant that The Queen's Proctor at the Strand, with Miss Violet Vanbrugh as Cyprienne, would have repaid me, had I been less in need of a holiday, for a return from the country. As it was, I thought it best to be content with having seen it before and praised it as it deserved. I had no reason to doubt the excellence of Mr Fred Horner's On Leave at the Avenue; and I thought it would be well perhaps not to risk a change in that friendly attitude by visiting it with a grudge against the management for bringing me away from the healing country air. So I stayed in the Surrey hills, and found myself thinking at odd moments about the relation between the country and the theatre. The country, it occurred to me, is very dull to those who spend much time there. And this is exactly the case with the theatre. Only, the country is better ventilated, and keeps healthier hours. If it is dull, at least it does not advertise itself as a lively place; and it is cheaper, because you are charged half a guinea for a chair in the theatre for three hours, whereas you can get a whole cottage for a week for that sum in the country. In point of scenery and weather the theatre is more to be depended on; but the successes of the country in these respects far surpass those of the theatre; and the view is not obstructed by *matinée* hats. Both, perhaps, may be described as places

> Where every prospect pleases
> And only Man is vile,

for agriculture is a failure because the agricultural laborer is underpaid and overworked and the farmer out of date, whilst the drama is a failure because the actor is overpaid and under-worked and the manager behind the times.

Here it is so certain that I shall be violently contradicted by the actor, that I sit down for a while on the hillside to consider whether it would not have paid me better to have gone on the stage instead of taking to criticism. In London, I understand, a "leading man" can get about £25 a week (discounted by a few weeks' gratuitous rehearsal) for physical qualifications no better than those of an average ranker in a smart cavalry regiment, for a degree of personal address and "style" just sufficient to bear the criticism of the Stock Exchange, for as much habituation to the mechanical routine of the stage as an office-boy could acquire in a few months, for a stage manner almost as dreadful as the "bedside manner" of an undistinguished suburban doctor in general practice, for a degree of personal comeliness which, though certainly more ravishing than that of the average dramatic critic (who is cut off from the aid of the make-up box), is resistible by a heroine of no more than ordinary strength of mind, and for the art of making an undertrained voice resound penetratingly in the nose.

Now if I could swoop down on the city-and-suburban trains any morning between half-past eight and half-past ten; capture the first-class carriages; and lay lands on all the adult male passengers under thirty who did not drop their aitches, I could with less than a year's drill work ninety per cent of them up to the £25 leading-man standard as certainly as a village lout can be worked up into a trim soldier or into the responsible and authoritative policeman in command of a London street crossing. But I should be very lucky if I found one sane man among them willing to consent to the process, although the rejected ten per cent would be composed mostly of stage-struck idiots. Their objections to embrace the actor's career would not arise from Puritanism, but from the undeniable fact that if the ninety per cent went through with my curriculum, the three with the most aptitude for getting engagements (*not* the three best actors) might get from £18 to £25 for six months in the year in London whilst they were in fashion; about twenty might get from £3 to £5 for four months or thereabouts in the provinces; and the rest would have to live solely by borrowing money from one another.

Under these circumstances, it is not worth anyone's while to train actors seriously. Hence there are no authoritative public schools of acting, and consequently no profession. There are the geniuses who train themselves—"forty-pound actors" who presently become actor-managers, and divide the command of our theatres with thrifty twenty-five pounders—but there is, I repeat, no profession.

Now the actor will not fail to remark that his "profession" in this respect is no worse than my own. Indeed, the comparison is too flattering to the critic, except in London and some half a dozen cities in which first-rate newspapers are published. In minor towns the actor may be what a carpenter or mason would contemptuously describe as "no tradesman"; but the critic is so abysmally beneath contempt that nobody would dream of taking him seriously enough to call him an impostor. At a well-known seaside resort the other day a newspaper suddenly let loose on the theatre a critic who did not choose to act as a mere puffster for advertisers. He wrote a notice of the local theatre which, though extremely indulgent, was nevertheless a critical notice. The manager, to whom such a thing had never happened before, discussed it excitedly with his friends until news came that the critic was brazenly walking through the streets of the town like any other citizen. He instantly sallied out with two retainers; smote the critic hip and thigh; and then threw himself as an insulted public man on the sympathy of his country, which callously fined him £3. I am devoutly thankful that critics are not quite so cheap in London; but yet I pitied that poor unaccustomed manager. If committees of deluded provincial playgoers were formed to trounce local puffsters, not forgetting the newspaper proprietors who are responsible for them, a fine of half a crown for assault, to be reduced to a shilling in cases of permanent disablement, would distinctly raise the tone of the provincial press.

Thus we have the unqualified actor criticized by a still less qualified critic, so that he misses the beneficent agony of having his shortcomings pointed out to him, and the public, ever diffident of its own judgment in artistic matters, left to believe that the theatre is the silly place the actors and critics make it. The only effective critic the actor has is his manager, who is generally either as ignorant as himself, or else, being also an actor, his professional rival. His best chance is to get into the hands of a manager of the old-fashioned Bateman-Daly type, who trains his company without competing personally with them, or of a capable author-actor-manager, like Mr Wilson Barrett, who, fonder of his plays than of himself, is conspicuous among our theatre chiefs for making the most of his company.

When William Morris founded the Kelmscott Press, and recovered for the world the lost art of making beautiful books, he had to make his printers do exactly the opposite of what they had been taught to regard as the perfection of tasty workmanship: in fact, a pressman whom he had broken in to his ways once remarked cheerfully that if he had "to go back to high art printing," he would be quite out of practice at first. But at least Morris had not to teach his printers composition and press-work: they were all skilled hands to begin with. Had they not been so, the Kelmscott Press could never have done what it did. He had no difficulty in finding men who could set type any way he wanted them to set it; and a manager could only rival the revolutionary rapidity of his results by finding actors who could play at least the routine of their parts in any way he wanted them played. As it is, the unfortunate manager must choose between people who have no skill at all, and our London circle of performers whose mannerisms have become public institutions, and who must have plays adapted to them instead of adapting themselves to the plays.

On the whole, I think I am safer off the stage than on it. An actor of the same standing in the theatres as I have in journalism would drop dead with indignation if he were offered my salary; but my engagements are long, and the better I write the better my editor is pleased. It is true that dramatists do not write their plays with a view to shewing me off to the best advantage by writing only what fits my style of criticism, and that I must know

114

my business all through and take it as the public demand it—
Shakespear and Ibsen one week, musical farce the next, light and
heavy, "character" and classical, instead of picking out what is
"in my line." But then, if I may not pick out my work, neither
must I wait to be picked out for it. Above all, my brain gets
exercised; and that is perhaps what really turns the scale between
the two departments of vagabondage—for your even Christian
looks askance on both actor and journalist.

As I break off these arid reflections to mark the decline of the
sun, and consider my distance from my roof-tree, it occurs to
me that if we had summer theatres here in the country, at which
fine performances of serious works could be given at least every
Saturday and Sunday, beginning in the afternoon, Bayreuth
fashion, how much better worth while the occupation of both
the critic and the actor would be! And with that Utopian vision,
and the consoling comment that, so far, my Utopian visions are
the only ones that have ever been carried out (because nobody
will ever take any real trouble about common-sense projects), I
turn to my iron steed, and speed over the hills and far away,
dinnerward.

HER MAJESTY'S

THE SEATS OF THE MIGHTY. In a prologue and three acts. Her
Majesty's Theatre (opening performance in the new building),
28 April 1897.

LOST, STOLEN, OR STRAYED. An original musical farce in three
acts, by J. Cheever Goodwin. Music by Woolson Morse.
Duke of York's Theatre, 27 April 1897.   [1 *May* 1897]

WHEN Mr Beerbohm Tree is called to his last audit by the Recording Angel, the account will shew two prominent items on
opposite sides. The credit one will be Her Majesty's Theatre; the
debit, Falstaff. And we can imagine Mr Tree thereupon exclaim-
ing, "You are a pretty sort of Recording Angel. Why, everybody—except one fool of a Saturday Reviewer—is agreed that
my Falstaff was a masterpiece, whereas that theatre nearly ruined
me and brought me no more thanks than if I had built a new

shop in Oxford Street." I may be in too great a hurry in anticipating such public ingratitude; but I have a very poor opinion of
London in its collective capacity. It is alike incapable of appreciating a benefit and of resenting an outrage. For example, one of the
finest views in the world is within a minute's walk of Charing
Cross. Go down Villiers Street and ascend the first stairs to your
right after you pass the music-hall. This brings you into the
loggia attached to the wall of the South-Eastern terminus, and
leading to the Hungerford footbridge. He who designed this
loggia was no Orcagna, though he had such a chance as Orcagna
never had in Florence. It is a dismal square hole in a mass of dirty
bricks, through which men hurry with loathing. Yet if you look
out through one of the holes—preferably the last but one—
made for the convenience of the east wind, you will find the view
magnificent. Right into one of the foci of that view, London,
without a murmur, permitted Mr Jabez Balfour to dump the
building which is now the Hotel Cecil, just as it allowed the
London Pavilion Music-hall to spoil Piccadilly Circus. If that
building had darkened the smallest window of a rag and bone
shop, the proprietor thereof would have been supported by all
the might of the State in maintaining his "ancient lights." But
because all London—nay, all the world that visits London—was
injured, there was no placard with "Ancient View" on it put up
in that grimy loggia. If the malefactor had confined himself to
injuring the public collectively, he would by this time have been
one of our most eminent citizens. Unfortunately, he trifled with
private property; and we instantly stretched out our hand to the
uttermost parts of the earth whither he had fled; seized him; and
cast him into prison. If the question had been one of beneficence
instead of maleficence, we should have shewn the same hyperæs-
thesia to a private advantage, the same anæsthesia to a public one.
Mr Tree has given London a theatre. There is nothing in that by
itself: a theatre is rather a promising speculation just at present;
and in England theatres can be built more cheaply than anywhere
else in the world: in fact, calculating the cost in the usual way
per head of the seating capacity of the house, we find that whereas

in some Continental cities, where the theatre rivals the parliament house or the cathedral as a public building, the cost is over £300 a head, in England we have achieved the commercial triumph of getting the cost down to £7. If Mr Tree had allowed his public spirit to carry him to the length of £10 per head, and then celebrated his first night by presenting every lady in the audience with a locket and every gentleman with a cigaret case (by arrangement with the advertising agents), his munificence would have been extolled to the skies, and the compliments to his public spirit and the handsomeness of his theatre would have been word for word just as they are at present; for to the Press a manager is a manager, and whether he gives you a theatre like Terry's or one like Daly's or the Garrick or the Palace, the acknowledgments are the same.

Under these circumstances the fact that Her Majesty's is no £7 commercial affair, but quite the handsomest theatre in London, must go altogether to the credit of Mr Tree's public spirit and artistic conscience. I do not mean that more money has been spent on Her Majesty's than Mr D'Oyly Carte lavished so splendidly on his New English Opera House, now the Palace Music-hall. I should not be surprised to hear that, if a few special items are left out of the question, Mr Tree has spent less in proportion than Mr Hare or Mr Daly. He has had the good sense—a very rare quality in England where artistic matters are in question—to see that a theatre which is panelled, and mirrored, and mantelpieced like the first-class saloon of a Peninsular and Oriental liner or a Pullman drawing room car, is no place for Julius Cæsar, or indeed for anything except tailor-made drama and farcical comedy. When you enter it you do not feel that you have walked into a Tottenham Court Road shop window, or smirk with a secret sense of looking as if you kept a carriage and belonged to a smart club; you feel that you are in a place where high scenes are to be enacted and dignified things to be done. And this is the first quality a theatre should have. The old theatres, with all their false notions of splendor and their barbarous disregard of modern ideas of health, comfort, and decency, always kept this in view;

and that is why the best of them, when supplemented by a couple of adjacent houses and modified by a little rearrangement and sanitary engineering, are better than the theatres of the Robertsonian era, with their first-class-carriage idealism. Nobody can say of Her Majesty's that it proclaims itself a place built by a snob for the entertainment of snobs with snobbish plays. It rises spaciously and brilliantly to the dignity of art; and if its way of doing so is still elegantly rhetorical and Renascent in conception, yet that style is not altogether the wrong one for a theatre; and it is wonderfully humanized and subtilized by the influence of modern anti-Renaissance ideas on the decoration. For this Mr Romaine-Walker cannot be too generously praised. He has stepped in just at the point where Mr Phipps might have spoiled as a decorator what he has wrought as an architect. M. Höfler's Fontainebleau chandelier fits into the decorative scheme perfectly; and Mr Dignam's stained canvas act drop, which produces the effect of an impossibly expensive Gobelins tapestry, is a convincing discovery of what an act drop ought to be, though I make no excuse for Coypel or for Dido and Eneas (Raphael's Parnassus, the act drop of the old theatre, was a much happier subject). And so we get the new beauty with the old elevation of sentiment. The Lyceum and Drury Lane, old as they are, would, if they were destroyed, be regretted as the Garrick and Daly's would never be regretted, but not more than Her Majesty's, which has as yet no associations.

Although the practical comfort of the audience has been carefully and intelligently looked after, there are one or two points in which I am not sure that I should exactly copy Her Majesty's if I were building a theatre myself. The perfectly horizontal stage is of course to be preferred for some purposes to the ordinary sloping one. Most playgoers have seen and laughed at the way in which a pencil, stick, or log of firewood accidentally dropped on the stage rolls down the stage to the footlights; but few of them understand the difficulties raised by the slope now that "flats" stand at angles to the footlights instead of parallel to them, as in the age of "wings." On the other hand, the more the stage slopes, the less steeply need the auditorium be banked up to command a view of it; and it must be confessed that the view of the stage from the back rows of the gallery at Her Majesty's is as foreshortened as that from the operatic altitudes of Covent Garden with its many tiers of boxes. This gallery will not, I understand, be always used; but it seems to me that it would be better, instead of wasting it on ordinary occasions, to set it apart at a charge of sixpence or even less for such faithful supporters of high art as the working-man with a taste for serious drama—especially Shakespear—and the impecunious student, male and female, who will go to the stalls or balcony later in life. These people would not, like the shilling god, expect the drama to be written down to them; and once they found their way to that gallery it would never be empty. For the working-men connoisseurs, though they represent a very small percentage of their class, yet belong to an enormously large class, and so are absolutely more numerous than might be expected from their relative scarcity.

Further, I would abolish all upholstery in the nature of plush and velvet. Its contact with the sitter is so clingingly intimate that it stops the circulation in the smaller vessels near the skin, so that the playgoer at last finds himself afflicted with "pins and needles" from the small of his back to his calves. At Bayreuth there is no upholstery—only a broad, cane-bottomed seat. This gets rid of the stuffiness which makes the stalls of some theatres less wholesome than the pit; but it would prove rather Spartan accommodation after a time if the audience did not leave the theatre for an hour between each act. In London we require cushions; but they should be covered with woollen cloth, and the stuffing should be unadulterated. At Her Majesty's the three rows of stalls next the pit, which are to be had for six shillings, are not plushy; so that to the man who sits down sensitively and knows the realities of things from the conventions, they are better upholstered then the half-guinea seats covered in velvet.

The first night was exceeding glorious. Our unique English

loyalty—consisting in a cool, resolute determination to get the last inch of advertisement out of the Royal Family—has seldom been better pushed. Not a man in the house but felt that the Jubilee was good for trade. Mr Tree told us that he would never disgrace the name the theatre bore; and his air as he spoke was that of a man who, on the brink of forgery, arson, and bigamy, was saved by the feeling that the owner of Her Majesty's Theatre must not do such things. Mr Alfred Austin contributed as straightforward and businesslike a piece of sycophancy in rhyme as ever a Poet Laureate penned; and Mrs Tree recited it with an absence of conviction that was only emphasized by her evident desire to please us all. Miss Clara Butt shewed what a Royal College of Music can make of a magnificent voice in singing God Save the Queen at full length (with a new verse thrown in) alternately with the Queen's Hall choir, the whole audience standing up determinedly meanwhile, with the Prince of Wales representing Royalty at one corner, Mr Labouchere representing Republicanism at the other, and the British Public representing Good Taste (formerly known as Hypocrisy) in the middle. The contents of the pay-boxes, it was announced, amid the enthusiasm of those who, like myself, had not paid for their seats, are to be handed over to the Prince of Wales's Ratepayers' Relief Fund. The proceedings terminated with a play, in which Mr and Mrs Tree, Miss Kate Rorke, Miss Janette Steer, Mr Lewis Waller, Mr Lionel Brough, Mr Brookfield, Mr Murray Carson, Mr Mollison, Mr Holmes-Gore, Mr Gerald Du Maurier, and about a dozen other artists had the honor of appearing.

Among the triumphs of Man over Nature I must reckon Mr Bourchier's reappearance in London—at The Strand—with a figure whose profile shews no trace of convexity. Whether it was done in a few seconds by a steam-roller, or by a month of hard training, I do not know: all I can say is that Mr Bourchier, whom I once reproached for physical redundance, is now a model of athletic grace. He now plays Dr Johnson as well as Sir Cecil Crofton; and an excellent piece of acting it is, wonderfully credible, and executed with the sort of skill and tact that stamp the born actor. The Queen's Proctor is as amusing as ever; but Miss Violet Vanbrugh is beginning to suffer from the necessity of pretending to be an Italian. The rage for assumed foreign accents on the stage now is worse than the rage for single eyeglasses in the day of H. J. Byron. On the first night, when the parts were only skin deep, Miss Vanbrugh's Stella was none the worse for being an Italian; but she would by this time have developed into something much more real and certainly more intelligible verbally, as an English-speaking woman, which Lady Crofton might easily be, volcanic temperament and all. This is probably why Miss Vanbrugh has not improved her part of the play as much as Mr Bourchier has improved his, though her performance is still very brilliant and fascinating. Besides, the Italian accent would not impose on an infant who had ever heard a real Italian speaking English. The other parts are as well done as they were at the Royalty, Mr Hendrie being replaced by that always more than competent actor, Mr Fred Thorne.

Lost, Stolen, or Strayed, the new musical farce at the Duke of York's Theatre, is a capital piece of its kind. The composer, Mr Woolson Morse, is a musician of resource, well up in Meyerbeer, Massenet, Verdi, and the operatic melodramatists: his score is just what is wanted. The acting is, if anything, too good. Mr Barnes and Mr de Lange, at any rate, ought to be better employed, even if Mr Robb Harwood may be regarded as in his proper grotesque element. Mr Arthur Styan's Cuban Borgia is a genuine bit of acting: the second scene of the second act, in which he is associated with Miss Decima Moore and Mr Barnes, achieved a perfectly legitimate comedy success. I was able to separate it from the accompanying pantomime business of Mr Wheeler on the ladder and Mr Harwood with the untameable clock all the better as I could not see either of these gentlemen, my stall not being one of those which have the advantage (like all the seats in Her Majesty's) of commanding a view of the stage. The dance in the last act would be an unalloyed success if the cruel, silly, forced, ugly high kicking were left out. The *jeune premier chantant*, Mr Appleby, is *not* a bore: his cues to the band are welcome; and Miss

Decima Moore is better than ever. The piece will probably run to the end of the century.

JOHN GABRIEL BORKMAN

JOHN GABRIEL BORKMAN. A play in four acts by Henrik Ibsen. English version by William Archer. Opening performance by the New Century Theatre at the Strand Theatre, 3 May 1897.

[8 *May* 1897]

THE first performance of John Gabriel Borkman, the latest masterpiece of the acknowledged chief of European dramatic art, has taken place in London under the usual shabby circumstances. For the first scene in the gloomy Borkman house, a faded, soiled, dusty wreck of some gay French salon, originally designed, perhaps, for Offenbach's Favart, was fitted with an incongruous Norwegian stove, a painted staircase, and a couple of chairs which were no doubt white and gold when they first figured in Tom Taylor's Plot and Passion or some other relic of the days before Mr Bancroft revolutionized stage furniture, but have apparently languished ever since, unsold and unsaleable, among secondhand keys, framed lithographs of the Prince Consort, casual fenders and stair-rods, and other spoils of the broker. Still, this scene at least was describable, and even stimulative— to irony. In Act II, the gallery in which Borkman prowls for eight years like a wolf was no gallery at all, but a square box ugly to loathsomeness, and too destructive to the imagination and descriptive faculty to incur the penalty of criticism. In Act III (requiring, it will be remembered, the shifting landscape from Parsifal), two new cloths specially painted, and good enough to produce a tolerable illusion of snowy pinewood and midnight mountain with proper accessories, were made ridiculous by a bare acre of wooden floor and only one set of wings for the two. When I looked at that, and thought of the eminence of the author and the greatness of his work, I felt ashamed. What Sir Henry Irving and Mr George Alexander and Mr Wilson Barrett feel about it I do not know—on the whole, perhaps, not altogether displeased to see Ibsen belittled. For my part, I beg the New Century Theatre, when the next Ibsen play is ready for mounting, to apply to me for assistance. If I have a ten-pound note, they shall have it: if not, I can at least lend them a couple of decent chairs. I cannot think that Mr Massingham, Mr Sutro, and Mr William Archer would have grudged a few such contributions from their humble cots on this occasion if they had not hoped that a display of the most sordid poverty would have shamed the public as it shamed me. Unfortunately their moral lesson is more likely to discredit Ibsen than to fill the New Century coffers. They have spent either too little or too much. When Dr Furnivall performed Browning's Luria in the lecture theatre at University College with a couple of curtains, a chair borrowed from the board-room, and the actors in their ordinary evening dress, the absence of scenery was as completely forgotten as if we had all been in the Globe in Shakespear's time. But between that and an adequate scenic equipment there is no middle course. It is highly honorable to the pioneers of the drama that they are poor; but in art, what poverty can only do unhandsomely and stingily it should not do at all. Besides, to be quite frank, I simply do not believe that the New Century Theatre could not have afforded at least a better couple of chairs.

I regret to say that the shortcomings of the scenery were not mitigated by imaginative and ingenious stage management. Mr Vernon's stage management is very actor-like: that is to say, it is directed, not to secure the maximum of illusion for the play, but the maximum of fairness in distributing good places on the stage to the members of the cast. Had he been selfish enough, as some actor-managers are accused of being, to manage the stage so as to secure the maximum of prominence for himself, the effect would probably have justified him, since he plays Borkman. But his sense of equity is evidently stronger than his vanity; for he takes less than his share of conspicuity, repeatedly standing patiently with his back to the audience to be declaimed at down the stage by Miss Robins or Miss Ward, or whoever else he deems entitled to a turn. Alas! these conceptions of fairness, honorable as they are to Mr Vernon's manhood, are far too simply quantitative for artistic purposes. The business of the stage manager of John Gabriel Borkman is chiefly to make the most of the title part; and if the actor of that part is too modest to do that for himself, some one else should stage-manage. Mr Vernon perhaps pleased the company, because he certainly did contrive that every one of them should have the centre of the stage to himself or herself whenever they had a chance of self-assertion; but as this act of green-room justice was placed before the naturalness of the representation, the actors did not gain by it, whilst the play suffered greatly.

Mr Vernon, I suspect, was also hampered by a rather old-fashioned technical conception of the play as a tragedy. Now the traditional stage management of tragedy ignores realism—even the moderate degree of realism traditional in comedy. It lends itself to people talking at each other rhetorically from opposite sides of the stage, taking long sweeping walks up to their "points," striking attitudes in the focus of the public vision with an artificiality which, instead of being concealed, is not only disclosed but insisted on, and being affected in all their joints by emotions which a fine comedian conveys by the faintest possible inflexion of tone or eyebrow. John Gabriel Borkman is no doubt technically a tragedy because it ends with the death of the leading personage in it. But to stage-manage or act it rhetorically as such is like drawing a Dance of Death in the style of Caracci or Giulio Romano. Clearly the required style is the homely-imaginative, the realistic-fateful—in a word, the Gothic. I am aware that to demand Gothic art from stage managers dominated by the notion that their business is to adapt the exigencies of stage etiquette to the tragic and comic categories of our pseudo-classical dramatic tradition is to give them an order which they can but dimly understand and cannot execute at all; but Mr Vernon is no mere routineer: he is a man of ideas. After all, Sir Henry Irving (in his Bells style), M. Lugné Poë, Mr Richard Mansfield, and Mr Charles Charrington have hit this mark (whilst missing the pseudo-classic one) nearly enough to shew that it is by no means unattainable. Failing the services of these geniuses, I beg the conventional stage manager to treat Ibsen as comedy. That will not get the business right; but it will be better than the tragedy plan.

As to the acting of the play, it was fairly good, as acting goes in London now, whenever the performers were at all in their depth; and it was at least lugubriously well intentioned when they were out of it. Unfortunately they were very often out of it. If they had been anti-Ibsenites they would have marked their resentment of and impatience with the passages they did not understand by an irritable listlessness, designed to make the worst of the play as far as that could be done without making the worst of themselves. But the Ibsenite actor marks the speeches which are beyond him by a sudden access of pathetic sentimentality and an intense consciousness of Ibsen's greatness. No doubt this devotional plan lets the earnestness of the representation down less than the sceptical one; yet its effect is as false as false can be; and I am sorry to say that it is gradually establishing a funereally unreal tradition which is likely to end in making Ibsen the most portentous of stage bores. Take, for example, Ella Rentheim. Here you have a part which up to a certain point almost plays itself—a sympathetic old maid with a broken heart. Nineteen-twentieths of her might be transferred to the stage of the Princess's tomorrow and be welcomed there tearfully by the audiences which delight in Two Little Vagabonds and East Lynne. Her desire to adopt Erhart is plainsailing sentimentalism: her reproach to Borkman for the crime of killing the "love life" in her and himself for the sake of his ambition is, as a *coup de théâtre*, quite within the range of playwrights who rank considerably below Mr Pinero. All this is presented intelligently by Miss Robins— at moments even touchingly and beautifully. But the moment the dialogue crosses the line which separates the Ibsen sphere from the ordinary sphere her utterance rings false at once. Here is an example—the most striking in the play:

ELLA [*In strong inward emotion*]. Pity! Ha ha! I have never known pity since you deserted me. I was incapable of feeling it.

If a poor starved child came into my kitchen, shivering and crying, and begging a morsel of food, I let the servants look to it. I never felt any desire to take the child to myself, to warm it at my own hearth, to have the pleasure of seeing it eat and be satisfied. And yet I wasnt like that when I was young: *that* I remember clearly. It is you that have created an empty, barren desert within me—and without me too!

What is there in this speech that might not occur in any popular novel or drama of sentiment written since Queen Anne's death? If Miss Millward were to introduce it into Black-Ey'd Susan, the Adelphi pit would accept it with moist eyes and without the faintest suspicion of Ibsen. But Ella Rentheim does not stop there. "You have cheated me of a mother's joy and happiness in life," she continues, "and of a mother's sorrows and tears as well. And perhaps that is the heaviest part of the loss to me. It may be that a mother's sorrows and tears were what I needed most." Now here the Adelphi pit would be puzzled; for here Ibsen speaks as the Great Man—one whose moral consciousness far transcends the common huckstering conception of life as a trade in happiness in which sorrows and tears represent the bad bargains and joys and happiness the good ones. And here Miss Robins suddenly betrays that she is an Ibsenite without being an Ibsenist. The genuine and touching tone of self-pity suddenly turns into a perceptibly artificial snivel (forgive the rudeness of the word); and the sentence, which is the most moving in the play provided it comes out simply and truthfully, is declaimed as a sentimental paradox which has no sort of reality or conviction for the actress. In this failure Miss Robins was entirely consistent with her own successes. As the woman in revolt against the intolerable slavery and injustice of ideal "womanliness" (Karin and Martha in Pillars of Society) or against the man treating her merely as his sexual prey (Mariana in the recital of her mother's fate) her success has had no bounds except those set by the commercial disadvantages at which the performances were undertaken. As the impetuous, imaginative New Woman in her first youth, free, unscrupulous through ignorance, demanding of life that it shall be "thrilling," and terribly dangerous to impressionable Master Builders who have put on life's chains without learning its lessons, she has succeeded heart and soul, rather by being the character than by understanding it. In representing poignant nervous phenomena in their purely physical aspect, as in Alan's Wife, and Mrs Lessingham, she has set up the infection of agony in the theatre with lacerating intensity by the vividness of her reproduction of its symptoms. But in sympathetic parts properly so called, where wisdom of heart, and sense of identity and common cause with others—in short, the parts we shall probably call religious as soon as we begin to gain some glimmering of what religion means—Miss Robins is only sympathetic as a flute is sympathetic: that is, she has a pretty tone, and can be played on with an affectation of sentiment; but there is no reality, no sincerity in it. And so Ella Rentheim, so far as she is sympathetic, eludes her. The fact is, Miss Robins is too young and too ferociously individualistic to play her. Ella's grievances come out well enough, also her romance, and some of those kindly amenities of hers—notably her amiable farewell to Erhart; but of the woman who understands that she has been robbed of her due of tears and sorrow, of the woman who sees that the crazy expedition through the snow with Borkman is as well worth trying as a hopeless return to the fireside, there is no trace, nothing but a few indications that Miss Robins would have very little patience with such wisdom if she met it in real life.

Mr Vernon's Borkman was not ill acted; only, as it was not Ibsen's Borkman, but the very reverse and negation of him, the better Mr Vernon acted the worse it was for the play. He was a thoroughly disillusioned elderly man of business, patient and sensible rather than kindly, and with the sort of strength that a man derives from the experience that teaches him his limits. I think Mr Vernon must have studied him in the north of Ireland, where that type reaches perfection. Ibsen's Borkman, on the contrary, is a man of the most energetic imagination, whose illusions feed on his misfortunes, and whose conception of his own power grows hyperbolical and Napoleonic in his solitude and impotence. Mr Vernon's excursion into the snow was the aberration of a respectable banker in whose brain a vessel had suddenly burst: the true Borkman meets the fate of a vehement dreamer who has for thirteen years been deprived of that daily contact with reality and responsibility without which genius inevitably produces unearthliness and insanity. Mr Vernon was as earthly and sane as a man need be until he went for his walk in the snow, and a Borkman who is that is necessarily a trifle dull. Even Mr Welch, though his scene in the second act was a triumph, made a fundamental mistake in the third, where Foldal, who has just been knocked down and nearly run over by the sleigh in which his daughter is being practically abducted by Erhart and Mrs Wilton, goes into ecstasies of delight at what he supposes to be her good fortune in riding off in a silver-mounted carriage to finish her musical education under distinguished auspices. The whole point of this scene, at once penetratingly tragic and irresistibly laughable, lies in the sincerity of Foldal's glee and Borkman's sardonic chuckling over it. But Mr Welch unexpectedly sacrificed the scene to a stage effect which has been done to death by Mr Harry Nicholls and even Mr Arthur Roberts. He played the heartbroken old man pretending to laugh—a descendant of the clown who jokes in the arena whilst his child is dying at home—and so wrecked what would otherwise have been the best piece of character work of the afternoon. Mr Martin Harvey, as Erhart, was clever enough to seize the main idea of the part—the impulse towards happiness—but not experienced enough to know that the actor's business is not to supply an idea with a sounding board, but with a credible, simple, and natural human being to utter it when its time comes and not before. He shewed, as we all knew he would shew, considerable stage talent and more than ordinary dramatic intelligence; but in the first act he was not the embarrassed young gentleman of Ibsen, but rather the "soaring human boy" imagined by Mr Chadband; and later on this attitude of his very nearly produced a serious jar at a critical point in the representation.

Miss Geneviève Ward played Gunhild. The character is a

very difficult one, since the violently stagey manifestations of maternal feeling prescribed for the actress by Ibsen indicate a tragic strenuousness of passion which is not suggested by the rest of the dialogue. Miss Ward did not quite convince me that she had found the temperament appropriate to both. The truth is, her tragic style, derived from Ristori, was not made for Ibsen. On the other hand, her conversational style, admirably natural and quite free from the Mesopotamian solemnity with which some of her colleagues delivered the words of the Master, was genuinely dramatic, and reminded me of her excellent performance, years ago with Mr Vernon, as Lona Hessel. Mrs Tree was clever and altogether successful as Mrs Wilton; and Miss Dora Barton's Frida was perfect. But then these two parts are comparatively easy. Miss Caldwell tried hard to modify her well-known representation of a farcical slavey into a passable Ibsenite parlormaid, and succeeded fairly except in the little scene which begins the third act.

On the whole, a rather disappointing performance of a play which cannot be read without forming expectations which are perhaps unreasonable, but are certainly inevitable.

A DOLL'S HOUSE AGAIN

A DOLL'S HOUSE. By Henrik Ibsen. Globe Theatre, 10 May 1897.
HAMLET. Olympic Theatre, 10 May 1897.
'CHAND D'HABITS. Musical play without words. By Catulle Mendès and Jules Bouval. Her Majesty's Theatre, 8 May 1897.

[15 *May* 1897]

AT last I am beginning to understand anti-Ibsenism. It must be that I am growing old and weak and sentimental and foolish; for I cannot stand up to reality as I did once. Eight years ago, when Mr Charrington, with A Doll's House, struck the decisive blow for Ibsen—perhaps the only one that has really got home in England as yet—I rejoiced in it, and watched the ruin and havoc it made among the idols and temples of the idealists as a young war correspondent watches the bombardment of the unhealthy quarters of a city. But now I understand better what it means to the unhappy wretches who can conceive no other life as possible to them except the Doll's House life. The master of the Doll's House may endure and even admire himself as long as he is called King Arthur and prodigiously flattered; but to paint a Torvald Helmer for him, and leave his conscience and his ever-gnawing secret diffidence to whisper "Thou art the man" when he has perhaps outlived all chance of being any other sort of man, must be bitter and dreadful to him. Dr Rank, too, with his rickets and his scrofula, no longer an example, like Herod, of the wrath of God, or a curiosity to be stared at as villagers stare at a sheep with two heads, but a matter-of-fact completion of the typical picture of family life by one of the inevitable congenital invalids, or drunkards, or lunatics whose teeth are set on edge because their fathers have eaten sour grapes: this also is a horror against which an agony of protest may well be excused.

It will be remarked that I no longer dwell on the awakening of the woman, which was once the central point of the controversy as it is the central point of the drama. Why should I? The play solves that problem just as it is being solved in real life. The woman's eyes are opened; and instantly her doll's dress is thrown off and her husband left staring at her, helpless, bound thenceforth either to do without her (an alternative which makes short work of his fancied independence) or else treat her as a human being like himself, fully recognizing that he is not a creature of one superior species, Man, living with a creature of another and inferior species, Woman, but that Mankind is male and female, like other kinds, and that the inequality of the sexes is literally a cock and bull story, certain to end in such unbearable humiliation as that which our suburban King Arthurs suffer at the hands of Ibsen. The ending of the play is not on the face of it particularly tragic: the alleged "note of interrogation" is a sentimental fancy; for it is clear that Helmer is brought to his senses, and that Nora's departure is no clap-trap "Farewell for ever," but a journey in search of self-respect and apprenticeship to life. Yet there is an underlying solemnity caused by a fact that the popular instinct has divined: to wit, that Nora's revolt is the end of a chapter of human history. The slam of the door behind her is more momentous than the cannon of Waterloo or Sedan, because when she comes back, it will not be to the old home; for when the patriarch no longer rules, and the "breadwinner" acknowledges his dependence, there is an end of the old order; and an institution upon which so much human affection and suffering have been lavished, and about which so much experience of the holiest right and bitterest wrong has gathered, cannot fall without moving even its destroyers, much more those who believe that its extirpation is a mortal wound to society. This moment of awe and remorse in A Doll's House was at first lightened by the mere Women's Rights question. Now that this no longer distracts us, we feel the full weight of the unsolved destiny of our Helmers, our Krogstads, our Ranks and our Rank ancestors, whom we cannot, like the Heavenly Twin, dispose of by breaking their noses and saying, "Take that, you father of a speckled toad."

It may be, however, that this difference between the impression made by the famous performance in 1889 and the present revival is due partly to artistic conditions. On Monday last Mr Courtenay Thorpe accomplished the remarkable feat of playing Helmer in the afternoon and the Ghost in Hamlet in the evening, and doing both better than we have seen them done before. Mr Waring, our original Helmer, realized the importance of this most unflattering part, and sacrificed himself to play it. But he could not bring himself to confess to it wholly. He played it critically, and realized it by a process of intentional self-stultification. The resultant performance, excellently convincing up to fully nineteen-twentieths, was, as regards the remaining twentieth obviously a piece of acting in which a line was drawn, as a matter of self-respect, between Mr Waring and Mr Helmer. Nevertheless, it was badly missed when Mr Charrington tried the part later on and achieved a record as the very worst Helmer in the world through sheer incompatibility of temperament. But Mr Courtenay Thorpe obliterates both records. He plays Helmer with passion. It is the first time we have seen this done; and the effect is overwhelming. We no longer study an object lesson in lord-of-creationism, appealing to our sociological interest only. We see a fellow-creature blindly wrecking his happiness and losing his "love life," and are touched dramatically. There were slips and blunders, it is true. Mr Courtenay Thorpe did not know his dialogue thoroughly; and when the words did not come unsought he said anything that came into his head (stark nonsense sometimes) sooner than go out of his part to look for them. And he succumbed to the temptation to utter the two or three most fatuously conceited of Helmer's utterances as "points," thereby destroying the naturalness that could alone make them really credible and effective. But it did not matter: the success was beyond being undone by trifles. Ibsen has in this case repeated his old feat of making an actor's reputation.

Miss Achurch's Nora is an old story by this time; and I leave its celebration to the young critics who saw it on Monday for the first time. It still seems to me to place her far ahead of any living English actress of her generation in this class of work—the only class, let me add, which now presents any difficulty to actresses who bring some personal charm to the aid of quite commonplace attainments. Here and there we have had some bits of newfashioned work on the stage—for instance, Mrs Kendal's extraordinarily fine and finished performance in The Greatest of These, and Miss Winifred Emery's last serious feat of acting in The Benefit of the Doubt. These shew that Miss Achurch's monopoly is not one of executive skill, but of the modernity of culture, the mental power and quickness of vision to recognize the enormous value of the opportunity she has seized. In the eight years since 1889 she has gained in strength and art; and her performance is more powerful, more surely gripped, and more expertly carried out than it used to be; but it has losses to shew as well as gains. In the old days Nora's first scene with Krogstad had a wonderful *naïveté*: her youthfully unsympathetic contempt for him, her certainty that his effort to make a serious business of the forgery was mere vulgarity, her utter repudiation of the notion that there could be any comparison between his case and hers, were expressed to perfection. And in the first half of the renowned final scene the chill "clearness and certainty" of the disillusion, the quite new tone of intellectual seriousness, announcing by its freshness and coolness a complete change in her as she calls her husband to account with her eyes wide open for the first time: all this, so vitally necessary to the novel truth of the scene and the convincing effect of the statement that she no longer loves him, came with lifegiving naturalness. But these two scenes have now become unmistakeably stale to Miss Achurch. In the Krogstad one she plays as if the danger of penal servitude were the whole point of it; and she agonizes over the cool opening of the explanation with Helmer with all the conventional pangs of parting in full play from the first. This ages her Nora perceptibly. Physically she is youthful enough: Helmer's "squirrel" still dances blithely, sings unmercifully, and wears reckless garments at which the modish occupants of the stalls stare in scandal and consternation (and which, by the way, are impossible for a snobbish bank manager's wife). But Miss Achurch can no longer content herself with a girl's allowance of passion and sympathy. She fills the cup and drains it; and consequently, though Nora has all her old vitality and originality, and more than her old hold on the audience, she is less girlish and more sophisticated with the passions of the stage than she was at the Novelty when she first captivated us.

Mr Charrington's Rank, always an admirable performance, is now better than ever. But it is also sterner and harder to bear. He has very perceptibly increased the horror of the part by a few touches which bring and keep his despair and doom more vividly before the audience; and he no longer softens his final exit by the sentimental business of snatching Nora's handkerchief.

The effect of a performance of the Doll's House with the three most important parts very well played, and the economy of the mounting—which involves a disembowelled sofa—got over by intelligent stage management and a little judicious hiring and borrowing, is almost painfully strong. It is mitigated by the earnest but mistaken efforts of Mr Charles Fulton and Miss Vane Featherstone as Krogstad and Mrs Linden. Mr Fulton, invaluable at the Adelphi, struggles with his part like a blacksmith mending a watch; and the style of play which makes Miss Vane Feather-stone so useful and attractive in the unrealistic drama produces, in a realistic part, exactly the effect that might have been expected. The flattering notion, still current in the profession, that anybody can play Ibsen, is hardly bearing the test of experience. Happily, the elements of strength in the performance triumph over all drawbacks. If The Wild Duck next week is as good as A Doll's House, the Independent Theatre (for which, as a small share-holder, I have a certain partiality) will have done very well.

I found Hamlet at the Olympic not a bad anodyne after the anguish of the Helmer household. Throwing off the critic, I in-dulged a silly boyish affection of mine for the play, which I know nearly by heart, thereby having a distinct advantage over Mr Nutcombe Gould, whose acquaintance with the text is extremely precarious. His aptitude for transposing the adverb "so" in such a way as to spoil the verse, not to mention putting in full stops where there is no stop, and no stop where there is a full stop, is calamitous and appalling. For example:

> For in that sleep of death what dreams may come [*full stop*].
> When we have shuffled off this mortal coil [*full stop*].
> Must give us pause.

And

> When the grass grows the proverb is somewhat musty.

The effect of changing "'tis" into "it is" was also fully exploited. Thus—

> Whether it is nobler in the mind to suffer.

Even Mr Foss, otherwise better than most Laerteses, said:

> O Heaven, is it possible a young maid's wits
> Should be as mortal as an old man's life?

Mr Nutcombe Gould gave us all Hamlet's appearance, something of his feeling, and but little of his brains. He died in the full possession of his faculties, and had but just announced with unimpaired vigor that the rest was silence when an elderly gentleman rose in the middle of the front row of the stalls, and addressed the house vehemently on burning political questions of the day. Miss Lily Hanbury went through the familiar ceremony of playing Ophelia with success, thanks to a delicate ear for the music and a goodly person. Mr Ben Greet was an exasperatingly placid Polonius, and Mr Kendrick an unwontedly spirited Horatio. The only really noteworthy feature of the performance was, as aforesaid, the Ghost. Mr Courtenay Thorpe's articulation deserted him towards the end; so that the last half-dozen lines of his long narrative and the whole of his part in the closet scene were a mere wail, in which no man could distinguish any words; but the effect was past spoiling by that time; and a very remarkable effect it was, well imagined and well executed.

What possessed Mr Beerbohm Tree to offer 'Chand d'Habits to the sort of audience that runs after stage versions of recent imitations of the "historical" novels of James Grant and Harrison Ainsworth? These plays without words only exist for people who are highly sensitive to music, color, and the complex art of physical expression. To offer them to barbarians with no senses at all, capable of nothing but sensational stories shouted at them in plain words, with plenty of guns and swords and silks and velvets, is to court ridicule, especially at half-past ten at night, and with the overture, which might have done something to attune the house, played as an *entr'acte*. For my part, I enjoyed 'Chand d'Habits immensely, and thought the insensibility and impatience of the audience perfectly hoggish. But then I had not to sit out Seats of the Mighty beforehand.

IBSEN TRIUMPHANT

[22 *May* 1897]

CAN it possibly be true that The Hobby Horse was produced so recently as 1886? More amazing still, was this the comedy—comedy, mark you—which suggested to me just such hopes of Mr Pinero's future as others built upon The Profligate and The Second Mrs Tanqueray, both of which I contemned as relapses into drawing room melodrama. Going back to it now after an interval of ten years, I find it, not a comedy, but a provincial farce in three acts, decrepit in stage convention, and only capable of appearing fresh to those who, like myself, can wrench themselves back, by force of memory, to the point of view of a period when revivals of London Assurance were still possible. What makes the puerilities of the play more exasperating nowadays is that it is clear, on a survey of the original production and the present revival, that Mr Pinero was not driven into them by any serious deficiency in the executive talent at his disposal. In Mrs Kendal and Mr Hare he had two comedians for whose combined services an unfortunate modern dramatic author might well sacrifice half his percentage. Yet the part of Spencer Jermyn is made so easy that one may well ask the people who rave about Mr Hare's performance as a masterpiece of art what they suppose really difficult acting to be. And imagine Mrs Kendal condemned to make London laugh by pretending to treat a grown-up stepson as a little boy, arranging his hair, telling him not to be afraid, that she will not punish him, and so forth! One gasps at these things nowadays. They may be pardonable in the part of Shattock, who, as comic relief—for even comedy in England must have comic relief—is not expected to do or say anything credible or possible; but here they were thrust into the part of the heroine, enacted by the most accomplished actress in London. What sort of barbarians were we in the days when we took this sort of thing as a matter of course, and made merry over it?

And yet I was right about The Hobby Horse. It has character,

humor, observation, genuine comedy, and literary workmanship
in it as unmistakeably as The Benefit of the Doubt has them.
What is the matter with the play is the distortion and debasement of all its qualities to suit the childishness and vulgarity of
the theatre of ten years ago. It will be asked scornfully whether
the theatre of today is any better—whether The Red Robe, for
instance, is half as good as The Hobby Horse? Before answering
that, let me compare The Hobby Horse with The Princess and
the Butterfly! Could Mr Pinero venture nowadays to present
to the St James's audience, as comedy, the humors of Mr Shattock
and the scene between Lady Jermyn and her stepson? You may
reply that the author who has given us the duel in The Princess
and the Butterfly is capable of anything; but I would have you
observe that the duel is a mere makeshift in the plot of The
Princess, whereas the follies of The Hobby Horse are presented
as flowers of comedy, and—please attend to this—are actually
very good of their kind. That such a kind should have been the
best of its day—nay, that the play should have suffered in 1886
because its comedy was rather too subtle for the taste of that
time—is a staggering thing to think of. But I am prepared to go
further as to our improvement by embracing even the comparison
with The Red Robe in support of my case. The nineteenth-
century novel, with all its faults, has maintained itself immeasurably above the nineteenth-century drama. Take the women
novelists alone, from Charlotte Brontë to Sarah Grand, and think
of them, if you can, in any sort of relation except that of a superior
species to the dramatists of their day. I unhesitatingly say that
no novelist could, even if there were any reason for it, approach
the writing of a novel with his mind warped, his hand shackled,
and his imagination stultified by the conditions which Mr
Pinero accepted, and even gloried in accepting, when he wrote
The Hobby Horse. The state of public taste which turns from
the first-rate comedies of the eighties to dramatizations of the
third-rate novels of the nineties is emphatically a progressive
state. These cloak-and-sword dramas, at their worst—if we have
reached their worst, which is perhaps too much to hope—are

only bad stories badly told: if they were good stories well told, there would be no more objection to them on my part than there is at present on that of the simple people for whom they are not too bad. But the sort of play they are supplanting, whether good or bad, was a wrong sort: the more craftily it was done the more hopelessly wrong it was. The dramatists who had mastered it despised the novelists, and said, "You may sneer at our craft, but let us see you do it yourselves." Just the sort of retort a card-sharper might make on a cardinal.

I need hardly go on to explain that Ibsen is at the back of this sudden explosion of disgusted intolerance on my part for a style of entertainment which I suffered gladly enough in the days of the Hare-Kendal management. On Monday last I sat without a murmur in a stuffy theatre on a summer afternoon from three to nearly half-past six, spellbound by Ibsen; but the price I paid for it was to find myself stricken with mortal impatience and boredom the next time I attempted to sit out the pre-Ibsenite drama for five minutes. Where shall I find an epithet magnificent enough for The Wild Duck! To sit there getting deeper and deeper into that Ekdal home, and getting deeper and deeper into your own life all the time, until you forget that you are in a theatre; to look on with horror and pity at a profound tragedy, shaking with laughter all the time at an irresistible comedy; to go out, not from a diversion, but from an experience deeper than real life ever brings to most men, or often brings to any man: that is what The Wild Duck was like last Monday at the Globe. It is idle to attempt to describe it; and as to giving an analysis of the play, I did that seven years ago, and decline now to give myself an antiquated air by treating as a novelty a masterpiece that all Europe delights in. Besides, the play is as simple as Little Red Ridinghood to anyone who comes to it fresh from life instead of stale from the theatre.

And now, what have our "passing craze" theorists to say to the latest nine-days' wonder, the tremendous effect this ultra-Ibsen play has just produced eight years after the craze set in? As for me, what I have to say is simply, "I told you so."

We have by this time seen several productions of A Doll's House, three of Rosmersholm, and two of The Wild Duck. The first performances of A Doll's House (Mr Charrington's at the Novelty) and of Rosmersholm (Miss Florence Farr's at the Vaudeville) gave the actors such an overwhelming advantage as the first revealers to London of a much greater dramatist than Shakespear, that even the vehemently anti-Ibsenite critics lost all power of discrimination, and flattered the performers as frantically as they abused the plays. But since then the performers have had to struggle against the unreasonable expectations thus created; and the effect of the plays has been sternly proportionate to the intelligence and skill brought to bear on them. We have learnt that an Ibsen performance in the hands of Lugné Poë or Mr Charrington is a perfectly different thing from one in which there is individual talent but practically no stage management. M. Lugné Poë established his reputation at once and easily, because he was under no suspicion of depending on the genius of a particular actress: his Rosmersholm with Marthe Mellot as Rebecca had the magic atmosphere which is the sign of the true manager as unmistakeably as his Master Builder with Suzanne Auclaire as Hilda. But Mr Charrington, like Mr Kendal and Mr Bancroft, has a wife; and the difference made by Miss Janet Achurch's acting has always been much more obvious than that made by her husband's management to a public which has lost all tradition of what stage management really is, apart from lavish expenditure on scenery and furniture. But for that his production of Voss's Alexandra would have established his reputation as the best stage manager of true modern drama in London—indeed the only one, in the sense in which I am now using the words: the sense, that is, of a producer of poetically realistic illusion. Now, however, we have him at last with Miss Janet Achurch out of the bill. The result is conclusive. The same insight which enables Mr Charrington, in acting Relling, to point the moral of the play in half a dozen strokes, has also enabled him to order the whole representation in such a fashion that there is not a moment of bewilderment during the development of a dramatic

action subtle enough in its motives to have left even highly
trained and attentive readers of the play quite addled as to what
it is all about. The dialogue, which in any other hands would have
been cut to ribbons, is given without the slightest regard to the
clock; and not even the striking of six produces the stampede that
would set in after a quarter-past five if the play were a "popular"
one. That is a real triumph of management. It may be said that it
is a triumph of Ibsen's genius; but of what use is Ibsen's genius
if the manager has not the genius to believe in it?

The acting, for a scratch company, was uncommonly good:
there was mettle in it, as there usually is where there is good
leadership. Mr Laurence Irving, who played Relling to Mr
Abingdon's Hjalmar Ekdal at the first production of the play by
Mr Grein, handed over Relling to Mr Charrington, and played
Hjalmar himself. In all dramatic literature, as far as I know it,
there is no other such part for a comedian; and I do not believe
any actor capable of repeating the lines intelligibly could possibly
fail in it. To say therefore that Mr Irving did not fail is to give
him no praise at all: to say that he quite succeeded would be to
proclaim him the greatest comedian in London. He was very
amusing, and played with cleverness and sometimes with considerable finesse. But though he did not overact any particular
passage, he overdid the part a little as a whole by making Hjalmar
grotesque. His appearance proclaimed his weakness at once: the
conceited ass was recognizable at a glance. This was not right:
Hjalmar should impose on us at first. The fact is, we all have to
look much nearer home for the originals of Ibsen's characters
than we imagine; and Hjalmar Ekdals are so common nowadays
that it is not they, but the other people, who look singular. Still,
Mr Irving's performance was a remarkable achievement, and
fairly entitles him to patronize his father as an old-fashioned actor
who has positively never played a leading Ibsen part. Mr Courtenay Thorpe, as Gregers Werle, confirmed the success he made
in A Doll's House as an Ibsen actor—that is, an actor of the
highest class in modern drama; but considering the length of the
play, he was too free in his use of repetitions and nervous

stumblings to give an air of naturalness and spontaneity to his dialogue. Miss Kate Phillips, who made her Ibsen début as Gina, was quite as natural; and yet she never wasted an instant, and was clear, crisp, and punctual as clockwork without being in the least mechanical. I am on the side of smart execution: if there are two ways of being natural in speech on the stage, I suggest that Miss Phillips's way is better than the fluffy way. As to her impersonation of Gina, Nature prevented her from making it quite complete. Gina is as unique in drama as Hjalmar. All Shakespear's matrons rolled into one, from Volumnia to Mrs Quickly, would be as superficial and conventional in comparison with Gina as a classic sybil by Raphael with a Dutch cook by Rembrandt. That waddling housewife, with her practical sense and sympathy, and her sanely shameless insensibility to the claims of the ideal, or to any imaginative presentment of a case whatever, could only be done by Gina herself; and Gina certainly could not act. If Miss Phillips were to waddle, or counterfeit insensitiveness, or divest her speech of artistic character, the result would only be such a caricature as a child gives of its grandmother, or, worse still, something stage-Shakespearean, like her Audrey. She wisely made no attempt to denaturalize herself, but played the part sincerely and with the technical skill that marks her off, as it marks Mrs Kendal and her school off, from our later generation of agreeable amateurs who do not know the A B C of their business. Once, in the second act, she from mere habit and professional sympathy played with her face to a speech of Hjalmar's which Gina would have taken quite stolidly; but this was her only mistake. She got no laughs of the wrong sort in the wrong place; and the speech in which the worried Gina bursts out with the quintessence of the whole comedy—"Thats what comes when crazy people go about making the claims of the what-d'yer-call-it"—went home right up to the hilt into our midriffs. Mr Welch's Ekdal left nothing to be said: it was faultless. Mr Charrington played Relling with great artistic distinction: nobody else got so completely free from conventional art or so convincingly behind the part and the play as he. The only failure of the cast was Molvik, who was well made up, but did not get beyond a crude pantomimic representation of sickness and drunkenness which nearly ruined the play at the most critically pathetic moment in the final act. Mr Outram was uninteresting as Werle: the part does not suit his age and style. Miss Ffolliott Paget was a capital Mrs Sörby.

Miss Winifred Fraser not only repeated her old triumph as Hedwig, but greatly added to it. The theatre could hardly have a more delicate talent at its service; and yet it seems to have no use for it. But Miss Fraser need not be discouraged. The British public is slow; but it is sure. By the time she is sixty it will discover that she is one of its best actresses; and then it will expect her to play Juliet until she dies of old age.

And this reminds me that I wandered away from The Hobby Horse without a word as to the acting of it. Mrs Kendal, always great in comedy, had an enchanting way of making Mrs Jermyn's silliness credible and attractive. Miss May Harvey is far too clever and too well acquainted with Mrs Kendal's methods to be at any great loss in replacing her; but she is no more specifically a comedian than Jane Hading is; and her decisive opportunity as an actress will evidently come in much more intense work. In technical skill she is far above the average of her generation—a generation, alas! of duffers—and I have no doubt that she will play a distinguished part in the theatrical history of the nineties and twenties. The lady who plays Miss Moxon cannot touch Mrs Beerbohm Tree's inimitable performance in that inglorious but amusing and lifelike part. On the other hand, Mr Fred Kerr has made the solicitor his own for ever. His acting is irresistibly funny, not because it is unscrupulously bad, as funny acting often is, but because it is perfectly in character and as good of its kind as can be. An actor of Mr Kerr's talent should not be allowed to waste himself on Miss Browns and Jedbury Juniors and such stuff. Mr Gilbert Hare has improved greatly, and is now as welcome for his own sake as he formerly was for his father's. Mr Groves of course does what can be done with the impossible but laughable Shattock; and the "pushin' little cad" whom he denounces, though *persona muta* and unnamed in the bill, is richly endowed by Nature for his humble part.

Secret Service at the Adelphi, with a smart American cast, is pure regulation melodrama. The fact that it is brightly and imaginatively done in the American style, instead of stupidly and only half literately in the Strand style, has imposed ludicrously on the English critics; but the article is the old article, only more aggressively machine-made than our clumsy hands would have left it. It has a capital situation, in Mr Gillette's best style, at the end of the second act. But this, like all the other situations, takes a huge deal of leading up to, and leads to nothing itself, being so speedily forgotten that before half an hour has elapsed the heroine quite forgets that it has involved, apparently, an act of fratricide on the part of the hero. The hero, by the way, is a spy; and why the intelligent gentleman (the only sensible man in the piece) who objects to him should be execrated as a villain, whilst all the rest rally round their betrayer and want to shake his hand repeatedly, is more than I can quite understand. I cannot even plead for him that—

> His honor rooted in dishonor stood;
> And faith unfaithful kept him falsely true;

for he first spies on the South and then, at the critical moment, betrays the North for purely personal reasons. Altogether an unredeemed rascal. But Mr Gillette plays him with so manly an air that the audience does not stop to ask what it is applauding; and everybody seems delighted. I confess I was disappointed; for I am an admirer of Mr Gillette's Held by the Enemy, which seemed to me a new departure in melodrama and an excellent play into the bargain. His Secret Service is certainly not to be compared to it. A Miss Odette Tyler almost bewitched us into believing that the comic relief was funny, especially in the scene with the telegraph operator (Mr W. B. Smith, I presume—there are several operators in the bill), who acted excellently.

Messrs John Lart and Charles Dickinson's Court of Honor must be a most thrilling and moving drama to those who, unlike myself, can place themselves at its evangelico-romantic point of view. I particularly admired the resolution and professional skill with which Miss Calhoun fought her way through a part which would have crushed any actress of no more than ordinary leading-ladyship.

MAINLY ABOUT SHAKESPEAR

OTHELLO. Lyric Theatre, 22 May 1897.
ANTONY AND CLEOPATRA. Olympic Theatre, 24 May 1897.
BELLE BELAIR. A new play in four acts. By R. R. Lumley.
    Avenue Theatre, 19 May 1897.   [29 *May* 1897]

IF only I were a moralist, like Shakespear, how I could improve the occasion of the fall of the once Independent Theatre! A fortnight ago that body, whose glory was its freedom from actor-managership and its repertory of plays which no commercial theatre would produce, was hanging the wreath on the tip-top of the Independent tower over its performance of the Wild Duck. This week it has offered us, as choice Independent fare, the thirty-year-old "acting version" of Shakespear's Antony and Cleopatra, with which Miss Janet Achurch made a sensation the other day in Manchester. I ask the directors of the Independent Theatre what they mean by this? I ask it as a shareholder who put down his hard-earned money for the express purpose of providing a refuge from such exhibitions. I ask it as a member of the body politic, whose only hope of dramatic nutrition is in the strict specialization of these newly and painfully evolved little organs, the Independent and New Century Theatres. I ask it as a critic who has pledged himself for the integrity of the Independent Theatre as recklessly as Falstaff did for Pistol's honesty. Even Pistol was able to retort on Falstaff, "Didst thou not share? Hadst thou not fifteen pence?" But I have not had fifteen pence: I have only had an afternoon of lacerating anguish, spent partly in contemplating Miss Achurch's overpowering experiments in rhetoric, and partly in wishing I had never been born.

If I speak intemperately on this matter, please to remember what I have endured throughout a quarter of a century of playgoing. Years ago—how many does not matter—I went to the theatre one evening to see a play called The Two Roses, and was much struck therein by the acting of one Henry Irving, who created a modern realistic character named Digby Grand in a manner which, if applied to an Ibsen play now, would astonish us as much as Miss Achurch's Nora astonished us. When next I saw that remarkable actor, he had gone into a much older established branch of his business, and was trying his hand at Richelieu. He was new to the work; and I suffered horribly; the audience suffered horribly; and I hope (though I am a humane man, considering my profession) that the actor suffered horribly. For I knew what rhetoric ought to be, having tasted it in literature, music, and painting; and as to the stage, I had seen great Italians do it in the days when Duse, like Ibsen, had not arrived. After a long period of convalescence, I ventured again to the Lyceum, and saw Hamlet. There was a change, Richelieu had been incessantly excruciating: Hamlet had only moments of violent ineptitude separated by lengths of dulness; and though I yawned, I felt none the worse next morning. When some unaccountable impulse led me to the Lyceum again (I suspect it was to see Miss Ellen Terry), The Lady of Lyons was in the bill. Before Claude Melnotte had moved his wrist and chin twice, I saw that he had mastered the rhetorical style at last. His virtuosity of execution soon became extraordinary. His Charles I, for instance, became a miracle of the most elaborate class of this sort of acting. It was a hard-earned and well-deserved triumph; and by it his destiny was accomplished; the anti-Irvingites were confuted; the caricaturists were disconcerted; and the foreign actor could no longer gasp at us when we talked of Irving as a master of his art. But suppose he had foregone this victory! Suppose he had said, "I can produce studies of modern life and character like Digby Grand. I can create weird supernatural figures like Vanderdecken (Vanderdecken, now forgotten, was a masterpiece), and all sorts of grotesques. But if I try this rhetorical art of making old-fashioned heroics impressive and even beautiful, I shall not only make a fool of myself as a beginner where I have hitherto shone as an adept, but—what is of deeper import to me and the world

—I shall give up a fundamentally serious social function for a fundamentally nonsensical theatrical accomplishment." What would have been the result of such a renunciation? We should have escaped Lyceum Shakespear; and we should have had the ablest manager of the day driven by life-or-death necessity to extract from contemporary literature the proper food for the modern side of his talent, and thus to create a new drama instead of galvanizing an old one and cutting himself off from all contact with the dramatic vitality of his time. And what an excellent thing that would have been both for us and for him!

Now what Sir Henry Irving has done, for good or evil, Miss Janet Achurch can do too. If she is tired of being "an Ibsenite actress" and wants to be a modern Ristori, it is clear that the public will submit to her apprenticeship as humbly as they submitted to Sir Henry Irving's. Mr Grossmith may caricature her at his recitals; flippant critics may pass jests through the stalls or pittites with an ungovernable sense of the ludicrous burst into guffaws; the orchestra may writhe like a heap of trodden worms at each uplifting of her favorite tragic wail; but now, as at the Lyceum of old, the public as a whole is clearly at her mercy; for in art the strength of a chain is its strongest link; and once the power to strike a masterstroke is clearly felt, the public will wait for it patiently through all extremities of experimental blundering. But the result will repeat itself as surely as the process. Let Miss Achurch once learn to make the rhetorical drama plausible, and thenceforth she will never do anything else. Her interest in life and character will be supplanted by an interest in plastique and execution; and she will come to regard emotion simply as the best of lubricants and stimulants, caring nothing for its specific character so long as it is of a sufficiently obvious and facile sort to ensure a copious flow without the fatigue of thought. She will take to the one-part plays of Shakespear, Schiller, Giacometti, and Sardou, and be regarded as a classic person by the Corporation of Stratford-on-Avon. In short, she will become an English Sarah Bernhardt. The process is already far advanced. On Monday last she was sweeping about, clothed with red Rossettian hair and beauty to match; revelling in the power of her voice and the steam pressure of her energy; curving her wrists elegantly above Antony's head as if she were going to extract a globe of gold fish and two rabbits from behind his ear; and generally celebrating her choice between the rare and costly art of being beautifully natural in lifelike human acting, like Duse, and the comparatively common and cheap one of being theatrically beautiful in heroic stage exhibition. Alas for our lost leaders! Shakespear and success capture them all.

Othello at the Lyric was a much less trying experience. Antony and Cleopatra is an attempt at a serious drama. To say that there is plenty of bogus characterization in it—Enobarbus, for instance —is merely to say that it is by Shakespear. But the contrast between Cæsar and Antony is true human drama; and Cæsar himself is deeper than the usual Shakespearean stage king. Othello, on the other hand, is pure melodrama. There is not a touch of character in it that goes below the skin; and the fitful attempts to make Iago something better than a melodramatic villain only make a hopeless mess of him and his motives. To anyone capable of reading the play with an open mind as to its merits, it is obvious that Shakespear plunged through it so impetuously that he had it finished before he had made up his mind as to the character and motives of a single person in it. Probably it was not until he stumbled into the sentimental fit in which he introduced the willow song that he saw his way through without making Desdemona enough of the "supersubtle Venetian" of Iago's description to strengthen the case for Othello's jealousy. That jealousy, by the way, is purely melodramatic jealousy. The real article is to be found later on in A Winter's Tale, where Leontes is an unmistakeable study of a jealous man from life. But when the worst has been said of Othello that can be provoked by its superficiality and staginess, it remains magnificent by the volume of its passion and the splendor of its word-music, which sweep the scenes up to a plane on which sense is drowned in sound. The words do not convey ideas: they are streaming ensigns and tossing branches to make the tempest of passion visible. In this passage, for instance:

> Like to the Pontic sea,
> Whose icy current and compulsive course
> Ne'er feels retiring ebb, but keeps due on
> To the Propontic and the Hellespont,
> E'en so my bloody thoughts, with violent pace,
> Shall ne'er look back, ne'er ebb to humble love
> Till that a capable and wide revenge
> Swallow them up,

if Othello cannot turn his voice into a thunder and surge of passion, he will achieve nothing but a ludicrously misplaced bit of geography. If in the last scene he cannot throw the darkness of night and the shadow of death over such lines as

> I know not where is that Promethean heat
> That can thy light relume,

he at once becomes a person who, on his way to commit a pettish murder, stops to philosophize foolishly about a candle end. The actor cannot help himself by studying his part acutely; for there is nothing to study in it. Tested by the brain, it is ridiculous: tested by the ear, it is sublime. He must have the orchestral quality in him; and as that is a matter largely of physical endowment, it follows that only an actor of certain physical endowments can play Othello. Let him be as crafty as he likes without that, he can no more get the effect than he can sound the bottom C on a violoncello. The note is not there, that is all; and he had better be content to play Iago, which is within the compass of any clever actor of normal endowments.

When I have said that Mr Wilson Barrett has not this special musical and vocal gift, I have said everything needful; for in this matter a miss is as good as a mile. It is of no use to *speak* "Farewell the tranquil mind"; for the more intelligently and reasonably it is spoken the more absurd it is. It must affect us as "Ora per sempre addio, sante memorie" affects us when sung by Tamagno. Mr Wilson Barrett is an unmusical speaker except when he is talking Manx. He chops and drives his phrases like a smart carpenter with a mallet and chisel, hitting all the preposi-

tions and conjunctions an extra hard tap; and he has a positive
genius for misquotation. For example:

> Of one that loved not wisely but well

and

> Drop tears down faster than the Arabian trees,

both of which appear to me to bear away the palm from Miss
Achurch's

> By the scandering of this pelleted storm.

It is a pity that he is not built to fit Othello; for he produces the
play, as usual, very well. At the Lyceum everyone is bored to
madness the moment Sir Henry Irving and Miss Terry leave the
stage: at the Lyric, as aforetime at the Princess's, the play goes
briskly from beginning to end; and there are always three or four
successes in smaller parts sparkling round Mr Barrett's big part.
Thus Mr Wigney Percyval, the first Cassio I ever saw get over
the difficulty of appearing a responsible officer and a possible
successor for Othello with nothing but a drunken scene to do it
in, divides the honors of the second act with Iago; and Mr Ambrose Manning is interesting and amusing all through as Roderigo. Mr Franklin McLeay, as Iago, makes him the hero of the
performance. But the character defies all consistency. Shakespear,
as usual, starts with a rough general notion of a certain type of
individual, and then throws it over at the first temptation. Iago
begins as a coarse blackguard, whose jovial bluntness passes as
"honesty," and who is professionally a routine subaltern incapable of understanding why a mathematician gets promoted
over his head. But the moment a stage effect can be made, or a
fine speech brought off by making him refined, subtle, and
dignified, he is set talking like Hamlet, and becomes a godsend to
students of the "problems" presented by our divine William's
sham characters. Mr McLeay does all that an actor can do with
him. He follows Shakespear faithfully on the rails and off them.
He plays the jovial blackguard to Cassio and Roderigo and the
philosopher and mentor to Othello just as the lines lead him,

with perfect intelligibility and with so much point, distinction, and fascination that the audience loads him with compliments, and the critics all make up their minds to declare that he shews the finest insight into the many-sided and complex character of the prince of villains. As to Miss Maud Jeffries, I came to the conclusion when she sat up in bed and said, "Why I should fear, I know not," with pretty petulance, that she did not realize the situation a bit; but her voice was so pathetically charming and musical, and she is so beautiful a woman, that I hasten to confess that I never saw a Desdemona I liked better. Miss Frances Ivor, always at her best in Shakespear, should not on that account try to deliver the speech about "lashing the rascal naked through the world" in the traditional Mrs Crummles manner. Emilia's really interesting speeches, which contain some of Shakespear's curious anticipations of modern ideas, were of course cut; but Miss Ivor, in what was left, proved her aptitude for Shakespearean work, of which I self-denyingly wish her all possible abundance.

Mr Barrett's best scene is that in which he reads the despatch brought by Lodovico. His worst—leaving out of account those torrential outbreaks of savagery for which he is too civilized—is the second act. The storm, the dread of shipwreck, the darkness, the fierce riot, the "dreadful bell that frights the isle from its propriety," are not only not suggested, but contradicted, by the scenery and management. We are shewn a delightful Mediterranean evening; the bell is as pretty as an operatic angelus; Othello comes in like a temperance lecturer; Desdemona does not appear; and the exclamation,

> Look, if my gentle love be not raised up—
> I'll make thee an example,

becomes a ludicrously schoolmasterly "I'll make thee an example," twice repeated. Here Mr Barrett makes the Moor priggish instead of simple, as Shakespear meant him to be in the moments when he meant anything beyond making effective stage points. Another mistake in management is the business of the portrait in the third act, which is of little value to Othello, and interrupts Iago's speeches in a flagrantly obvious manner.

Belle Belair at the Avenue is a primitive and not very robust specimen of modern comedy, pleasantly held up by a cast which includes Mrs John Wood, Mr Weedon Grossmith, Mr Martin Harvey, and Miss Irene Vanbrugh. The title part was probably meant for Miss Ada Rehan rather than for Mrs John Wood; but Mrs John Wood can translate all sorts of parts into Mrs John Wood parts; so it does not greatly matter. Miss Louise Moodie, Mr Farquharson, and Mr Beauchamp are also in the cast; so if the piece fails it will not be from underplaying.

QUICKWIT ON BLOCKHEAD

THE ENGLISH STAGE. An account of the Victorian drama by Augustin Filon, translated by Frederic Whyte, with an introduction by Henry Arthur Jones. London: John Milne. 1897.
THE THEATRICAL "WORLD" OF 1896. By William Archer. London: Walter Scott. 1897.   [5 *June* 1897]

As I have not the pleasure of knowing M. Augustin Filon personally, I am rather at a loss to place him. On the one hand, he seems too young to know that the electric light was never dreamt of in the old Prince of Wales' Theatre (the Tottenham Court Road house) in the sixties, or to be unable to see any merit in Ibsen. On the other, his occasional errors as to the order of events during the last thirty years are more like mistakes of memory than the inaccuracies of a young man who has just read up his subject. In many places, too, there are evidences of that amiable and shameless friendliness which gradually and inevitably mollifies criticism in London as the writer in the course of years comes to know personally nearly all the people he has to write about, except, perhaps, the rising generation towards which advancing age makes us all paternally indulgent and sentimental instances of the law that there is no fool like an old fool.

On the whole, I conclude, in spite of the electric light, that M. Filon, though a Frenchman, is an old London playgoer; and that not to have known this before argues myself unknown. His period begins with the advent of Robertson and the appearance on the stage of walls, doors, ceilings, fashionable tailoring and millinery, fashionable colloquialism, and a drama which proposed to live on these things as confidently as a child feels that it could live on confectionery. Thanks to his nationality, his vision of our theatre is quite unclouded by our own stupidity: he says what he has to say and thinks what he has to think instead of what he vaguely feels he ought to say and think; and he is simply and sincerely adroit and clever because he writes for French readers, and can afford to laugh at the fact that such qualities are neither safe nor decent in England. So far, his French differentia are all in his favor. But he also writes about the theatre as if it were merely a self-contained artistic contrivance, falling from time to time into more or less intelligent or gifted hands, and being more or less interestingly handled accordingly. No doubt it is that; and it would be well for us if our critics and playgoers had more of M. Filon's fine connoisseurship in this aspect of it! But the theatre is also a response to our need for a sensible expression of our ideals and illusions and approvals and resentments. As such it is bound to affect our ideas, and finally our conduct, even to the extent of setting on foot the strangest functional adaptations in society to the morality it imposes on us through our imaginations. Now, English criticism, though so deficient in technical connoisseurship that brilliant French critics, whatever they may politely pretend, always really see in an English colleague another Monsieur Jourdain, is never insensible or indifferent to what it calls "the moral tendency" of the drama. We may have, artistically speaking, neither eyes, nor ears, nor brains; we may be insensible to the differences between the color of a face on a badly lighted stage and on a hillside in the sun, between the English of the Bible and that of The Sign of the Cross, the blank verse of Sheridan Knowles and that of Shakespear, a pure vowel and a corrupt diphthong, a fifteenth-century Florentine or Venetian costume and the tunic of a provincial opera chorister, a copybook platitude and the Parerga and Paralipomena of Schopenhauer, between, in short, the two crudest polar opposites in art that can be propounded for our discrimination; but the dulness of all our other senses is more than made up by the hyperacuteness of our sense of the importance of moral tendency. Touch that nerve ever so lightly, and we shriek, seeing the downfall of all civil society imminent upon the least countenance given to a bad example set in serious drama on the stage. Thus we may be bad critics; but we are earnest agitators, whether conservative or revolutionary, and can uphold, even at our blunderingest, our reputation as sons of the nation with a hundred religions and only one sauce: that is, a greater nation than the nation with only ninety-nine religions and two sauces, and prodigiously greater than the nation, if any such could exist for a week, with a hundred and one sauces and no religion.

M. Filon is too French to comprehend this distinction, though his consciousness of its existence is seen in the passage in which he attempts to shew how Mr William Archer differs from Sarcey and Lemaître. "The province of the theatre," he explains, "is to Mr Archer co-extensive with life itself. He welcomes all forms and all kinds, provided they are not exotic growths and answer to some need of the soul of the people. MM. Sarcey and Lemaître are with us the guardians and interpreters of a tradition consecrated by masterpieces. They strengthen and refine it—now by the vivacity and gaiety, now by the delicacy and grace, of their personal impressions." Here M. Filon gives as characteristic of Mr Archer that very officious concern for the soul of the people from which he is so conspicuously free, though it is undoubtedly common to the general body of critics among whom he figures with so much intellectual distinction. And he quite breaks down over his own countrymen; for the neatly turned phrases quoted above mean no more than an average vote of thanks. It is the old difficulty: we cannot taste water because we were born with it in our mouths; and M. Filon does not know what a French critic is like because he is a French critic himself. I myself should not know what an English critic is like if I were an Englishman; and I suspect that Mr Archer's clear consciousness of the English theatre is due to his being a Scotchman.

At all events, it is certain that the one figure whose appearance on the stage is certain to be received by the English critics with a blank stare of unrecognition, presently giving way to a tumultuous protest against the dramatist's love of the morbid and monstrous in tragedy and of the paradoxical in comedy, is the typical Englishman or Englishwoman whom the French dweller among us recognizes with a chuckle at once. For example, read the English critics on Ibsen and then turn to the Frenchman. M. Filon revels in Ibsen—guess why. Because Ibsen is the first great dramatist who has put English society on the stage. M. Filon gives a rapid series of character sketches from Ibsen's plays, and ends with the exclamation, "If these traits are not English, I dont know what the English character is!" "But," he adds, "it is English women that Ibsen seems to have divined best of all. . . . I shall not go so far as to say that Ibsen has taught the English dramatists to understand the women of their race; but at least he has brought out certain aspects of them which had remained unportrayed." This reminds us of Mr Grant Allen's saying, "I am interested in Hedda Gabler because I take her in to dinner twice a week." Mr Grant Allen, be it observed, is not an Englishman, but a Canadian.

On Sir Henry Irving M. Filon pours out a chapter of international courtesy, carried to the length of extolling him as a literary genius on the strength of his "acting editions of the Shakespearean masterpieces." Sir Henry has rarely been more thickly buttered; but the chapter is worth reading, not only for those eulogies which are also criticisms, but for the shrewd remark that "Irving was not only able to impart more meaning to his words than they expressed in themselves, but was addicted even to making them subservient to his own ideas, and making the public accept his conception in face of a text which was in flat contradiction to it." If M. Filon had said not only that Sir Henry Irving is able to do this, but that he is not able to do anything else; that he is the despair of all authors and true Shakespeareans in consequence; that he has practically abolished interpretation on the Lyceum stage and substituted the acting of his own fancies for it; and that his constitutional imperviousness to literature is the mainstay of his originality and of his Chinese conservatism in that originality, he would have said nothing that is not latent in his observation about the power to act in flat contradiction to the text—or what is left of the text—in the Lyceum "acting editions."

Perhaps the most astonishing remark in the book, and one highly personal to myself, is that "dramatic criticism and musical criticism, owing to the natural gifts they require, are two absolutely different callings." Here you have your typical nineteenth-century Frenchman, always cleverer than your stupid Englishman, and always fifty years behind him. The twentieth-century Frenchman may retrieve the situation; for young France today has fallen in love with Germany, and shocks the generation of the war. M. Noufflard, for instance, if he were only twenty-five, would not now feel bound to preface his admirable work on Wagner with a careful explanation that his appreciation of Der Ring des Nibelungen must not be taken to indicate any slackness in his resolve to have back Alsace and Lorraine at all hazards. But to the generation represented by M. Filon, Wagner was only a Prussian, author of an opera called Tannhäuser, which failed in Paris, and of a pamphlet called A Capitulation, written to revenge that failure. Still, Gluck, Meyerbeer, Gounod, Massenet, and Bruneau ought to have made it impossible for any French writer to suppose that even opera, to say nothing of music drama, lies out of the dramatic critic's province. The promoted police-court reporter is not, as M. Filon implies, the typical person who undertakes both drama and opera. Lewes, the most able and brilliant critic between Hazlitt and our own contemporaries, undertook the two. Mr William Archer, for whom M. Filon's admiration knows no bounds, began his career with a Life of Wagner, and is a Bayreuth pilgrim. Mr Walkley, whose nose is apt to turn up at the theatre, is on terms of simple affection with music. Modesty forbids me to cite another obvious case. The reason that Mr Archer, Mr Walkley, and myself do not, like Lewes, include the opera, or our musical colleagues the drama, in our operations is simply that we cannot be in two places at the same time. No man can now do the whole work of a London musical critic single-handed; and even the dramatic critic, whose task is child's play in comparison, must often have his under-studies, at least for the daily papers. But this specialization, if inevitable, is a misfortune: it has led at the Opera to the toleration of acting and stage arrangements as obsolete as Richardson's Show, and in the theatre to the triumph of amateur affability over skilled professionalism. If our musical critics had formed their standards of stage representation at the Lyceum, St James's, Criterion, and Haymarket; and our dramatic critics learned what trained skill can do, and sharpened their senses and their power of analysing sense impressions on comparisons of Paderewski with Stavenhagen and Sapellnikoff, or of Sarasate with Isaye and Joachim, half the absurdities of the Opera would have been laughed to death by this time; and we should be spared a great deal of that diffidence and ineffectiveness which paralyses most of our dramatic criticism when it has to deal with the technical work of the stage instead of gossiping cleverly about the ideas of Mr Jones, Mr Pinero, and Mr Grundy.

I regret that I have not room to do much more than mention the remarkable preface by Mr Henry Arthur Jones—remarkable as the outpouring of the only one of our popular dramatists whose sense of the earnestness of real life has been deep enough to bring him into serious conflict with the limitations and levities of our theatre. "In all matters of the modern drama," he cries, "England is no better than a parish, with 'porochial' judgments, 'porochial' instincts, and 'porochial' ways of looking at things. There is not a breath of national feeling, of width of view, in the way English playgoers regard their drama." On this text he preaches his sermon with refreshing vitality, passing the word finally to Mr George Meredith, from whom he borrows a stirring passage (in Diana of the Crossways). After all, things must be mending when a dramatist capable of recognizing the voice of his own need in a Meredith novel can also be popular. Robertson or H. J. Byron quoting George Meredith—except to raise that

sort of laughter which is like the crackling of thorns under a pot
—would have been as probable a phenomenon as a professional
cricketer quoting Hegel.

Mr William Archer, who has evidently alone saved the credit
of English criticism with M. Filon, has just issued his annual
volume of criticisms, with the usual lists and dates by Mr Hibbert
which make it an indispensable book of reference as well as an
unrivalled history of the stage. It is a pity that the volumes do
not stretch back to the days—they must be nearly twenty years
removed by this time—when Mr Archer made his mark in the
London Figaro, under the editorship of Mr Mortimer, to whose
services in letting loose young lions both in musical and dramatic
criticism long before "the New Journalism" was heard of,
justice, too long delayed, is done by M. Filon. Some day, if I
have time, I will complete M. Filon's genealogy, and fit Mr
Archer into his niche in the complete critical edifice of the century. The value of Mr Archer's steady adherence to an unvarying
ideal standard is shewn by the fact that the articles he reprints are
as true now as they were last year. Look up any of *my* last year's
articles—especially one which you may have preferred then to
Mr Archer's on the same subject—and you will see the difference
in permanence between his classic method and my demagogic
one. Indeed none of us would reprint as well as Mr Archer. Mr
Clement Scott is as incapable as I am of keeping out of a scrim-
mage: he is an agitator, an advocate, a champion, a man of enthusiasms and generosities, abhorrences and defiances, always,
of course, within the limits imposed by his experience, his responsibility, and his conscience. Mr Walkley is a scoffer, a
banterer: he treats the theatre *de haut en bas*—and serve it right!
—but one does not need a Snubbing Annual. And nobody else
cares enough about the theatre to spend ten times more thought
on it than it is worth. So Mr Archer will stand on the shelves with
Genest when we are all buried in extinct newspapers and happily
forgotten.

Mr Archer, by the way, writes his own preface this time, and
makes it a renewed plea for an endowed theatre. I am quite of

his opinion in that matter, but have said my say in this column too recently to return to it just yet.

ALEXANDER THE GREAT

A MARRIAGE OF CONVENIENCE. A version of Alexandre Dumas's Mariage sous Louis XV. By Sydney Grundy. Haymarket Theatre, 5 June 1897.

THE TEMPEST. Reading by the Elizabethan Stage Society. Steinway Hall, 4 June 1897.

SETTLED OUT OF COURT. A play in four acts. By Estelle Burney. Globe Theatre, 3 June 1897. [12 *June* 1897]

THE Haymarket management no doubt had its reason unsettled by several hundred performances of The Red Robe when it recently threatened London with a New Drama by a critic-dramatist. In a happy hour it was turned from this road to ruin by the genius of Dumas—not *fils*, but Alexander the Great—who, though dead, yet speaketh with most miraculous organ. Nothing could have been better timed. Our playgoing public, who in Dumas's own time, incapable of appreciating his witty and wise-hearted humanity, were still barbarously rioting in stories of crimes and passions enacted by crude stage idols and devils, are now becoming civilized enough to feel his charm. Dumas was not, like his son, a man of problems. He had no need for them, being full of stories about charming imaginary people, whose affairs he manipulated with such delicacy, geniality, and humor, that nothing that they could do ever raised any moral questions. What in the son's work is murder, adultery, and the rest of the seven deadly sins, is in the father's simply natural history. Not that Dumas by any means flatters humanity. If he is quite free from cynicism, it is because he did not begin with credulity, and is interested and amused where the credulous are disappointed and embittered. There is no goody-goody optimism or vulgar Jingo patriotism about him. His kings are spoiled children; his heroes lapse into follies and petty rascalities, and have a quite unheroic estimate of the value of money and of their own skins (witness D'Artagnan making a "corner" in straw when the Court unexpectedly sleeps out, and Henri Quatre's fright at the siege of Cahors); he is on sufficiently familiar terms with women to make his most ravishing heroines much less suggestive of sex illusion on the author's part than Cesarine or Becky Sharp; and his villains are not monsters, but simply defective men, on whose account he does not fear that the world will fall to pieces. But if he does not idolize humanity, he is never unkind to it, and is generally willing to lend it some of his own pleasantest qualities to make a show with. He finds a point of view for everybody that makes them bearable; and he is always considerate to his audience: for example, his account of the torturing of La Mole and Coconnas, though it leaves a sufficiently vivid impression of the atrocity of the process, is much more agreeable reading than the love scenes of Dumas *fils*; and his own love scenes are unembarrassing and unembarrassed without being the least prudish. On the whole, Dumas is the best of all the storytellers; and as he was as apt at dialogue as at narrative, he is an unrivalled storytelling playwright. If our playgoing public takes to his historical romances instead of to clumsy modern imitations of them, and to translations of his plays by Mr Grundy instead of to stage versions of those imitations, why, so much the better!

To be thoroughly convinced that Dumas is congenial to our actors, all that is necessary is a visit to the Haymarket to see how perfectly happy the company there is in A Marriage of Convenience. It is an ideal play for them. They escape the jar of new ideas, the bewilderment of new standards, and the terrible doubt as to whether the comparative frankness and rudeness of the more equal terms of modern intercourse between men and women may not be mistaken for the bad manners of the period when women were childish enough to think it worth their while to exchange all the genuine consideration which men require from one another for the obsequiousness a shopwalker shews to the customer he intends to cheat. And instead of escaping all this, as actors must in plays by contemporary authors, at the cost of having stupid, common, behindhand parts in third-rate sincere plays, or else unreal parts in venally conventional ones, they have brilliant, witty, delicate dialogue, flattering characterization, and an atmosphere of artistic and literary distinction. You cannot now say that Miss Winifred Emery and Mr Terriss are wasting their talent on stuff that might be served up in penny numbers to the Boy Brotherhoods of Hoxton and Bethnal Green, as they certainly were in One of the Best and Under the Red Robe. Dumas *père* is good enough for anybody: literary connoisseurs of all kinds, from Morris and Rossetti to Henley and Stevenson, and nameless thousands of lovers of the highest fiction, have revelled in him and scorned as prigs and pedants the dullards who did not know the histories of D'Artagnan, Chicot, Balsamo, Henri Trois, and Louis Treize by heart—or, if they did, were afraid to own to a taste shared by boys and girls. Dumas has always kept the best company—company which was apt to be bored by his son (for whom, one fancies, he must have felt much as Alexander VI for the correct and serious Cæsar Borgia); and to that company the Haymarket stars can conclusively refer anyone who disparages the rank of their author.

An incidental advantage of the substitution of A Marriage of Convenience for Under the Red Robe is that it does not debauch the public by setting it to admire spurious and vulgar imitations of chivalry and gallantry, and, as an inevitable consequence, histrionic guff and bugaboo instead of fine acting. When the public was encouraged to think Gil de Berault a fine fellow, and to fall in love with a senseless stage doll like Renée de Cocheforêt, it was impossible not to feel that its education was being neglected, and its childishness exploited. Let us rejoice, therefore, that A Marriage of Convenience is an educative piece as well as a captivating one. The Countess de Candale is not a New Woman; but she is a human being; and Miss Winifred Emery, in impersonating her, is really acting—for the first time for eighteen months —and acting very delightfully. Candale is a real gallant gentleman; and such sense of inadequacy as that obsolescent ideal leaves nowadays is fully satisfied by the delicate irony of his point of honor —"Remember: I will not be made ridiculous." But he is still a gentleman according to his lights; and Mr Terriss can play him with perfect self-respect, not forcing his own grace, skill, and distinction of sympathetic sentiment on a stuffed Guy, but realizing a quite natural and interesting picture of humanity at its pleasantest.

The audience, to its credit be it said, enjoyed the change from sawdust to flesh and blood immensely. That is the good side of our playgoers. They are invariably unfaithful to fine art when it is absent, and will console themselves uproariously and shamelessly with the vilest illicit substitutes. But when it is brought back to them they heartily admit that there is nothing like it after all, and settle down lovingly with it until its next holiday.

There is of course a side on which A Marriage of Convenience is vulnerable to advanced criticism. Its characterization is the trait-mimicry of Shakespear and Scott, not the life-study of Balzac, Meredith, and Ibsen. The play is an entertainment, not a serious revelation of humanity to itself. It has a happy ending, as inorganic as a pseudo-Mozartian coda in an old concert version of a Gluck overture. Everything in the play happens because it is the amusing or touching thing to happen, not because it must happen so, given the characters and circumstances, whether we like it or not. Consequently, if you have acquired from Ibsen the taste for glimpses into the engine-room under the decks of society, you may find that you have left Dumas behind in Scott's and Shakespear's company. In any case you are likely to feel that certain passages, like old pastel pictures, have retained their color but lost their bloom and sparkle. The happy ending is trite; the choleric old general is an exploded convention; the levity of the amended marriage relations is less credible and more shocking nowadays than the profligacy of the original "convenient" ones. But it is wonderful how little of this wear and tear there is after the lapse of half a century; and how perfectly Dumas seems to be in our confidence as to all shortcomings, as if he knew perfectly well about these serious matters, but would not trouble us, his guests, with them after dinner. For my part, I hope Mr Grundy will pursue his researches into the works of the Immortal Alick, and that the Haymarket may long keep them between us and his degenerate imitators.

The performance on the first night was as successful as the hearts of the managers could desire. The audience rose with un-expected buoyancy to Dumas's high comedy; and when Miss Emery gave it a lump of sugar in the shape of a little shower of tears in one of the most effective episodes in the third act, its enthusiasm knew no bounds. At the end, it remained frantically demonstrating until the company revolted against further calls; though even then Mr Terriss was dragged from his washhand basin and forced, soap in hand, on the stage, to receive a final salvo. The soubrette part was played by Miss Adrienne Dairolles, who did not find, as she easily might in a new play, her cleverness and address hindering instead of helping her. Mr Cyril Maude amused himself with the part of Valclos to an extent that would have considerably astonished the author; but as the audience was equally amused, remonstrance is vain. I always give myself away to Mr Maude by laughing under the spell of his genuine comic force and impersonative faculty, though he shocks my critical pedantry unmercifully by his naïve incapacity for distinguishing between acting and clowning. He mixes up genuine strokes of character, executed with perfect artistic dignity, with the galvanic grins and knock-kneed attitudes of a funny man at a children's party. And both are undertaken with the same unsparing con-scientiousness, and without the faintest apparent suspicion that there is any difference in their class or value. In this play, for instance, he has to sit for a few minutes on a sofa whilst Mr Terriss tells a story which makes him acutely ridiculous. It is not necessary for him to meddle in the effect: a Lord Chief Justice in his robes and at his gravest would be laughed at in such a situation. But Mr Maude likes acting, and has no belief in letting the play do its own work. He comically draws up his heels, knees, and shoulders, and drags down the corners of his mouth, with the fullest persuasion that unless he did this there would be nothing to laugh at. At such moments I pull out handfuls of my hair, and sit contemplating them vacantly, asking myself what I am doing in such an absurd place as the British theatre. But, after all, this is the fault of Mr Maude's quality. The last thing an artist with a strong sense of fun learns to do is to go over his work and resolutely cut out every stroke, however uproariously laughable, that is not perfectly possible and natural. It is the neglect of this critical process that disqualifies Mr Maude from the classical rank as a comedian which is easily within his reach. Now that he is a manager, and that the author is dead, it rests with himself alone to keep himself to a strict account, and not accept farcical currency in payment of his obligations to comedy.

The performance of The Tempest at Steinway Hall by the Elizabethan Stage Society was only an ordinary platform reading, with the human personages in modern evening dress and the pageant-figures in grotesque costumes. It would have been more impressive had Mr Hermann Vezin been able to bring himself to take Prospero seriously: as it was, he dosed him with dry common sense and colloquial realism to the verge of guying him. Mr Poel's little brigade of Elizabethans got through the other parts very creditably. Mr Dolmetsch has mastered a new instrument—the penny whistle—on which, aided by Miss Hélène Dolmetsch on the drum, he discoursed excellent pipe and tabor music for Ariel. His reproduction of the original music on viols and virginals gave a unique interest to the occasion, and led to the hall being crowded.

Miss Estelle Burney's Settled Out of Court, produced last week at a Globe *matinée*, has some admirable points. As a piece of crisp, deft, vivid scenic projection of such character and situation as there is in it to project, neither Mr Pinero nor Mr Grundy could have done it better—in fact, they would probably have done it worse. The action is handled with abundant nervous energy and perfect clear-headedness. Unfortunately Miss Burney has let her imagination waver between two incompatible planes. Her heroine is a figment of the old operatic school. She might have been set to music, with variations and flute *obbligato*, by Donizetti, or haunted the early novels of Miss Braddon and Wilkie Collins. The hero and his mistress, on the other hand, belong to the realistic repertory of the Independent Theatre. The result is that there is no real drama; for it is impossible to seriously connect a lady who is obviously working up towards a dagger, a maniac laugh, and a homicide, with an ultra-modern husband. The husband himself, though drawn from a contemporary point of view, is morally judged from that of Sir Walter Scott. Our drama is getting fuller and fuller of this sort of confusion; for the daily observation of our dramatists keeps them up to date in personal descriptions, whilst there is nothing to force them to revise the morality they inherit from their grandmothers. Confusion is always an element of failure, and is especially so in the case of Miss Burney, who is too clever to succeed as a half-and-half playwright. With some solid opinions, and an utter disregard of the theatre and the public, Miss Burney might, I think, give us some excellent plays.

Mr Lewis Waller, who has been for some time past shewing all sorts of valuable qualities as an actor—I mean, of course, above and beyond his old-established presentability as a fashionable leading man, by which I set no store whatever—played the hero in a highly skilful and interesting way, and rescued the performance from the fate which would certainly have overtaken it had its charm depended on the Donizetti heroine, through whose part Miss Janette Steer, frightfully misfitted, ranted and lachrymosed with a conscientiousness all the more admirable as it was unsustained by a ray of conviction.

ROBERTSON REDIVIVUS

AN IRISH GENTLEMAN. A play in three acts. By David Christie Murray and John L. Shine. Globe Theatre, 9 June 1897.

FOR THE HONOUR OF THE FAMILY. Anonymous adaptation of Émile Augier's Mariage d'Olympe. Comedy Theatre, 10 June 1897.

CASTE. By T. W. Robertson. Revival. Court Theatre, 10 June 1897.   [19 *June* 1897]

THE revival of Caste at the Court Theatre is the revival of an epoch-making play after thirty years. A very little epoch and a very little play, certainly, but none the less interesting on that account to mortal critics whose own epochs, after full deductions for nonage and dotage, do not outlast more than two such plays. The Robertsonian movement caught me as a boy; the Ibsen movement caught me as a man; and the next one will catch me as a fossil.

It happens that I did not see Mr Hare's revival of Caste at the Garrick, nor was I at his leave-taking at the Lyceum before his trip to America; so that until last week I had not seen Caste since the old times when the Hare-Kendal management was still in futurity, and the Bancrofts had not left Tottenham Court Road. During that interval a great many things have happened, some of which have changed our minds and morals more than many of the famous Revolutions and Reformations of the historians. For instance, there was supernatural religion then; and eminent physicists, biologists, and their disciples were "infidels." There was a population question then; and what men and women knew about one another was either a family secret or the recollection of a harvest of wild oats. There was no social question—only a "social evil"; and the educated classes knew the working classes through novels written by men who had gathered their notions of the subject either from a squalid familiarity with general servants in Pentonville kitchens, or from no familiarity at all with the agricultural laborer and the retinues of the country house and west end mansion. Today the "infidels" are bishops and church-wardens, without change of view on their part. There is no population question; and the young lions and lionesses of Chronicle and Star, Keynote and Pseudonym, without suspicion of debauchery, seem to know as much of erotic psychology as the most liberally educated Periclean Athenians. The real working classes loom hugely in middle-class consciousness, and have pressed into their service the whole public energy of the time; so that now even a Conservative Government has nothing for the classes but "doles," extracted with difficulty from its pre-occupation with instalments of Utopian Socialism. The extreme reluctance of Englishmen to mention these changes is the measure of their dread of a reaction to the older order which they still instinctively connect with strict applications of religion and respectability.

Since Caste has managed to survive all this, it need not be altogether despised by the young champions who are staring contemptuously at it, and asking what heed they can be expected to give to the opinions of critics who think such stuff worth five minutes' serious consideration. For my part, though I enjoy it more than I enjoyed The Notorious Mrs Ebbsmith, I do not defend it. I see now clearly enough that the eagerness with which it was swallowed long ago was the eagerness with which an ocean castaway, sucking his bootlaces in an agony of thirst in a sublime desert of salt water, would pounce on a spoonful of flat salutaris and think it nectar. After years of sham heroics and superhuman balderdash, Caste delighted everyone by its freshness, its nature, its humanity. You will shriek and snort, O scornful young men, at this monstrous assertion. "Nature! Freshness!" you will exclaim. "In Heaven's name [if you are not too modern to have heard of Heaven], where is there a touch of nature in Caste?" I reply, "In the windows, in the doors, in the walls, in the carpet, in the ceiling, in the kettle, in the fireplace, in the ham, in the tea, in the bread and butter, in the bassinet, in the hats and sticks and clothes, in the familiar phrases, the quiet, unpumped, everyday utterance: in short, the commonplaces that are now spurned because they are commonplaces, and were then inexpressibly welcome because they were the most unexpected of novelties."

And yet I dare not submit even this excuse to a detailed examination. Charles Mathews was in the field long before Robertson and Mr Bancroft with the art of behaving like an ordinary gentleman in what looked like a real drawing room. The characters are very old stagers, very thinly "humanized." Captain Hawtrey may look natural now in the hands of Mr Fred Kerr; but he began by being a very near relation of the old stage "swell," who pulled his moustache, held a single eyeglass between his brow and cheekbone, said "Haw, haw" and "By Jove," and appeared in every harlequinade in a pair of white trousers which were blacked by the clown instead of his boots. Mr Henry Arthur Jones, defending his idealized early impressions as Berlioz defended the forgotten Dalayrac, pleads for Eccles as "a great and vital tragi-comic figure." But the fond plea cannot be allowed. Eccles is caricatured in the vein and by the methods which Dickens had made obvious; and the implied moral view of his case is the common Pharisaic one of his day. Eccles and Gerridge together epitomize mid-century Victorian shabby-genteel ignorance of the working classes. Polly is comic relief pure and simple; George and Esther have nothing but a milkcan to differentiate them from the heroes and heroines of a thousand sentimental dramas; and though Robertson happens to be quite right—contrary to the prevailing opinion among critics whose conception of the aristocracy is a theoretic one—in representing the "Marquizzy" as insisting openly and jealously on her rank, and, in fact, having an impenitent and resolute flunkeyism as her class characteristic, yet it is quite evident that she is not an original study from life, but simply a ladyfication of the conventional haughty mother whom we lately saw revived in all her original vulgarity and absurdity at the Adelphi in Maddison Morton's All that Glitters is not Gold, and who was generally associated on the stage with the swell from whom Captain Hawtrey is evolved. Only, let it not be forgotten that in both there really is a humanization, as humanization was understood in the 'sixties: that is, a discovery of saving sympathetic qualities in personages thitherto deemed beyond redemption. Even theology had to be humanized then by the rejection of the old doctrine of eternal punishment. Hawtrey is a good fellow, which the earlier "swell" never was; the Marquise is dignified and affectionate at heart, and is neither made ridiculous by a grotesque headdress nor embraced by the drunken Eccles; and neither of them is attended by a supercilious footman in plush whose head is finally punched powderless by Sam Gerridge. And if from these hints you cannot gather the real nature and limits of the tiny theatrical revolution of which Robertson was the hero, I must leave you in your perplexity for want of time and space for further exposition.

Of the performance I need say nothing. Caste is a task for amateurs: if its difficulties were doubled, the Court company could without effort play it twice as well as it need be played. Mr Hare's Eccles is the *tour de force* of a refined actor playing a coarse part; but it is all the more enjoyable for that. Of the staging I have one small criticism to offer. If George D'Alroy's drawing room is to be dated by a cluster of electric lights, Sam Gerridge must not come to tea in corduroy trousers, dirty shirt-sleeves, and a huge rule sticking out of his pocket. No "mechanic" nowadays would dream of doing such a thing. A stockbroker in moleskins would not be a grosser solecism.

But if Robertson begins to wear a little, what is to be said of Augier? The version of his Mariage d'Olympe produced last week at the Comedy was ten times more obsolete than Caste, though Augier's was a solider talent than Robertson's. The Robertsonian "humanity," with its sloppy insistence on the soft place that is to be found in everybody—especially in the most hopelessly worthless people—was poor enough; but it was better than the invincible ignorance which could conscientiously produce such a tissue of arrant respectability worshipping folly as Le Mariage d'Olympe. Augier was a true bourgeois: when he observed a human impulse that ran counter to the habits of his class, it never occurred to him that it opened a question as to their universal propriety. To him those habits were "morality"; and what was counter to them was "nostalgie de la boue." Accordingly, the play is already a ridiculous inversion of moral order. Stupid and prejudiced old gentlemen are doubtless childish enough in their objection to rowdy daughters-in-law to wish occasionally that they would die; but they dont shoot them on principle; and the fact that Augier was driven to such a foolish solution is in itself a damning criticism of his play. But it is amusing and not uninteresting to watch Olympe nowadays, and note how completely her "nostalgie de la boue" is justified as against the dull and sensual respectability of the father-in-law. In fact, the play now so plainly shews that it is better for a woman to be a liar and a rapscallion than a mere lady, that I should be inclined to denounce it as dangerously immoral if there were no further and better alternatives open to her.

Miss Eleanor Lane, a very capable American actress, played Olympe efficiently; and Mrs Rose Vernon-Paget made a distinct hit by giving a character sketch of the detrimental mother on which Granny Stephens at her best could not have improved. Mr Bell played the dashing man-about-town as such parts used to be played in the days of H. J. Byron; and Mrs Theodore Wright was particularly good as the wife of the Vindicator of Family Honor, who was better treated by Mr Gurney than he deserved.

An Irish Gentleman at the Globe is a typical product of our theatre. It has been evident for some time that we have in Mr J. L. Shine a comedian capable of restoring the popularity which Boucicault won for sketches of Irish character on the English stage. Accordingly, Mr Shine, who, like all experienced actors, knows just what will go down with the public, calls in Mr Christie Murray to act as penman, and manufactures a "drama" with heroes, heroines, villains, Irish retainers, comic relief, incidental songs, and all needful accessories for the exploitation of his talent. And I have no doubt that Mr Shine and his backers were convinced that they had a fortune in the product, although they would have laughed to scorn a proposal to invest thirty shillings in an Ibsen production. They are wiser now. Fate was in her ironical mood on the first night. Neither Mr Shine nor any other of the stage Irishmen raised a smile: all the honors went to the Scotch villain (Mr J. B. Gordon) and to Miss Eva Moore, who was very charming and very English as the heroine.

Mr Hermann Vezin informs me that the "view" of Prospero with which I credited him last week was less the result of his attitude towards Shakespear than of a startling bicycle accident which prevented him from having any views beyond a conviction of the extreme desirability of getting back as soon as possible to his bed, his doctor, and his nurse. I am happy to be able to add that he is out of their hands now, and none the worse for his mishap.

LORENZACCIO

ALL ALIVE, OH! A farce in three acts. By A. Bisson and A. Sylvaine. Strand Theatre, 16 June 1897.

LORENZACCIO. A drama in five acts. By Alfred de Musset. Adapted for the stage by M. Armand d'Artois. Adelphi Theatre, 17 June 1897.   [26 *June* 1897]

WHAT was the Romantic movement? I dont know, though I was under its spell in my youth. All I can say is that it was a freak of the human imagination, which created an imaginary past, an imaginary heroism, an imaginary poetry out of what appears to those of us who are no longer in the vein for it as the show in a theatrical costumier's shop window. Everybody tells you that it began with somebody and ended with somebody else; but all its beginners were anticipated; and it is going on still. Byron's Laras and Corsairs look like the beginning of it to an elderly reader until he recollects The Castle of Otranto; yet The Castle of Otranto is not so romantic as Otway's Venice Preserved, which, again, is no more romantic than the tales of the knights errant beloved of Don Quixote. Romance is always, I think, a product of *ennui*, an attempt to escape from a condition in which real life appears empty, prosaic, and boresome—therefore essentially a gentlemanly product. The man who has grappled with real life, flesh to flesh and spirit to spirit, has little patience with fools' paradises. When Carlyle said to the emigrants, "Here and now is your America," he spoke as a realist to romanticists; and Ibsen was of the same mind when he finally decided that there is more tragedy in the next suburban villa than in a whole imaginary Italy of unauthentic Borgias. Indeed, in our present phase, romance has become the literary trade of imaginative weaklings who have neither the energy to gain experience of life nor the genius to divine it: wherefore I would have the State establish a public Department of Literature, which should affix to every romance a brief *dossier* of the author. For example: "The writer of this story has no ascertainable qualifications for dealing with the great personages and events of history. His mind is stored with fiction, and his imagination inflamed with alcohol. His books, full of splendid sins, in no respect reflect his life, as he is too timid not to be conventionally respectable, and has never fought a man or tempted a woman. He cannot box, fence, or ride, and is afraid to master the bicycle. He appears to be kept alive mainly by the care of his wife, a plain woman, much worn by looking after him and the children. He is unconscious that he has any duties as a citizen; and the Secretary of State for Literature has failed to extract from him any intelligible answer to a question as to the difference between an Urban Sanitary Authority and the Holy Roman Empire. The public are therefore warned to attach no practical importance to the feats of swordsmanship, the break-neck rides, the intrigues with Semiramis, Cleopatra, and Catherine of Russia, and the cabinet councils of Julius Cæsar, Charlemagne, Richelieu, and Napoleon, as described in his works; and he is hereby declared liable to quadruple assessment for School Board rates in consideration of his being the chief beneficiary, so far, by the efforts made in the name of popular education to make reading and writing coextensive with popular ignorance."

For all that, the land of dreams is a wonderful place; and the great Romancers who found the key of its gates were no Alnaschars. These artists, inspired neither by faith and beatitude, nor by strife and realization, were neither saints nor crusaders, but pure enchanters, who conjured up a region where existence touches you delicately to the very heart, and where mysteriously thrilling people, secretly known to you in dreams of your childhood, enact a life in which terrors are as fascinating as delights; so that ghosts and death, agony and sin, become, like love and victory, phases of an unaccountable ecstasy. Goethe bathed by moonlight in the Rhine to learn this white magic, and saturated even the criticism and didacticism of Faust with the strangest charm by means of it. Mozart was a most wonderful enchanter of this kind: he drove very clever men—Oublicheff, for example—clean out of their wits by his airs from heaven and blasts from hell in Le Nozze di Figaro and Don Giovanni. From the middle of the eighteenth to the middle of the nineteenth century Art went crazy in its search for spells and dreams; and many artists who, being neither Mozarts nor Goethes, had their minds burnt up instead of cleansed by "the sacred fire," yet could make that fire cast shadows that gave unreal figures a strange majesty, and phantom landscapes a "light that never was on sea or land." These phrases which I quote were then the commonplaces of critics' rhapsodies.

Today, alas!—I mean thank goodness!—all this rhapsodizing makes people stare at me as at Rip Van Winkle. The lithographs of Delacroix, the ghostly tam-tam march in Robert the Devil, the tinkle of the goat's bell in Dinorah, the illustrations of Gustave Doré, mean nothing to the elect of this stern generation but an unintelligible refuse of bad drawing, barren, ugly orchestral tinkering, senseless, and debased ambition. We have been led forth from the desert in which these mirages were always on the horizon to a land overflowing with reality and earnestness. But if I were to be stoned for it this afternoon by fervent Wagnerites and Ibsenites, I must declare that the mirages were once dear and beautiful, and that the whole Wagnerian criticism of them, however salutary (I have been myself one of its most ruthless practitioners), has all along been a pious dialectical fraud, because it applies the tests of realism and revelation to the arts of illusion and transfiguration. From the point of view of the Building Act the palaces built by Mr Brock, the pyrotechnist, may be most pestilent frauds; but that only shews that Mr Brock's point of view is not that of the Building Act, though it might be very necessary to deliberately force that criticism on his works if real architecture shewed signs of being seduced by the charms of his colored fires. It was just such an emergency that compelled Wagner to resort to the pious dialectical fraud against his old romanticist loves. Their enchantments were such that their phantasms, which genuis alone could sublimate from real life, became the models after which the journeyman artist worked and was taught to work, blinding him to nature and reality, from which alone his talent could gain nourishment and originality, and setting him to waste his life in outlining the shadows of shadows, with the result that Romanticism became, at second hand, the blight and dry rot of Art. Then all the earnest spirits, from Ruskin and the pre-Raphaelites to Wagner and Ibsen, rose up and made war on it. Salvator Rosa, the romantic painter, went down before the preaching of Ruskin as Delacroix has gone down before the practice of John Maris, Von Uhde, and the "impressionists" and realists whose work led up to them. Meyerbeer was brutally squelched, and Berlioz put out of countenance, by the preaching and practice of Wagner. And after Ibsen—nay, even after the cup-and-saucer realists—we no longer care for Schiller; Victor Hugo, on his spurious, violently romantic side, only incommodes us; and the spirit of such a wayward masterpiece of Romanticism as Alfred de Musset's Lorenzaccio would miss fire with us altogether if we could bring ourselves to wade through the morass of pseudo-medieval Florentine chatter with which it begins.

De Musset, though a drunkard, with his mind always derelict in the sea of his imagination, yet had the sacred fire. Lorenzaccio is a reckless play, broken up into scores of scenes in the Shakespearean manner, but without Shakespear's workmanlike eye to stage business and to cumulative dramatic effect; for half these scenes lead nowhere; and the most gaily trivial of them—that in which the two children fight—is placed in the fifth act, *after* the catastrophe, which takes place in the fourth. According to all the rules, the painter Tebaldeo must have been introduced to stab somebody later on, instead of merely to make Lorenzaccio feel like a cur; Filippo Strozzi is a Virginius-Lear wasted; the Marquise was plainly intended for something very fine in the seventeenth act, if the play ever got so far; and Lorenzaccio's swoon at the sight of a sword in the first act remains a mystery to the end of the play. False starts, dropped motives, no-thoroughfares, bewilder the expert in "construction" all through; but none the less the enchanter sustains his illusion: you are always in the Renaissant Italian city of the Romanticist imagination, a murderous but fascinating place; and the characters, spectral as they are, are yet as distinct and individual as Shakespear's, some of them—Salviati, for instance—coming out with the rudest force in a mere mouthful of lines. Only, the force never becomes realism: the romantic atmosphere veils and transfigures everything: Lorenzaccio himself, though his speeches bite with the suddenest vivacity, never emerges from the mystic twilight of which he seems to be only a fantastic cloud, and no one questions the consistency of the feet stealing through nameless infamy and the head raised to the stars. In the Romantic school horror was naturally akin to sublimity.

In the Romantic school, too, there was nothing incongruous in the man's part being played by a woman, since the whole business was so subtly pervaded by sex instincts that a woman never came amiss to a romanticist. To him she was not a human being or a fellow-creature, but simply the incarnated divinity of sex. And I regret to add that women rather liked being worshipped on false pretences at first. In America they still do. So they play men's parts fitly enough in the Romantic school; and the contralto in trunk hose is almost a natural organic part of romantic opera. Consequently, the announcement that Sarah Bernhardt was to play Lorenzaccio was by no means incongruous and scandalous, as, for instance, a proposal on her part to play the Master Builder would have been. Twenty years ago, under the direction of a stage manager who really understood the work, she would probably have given us a memorable sensation with it. As it is—well, as it is, perhaps you had better go and judge for yourself. A stall will only cost you a guinea.

Perhaps I am a prejudiced critic of French acting, as it seems to me to be simply English acting fifty years out of date, always excepting the geniuses like Coquelin and Réjane, and the bold pioneers like Lugné Poë and his company. The average Parisian actor was quaint and interesting to me at first; and his peculiar mechanical cadence, which he learns as brainlessly as a coster-monger learns his street cry, did not drive me mad as it does now. I have even wished that English actors were taught their alphabet as he is taught his. But I have worn off his novelty by this time;

and I now perceive that he is quite the worst actor in the world. Every year Madame Bernhardt comes to us with a new play, in which she kills somebody with any weapon from a hairpin to a hatchet; intones a great deal of dialogue as a sample of what is called "the golden voice," to the great delight of our curates, who all produce more or less golden voices by exactly the same trick; goes through her well-known feat of tearing a passion to tatters at the end of the second or fourth act, according to the length of the piece; serves out a certain ration of the celebrated smile; and between whiles gets through any ordinary acting that may be necessary in a thoroughly businesslike and competent fashion. This routine constitutes a permanent exhibition, which is refurnished every year with fresh scenery, fresh dialogue, and a fresh author, whilst remaining itself invariable. Still, there are real parts in Madame Bernhardt's repertory which date from the days before the travelling show was opened; and she is far too clever a woman, and too well endowed with stage instinct, not to rise, in an offhanded, experimental sort of way, to the more obvious points in such an irresistible new part as Magda. So I had hopes, when I went to see Lorenzaccio, that the fascination which, as Dona Sol, she once gave to Hernani, might be revived by De Musset's romanticism. Those hopes did not last a minute after her first entry. When the retort *"Une insulte de prêtre doit se faire en latin"* was intoned on one note with Melissindian sweetness, like a sentimental motto out of a cracker, I concluded that we were to have no Lorenzaccio, and that poor De Musset's play was only a new pretext for the old exhibition. But that conclusion, though sound in the main, proved a little too sweeping. Certainly the Lorenzaccio of De Musset, the filthy wretch who is a demon and an angel, with his fierce, serpent-tongued repartees, his subtle blasphemies, his cynical levity playing over a passion of horror at the wickedness and cowardice of the world that tolerates him, is a conception which Madame Bernhardt has failed to gather from the text—if she has troubled herself to gather any original imaginative conception from it, which I cannot help doubting. But the scene of the stealing of the coat of mail, with its incorporated fragment of the earlier scene with the painter, was excellently played; and the murder scene was not a bad piece of acting of a heavy conventional kind, such as a good Shakespearean actor of the old school would turn on before killing Duncan or Desdemona, or in declaiming "Oh that this too too solid flesh would melt!" I seriously suggest to Madame Bernhardt that she might do worse than attempt a round of Shakespearean heroes. Only, I beg her not to get M. Armand d'Artois to arrange Shakespear's plays for the stage as he has so kindly arranged Lorenzaccio.

The company supporting Madame Bernhardt is, as far as I can judge, up to standard requirements. They delivered De Musset's phrases in the usual French manner, so that the words "Alexandre de Médicis" rang through my head all night like "extra special" or "Tuppence a barskit." Only one actor succeeded in pronouncing "Strozzi" properly; and even he drew the line at Venturi, which became frankly French. And yet when Mr Terriss, with British straightforwardness, makes the first syllable in Valclos rhyme to "hall," and pronounces "Comtesse" like contest with the final *t* omitted, the British playgoer whispers that you would never hear a French actor doing such a thing. The truth is that if Mr Terriss were to speak as we have often heard M. Mounet Sully speak, he would be removed to an asylum until he shewed signs of returning humanity. As a rule, when an Englishman can act, he knows better than to waste that invaluable talent on the stage; so that in England an actor is mostly a man who cannot act well enough to be allowed to perform anywhere except in a theatre. In France, an actor is a man who has not common sense enough to behave naturally. And that, I imagine, is just what the English actor was half a century ago.

All Alive, Oh at the Strand (the name reminds me of "Alex*an*dre de Méd'cis-is-is-is") is a piece of tomfoolery with which criticism on its high horse absolutely declines to concern itself. There are one or two funny notions in it, at which I confess to having laughed; and the acting is much better than the play. Mr James Leigh's auctioneer is a capital piece of mimicry; and Mr Compton Coutts makes a good deal of the solicitor who lost his memory immediately after passing his examination. Mr King-horne and Mr Fred. Thorne also do wonders; but Mr Bourchier's part is beyond redemption: it is as much as he can do to prevent it from absolutely discrediting him.

GHOSTS AT THE JUBILEE

GHOSTS. By Henrik Ibsen. The Independent Theatre, Queen's Gate Hall, South Kensington, 24, 25, and 26 June 1897.

[3 *July* 1897]

THE Jubilee and Ibsen's Ghosts! On the one hand the Queen and the Archbishop of Canterbury: on the other, Mrs Alving and Pastor Manders. Stupendous contrast! how far reflected in the private consciousness of those two august persons there is no means of ascertaining. For though of all the millions for the nourishment of whose loyalty the Queen must submit to be carried through the streets from time to time, not a man but is firmly persuaded that her opinions and convictions are exact fac-similes of his own, none the less she, having seen much of men and affairs, may quite possibly be a wise woman and worthy suc-cessor of Canute, and no mere butt for impertinent and senseless Jubilee odes such as their perpetrators dare not, for fear of in-tolerable domestic scorn and ridicule, address to their own wives or mothers. I am myself cut off by my profession from Jubilees; for loyalty in a critic is corruption. But if I am to avoid idolizing kings and queens in the ordinary human way, I must carefully realize them as fellow-creatures. And so, whilst the nation was burning war incense in a thousand cannons before the throne at Spithead, I was wondering, on my way home from Ghosts, how far life had brought to the Queen the lessons it brought to Mrs Alving. For Mrs Alving is not anybody in particular: she is a typical figure of the experienced, intelligent woman who, in pass-ing from the first to the last quarter of the hour of history called the nineteenth century, has discovered how appallingly oppor-tunities were wasted, morals perverted, and instincts corrupted, not only—sometimes not at all—by the vices she was taught to abhor in her youth, but by the virtues it was her pride and up-rightness to maintain.

Suppose, then, the Queen were to turn upon us in the midst of our jubilation, and say, "My Lords and Gentlemen: You have been good enough to describe at great length the changes made during the last sixty years in science, art, politics, dress, sport, locomotion, newspapers, and everything else that men chatter about. But you have not a word to say about the change that comes home most closely to me? I mean the change in the number, the character, and the intensity of the lies a woman must either believe or pretend to believe before she can graduate in polite society as a well-brought-up lady." If Her Majesty could be persuaded to give a list of these lies, what a document it would be! Think of the young lady of seventy years ago, systematically and piously lied to by parents, governesses, clergymen, servants, everybody; and slapped, sent to bed, or locked up in the be-devilled and beghosted dark at every rebellion of her common sense and natural instinct against sham religion, sham propriety, sham decency, sham knowledge, and sham ignorance. Surely every shop-window picture of "the girl Queen" of 1837 must tempt the Queen of 1897 to jump out of her carriage and write up under it, "Please remember that there is not a woman earning twenty-four shillings a week as a clerk today who is not ten times better educated than this unfortunate girl was when the crown dropped on her head, and left her to reign by her mother wit and the advice of a parcel of men who to this day have not sense enough to manage a Jubilee, let alone an Empire, without offending everybody." Depend on it, seventy-eight years cannot be lived through without finding out things that queens do not mention in Adelphi melodramas. Granted that the Queen's consort was not a Chamberlain Alving, and that too few of her wide, numerous and robust posterity have perished for even Ibsen to see in the dissoluteness of the ancestors of the First Gentleman in Europe any great menace to the longevity of their descendants; still nineteenth-century life, however it may stage-manage itself tragically and sensationally here, or settle itself happily and

178

domestically there, is yet all of one piece; and it is possible to have better luck than Mrs Alving without missing all her conclusions.

Let us therefore guard ourselves against the gratuitous, but just now very common, assumption that the Queen, in her garnered wisdom and sorrow, is as silly as the noisiest of her subjects, who see in their ideal Queen the polar opposite of Mrs Alving, and who are so far right that the spirit of Ghosts is unquestionably the polar opposite of the spirit of the Jubilee. The Jubilee represents the nineteenth century proud of itself. Ghosts represents it loathing itself. And how it *can* loathe itself when it gets tired of its money! Think of Schopenhauer and Shelley, Lassalle and Karl Marx, Ruskin and Carlyle, Morris and Wagner and Ibsen. How fiercely they rent the bosom that bore them! How they detested all the orthodoxies, and respectabilities, and ideals we have just been jubilating! Of all their attacks, none is rasher or fiercer than Ghosts. And yet, like them all, it is perfectly unanswerable. Many generations have laughed at comedies like L'Etourdi, and repeated that hell is paved with good intentions; but never before have we had the well-brought-up, high-minded nineteenth-century lady and her excellent clergyman as the mischief-makers. With them the theme, though still in its essence comic, requires a god to laugh at it. To mortals who may die of such blundering it is tragic and ghastly.

The performance of Ghosts by the Independent Theatre Society left the two previous productions by the same society far behind. As in the case of The Wild Duck, all obscurity vanished; and Ibsen's clearness, his grip of his theme, and the rapidity, directness, and intensity of the action of the piece produced the effect they can always be depended on to produce in capable hands, such as Mr Charrington's (so far alone among those of Ibsenite stage-managers) have proved to be. Mrs Theodore Wright's Mrs Alving, originally an achievement quite beyond the culture of any other actress of her generation, is still hardly less peculiar to her. Mrs Wright's technique is not in the least that of the Ibsen school. Never for a moment would you suspect her of having seen Miss Janet Achurch or anyone remotely resembling her. She is unmistakeably a contemporary of Miss Ellen Terry. When I first saw her act she was playing Beatrice in Much Ado About Nothing, with a charm and intuition that I have not seen surpassed, and should not have seen equalled if I had never seen Miss Terry wasting her gifts on Shakespear. As it happened, Mrs Theodore Wright, perhaps because she was so fond of acting that the stage, where there is less opportunity for it than anywhere else in England, bored her intolerably, found her way behind the scenes of the revolutionary drama of the century at a time when the happy ending now in progress had not been reached, and played Shakespear and recited Shelley, Hood, and George Eliot before Karl Max, Morris, Bradlaugh, and other volcanic makers of the difference between 1837 and 1897, as proudly as Talma played to his pit of kings. Her authors, it will be seen, were not so advanced as her audiences; but that could not be helped, as the progressive movement in England had not produced a dramatist; and nobody then dreamt of Norway, or knew that Ibsen had begun the drama of struggle and emancipation, and had declared that the really effective progressive forces of the moment were the revolt of the working classes against economic, and of the women against idealistic, slavery. Such a drama, of course, immediately found out that weak spot in the theatrical profession which Duse put her finger on the other day in Paris—the so-called stupidity of the actors and actresses. Stupidity, however, is hardly the word. Actors and actresses are clever enough on the side on which their profession cultivates them. What is the matter with them is the characteristic narrowness and ignorance of their newly conquered conventional respectability. They are now neither above the commonplaces of middle-class idealism, like the aristocrat and poet, nor below them, like the vagabond and Bohemian. The theatre has become very much what the Dissenting chapel used to be: there is not a manager in London who, in respect of liberality and enlightenment of opinion, familiarity and sympathy with current social questions, can be compared with the leaders of Nonconformity. Take Sir Henry Irving and Dr Clifford for example. The Dissenter is a couple of centuries ahead of the actor: indeed, the comparison seems absurd, so grotesquely is it to the disadvantage of the institution which still imagines itself the more cultured and less prejudiced of the two. And, but for Mr Henry Arthur Jones, the authors would cut as poor a figure from this point of view as the actors. Duse advises actors to read; but of what use is that? They *do* read—more than is good for them. They read the drama, and are eager students of criticism, though they would die rather than confess as much to a critic. (Whenever an actor tells me, as he invariably does, that he has not seen any notices of his performance, I always know that he has the Saturday Review in his pocket; but I respect the delicacy of an evasion which is as instinctive and involuntary as blushing.) When the drama loses its hold on life, and criticism is dragged down with it, the actor's main point of intellectual contact with the world is cut off; for he reads nothing else with serious attention. He then has to spin his culture out of his own imagination or that of the dramatist and critics, a facile but delusive process which leaves him nothing real to fall back on but his technical craft, which may make him a good workman, but nothing else.

If even technical craft became impossible at such a period—say through the long run and the still longer tour destroying the old training without replacing it by a new one—then the gaps in the actor's cultivation and the corresponding atrophied patches in his brain would call almost for a Mission for his Intellectual Reclamation. Something of this kind might have happened in our own time—I am not sure that a few cases of it did not actually happen—if Ibsen had not come to the rescue. At all events, things had gone so far that the reigning generation of actor-managers were totally incapable of understanding Ibsen: his plays were not even grammar and spelling to them, much less drama. That what they found there was the life of their own time; that its ideas had been seething round their theatres for years past; that they themselves, chivalrously "holding up the banner of the ideal" in the fool's paradise of theatrical romance and sentiment, had served Ibsen, as they formerly served Goethe, as reductions-to-absurdity of that divorce of the imagined life from the real which is the main peril of an age in which everybody is provided with the means of substituting reading and romancing for real living: all this was quite outside their comprehension. To them the new phenomenon was literally "the Ibsen craze," a thing bound to disappear whilst they were rubbing their eyes to make sure that they saw the absurd monster clearly. But that was exactly Mrs Theodore Wright's opportunity. A lady who had talked over matters with Karl Marx was not to be frightened by Pastor Manders. She created Mrs Alving as easily, sympathetically, and intelligently as Miss Winifred Emery or Miss Kate Rorke will create the heroine of the next adaptation from the French drama of 1840 by Mr Grundy; and by that one step she walked over the heads of the whole profession, I cannot say into the first intellectual rank as an English actress, because no such rank then existed, but into a niche in the history of the English stage the prominence of which would, if they could foresee it, very considerably astonish those who think that making history is as easy as making knights. (The point of this venomous allusion will not be missed. It is nothing to be a knight-actor now that there are two of them. When will Sir Henry Irving bid for at least a tiny memorial inscription in the neighborhood of Mrs Theodore Wright's niche?)

The remarkable success of Mr Courtenay Thorpe in Ibsen parts in London lately, and the rumors as to the sensation created by his Oswald Alving in America, gave a good deal of interest to his first appearance here in that part. He has certainly succeeded in it to his heart's content, though this time his very large share of the original sin of picturesqueness and romanticism broke out so strongly that he borrowed little from realism except its pathologic horrors. Since Miss Robins's memorable exploit in Alan's Wife we have had nothing so harrowing on the stage; and it should be noted, for guidance in future experiments in audience torture, that in both instances the limit of the victim's susceptibility was reached before the end of the second act, at which exhaustion produced callousness. Mrs Alving, who spared us by making the best of her sorrows instead of the worst of them, preserved our sympathy up to the last; but Oswald, who shewed no mercy, might have been burnt alive in the orphanage without a throb of compassion. Mr Leonard Outram improved prodigiously on his old impersonation of Pastor Manders. In 1891 he was still comparatively fresh from the apprenticeship as a rhetorical actor which served him so well when he played Valence to Miss Alma Murray's Colombe for the Browning Society; and his stiff and cautious performance probably meant nothing but cleverly concealed bewilderment. This time Mr Outram really achieved the character, though he would probably please a popular audience better by making more of that babyish side of him which excites the indulgent affection of Mrs Alving, and less of the moral cowardice and futility posing as virtue and optimism which brings down on him the contemptuous judgment of Ibsen himself. Miss Kingsley's attractions, made as familiar to us by the pencil of Mr Rothenstein as Miss Dorothy Dene's by that of Leighton, were excellently fitted to Regina; and Mr Norreys Connell, after a somewhat unpromising beginning, played Engstrand with much zest and humor.

THE SHOOTING STAR SEASON

La Douloureuse. By Maurice Donnay. Madame Réjane's season at the Lyric Theatre, 21 June 1897.
The Vienna Volkstheater Company's season at Daly's Theatre, 21 June 1897.   [10 *July* 1897]

This is the season when the foreign actor and the native travelling star come to London that they may be recognized in other places as coming from London. It is assumed by a thoughtless public that they come because London wants them. But London never wants anything: the greatest artists in the world throw their best at its head without making the smallest impression on its "verdammte Bedürflosigkeit." Only, just as we will stamp an agreement for you at Somerset House for sixpence, so, if you take a West End theatre or a Bond Street gallery for your show, and advertise and invite the Press according to a well-established and frightfully expensive routine, we will send down a horde of dreary, disillusioned men whose devoted calling it is to sample the pleasures of others in the sweat of their brow, attending entertainments as waiters attend civic banquets, with this horrible difference, that they are compelled to eat all the dishes and drain all the wines to the very dregs, whether they like them or not, so that they may advise the guests as to which they had better order. These unhappy men will write you up or write you down, as the case may be, in the newspapers; but they are pretty sure to write you up, because in writing you down they have to be extremely careful what they say lest you should have the law of them, whereas in paying you compliments they may say what they please without the least anxiety to themselves or their editors. When they have done their worst or best, as the case may be, a few of the public will come and make a small contribution to-wards your expenses at the doors—enough to pay your gas bill and half your rent if you are lucky; and then off you go on tour to recoup your losses on the strength of your London reputation.

In short, a London season is an advertisement, and nothing else. I sometimes wonder whether it is worth what it costs. It is not very easy for a Londoner to prove to Londoners that it is possible to do without London, because neither party knows anything of the people who try the experiment; but I cannot help suspecting that the more able an actor "starring" with a repertory is, the less frequently he meets with those checks to his career of provincial and colonial moneymaking which force him to pause and sacrifice a large sum to procure a fresh coat of London paint for his reputation. Mrs Kendal, who is one of our very finest artists, might be said to have simply dropped London if it were not for the faint compliment she paid us some time ago by playing Mr Grundy's Greatest of These at the Garrick. America used to send us Miss Ada Rehan, an actress of genius as well as of extra-ordinary technical accomplishment, who could actually make responsible critics polite to Dollars and Cents, Countess Gucki, and the exasperating manager who wasted her on those plays;

but Miss Rehan informs us now that if we want to see her we can do so by going to Newcastle. Even Mrs Patrick Campbell is vanishing. Now that she is no longer content to be a mere piece of trimming for fashionable dramas, but asserts herself as an actress, we see as little of her as of Miss Janet Achurch, who has always "starred." What has become of Miss Alma Murray, who has an exceptional record as an actress, and is quite capable of what is naïvely disparaged behind the scenes as "the sort of thing that authors want"—that is, skilled acting? Why have we seen so little of the incomparable Mrs Calvert, and so much of the very mediocre old ladies who are never tempted out of London? It is the same with the men. Mr Benson apparently finds, as Barry Sullivan did, that it is better to reign in the provinces than to serve "backers" for fifteen years or so for an uneasy position as a London manager. Mr Wilson Barrett disappears for years to amass the means of giving ruinous treats to us cockneys. Mr Willard has not thought us worth troubling about this season; Mr Hare's opinion as to the value of playing The Hobby Horse and Caste at the Court has not been ascertained; and Mr Forbes Robertson has been busily comparing the successes of the actor throughout the kingdom with the failures of the dramatist in the capital. It seems that the moment an actor becomes sufficiently master of his art to be independent of speculation in fashionable drama—that is, of London management—we see less and less of him, especially since the recent discoveries of America and the Cape, to which, however, we can fortunately add "provincial London"—Camberwell and Islington and so on. Of course complete impermanence is not possible in so gigantic a capital as London. The Lyceum, the Criterion, the Haymarket, and the Adelphi can boast that, given a tolerable play, new or old, their reputation and the acting of their companies will pull it through, even triumphantly. Thus, roughly speaking, the West End of London seems capable of maintaining about four theatres, one classical, one popular, and two intermediate, in tolerable security; for Sir Henry Irving is completely independent of the dramatist, and only approaches him in moments of aberration; Mr Wyndham and Messrs Harrison and Cyril Maude can always fall back safely on the French theatre of the middle of the century when they are at a loss; and the Adelphi plays are like Messrs Chubb's locks: each of them presents a fresh combination and permutation of the standard component parts, and so can be described as "new and original"; but the parts are the same, and the manufacture would probably be carried on by machinery if hand labor were not cheaper. The other houses, though they number among them the best managed theatre in London (the St James's) and the handsomest stage and auditorium (Her Majesty's), are in the desperately precarious position of depending on their luck and judgment in getting hold of interesting plays so contrived that the illusion can be sufficiently suggested to the audience, without anything worth calling acting, by people of agreeable personality and cultivated tact and command of manner. Genius and impersonative faculty, being expensive and apt to be troublesome to the management, are dispensed with, and go on tour.

Under these circumstances I cannot but be thankful that there is still glamor enough about this neglected metropolis to induce a foreign actor or actress to look in upon us occasionally for an advertisement. Duse, the greatest actress we have ever seen, has unfortunately selected Paris for her hoarding, so to speak, this year; but if I am cut off from her acting, I can at least admire her advertising. It is magnificent. Other actresses court journalists, receive interviewers and bewitch them, dine with royal families, wear orders or bediamonded miniatures of kings, and send their latest portraits to every illustrated paper in Europe. Duse knows better than that. She treats the Press with such unbearable contempt that it can talk of nobody else. "I detest journalists," she says; and instantly every journalist in the world chronicles the outrage. She shews interviewers the door, indignantly proclaiming that her private life is her own, and that "the public do not need to see the strings of the marionette." Next day every living editor either publishes the epigram and feels that he must have some details about her private life or be for ever disgraced. And the details come, not from vulgar journalists, but from ancient friends of noble family who have enjoyed the rare privilege of her friendship, and who betray her confidence in a shocking manner, publishing snapshots of her in her hammock, giving the names of her books, the gems of her conversation, the anecdotes of her early struggles, and everything that the most inquisitive of interviewers could extract from the most communicative of prima donnas. Kings send their chamberlains to conduct her to the royal box; she replies to the effect that an introduction to her is the privilege of her friends, not of official persons in crowns and other fripperies. The kings humble themselves to go in search of the scorner, and even tap at the door of her dressing room. "Who is there?" says the Signora. "The king." "Excuse me: I am changing my dress." "I will wait." "Useless, sire. I cannot receive you. Very sorry. Go away." "D——!" And the king goes away furious, and gives orders that Duse is never to be allowed to play at the Court Theatre again, which has precisely the same effect as if she had clapped a couple of boards on the royal back and breast and sent him through Europe as one of her sandwich-men. If she had been here last month she would have snubbed the Jubilee; and from that moment we should have heard no more of the Queen: the whole business would have become a colossal puff for her, beginning with a Duse Jubilee number of the Daily Chronicle. I am myself a hardened and passably expert advertiser; but I positively blush at the scale of Duse's operations, especially this Paris campaign. Patti and Sarah Bernhardt have written their names across the heavens in their day with remarkable persistence and success; but they are as much babies compared to Duse in the art of publicity as in the art of acting. Others may flatter and smile and gush and bribe, and cover continents with a network of agents to do the same by deputy. Duse simply turns her back superbly on the whole business; and lo! it is done before she can turn round again.

In the absence of Duse, we have Bernhardt, Réjane, and Odilon. Odilon is the Ada Rehan of the Vienna Volkstheater Company, which may now be seen of an afternoon at Daly's

Theatre, where The Geisha (whatever that may be—no doubt something musical) still occupies the evening. They play harmless German comedies of the kind beloved by Mr Daly. Such dramatic mediocrity may distress our Ibsen enthusiasts; but, as Wagner pointed out twenty years ago, mediocre work is the only work that our modern theatre can present perfectly. An amusing mediocre play, done as well as it can be done, and indeed much better than it deserves to be done, passes the afternoon very pleasantly; and that is what the Vienna company gives us. The actors are skilled professionals, and not amateurs who train themselves by imitating one another's mannerisms, like our unhappy stage casuals. Madame Odilon's qualifications hardly leap to English eyes at first sight: her person, voice, and address will hardly be considered uncommon here, certainly not distinguished; for she makes no effort to be either picturesque or ladylike. But she wins her way irresistibly as an actress, her Gold'ne Eva being quite the best piece of comedy we have had from abroad since Duse's Mirandolina. Her comic power, which has the vivacity of Lady Bancroft's and the breadth of Mrs John Wood's, has a full reserve of strength, natural dignity, and depth of sentiment behind it. After Mesdames Réjane and Bernhardt the very plainnesses of her style are specially welcome. Herr Christian, the John Drew of the company, does no more perhaps than we have a right to expect from any well-graced and competent actor in his position; but in London the mere fact that he knows his business fills the natives with astonishment and admiration.

Réjane has brought us M. Maurice Donnay's La Douloureuse, in which a circle of disreputable people are represented as gaily sitting down to a champagne supper whilst the host lies suicided. Such false sociology is unpardonable. I can assure M. Donnay that disreputable people, having no nerves and no character, are always full of "heart." If their host committed suicide, they would burst into tears, see his ghost, commiserate his wife and children, and drink brandy very apologetically on the plea of being quite upset. And they would send all the flowers they could beg or buy on credit to heap on the coffin. However, it does not matter: the whole play is only an excuse for a very effective and touchingly executed stroke of stage business at the end of the third act, when Réjane tries in vain to put on a heavy cloak without assistance from her lover, with whom she has just had a tearing scene. The rest is the familiar Réjanesque routine. The old allurements, including the vulgarities of Sans-Gêne without any of the momentary delicacies and dignities which have occasionally redeemed the trivial side of her repertory in the eyes of audiences who know how to appreciate the comparative self-respect of English actresses of her rank, are in full play throughout. Their repetition would become intolerable if it were possible to dislike Réjane. Fortunately for her, her cleverness, good-fellowship, and queer personal charm put that out of the question. She is supported by an excellent company. I hope she will give me the opportunity of returning to the subject by redeeming her promise to play Nora Helmer; for of Sans-Gêne I have had enough.

MR GRUNDY'S IMPROVEMENTS ON DUMAS

THE SILVER KEY. A comedy in four acts, adapted from Alexandre Dumas' Mlle de Belleisle by Sydney Grundy. Her Majesty's Theatre, 10 July 1897.   [17 *July* 1897]

I MUST say I take the new Dumas adaptation in anything but good part. Why on earth cannot Mr Grundy let well alone? Dumas *père* was what Gounod called Mozart, a summit of art. Nobody ever could, or did, or will improve on Mozart's operas; and nobody ever could, or did, or will improve on Dumas' romances and plays. After Dumas you may have Dumas-and-water, or you may have, in Balzac, a quite new and different beginning; but you get nothing above Dumas on his own mountain: he is the summit, and if you attempt to pass him you come down on the other side instead of getting higher. Mr Grundy's version of the Mariage sous Louis Quinze did not suggest that he was in the absurd position of being the only expert in the world who did not know this; but the chorus of acclamation with which we greeted that modest and workmanlike achievement seems to have dazzled him; for in his version of Mademoiselle de Belleisle he treats us to several improvements of his own, some of them pruderies which spare us nothing of the original except its wit; others, like the dreams and the questioning of the servant in her mistress's presence by the jealous lover, wanton adulterations; and all, as it seems to me, blunders in stagecraft. They remind me of the "additional accompaniments" our musicians used to condescend to supply when an opera by some benighted foreigner of genius was produced here. If Mr Grundy were a painter and composer as well as a dramatist, I dare say he could rescore Don Giovanni and repaint Velasquez' Philip to the entire satisfaction of people who know no better; but if he were an artist, he would not want to do so, and would feel extremely indignant with anyone who did. I hope I am no fanatic as to the reverence with which the handiwork of a great man should be treated. If Dumas had failed to make any point in his story clear, then I should no more think of blaming Mr Grundy for putting in a speech, or even a little episode, to elucidate it, than I blame Wagner for helping out Beethoven in the Ninth Symphony in places where the most prominent melody in the written score was, as a matter of physical fact, inaudible when performed, or where there were distortions caused by deficiencies in instruments since provided with a complete scale. But Mademoiselle de Belleisle is expounded by its author with a dramatic perspicacity far beyond our most laborious efforts at play construction; and the net result of Mr Grundy's meddling is that the audience does not fully understand until the end of the third act (the original fourth) the mistake on which the whole interest of the scene in the second (third) between Richelieu and the two lovers depends. It is almost as if Mr Grundy were to adapt Cymbeline, which is the same play with a slight difference of treatment, and to send the audience home with the gravest doubts as to what really took place between Iachimo and Imogen. The resource of "construction" cannot reasonably be denied to authors who have not the natural gift of telling a story; but when the whole difficulty might have been avoided by dealing faithfully with the work of one of the best storytellers, narrative or dramatic, that ever lived, I feel driven to express myself shrewishly. As to the ending of the play with a crudely dragged in title-tag (The Silver King, or something like it), it is—well, I do not wish to be impolite; so I will simply ask Mr Grundy whether he really thinks highly of it himself.

The acting at Her Majesty's is not precisely what one calls exquisite; and for perfect interpretation of Dumas acting should be nothing less. Such delicacy of execution as there is on our stage never comes within a mile of virtuosity. As virtuosity in manners was the characteristic mode of eighteenth-century smart society, it follows that we get nothing of the eighteenth century at Her Majesty's, except that from time to time the persons of the drama alarm us by suddenly developing symptoms of strychnine poisoning, which are presently seen to be intended for elaborate bows and curtseys. This troubles the audience very little. The manners of Mr Tree and Mr Waller are better than eighteenth-century manners; and I, for one, am usually glad to exchange old lamps for new ones in this particular. But it takes no very subtle critic to see that the exchange makes the play partly incredible. Mr Waller suffers more in this respect than Mr Tree, because his late-nineteenth-century personality is hopelessly incompatible with the eighteenth-century cut-and-dried ideals of womanhood and chivalry of the hero he represents. Mr Tree is in no such dilemma. The lapse of a century has left Richelieu (described by Macaulay as "an old fop who had passed his life from sixteen to sixty in seducing women for whom he cared not one straw") still alive and familiar. What people call vice is eternal: what they call virtue is mere fashion. Consequently, though Mr Waller's is the most forcible acting in the piece—though he alone selects and emphasizes the dramatically significant points which lead the spectator clearly through the story, yet his performance stands out flagrantly as a *tour de force* of acting and not as life; whilst Mr Tree, who makes no particular display of his powers as an actor except for a moment in the duel with dice, produces a quite sufficient illusion.

There is one quality which is never absent in Dumas, and never present in English performances of him; and that is a voluntary naïveté of humorous clearsightedness. Dumas' invariable homage to the delicacy of his heroines and the honor of his heroes has something in it of that *maxima reverentia* which the disillusionment of mature age pays to the innocence of youth. He handles his lovers as if they were pretty children, giving them the charm of childhood when he can, and unconsciously betraying a wide distinction in his own mind between the ideal virtues which he gives them as a romantic sinner might give golden candlesticks to a saint's altar, and the real ones which he is prepared to practise as well as preach—high personal loyalty, for instance. Hence it is that his stories are always light-hearted and free from that pressure of moral responsibility without which an Englishman would burst like a fish dragged up from the floor of the Atlantic deeps. At Her Majesty's the two performers with the strongest sense of comedy—Mrs Tree and Mr Lionel Brough—do contrive to bear the burden of public morality easily; but the rest carefully clear themselves of all suspicion of Continental levity: even Richelieu contrives to convey that whatever may happen in the Marquise's bedroom, he will be found at the strait gate in the narrow way punctually at eleven next Sunday morning. As to Miss Millard, she impersonated Mademoiselle de Belleisle with the most chastising propriety. She evidently knew all about Richelieu's ways from the beginning, and was simply lying in wait for effective opportunities of pretending to be amazed and horrified at them. I have seen nothing more ladylike on the stage. It was magnificent; but it was not Dumas.

Miss Gigia Filippi—sister, I presume, to that clever actress Miss Rosina Filippi—played the waiting-maid Mariette according to a conception of her art upon which I shall preach a little sermon, because I believe it to be a misleading conception, and because nevertheless it is one which no less an exponent of stage art than Miss Ellen Terry has carried out with undeniable success. It came about, as I guess, in this way. Miss Terry, as we all know, went on the stage in her childhood, and not only "picked up" her profession, but was systematically taught it by Mrs Charles Kean, with the result that to this day her business is always thoroughly well done, and her part gets over the footlights to the ends of the house without the loss of a syllable or the waste of a stroke. But if Mrs Charles Kean qualified her to be the heroine of a play, Nature presently qualified her to be the heroine of a picture by making her grow up quite unlike anybody that had ever been seen on earth before. I trust Nature has not broken the mould: if she has, Miss Terry's portraits will go down to posterity as those of the only real New Woman, who was never repeated afterwards. The great painters promptly pounced on her as they did on Mrs Morris and Mrs Stillman. She added what she learnt in the studio to what she had already learnt on the stage so successfully that when I first saw her in Hamlet it was exactly as if the powers of a beautiful picture of Ophelia had been extended to speaking and singing. It was no doubt her delight in this pictorial art that made her so easily satisfied with old-fashioned rhetorical characters which have no dramatic interest for any intelligent woman nowadays, much less for an ultra-modern talent like Miss Terry's. When she came to the "touches of nature" in such characters (imagine a school of drama in which nature is represented only by "touches"!) she seized on them with an enjoyment and a tender solicitude for them that shewed the born actress; but after each of them she dropped back into the pictorial as unquestioningly as Patti, after two bars of really dramatic music in an old-fashioned aria, will drop back into purely decorative roulade. And here you have the whole secret of the Lyceum: a drama worn by age into great holes, and the holes filled up with the art of the picture gallery. Sir Henry Irving as King Arthur, going solemnly through a Crummles broadsword combat with great beauty of deportment in a costume designed by Burne-Jones, is the *reductio ad absurdum* of it. Miss Ellen Terry as a beautiful living picture in the vision in the prologue is its open reduction to the art to which it really belongs. And Miss Ellen Terry as Madame Sans-Gêne is the first serious struggle of dramatic art to oust its supplanter and reclaim the undivided service of its wayward daughter.

The most advanced audiences today, taught by Wagner and Ibsen (not to mention Ford Madox Brown), cannot stand the drop back into decoration after the moment of earnest life. They want realistic drama of complete brainy, passional texture all through, and will not have any pictorial stuff or roulade at all—will not even have the old compromise by which drama was disguised and denaturalized in adaptations of the decorative forms. The decorative play, with its versified rhetoric, its timid little moments of feeling and blusterous big moments of raving nonsense, must now step down to the second-class audience, which is certainly more numerous and lucrative than the first-class, but is being slowly dragged after it, in spite of the reinforcement of its resistance by the third-class audience hanging on to its coat tails. It screams and kicks most piteously during the process; but it will have to submit; for the public must finally take, willy-nilly, what its greatest artists choose to give it, or else do without art. And so even the second-class public, though it still likes plenty of pictorial beauty and distinction (meaning mostly expensiveness and gentility) in the setting, and plenty of comfortable optimistic endearment and cheap fun in the substance, nevertheless needs far more continuous drama to bind the whole together and compel sustained attention and interest than it did twenty years ago. Consequently the woman who now comes on the stage with carefully cultivated qualifications as an artist's model, and none as an actress, no longer finds herself fitting exactly into leading parts even in the fashionable drama of the day, and automatically driving the real actresses off the stage. Miss Ellen Terry innocently created a whole school of such pictorial leading ladies. They went to the Lyceum, where, not being skilled critics, they recognized the heroine's pictorial triumphs as art, whilst taking such occasional sallies of acting as the Shakespearean "touches of nature" admitted of as the spontaneous operation of Miss Terry's own charming individuality. I am not sure that I have not detected that simple-minded Terry theory in more critical

194

quarters. The art, of course, lay on the side where it was least suspected. The nervous athleticism and trained expertness which have enabled Miss Terry, without the least appearance of violence to hold her audiences with an unfailing grip in a house which is no bandbox, and where really weak acting, as we have often seen, drifts away under the stage door and leaves the audience coughing, are only known by their dissimulative effect: that is, they are not known at all for what they really are; whereas the pictorial business, five-sixths of which is done by trusting to nature, proceeds, as to the other sixth, by perfectly obvious methods. In this way, an unenlightened observation of Miss Ellen Terry produced the "æsthetic" actress, or living picture. Such a conception of stage art came very easily to a generation of young ladies whose notions of art were centred by the Slade School and the Grosvenor Gallery.

Now Miss Gigia Filippi is original enough not to directly imitate Miss Terry or any other individual artist. But I have never seen the pictorial conception carried out with greater industry and integrity. Miss Filippi was on the stage when the curtain went up; and before it was out of sight I wanted a kodak. Every movement ended in a picture, not a Burne-Jones or Rossetti, but a dark-eyed, red-cheeked, full-lipped, pearly-toothed, coquettish Fildes or Van Haanen. The success of the exhibition almost justified the labor it must have cost. But that is not acting. It is a string that a finished actress may add to her bow if she has the faculty for it, like Miss Terry; but as a changeling for acting it will not do, especially in a play by Dumas. When Miss Filippi speaks, she takes pains to make her voice soft and musical; but as she has never had a competent person sitting in the gallery to throw things at her head the moment she became unintelligible, the consonants often slip away unheard, and nothing remains but a musical murmur of vowels, soothing to the ear, but baffling and exasperating to people whose chief need at the moment is to find out what the play is about. On the other side of the Haymarket Miss Dairolles has a precisely similar part. Miss Dairolles seeks first to live as the clever lady's-maid of the play in the imagination of the audience; and all the other things are added unto her without much preoccupation on her part. Miss Filippi prefers to stand composing pretty pictures, and exhibiting each of them for nearly half a minute, instead of for the tenth part of a second, as a skilled actress would. Now an effect prolonged for even an instant after artist and audience have become conscious of it is recognized as an end with the artist instead of a means, and so ceases to be an effect at all. It is only applauded by Partridge, with his "anybody can see that the king is an actor," or, in Miss Filippi's case, by dramatically obtuse painters and Slade School students on the watch for pictures everywhere. I earnestly advise Miss Filippi to disregard their praises and set about finding a substitute for Mrs Charles Kean at once.

THE LAST GASP OF THE SEASON

FOUR LITTLE GIRLS. A new and original farce in three acts. By Walter Stokes Craven. Criterion Theatre, 17 July 1897.
THE KANGAROO GIRL. Mr Oscar Barrett's musical version of Dr Bill. Théâtre Métropole, Camberwell, 19 July 1897.

[24 *July* 1897]

THE departing theatrical season has aimed a Parthian shaft at me in the shape of a farcical comedy at the Criterion, and brought me down groaning with it. When pantomime was at its desperatest they doubled the harlequinade and had two clowns, two pantaloons, two harlequins, and two columbines, neither of any of the pairs being good enough to bear the undivided attention of the audience. And now they are doubling the farcical comedies and giving us two scapegraces, two fathers, two comic old women, and actually four disingenuous young ones. This horrible uncoordinated binocular vision of a farce plot would have made me doubt my sobriety at the Criterion but for the single figure of Mr Welch as a Scotch version of the tutor out of Betsy. There would certainly have been two tutors had a second Mr Welch been available; as it was, the author had to content himself with giving Mr Welch work enough for two. And what an actor could do for his author in return, Mr Welch did. He pretended to drink pints of whisky; he suffered himself to be dragged about the floor by a grimy maid-of-all-work; he got under the table, fell over the sofa, and wrestled fitfully with a far from deep-seated Scotch accent. But though he was supported by Mr Barnes and Mr Blakeley, Miss Victor and Miss Fairbrother, against the racketings, mostly inept and humorless, of a noisy junior contingent, his labor was in vain as far as I was concerned. The theatre resounded with autumnal laughter; but my soul grew heavier and heavier. I have no doubt that the play was a passable piece of harmless tomfoolery; but I could not enjoy it. The spectacle of Mr Wyndham coming into the stalls with an elaborate air of enjoying himself tantalized me almost to madness. Clearly my dramatic receptiveness is exhausted. I can only pack up my holiday traps and apologize to the author and the company for my inability to rise to the occasion.

One other entertainment have I suffered since. Mr Mulholland beguiled me to Camberwell to see The Kangaroo Girl, an operatic version of Mr Alexander's old success Dr Bill. By Dr Bill's time the doubling process had begun. Two music-hall ladies, two Lotharios, two keys put down the backs of the principal personages, and two lockings into two rooms of two couples supposed to be under two identical sets of circumstances constituted between them the second act of the play. I condescended to be faintly amused; for I had seen worse plays and much worse companies on West End stages. Miss Nellie Ganthony's in particular was a pleasing talent; and her digressive way of enlivening the tedium of the comedy by an occasional coon song struck me as happy. But I did not wait for the third act—why should I? knowing, as I did, that nothing could possibly happen in it.

The Kangaroo Girl reminds me of the prevalence of plays with actresses in them. Let me be understood: I do not mean real actresses, but stage actresses. The author wants to present a loose woman on the stage; and he has not the courage to say what he means, or perhaps he is afraid of the Licenser. So he adopts the subterfuge of the woman of the streets who calls herself "an actress" when she gets into trouble with the police. No musical farce seems to be complete without the introduction of a travelling company of "Gaiety Girls," to whom life is one intolerably long skirt dance. And the odd thing is that actresses and ladies of the chorus, instead of resenting these parts, help the author to identify them with professionally improper persons as eagerly as they might play Magda or Adrienne if anybody would let them. They have scruples about Mrs Tanqueray, or Regina in Ghosts. But represent Paula or Regina as being one of themselves and they are delighted, and will put on fifty pink silk petticoats in honor of the happy invention.

It is a heavy lot, that of the dramatic critic. Nobody can imagine what excessive playgoing has done to this once keen intellect, once alert susceptibility, once maliciously buoyant humor. I have lavished ideas on the theatre; and now, in the moment of my bankruptcy, the wretched institution cannot supply me with half a one to go on with. I cannot review the work of the season—I had rather die than retaste its bitterness—but I dare say the theatre has something to congratulate itself on. For instance, it has got as far as Dumas *père*, a real dramatic author of the first rank, hardly more than half a century behind our time in his ideas about womanhood and chivalry and the like. Hamlet has not been played; and The Wild Duck has. Quite a number of performances of plays by me have been announced, and have not come off—an infallible symptom of high intellectual activity behind the scenes. Mr Henry Arthur Jones, after outrunning the powers of our actors in 1896, has been caught up by Mr Wyndham and the Criterion company—some of them a good deal out of breath, but still close enough to avoid a renewal of last year's collapses. Mr Pinero has managed to get a couple of pleasant scenes into one of those vast philosophic dramas in which he shews us wantons blushing in the presence of young girls from convents, agnostic platform women reclaimed by low-necked dresses and burning Bibles, men and women about town turning forty, and other themes that seem profound to a mind blunted by a petulant substitution of the Mining Journal for the

Saturday Review. We have had the New Century Theatre created and the Independent Theatre revived vigorously and actually starting on tour with Ibsen. A lady has presented us with a play about Nelson and Lady Hamilton, so advanced that my modest description of it in these columns has been reprinted in America as a tract, with certain alterations designed to give me the proper Pharisaic tone essential to moral influence across the Atlantic. And we have had a really imposing new theatre from Mr Tree. On the whole, we might have done worse.

But, after all, the great thing about the season is that it is over. In bowing it out, may I take this opportunity of acknowledging the letters from readers of this column which I have been unable to answer. The information they contain has not been lost on my ignorance, nor the flattery on my conceit. Up to two or three years ago I was seldom more than six months in arrear with my correspondence. But like all the people in The Princess and the Butterfly I am getting old: my endurance is failing and my conscience clean gone. When my curiosity goes too I shall no longer even read my letters; but I have not reached that stage yet; and I beg my unanswered correspondents to believe that it is exhaustion and not indifference that prevents me from privately acknowledging communications which are often useful and interesting to me. Even people who only want my autograph sometimes amuse me, though I hold that a collection of autographs acquired, not by the collector's tact and luck in making friends, or by honest purchase, but by shamelessly asking illustrious persons to forge their own signatures (for a signature without a document is a forgery), is like money acquired by cheating at cards. I never observe rules of conduct, and therefore have given up making them; but I am rather apt to answer autograph collectors who collect unfairly with my typewriter when I answer them at all. Nevertheless I do not wish to discourage them, as they often send me stamps, neat cards, envelopes, and other useful trifles.

HAMLET

[2 *October* 1897]

THE Forbes Robertson Hamlet at the Lyceum is, very unexpectedly at that address, really not at all unlike Shakespear's play
of the same name. I am quite certain I saw Reynaldo in it for a
moment; and possibly I may have seen Voltimand and Cornelius;
but just as the time for their scene arrived, my eye fell on the
word "Fortinbras" in the program, which so amazed me that I
hardly know what I saw for the next ten minutes. Ophelia, instead of being a strenuously earnest and self-possessed young
lady giving a concert and recitation for all she was worth, was
mad—actually mad. The story of the play was perfectly intelligible, and quite took the attention of the audience off the principal actor at moments. What is the Lyceum coming to? Is it for
this that Sir Henry Irving has invented a whole series of original
romantic dramas, and given the credit of them without a murmur
to the immortal bard whose profundity (as exemplified in the
remark that good and evil are mingled in our natures) he has just
been pointing out to the inhabitants of Cardiff, and whose works
have been no more to him than the word-quarry from which he
has hewn and blasted the lines and titles of masterpieces which
are really all his own? And now, when he has created by these
means a reputation for Shakespear, he no sooner turns his back
for a moment on London than Mr Forbes Robertson competes
with him on the boards of his own theatre by actually playing off
against him the authentic Swan of Avon. Now if the result had
been the utter exposure and collapse of that impostor, poetic
justice must have proclaimed that it served Mr Forbes Robertson
right. But alas! the wily William, by literary tricks which our
simple Sir Henry has never quite understood, has played into
Mr Forbes Robertson's hands so artfully that the scheme is a
prodigious success. The effect of this success, coming after that
of Mr Alexander's experiment with a Shakespearean version of
As You Like It, makes it almost probable that we shall presently

find managers vying with each other in offering the public as much of the original Shakespearean stuff as possible, instead of, as heretofore, doing their utmost to reassure us that everything that the most modern resources can do to relieve the irreducible minimum of tedium inseparable from even the most heavily cut acting version will be lavished on their revivals. It is true that Mr Beerbohm Tree still holds to the old scepticism, and calmly proposes to insult us by offering us Garrick's puerile and horribly caddish knockabout farce of Katharine and Petruchio for Shakespear's Taming of the Shrew; but Mr Tree, like all romantic actors, is incorrigible on the subject of Shakespear.

Mr Forbes Robertson is essentially a classical actor, the only one, with the exception of Mr Alexander, now established in London management. What I mean by classical is that he can present a dramatic hero as a man whose passions are those which have produced the philosophy, the poetry, the art, and the statecraft of the world, and not merely those which have produced its weddings, coroners' inquests, and executions. And that is just the sort of actor that Hamlet requires. A Hamlet who only understands his love for Ophelia, his grief for his father, his vindictive hatred of his uncle, his fear of ghosts, his impulse to snub Rosencrantz and Guildenstern, and the sportsman's excitement with which he lays the "mousetrap" for Claudius, can, with sufficient force or virtuosity of execution, get a great reputation in the part, even though the very intensity of his obsession by these sentiments (which are common not only to all men but to many animals) shews that the characteristic side of Hamlet, the side that differentiates him from Fortinbras, is absolutely outside the actor's consciousness. Such a reputation is the actor's, not Hamlet's. Hamlet is not a man in whom "common humanity" is raised by great vital energy to a heroic pitch, like Coriolanus or Othello. On the contrary, he is a man in whom the common personal passions are so superseded by wider and rarer interests, and so discouraged by a degree of critical self-consciousness which makes the practical efficiency of the instinctive man on the lower plane impossible to him, that he finds the duties dictated by con-

ventional revenge and ambition as disagreeable a burden as commerce is to a poet. Even his instinctive sexual impulses offend his
intellect; so that when he meets the woman who excites them he
invites her to join him in a bitter and scornful criticism of their
joint absurdity, demanding "What should such fellows as I do
crawling between heaven and earth?" "Why wouldst thou be a
breeder of sinners?" and so forth, all of which is so completely
beyond the poor girl that she naturally thinks him mad. And,
indeed, there is a sense in which Hamlet is insane; for he trips
over the mistake which lies on the threshold of intellectual self-
consciousness: that of bringing life to utilitarian or Hedonistic
tests, thus treating it as a means instead of an end. Because
Polonius is "a foolish prating knave," because Rosencrantz and
Guildenstern are snobs, he kills them as remorselessly as he
might kill a flea, shewing that he has no real belief in the superstitious reason which he gives for not killing himself, and in fact
anticipating exactly the whole course of the intellectual history
of Western Europe until Schopenhauer found the clue that
Shakespear missed. But to call Hamlet mad because he did not
anticipate Schopenhauer is like calling Marcellus mad because he
did not refer the Ghost to the Psychical Society. It is in fact not
possible for any actor to represent Hamlet as mad. He may (and
generally does) combine some notion of his own of a man who
is the creature of affectionate sentiment with the figure drawn by
the lines of Shakespear; but the result is not a madman, but simply
one of those monsters produced by the imaginary combination
of two normal species, such as sphinxes, mermaids, or centaurs.
And this is the invariable resource of the instinctive, imaginative,
romantic actor. You will see him weeping bucketsful of tears
over Ophelia, and treating the players, the gravedigger, Horatio,
Rosencrantz, and Guildenstern as if they were mutes at his own
funeral. But go and watch Mr Forbes Robertson's Hamlet seizing
delightedly on every opportunity for a bit of philosophic discussion or artistic recreation to escape from the "cursed spite"
of revenge and love and other common troubles; see how he
brightens up when the players come; how he tries to talk phil-

osophy with Rosencrantz and Guildenstern the moment they come into the room; how he stops on his country walk with Horatio to lean over the churchyard wall and draw out the grave-digger whom he sees singing at his trade; how even his fits of excitement find expression in declaiming scraps of poetry; how the shock of Ophelia's death relieves itself in the fiercest intellectual contempt for Laertes's ranting, whilst an hour afterwards, when Laertes stabs him, he bears no malice for that at all, but embraces him gallantly and comradely; and how he dies as we forgive everything to Charles II for dying, and makes "the rest is silence" a touchingly humorous apology for not being able to finish his business. See all that; and you have seen a true classical Hamlet. Nothing half so charming has been seen by this generation. It will bear seeing again and again.

And please observe that this is not a cold Hamlet. He is none of your logicians who reason their way through the world because they cannot feel their way through it: his intellect is the organ of his passion: his eternal self-criticism is as alive and thrilling as it can possibly be. The great soliloquy—no: I do NOT mean "To be or not to be": I mean the dramatic one, "O what a rogue and peasant slave am I!"—is as passionate in its scorn of brute passion as the most bull-necked affirmation or sentimental dilution of it could be. It comes out so without violence: Mr Forbes Robertson takes the part quite easily and spontaneously. There is none of that strange Lyceum intensity which comes from the perpetual struggle between Sir Henry Irving and Shakespear. The lines help Mr Forbes Robertson instead of getting in his way at every turn, because he wants to play Hamlet, and not to slip into his inky cloak a changeling of quite another race. We may miss the craft, the skill double-distilled by constant peril, the subtlety, the dark rays of heat generated by intense friction, the relentless parental tenacity and cunning with which Sir Henry nurses his own pet creations on Shakespearean food like a fox rearing its litter in the den of a lioness; but we get light, freedom, naturalness, credibility, and Shakespear. It is wonderful how easily everything comes right when you have the right man with the right mind for it—how the story tells itself, how the characters come to life, how even the failures in the cast cannot confuse you, though they may disappoint you. And Mr Forbes Robertson has certainly not escaped such failures, even in his own family. I strongly urge him to take a hint from Claudius and make a real ghost of Mr Ian Robertson at once; for there is no sort of use in going through that scene night after night with a Ghost so solidly, comfortably, and dogmatically alive as his brother. The voice is not a bad voice; but it is the voice of a man who does not believe in ghosts. Moreover, it is a hungry voice, not that of one who is past eating. There is an indescribable little complacent drop at the end of every line which no sooner calls up the image of purgatory by its words than by its smug elocution it convinces us that this particular penitent is cosily warming his shins and toasting his muffin at the flames instead of expiating his bad acting in the midst of them. His aspect and bearing are worse than his recitations. He beckons Hamlet away like a beadle summoning a timid candidate for the post of junior footman to the presence of the Lord Mayor. If I were Mr Forbes Robertson I would not stand that from any brother: I would cleave the general ear with horrid speech at him first. It is a pity; for the Ghost's part is one of the wonders of the play. And yet, until Mr Courtenay Thorpe divined it the other day, nobody seems to have had a glimpse of the reason why Shakespear would not trust anyone else with it, and played it himself. The weird music of that long speech which should be the spectral wail of a soul's bitter wrong crying from one world to another in the extremity of its torment, is invariably handed over to the most squaretoed member of the company, who makes it sound, not like Rossetti's Sister Helen, or even, to suggest a possible heavy treatment, like Mozart's statue-ghost, but like Chambers's Information for the People.

Still, I can understand Mr Ian Robertson, by sheer force of a certain quality of sententiousness in him, overbearing the management into casting him for the Ghost. What I cannot understand is why Miss Granville was cast for the Queen. It is like setting a fashionable modern mandolinist to play Haydn's sonatas. She does her best under the circumstances; but she would have been more fortunate had she been in a position to refuse the part.

On the other hand, several of the impersonations are conspicuously successful. Mrs Patrick Campbell's Ophelia is a surprise. The part is one which has hitherto seemed incapable of progress. From generation to generation actresses have, in the mad scene, exhausted their musical skill, their ingenuity in devising fantasias in the language of flowers, and their intensest powers of portraying anxiously earnest sanity. Mrs Patrick Campbell, with that complacent audacity of hers which is so exasperating when she is doing the wrong thing, this time does the right thing by making Ophelia really mad. The resentment of the audience at this outrage is hardly to be described. They long for the strenuous mental grasp and attentive coherence of Miss Lily Hanbury's conception of maiden lunacy; and this wandering, silly, vague Ophelia, who no sooner catches an emotional impulse than it drifts away from her again, emptying her voice of its tone in a way that makes one shiver, makes them horribly uncomfortable. But the effect on the play is conclusive. The shrinking discomfort of the King and Queen, the rankling grief of Laertes, are created by it at once; and the scene, instead of being a pretty interlude coming in just when a little relief from the inky cloak is welcome, touches us with a chill of the blood that gives it its right tragic power and dramatic significance. Playgoers naturally murmur when something that has always been pretty becomes painful; but the pain is good for them, good for the theatre, and good for the play. I doubt whether Mrs Patrick Campbell fully appreciates the dramatic value of her quite simple and original sketch—it is only a sketch—of the part; but in spite of the occasional triviality of its execution and the petulance with which it has been received, it seems to me to settle finally in her favor the question of her right to the very important place which Mr Forbes Robertson has assigned to her in his enterprises.

I did not see Mr Bernard Gould play Laertes: he was indisposed when I returned to town and hastened to the Lyceum; but he was replaced very creditably by Mr Frank Dyall. Mr Martin Harvey is the best Osric I have seen: he plays Osric from Osric's own point of view, which is, that Osric is a gallant and distinguished courtier, and not, as usual, from Hamlet's, which is that Osric is "a waterfly." Mr Harrison Hunter hits off the modest, honest Horatio capitally; and Mr Willes is so good a Gravedigger that I venture to suggest to him that he should carry his work a little further, and not virtually cease to concern himself with the play when he has spoken his last line and handed Hamlet the skull. Mr Cooper Cliffe is not exactly a subtle Claudius; but he looks as if he had stepped out of a picture by Madox Brown, and plays straightforwardly on his very successful appearance. Mr Barnes makes Polonius robust and elderly instead of aged and garrulous. He is good in the scenes where Polonius appears as a man of character and experience; but the senile exhibitions of courtierly tact do not match these, and so seem forced and farcical.

Mr Forbes Robertson's own performance has a continuous charm, interest, and variety which are the result not only of his well-known grace and accomplishment as an actor, but of a genuine delight—the rarest thing on our stage—in Shakespear's art, and a natural familiarity with the plane of his imagination. He does not superstitiously worship William: he enjoys him and understands his methods of expression. Instead of cutting every line that can possibly be spared, he retains every gem, in his own part or anyone else's, that he can make time for in a spiritedly brisk performance lasting three hours and a half with very short intervals. He does not utter half a line; then stop to act; then go on with another half line; and then stop to act again, with the clock running away with Shakespear's chances all the time. He plays as Shakespear should be played, on the line and to the line, with the utterance and acting simultaneous, inseparable and in fact identical. Not for a moment is he solemnly conscious of Shakespear's reputation or of Hamlet's momentousness in literary history: on the contrary, he delivers us from all these boredoms instead of heaping them on us. We forgive him the platitudes, so engagingly are they delivered. His novel and astonishingly effective and touching treatment of the final scene is an inspiration, from the fencing match onward. If only Fortinbras could also be inspired with sufficient force and brilliancy to rise to the warlike splendor of his helmet, and make straight for that throne like a man who intended to keep it against all comers, he would leave nothing to be desired. How many generations of Hamlets, all thirsting to outshine their competitors in effect and originality, have regarded Fortinbras, and the clue he gives to this kingly death for Hamlet, as a wildly unpresentable blunder of the poor foolish old Swan, than whom they all knew so much better! How sweetly they have died in that faith to slow music, like Little Nell in The Old Curiosity Shop! And now how completely Mr Forbes Robertson has bowled them all out by being clever enough to be simple.

By the way, talking of slow music, the sooner Mr Hamilton Clark's romantic Irving music is stopped, the better. Its effect in this Shakespearean version of the play is absurd. The four Offenbachian young women in tights should also be abolished, and the part of the player-queen given to a man. The courtiers should be taught how flatteringly courtiers listen when a king shews off his wisdom in wise speeches to his nephew. And that nice wooden beach on which the ghost walks would be the better for a sea-weedy looking cloth on it, with a handful of shrimps and a pennorth of silver sand.

AT SEVERAL THEATRES

FRANCILLON. From the French of Alexander Dumas *fils*. A comedy in three acts. Duke of York's Theatre.

Triple Bill at the Avenue Theatre, 2 October 1897.

As You Like It. Grand Theatre, Islington, 4 October 1897.

OH, SUSANNAH! Farcical comedy in three acts. By Messrs Ambient, Atwood, and Vaun. Royalty Theatre, 5 October 1897.

THE LIARS. A new and original comedy. By Henry Arthur Jones. Criterion Theatre, 6 October 1897.

[9 *October* 1897]

I NEVER see Miss Ada Rehan act without burning to present Mr Augustin Daly with a delightful villa in St Helena, and a commission from an influential committee of his admirers to produce at his leisure a complete set of Shakespear's plays, entirely rewritten, reformed, rearranged, and brought up to the most advanced requirements of the year 1850. He was in full force at the Islington Theatre on Monday evening last with his version of As You Like It just as I dont like it. There I saw Amiens under the greenwood tree, braving winter and rough weather in a pair of crimson plush breeches, a spectacle to benumb the mind and obscure the passions. There was Orlando with the harmony of his brown boots and tunic torn asunder by a piercing discord of dark volcanic green, a walking tribute to Mr Daly's taste in tights. There did I hear slow music stealing up from the band at all the well-known recitations of Adam, Jacques, and Rosalind, lest we should for a moment forget that we were in a theatre and not in the forest of Arden. There did I look through practicable doors in the walls of sunny orchards into an abyss of pitchy darkness. There saw I in the attitudes, grace, and deportment of the forest dwellers the plastique of an Arcadian past. And the music synchronized with it all to perfection, from La Grande Duchesse and Dichter und Bauer, conducted by the leader of the band, to the inevitable old English airs conducted by the haughty musician who is Mr Daly's special property. And to think that Mr Daly will die in his bed, whilst innocent presidents of republics, who never harmed an immortal bard, are falling on all sides under the knives of well-intentioned reformers whose only crime is that they assassinate the wrong people! And yet let me be magnanimous. I confess I would not like to see Mr Daly assassinated: St Helena would satisfy me. For Mr Daly was in his prime an advanced man relatively to his own time and place, and was a real manager, with definite artistic aims which he trained his company to accomplish. His Irish-American Yanko-German comedies, as

208

played under his management by Ada Rehan and Mrs Gilbert, John Drew, Otis Skinner and the late John Lewis, turned a page in theatrical history here, and secured him a position in London which was never questioned until it became apparent that he was throwing away Miss Rehan's genius. When, after the complete discovery of her gifts by the London public, Mr Daly could find no better employment for her than in a revival of Dollars and Cents, his annihilation and Miss Rehan's rescue became the critic's first duty. Shakespear saved the situation for a time, and got severely damaged in the process; but The Countess Gucki convinced me that in Mr Daly's hands Miss Rehan's talent was likely to be lost not only to the modern drama, but to the modern Shakespearean stage: that is to say, to the indispensable conditions of its own fullest development. No doubt starring in Daly Shakespear is as lucrative and secure as the greatest of Duse's achievements are thankless and precarious; but surely it must be better fun making money enough by La Dame aux Camélias to pay for Heimat and La Femme de Claude, and win the position of the greatest actress in the world with all three, than to astonish provincials with versions of Shakespear which are no longer up even to metropolitan literary and dramatic standards.

However, since I cannot convert Miss Rehan to my view of the position, I must live in hope that some day she will come to the West End of London for a week or two, just as Réjane and Sarah Bernhardt do, with some work of sufficient novelty and importance to make good the provincial wear and tear of her artistic prestige. Just now she is at the height of her powers. The plumpness that threatened the Countess Gucki has vanished: Rosalind is as slim as a girl. The third and fourth acts are as wonderful as ever—miracles of vocal expression. If As You Like It were a typical Shakespearean play, I should unhesitatingly declare Miss Rehan the most perfect Shakespearean executant in the world. But when I think of those plays in which our William anticipated modern dramatic art by making serious attempts to hold the mirror up to nature—All's Well, Measure for Measure, Troilus and Cressida, and so on—I must limit the tribute to

Shakespear's popular style. Rosalind is not a complete human being: she is simply an extension into five acts of the most affectionate, fortunate, delightful five minutes in the life of a charming woman. And all the other figures in the play are cognate impostures. Orlando, Adam, Jacques, Touchstone, the banished Duke, and the rest play each the same tune all through. This is not human nature or dramatic character; it is juvenile lead, first old man, heavy lead, heavy father, principal comedian, and leading lady, transfigured by magical word-music. The Shakespearolators who are taken in by it do not know drama in the classical sense from "drama" in the technical Adelphi sense. You have only to compare Orlando and Rosalind with Bertram and Helena, the Duke and Touchstone with Leontes and Autolycus, to learn the difference from Shakespear himself. Therefore I cannot judge from Miss Rehan's enchanting Rosalind whether she is a great Shakespearean actress or not: there is even a sense in which I cannot tell whether she can act at all or not. So far, I have never seen her create a character: she has always practised the same adorable arts on me, by whatever name the playbill has called her—Nancy Brasher (ugh!), Viola, or Rosalind. I have never complained: the drama with all its heroines levelled up to a universal Ada Rehan has seemed no such dreary prospect to me; and her voice, compared to Sarah Bernhardt's *voix d'or*, has been as all the sounds of the woodland to the chinking of twenty-franc pieces. In Shakespear (what Mr Daly leaves of him) she was and is irresistible: at Islington on Monday she made me cry faster than Mr Daly could make me swear. But the critic in me is bound to insist that Ada Rehan has as yet created nothing but Ada Rehan. She will probably never excel that masterpiece; but why should she not superimpose a character study or two on it! Duse's greatest work is Duse; but that does not prevent Césarine, Santuzza, and Camille from being three totally different women, none of them Duses, though Duse is all of them. Miss Rehan would charm everybody as Mirandolina as effectually as Duse does. But how about Magda? It is because nobody in England knows the answer to that question that nobody in England as yet knows whether Ada Rehan is a creative artist or a mere virtuosa.

The Liars, Mr Henry Arthur Jones's new comedy, is one of his lighter works, written with due indulgence to the Criterion company and the playgoing public. Its subject is a common enough social episode—a married lady sailing too close to the wind in a flirtation, and her friends and relatives interposing to half hustle, half coax the husband and wife into a reconciliation, and the gallant off to Africa. Mr Jones has extracted from this all the drama that can be got from it without sacrificing verisimilitude, or spoiling the reassuring common sense of the conclusion. Its interest, apart from its wealth of comedy, lies in its very keen and accurate picture of smart society. Smart society will probably demur, as it always does to views of it obtained from any standpoint outside itself. Mr Jones's detachment is absolute: he describes Mayfair as an English traveller describes the pygmies or the Zulus, caring very little about the common human perversities of which (believing them, of course, to be the caste-mark of their class) they are so self-importantly conscious, and being much tickled by the morally significant peculiarities of which they are not conscious at all. "Society" is intensely parochial, intensely conceited, and, outside that art of fashionable life for which it has specialized itself, and in which it has acquired a fairly artistic technique, trivial, vulgar, and horribly tiresome. Its conceit, however, is not of the personally self-complacent kind. Within its own limits it does not flatter itself: on the contrary, being chronically bored with itself, it positively delights in the most savage and embittered satire at its own expense from its own point of view. For example, Thackeray, who belonged to it and hated it, is admired and endorsed by it, because, with all his rancor against its failings, he took Hyde Park Corner as the cosmic headquarters, a Ptolemaic mistake which saved his gentility throughout all his Thersites railings at it. Charles Dickens, on the other hand, could never be a gentleman, because it never occurred to him to look at fashionable society otherwise than from the moral and industrial centres of the community, in which position he was necessarily "an outsider" from the point of view of the parishioners of St James of Piccadilly and St George of Hanover Square. That this outside position could be a position of advantage, even to a literary lion flatteringly petted and freely fed at the parish tables, is a conception impossible to the insider, since if he thought so, he would at once, by that thought, be placed outside. All fiction which deals with fashionable society as a class exhibits this division into Thackeray and Dickens—into the insider and the outsider. For my own part I recommend the outside, because it is possible for the outsider to comprehend and enjoy the works of the insiders, whereas they can never comprehend his. From Dickens's point of view Thackeray and Trollope are fully available, whilst from their point of view Dickens is deplorable. Just so with Mr Jones and Mr Pinero. Mr Jones's pictures of society never seem truthful to those who see ladies and gentlemen as they see themselves. They are restricted to Mr Pinero's plays, recognizing in them alone poetic justice to the charm of good society. But those who appreciate Mr Jones accommodate themselves without difficulty to Mr Pinero's range, and so enjoy both. In the latest plays of these two authors the difference is very marked. The pictures of fashionable life in The Princess and the Butterfly, containing, if we except the mere kodaking, not one stroke that is objectively lifelike or even plausible, is yet made subjectively appropriate in a most acceptable degree by the veil of sentimental romance which it casts over Mayfair. In The Liars, the "smart" group which carries on the action of the piece is hit off to the life, with the result that the originals will probably feel brutally misrepresented.

And now comes in the oddity of the situation. Mr Jones, with a wide and clear vision of society, is content with theories of it that have really no relation to his observation. The comedic sentiment of The Liars is from beginning to end one of affectionate contempt for women and friendly contempt for men, applied to their affairs with shrewd worldly common sense and much mollifying humor; whilst its essentially pious theology and its absolute conceptions of duty belong to a passionately anti-comedic conception of them as temples of the Holy Ghost. Its observations could only have been made today; its idealism might have been made yesterday; its reflections might have been made a long time ago. Against this I am inclined to protest. It is surely immoral for an Englishman to keep two establishments, much more three.

The incongruities arising from the different dates of Mr Jones's brain compartments have, happily, the effect of keeping his sense of humor continually stirring. I am sure The Liars must be an extremely diverting play on the stage. But I have not seen it there. Mr Wyndham's acting-manager wrote to ask whether I would come if I were invited. I said Yes. Accordingly I was *not* invited. The shock to my self-esteem was severe and unexpected. I desire it to be distinctly understood, however, that I forgive everybody.

The conscientious transliteration (for the most part) of the Francillon of Dumas *fils* at the Duke of York's Theatre makes a very tolerable evening's amusement. It is, of course, only here to get hallmarked as a London success, and is planned to impress unsophisticated audiences as an exceedingly dashing and classy representation of high life. Mrs Brown Potter is unsparing of the beauties of her wardrobe, and indeed of her own person. She seems, as far as I can judge, congenitally incapable of genuine impersonation; but she has coached herself into a capital imitation of a real French actress playing the part, which she thoroughly understands. Saving one or two lapses into clowning for provincial laughs, her performance is not a bad specimen of manufactured acting. The best manufactured acting I ever saw was Modjeska's. It was much stricter, adroiter, finer, cleverer, more elaborate and erudite than Mrs Brown Potter's; but Modjeska was not genial. Mrs Brown Potter is genial. Her good looks are unimpaired; and only the very hard-hearted will feel much ill used by her shortcomings, especially as she is well supported in a good play, carefully managed and staged up to the point of making several prolonged passages of pure pantomime quite successful. Mr Bellew should stay in London a while, to brush away a few trifling stage habits which, like the comedy itself, begin to date a little. He plays with his old grace and much more than his old skill and ease, in the quiet style of the eighties, which is also revived with success by Messrs Elwood, Thursby, and Beauchamp. Mr J. L. Mackay keeps to his own somewhat later date, not unwisely, as Stanislas.

Oh, Susannah! at the Royalty, by Messrs Mark Ambient, A. Atwood, and R. Vaun, would be an extremely ingenious farce if its authors had contrived to make the incidents credible or even possible. It is nevertheless made positively thrilling by the genius of a Miss Louie Freear, who flings down a weedy glove on the stage and exclaims, "Aw chucks dahn me gimlet" (I throw down my gauntlet), and makes the audience scream—made *me* scream—frantically with laughter at this simple-minded pleasantry. She has sense of character, enormous comic force of the rare *pathetic* kind, wonderful powers of mimicry, instinctive good judgment as an executant, and unrivalled artistic command of all the humors of the slum and back kitchen. The popular history of the English stage for the next ten years will be the history of Miss Freear and Mr Dan Leno.

The triple bill at the Avenue begins with a trivial comedietta in eighteenth-century costume which any well-trained footman and lady's-maid could move through with credit. If actors would only learn their business as footmen do, such trifles would be more popular. My Lady's Orchard, by Mrs Oscar Beringer, is a little tale of chivalry of the naïve Waverley school—a play for children. Miss Esme Beringer, by some desperate and very clever and striking overplaying as the troubadour, undertakes to force it up to concert pitch, a heroic but impossible task. Mr Brookfield's part misfits him amusingly. In The Mermaid there is some bearable music, especially a new version of that charming old song I've been roaming. With Miss Lottie Venne and Mr Wyatt to act, and an agreeably grave young lady named Miss Davenport to provide serious relief as prima donna, the piece, which is of just the right length for its kind, serves its turn better than the usual overdose.

THE THEATRES

NEVER AGAIN. A farcical comedy in three acts. By Maurice Desvallières and Antony Mars. Vaudeville Theatre, 11 October 1897.

ONE SUMMER'S DAY. A love story in three acts. By H. V. Esmond. Comedy Theatre.

THE WHITE HEATHER. By Cecil Raleigh and Henry Hamilton. Drury Lane Theatre.   [16 *October* 1897]

I CAN hardly estimate offhand how many visits to Never Again at the Vaudeville would enable an acute acrostician to unravel its plot. Probably not less than seventeen. It may be that there is really no plot, and that the whole bewildering tangle of names and relationships is a sham. If so, it shews how superfluous a real plot is. In this play everyone who opens a door and sees somebody outside it utters a yell of dismay and slams the door to as if the fiend in person had knocked at it. When anybody enters a room, he or she is received with a roar of confusion and terror, and frantically ejected by bodily violence. The audience does not know why; but as each member of it thinks he ought to, and believes that his neighbor does, he echoes the yell of the actor with a shout of laughter; and so the piece "goes" immensely. It is, to my taste, a vulgar, stupid, noisy, headachy, tedious business. One actor, Mr Ferdinand Gottschalk, shews remarkable talent, both as actor and mimic, in the part of a German musician; but this character is named Katzenjammer, which can produce no effect whatever on those who do not know what it means, and must sicken those who do. There is of course a Shakespearean precedent in Twelfth Night; but even in the spacious times of great Elizabeth they did not keep repeating Sir Toby's surname all over the stage, whereas this play is all Katzenjammer: the word is thrown in the face of the audience every two or three minutes. Unfortunately this is only part of the puerile enjoyment of mischief and coarseness for their own sakes which is characteristic not so much of the play as of the method of its presentation.

And as that method is aggressively American, and is apparently part of a general design on Mr Charles Frohman's part to smarten up our stage habits by Americanizing them, it raises a much larger question than the merits of an insignificant version of a loose French farce.

I need hardly point out to intelligent Americans that any difference which exists between American methods and English ones must necessarily present itself to the American as an inferiority on the part of the English, and to the Englishman as an inferiority on the part of the Americans; for it is obvious that if the two nations were agreed as to the superiority of any particular method, they would both adopt it, and the difference would disappear, since it can hardly be seriously contended that the average English actor cannot, if he chooses, do anything that the average American actor can do, or vice versa. Consequently nothing is more natural and inevitable than that Mr Frohman, confronted with English stage business, should feel absolutely confident that he can alter it for the better. But it does not at all follow that the English public will agree with him. For example, if in a farcical comedy a contretemps is produced by the arrival of an unwelcome visitor, and the English actor extricates himself from the difficulty by half bowing, half coaxing the intruder out, it may seem to Mr Frohman much funnier and livelier that he should resort to the summary and violent methods of a potman, especially if the visitor is an elderly lady. Now I do not deny that Mr Frohman may strike on a stratum of English society which will agree with him, nor even that for twenty years to come the largest fortunes made in theatrical enterprise may be made by exploiting that stratum; but to English people who have learnt the art of playgoing at our best theatres, such horseplay is simply silly. Again, it may seem to Mr Frohman, as it did once (and probably does still) to Mr Augustin Daly, that the way to work every act of a comedy up to a rattling finish is to upset chairs, smash plates, make all the women faint and all the men tumble over one another. But in London we are apt to receive that sort of thing so coldly even in its proper place in the rallies of a harlequinade that there is no temptation to West End managers to condescend to it. The truth is, all this knockabout stuff, these coarse pleasantries about women's petticoats, Katzenjammer, and so forth, belong, not to American civilization, but to American barbarism. It converts what might be, at worst, a wittily licentious form of comedy for licentiously witty people into a crude sort of entertainment for a crude sort of audience. The more it tries to hustle and bustle me into enjoying myself, the more does it put me on my most melancholy dignity, and set me reflecting funereally on the probable future of a race nursed on such amusements. To save myself from pessimism I have to remind myself that neither in America nor here is the taste for them a mature taste, and that the Americans in particular are so far from being its partisans that they rate English acting and English methods far higher than we do ourselves.

There is, however, a heavy account on the other side. The routine of melodrama and farcical comedy is not a fine art: it is an industry; and in it the industrial qualities of the Americans shine out. Their companies are smarter, better drilled, work harder and faster, waste less time, and know their business better than English companies. They do not select duffers when they can help it; and though the duffer may occasionally get engaged *faute de mieux*, as a dog gets eaten during a siege, he does not find that there is a living for him in melodrama, and so gets driven into the fashionable drama of the day, in which he will easily obtain engagements if he convinces the manager that he is a desirable private acquaintance. A good deal of the technique acquired by American actors no doubt makes one almost long for the fatuous complacency of the British "walker-on"; but still it is at least an accomplishment which raises its possessor above the level of an unskilled laborer; and the value of a well-directed systematic cultivation of executive skill will be appreciated by anyone who compares the speech of Miss Maud Jeffries and the physical expertness of Miss Fay Davis with those of English actresses of their own age and standing. Now in so far as Mr Frohman's Americanizations tend to smarten the organization of English stage business, and to demand from every actor at least some scrap of trained athleticism of speech and movement, they are welcome. So far, too, as the influence of a bright, brainy people, full of fun and curiosity, can wake our drama up from the half-asleep, half-drunk delirium of brainless sentimentality in which it is apt to wallow, it will be a good influence. But in so far as it means mechanical horseplay, prurient pleasantries, and deliberate nastinesses of the Katzenjammer order, it is our business to reform the Americans, not theirs to reform us. When it comes to the stupidities, follies, and grossnesses of the stage, we may safely be left to our native resources, which have never yet failed us in such matters.

The only notable addition to the Vaudeville company is Mr Allan Aynesworth, who keeps up the fun with an unsparing devotion to a bad play which must be extremely touching to the author. I do not believe he understands the plot, because no man can do what is impossible; but he quite persuades the audience that he does.

One Summer's Day at the Comedy Theatre is a play written by Mr Esmond to please himself. Some plays are written to please the author; some to please the actor-manager (these are the worst); some to please the public; and some—my own, for instance—to please nobody. Next to my plan, I prefer Mr Esmond's; but it undoubtedly leads to self-indulgence. When Mr Esmond, in the third act of a comedy, slaughters an innocent little boy to squeeze two pennorth of sentiment out of his mangled body, humanity protests. If Mr Esmond were hard to move, one might excuse him for resorting to extreme measures. But he is, on the contrary, a highly susceptible man. He gets a perfect ocean of sentiment out of Dick and Dick's pipe. If you ask who Dick was, I reply that that is not the point. It is in the name Dick—in its tender familiarity, its unaffected good-nature, its modest sincerity, its combination of womanly affectionateness with manly strength, that the charm resides. If you say that the name Dick does not convey this to you, I can only say that it does to Mr Esmond when associated with a pipe; and that if

your imagination is too sluggish or prosaic to see it, then that is
your misfortune and not Mr Esmond's fault. He cherishes Dick
more consistently than Thackeray cherished Colonel Newcome;
for he tells you nothing unpleasant, and indeed nothing credible,
about him; whereas Thackeray, being daimonic as well as sentimental, must paint his Colonel remorselessly as a fool, humbug,
and swindler with one hand, whilst vainly claiming the world's
affection for him with the other. Dick's drawbacks are not hinted
at. Provided you take him on trust, and Maysie on trust, and
indeed everybody else on trust, One Summer's Day is a quite
touching play. Mr Hawtrey has finally to dissolve in tears, like
the player in Hamlet; and he does it like a true comedian: that is,
in earnest, and consequently almost distressingly. That is the
penalty of comedianship: it involves humanity, which forbids
its possessor to enjoy grief. Your true pathetic actor is a rare
mixture of monstrous callousness and monstrous vanity. To him
suffering means nothing but a bait to catch sympathy. He enjoys
his malingering; and so does the audience. Mr Hawtrey does not
enjoy it; and the result is an impression of genuine grief, which
makes it seem quite brutal to stare at him. Fortunately, this is
only for a moment, at the end of the play, just after Mr Esmond's
massacre of the innocent. For the rest, he is as entertaining as
ever, and happily much smoother, pleasanter, sunnier, and
younger than Mr Esmond evidently intended Dick to be. I really
could not have stood Dick if he had gone through with the
Dobbin-Newcome formula, and robbed good-nature of grace
and self-respect. The comic part of the play has a certain youthfully mischievous quality, which produces good entertainment
with a lovesick schoolboy, excellently played by Mr Kenneth
Douglas, and an impossible but amusing urchin impersonated
by Master Bottomley. But Mrs Bendyshe, whose part is so poor
that it would conquer Mrs Charles Calvert if she were conquer-
able, which it seems she is not, and Mr Bendyshe, one of her
husbands (she seemed to have two), exhibit Mr Esmond as
descending from the dignity of dramatic authorship to lark
boyishly at the expense of his elderly fellow-creatures. Miss Eva

Moore's Maysie secures the success of the piece, though the part is not difficult enough to tax her powers seriously.

The Drury Lane play proves Mr Arthur Collins to be every whit as competent a manager of Harrisian drama as the illustrious founder of that form of art was himself. In fact, Mr Collins, as a younger man, with a smarter and more modern standard, does the thing rather better. Sir Augustus, lavish as to the trappings and suits of his fashionable scenes, was reckless as to the presentability of their wearers. Compare Mr Collins's cycling parade in Battersea Park, for instance, with Sir Augustus's church parade in Hyde Park! There is no reason to suppose that Battersea has cost a farthing more; yet it is ten times more plausible. It is not given to all "extra ladies" to look ladylike in proportion to the costliness of their attire: on the contrary, many of them have the gift of looking respectable in the uniform of a parlormaid, or even in a shawl, gown, apron, and ostrich-feathered hat, but outrageous and disreputable in a fashionable frock confected by an expensive modiste. Now whether Sir Augustus knew the difference, and cynically selected the disreputable people as likely to be more attractive to the sailorlike simplicity of the average playgoer, or whether he had a bad eye for such distinctions, just as some people have a bad ear for music, there can be no doubt that not even the Vicar of Wakefield could have been imposed on by his fashionable crowds. Mr Collins is much more successful in this respect. As I saw The White Heather from a rather remote corner of the stalls, distance may have lent my view some enchantment; but as far as I could see, Mr Collins does not, if he can help it, pay an extravagant sum for a dress, and then put it on the back of a young lady who obviously could not have become possessed of it by ladylike means. His casting of principal parts is also much better: he goes straight to the mark with Mrs John Wood where Sir Augustus would have missed it with Miss Fanny Brough (an habitually underparted tragi-comic actress); and he refines the whole play by putting Miss Kate Rorke and Miss Beatrice Lamb into parts which would formerly have been given respectively to a purely melodramatic heroine and villainess. Indeed he has in one instance overshot the mark in improving the company; for though he has replaced the usual funny man with a much higher class of comedian in Mr De Lange, the authors have abjectly failed to provide the actor with anything better than the poorest sort of clowning part; and as Mr De Lange is not a clown, he can only help the play, at a sacrifice of "comic relief," by virtually suppressing the buffoonery with which the authors wanted to spoil it. In short, everything is improved at Drury Lane except the drama, which, though very ingeniously adapted to its purpose, and not without flashes of wit (mostly at its own expense), remains as mechanical and as void of real dramatic illusion as the equally ingenious contrivances of the lock up the river, the descent of the divers and their combat under the sea, the Stock Exchange, and the reproduction of the costume ball at Devonshire House.

Naturally, though there is plenty of competent acting that amply fulfils the requirements of the occasion, the principals have nothing to do that can add to their established reputations. Mr Robert Loraine as Dick Beach was new to me; but he played so well that I concluded that it was I, and not Mr Loraine, who was the novice in the matter.

ROMANCE IN ITS LAST DITCH

THE VAGABOND KING. A play in four acts. By Louis N. Parker. Théâtre Métropole, Camberwell, 18 October 1897.

[23 October 1897]

THE production of Mr Louis Parker's play at a suburban theatre last Monday was an expected development in an unexpected place. A few years ago some of the central theatres began trying very hard which could stoop lowest to meet the rising tide of popular interest in fiction of all sorts. Most of the attempts failed because they went back to the obsolete methods of the days when audiences were illiterate as well as ignorant. Now audiences are still ignorant; but they are no longer illiterate: on the contrary, they are becoming so bookish that they actually repudiate and ridicule claptrap and sentiment of purely theatrical extraction, and must have both adapted to a taste educated by inveterate novel-reading. Formerly a man who had never read a novel, but knew the stage and the playgoing public, was a more trustworthy provider of artificial substitutes for genuine drama than the cleverest novelist. Nowadays the old stager is the most fatal of advisers; and The Prisoner of Zenda, Trilby, and Under the Red Robe, all three specifically literary plays, have swept from the boards the rival attempts that were being made to Whitechapelize the West End theatres on the old stagy lines. And it is significant that when a literary play failed, however deservedly, it was respected in the midst of its misfortunes, whereas the stagy plays failed with the extremity of derision, disgrace, and loss of caste for their promoters.

One of the advantages of the literary play was that it was very easy to act. It completed the process, by that time far advanced, of adapting the drama to the incompetent acting produced by the long run and tour system. But it is not possible under a system of competitive commerce in theatrical entertainments to maintain extravagant prices for cheap commodities and facile services. Time was when I demanded again and again what the theatres were offering that could induce any sensible person to leave his comfortable suburban fireside, his illustrated magazines and books, his piano and his chessboard, to worry his way by relays of omnibus, train, and cab to seek admission to a stuffy theatre at a cost of a guinea for comfortable seats for himself and his wife. I prophesied the suburban theatre, following my usual plan of prophesying nothing that is not already arrived and at work (and therefore sure to be discovered by the English Press generally in from ten to fifty years). Well, the suburban theatre has come with a rush. The theatre within ten minutes' walk, the four-shilling stall, the twopenny program, the hours admitting of bed before midnight, have only to be combined with an entertainment equal in quality to that of the West End houses to beat them out of the field. So far from there being any difficulty about such a combination, the suburban theatres may be safely defied to produce anything worse than many of the central theatres have been unblushingly offering for some years past. The acting is as likely as not to be better; for snobbery behind the scenes at the West End houses has led to a steady squeezing-out of the trained and skilled actor who makes no pretension to fashion in private life, as well as the artistic enthusiast who is necessarily unconventional and revolutionary in personal ideas and conduct, and the replacement of both by society-struck actors and stage-struck wealthy amateurs. In tailor-made plays the man who is an actor off the stage and a man of fashion on it gets displaced by the competitor who is a man of fashion off the stage and a duffer on it. I say nothing of the preference of actor-managers for nice fellows and moderately good actors, since the superseded actors are not likely to let that be forgotten, though they are naturally slow to confess that what they lack is an air of belonging to "the Marlborough House set" or some such nonsense. If an exact estimate could be made of the average skill of the well-known actors who have been for the last few years mostly out of engagement and those who have been mostly in it, the balance would perhaps not be against the unemployed. Such unemployment is the opportunity of the suburban manager, who does not concern himself with the set to which the members of his company belong, and has no interest in preventing them from attaining the maximum of popularity. Consequently, when once the good actors who do not affect smart society are starved out of waiting vainly for West End engagements, it is possible that the suburban actor may beat the fashionable actor out of the field too.

Finally, let us hope, the cards will be completely reshuffled, and the central theatres will have either to shut up shop or else give an entertainment beyond the reach of suburban art and suburban prices. Mr Forbes Robertson is doing that at the Lyceum at present: consequently the suburban theatres, far from damaging him, are, as Sir Henry Irving foresaw, simply acting as nurseries of playgoers for him. But take the case of the "triple bill" which has just vanished from the Avenue, perhaps as a judgment for playing Mozart's Figaro overture between the acts with big drum and cymbals *ad lib.* à la Offenbach. The triple bill was not bad of its kind: seen from a half-crown seat at the Lyric Hall, Ealing, it would have been excellent value. But why should any man in his senses have gone miles and paid half a guinea to see it? Take, again, such a play as My Friend the Prince. Is it conceivable that the actors now performing it at the Fulham Grand Theatre, even if they do not play it quite as well as the original company at the Garrick (and I have no reason to suppose they dont), do not at least act it as well as it need be acted, and get just as loud laughs when the gentleman sits down on his spur, and all the men come in at the end in the same disguise? Or take the rough-and-tumble farcical comedy at the Vaudeville! Am I to be told that Mr Mulholland could not do everything for that piece at Camberwell that Mr Frohman is doing for it in the Strand, without raising his prices one farthing, or even making any particularly expensive engagement?

It looks, then, as if the West End theatre were to be driven back on serious dramatic art after all. Of course there will always be the sort of West End production, supported by deadheads, which is nothing but a preliminary advertisement for the tour of "a London success." Personal successes will be made in very bad plays by popular favorites like Miss Louie Freear and Mr Penley. But legitimate business at high-priced West End houses must at last be forced in the direction of better plays, probably with the extreme runs shorter than at present, but most likely with the average run longer. And the better plays will make short work of the incompetent fashionable actor. When Mr Forbes Robertson was wasting his energies on fashionable plays at the Garrick with Miss Kate Rorke, there was not a pin to choose between him and any other fashionable leading man. In Hamlet and Joseph Surface there are a good many thousand pounds to choose. When the plays that are no plays are all driven to the suburbs, the actors who are no actors will have to go after them; and then perhaps the actors who are actors will come back.

This is why I began by saying that what has just happened at the Camberwell Theatre was the expected coming in an unexpected place. The higher class of play has appeared, not at the West End, but in the suburbs. The reappearance of a once famous actress for whom the fashionable stage found no use, and of a few younger people who had exposed themselves to West End managerial suspicion by the exhibition of a specific professional talent and skill, has occurred on the same occasion. That, however, is a mere accident. A year ago no West End manager would have considered a play of the class of The Vagabond King commercially practicable. A year or so hence managers in search of "high-class drama" will probably be imploring Mr Parker to let them have something as high as possible above the heads of the public. Thus does the whirligig of time bring its revenges.

Whoever has glanced at the notices of Mr Parker's play will have gathered here and there that there is something wrong with it. Now what I wish to convey is that there is something right with it, and that this something right is exactly the something wrong of which my romantic colleagues complain. It is true that they too find something right with it—something "beautiful and true," as they call it; but to me this bit of romantic beauty and truth is a piece of immoral nonsense that spoils the whole work. If Mr Parker wishes to get on safe ground as a dramatist, he must take firm hold of the fact that the present transition from romantic to sincerely human drama is a revolutionary one, and that those who make half-revolutions dig their own graves. Nothing is easier than for a modern writer only half weaned from Romance to mix the two, especially in his youth, when he is pretty sure to have romantic illusions about women long after he has arrived at a fairly human view of his own sex. This is precisely what has happened to Mr Parker. Into the middle of an exiled court which has set up its mock throne in furnished lodgings in London, and which he has depicted in an entirely disillusioned human manner, he drops an ultra-romantic heroine. If this were done purposely, with the object of reducing the romantic to absurdity, and preaching the worth of the real, there are plenty of works, from Don Quixote to Arms and the Man, to justify it as the classic formula of the human school in its controversial stage. Or if it were done with the shallower purpose of merely enjoying the fantastic incongruity of the mixture, then we should have at once the familiar formula of comic opera. But when it is done unconsciously—when the artist designs his heroine according to an artificial convention of moral and physical prettiness, and confessedly draws all the rest in the light of a perception of "the true meaning of life," the result is the incongruity of comic opera without its fun and fantasy, and the Quixotic belittlement of romance without its affirmation of the worth of reality. Mr Parker's Vagabond King married to Stella Desmond is like Balzac's Mercadet married to Black Eyed Susan. Whoever has come to a clear understanding with himself as between romance and reality will be able to follow with perfect intelligence the waverings of Mr Louis Parker's play between failure and success. When Miss Lena Ashwell gets the play completely on the romantic plane, and makes the audience for the moment unconscious of all other planes by acting so beautifully saturated with feeling as to appear almost religious (it has been plain to the wise, any time these two years, that Miss Ashwell was on the way to a high place in her art), the audience is satisfied and delighted to the seventh heaven. But she makes it impossible for the King and the parasites of the exiled Court to get their scenes definitely on the realistic plane. At her romantic pitch they are out of tune; for the audience, accustomed to that pitch, conceives that they are flat rather than she sharp. If the effect were reversed, the play would be irretrievably ruined by their reduction of her to absurdity. For, judged by serious human standards, she is an objectionable and mischievous person. She begins by conniving with the King's mother to entrap him into prostitution. She allows him to ruin and degrade himself, and to beggar her, in the true romantic manner, so that she may be able to make a "sacrifice." In the end she spoils the moral of the play and utterly discredits his discovery of "the true meaning of life," and his resolution to live by honest toil, by enabling him to face their stern realities from the comfortable vantage ground of a pretty cottage at Highgate and a charming wife with money enough

226

left to indulge in the smartest frocks. Nothing could be further from the true meaning of life: nothing could pander more amiably and abjectly to that miserable vital incapacity to which life at its imagined best means only what a confectioner's shop window means to a child. It is quite clear that no such experience as that of the Vagabond King could redeem any man: one might as well try to refine gold by holding it to the spark of a glowworm. The woman declares that she has sacrificed this, that, and the other, and has nothing left but love (the cottage and dresses not being worth mentioning); but as a matter of fact she has neither lost nor gained one jot or tittle, being exactly the same unmeaning romantic convention at the end of the play as at the beginning.

When the world gets a serious fit, and the desire for a true knowledge of the world and a noble life in it at all costs arises in men and lifts them above lusting for the trivial luxuries and ideals and happy endings of romance, romance, repudiated by art and challenged by religion, falls back on its citadel, and announces that it has given up all the pomps and vanities of this wicked world, and recognizes that nothing is eternally valid and all-redeeming but Love. That is to say, the romanticist is blind enough to imagine that the humanist will accept the abandonment of all his minor lies as a bribe for the toleration of the most impudent of all lies. "I am willing to be redeemed, and even religious," says the converted romanticist, "if only the business be managed by a pretty woman who will be left in my arms when the curtain falls." And this is just how the Vagabond King gets out of his difficulties. Has Mr Parker, a disciple of Richard Wagner, forgotten these lines?—

> Nicht Gut, nicht Gold, noch göttliche Pracht;
> nicht Haus, nicht Hof, noch herrischer Prunk;
> nicht trüber Verträge trügender Bund,
> noch heuchelnder Sitte hartes Gesetz:
> selig in Lust und Leid *lässt die Liebe nur sein*.

There is the arch lie formulated by the master's hand! But when he completed the work by finding the music for the poem, he found no music for that: the Nibelungen score is guiltless of it. I presume Wagner had by that time made up his mind that a world in which all the women were piously willing to be redeemed by a Siegfried, and all the men by a Brynhild, would find their way to the bottomless pit by quite as short a cut as the most cynical of the voluptuaries who enjoy themselves without claiming divine honours for their passions. Mr Parker may take my word for it, that Vagabond King of his will be damned yet, in spite of pretty Stella Desmond, unless he can find a means to save himself. He that would save his soul (not get it saved for him, mind) must first lose it; and he must lose it in earnest, and not keep back a pretty woman and a cottage at Highgate after the prudent manner of Ananias.

Though this be an adverse criticism, yet it is no small compliment to Mr Parker that he has come within reach of it. He has fallen, like many another artist before him, through woman worship, "arter all, an amiable weakness," as the elder Weller observed of wife-beating, which is another mode of the same phenomenon. However "beautiful and true" may be his assumption that the best woman is far better than the best man, and however loathsome and cynical may be my assumption that she is not—nay, that as women are treated at present she is almost certain, other things being equal, to be a good deal worse—I venture to think that Mr Parker will find that more convincing plays can be got out of my assumption than out of his. At the same time I am bound to add that the very worst real woman I ever knew was better than Mr Parker's paragon, whose conduct, like that of all romantic heroines, will not stand a moment's serious investigation.

The play has a cast which would rank as a strong one at any West End theatre. Besides Miss Bateman and Miss Lena Ashwell, there is Miss Phyllis Broughton. Mr Murray Carson is the Vagabond King; Mr George Grossmith, junior, the other King, both supported by a Court including Mr Sidney Brough, Mr Gilbert Farquhar, and Mr L. D. Mannering, who will be remembered for some remarkable work in Elizabethan drama.

VEGETARIAN AND ARBOREAL

THE FANATIC. A new and original play, in four acts. By John T.
  Day. Strand Theatre, 21 October 1897.
THE TREE OF KNOWLEDGE. A new and original play, in five acts.
  By R. C. Carton. St James's Theatre, 25 October 1897.

[30 *October* 1897]

AN anti-vegetarian play is an unexpected but not unwelcome
novelty. Hitherto the ideas of dramatists on the food question
have been limited to a keen sense of the effect on the poorer
section of the audience of a liberal display at every possible opportunity of spirit stands, siphons, and bottles; so that the elaborate
interiors may combine the charms of the private and the public
house. I am always asking myself whether it is toast and water or
whether it is real; and, if the latter, how much extra salary an actor
receives for the injury to his liver involved in repeated exhibitions to the gallery of the never-palling spectacle of a gentleman
taking an expensive drink. But now we have a dramatist who
makes the whole interest of his play depend on a passionate faith
in the nutritiousness of a cutlet and a glass of wine. The result is
at least more real and interesting than Mr Carton's five-act stage
romance at the St James's. But for an unsound theory of alimenta-
tion, and an unhappy relapse into more-than-Cartonic romance at
the end, it would be an excellent comedy.

The heroine of The Fanatic marries a vegetarian teetotaller
who proceeds to feed her at a rate which may be faintly estimated
from the fact that her breakfast alone consists of hominy porridge,
tapioca omelette, and cucumber pie. If she were an elephant working out a sentence of hard labor, she might possibly be able to
get exercise enough to keep pace with such Gargantuan meals. As
she is only a rather sedentary lady, they speedily ruin her complexion and render her incapable of assimilating any nourishment
at all. The doctor is called in; and I should unhesitatingly rank Mr
Day with Molière as a delineator of doctors if I could pretend not
to see that he takes his modern Diafoirus with awestruck serious-

229

ness, and without the least comedic intention. Nevertheless we have had no better bit of comedy this season, nor any truer to life, than this foolish fashionable doctor instantly diagnosing a glaring case of over-feeding as one of "starvation," and flying Diafoiresquely into a raging condition of academic indignation with the husband for repudiating his prescription of the glass of wine and the cutlet. It is to be observed, as a curious illustration of our notions of family morals, that it never occurs to the doctor or to anyone else in the play to question the husband's right to dictate what his wife shall eat as absolutely as if she were a convict and he the prison doctor—nay, almost as if he were a farmer and she one of his ewes being fattened for market. And the doctor's right to dictate what the husband shall order is only disputed in order to prove the lunacy of the man who questions it. The unfortunate patient's own views are left completely out of account. "She shall have cutlet and marsala," says the doctor. "She shant," says the husband: "she shall have cucumber pie and cocoa." "Cucumber pie isnt food: she'll die of it," says the doctor. "Cucumber pie *is* food," retorts the husband: "heres a pamphlet which proves it." And so on. The question is one of cucumbers versus corpses, of the husband's authority versus the doctor's authority: never for a moment is it suggested that a short way out of the difficulty would be to allow the lady to order her own dinner. When they go on from the food question to the drink question they reach the summit of conceited absurdity. "I insist on her having wine," screams the doctor: "if she dont, she'll die." "Let her die," says the husband: "I'm a teetotaller, and would rather see her in her grave than allow her to drink alcohol."

Here you have the comedy in which Molière delighted—the comedy of lay ignorance and incapacity confronting academic error and prejudice: the layman being right in theory and wrong in practice, the academician wrong in theory but right in practice. Unfortunately, though Mr Day observes the conflict very accurately, he does not understand it, and takes sides vehemently with the doctor, even whilst faithfully dramatizing the dispute on the lines of a wrangle between two African witches as to the merits of their rival incantations. The doctor prescribes his diet of cutlet and wine (which, by the way, would almost at once cure the patient) quite superstitiously, as a charm. The vegetarian prescribes his hominy porridge diet (which he is quite right in supposing to be just as nutritious as a dead sheep) in the same way. Both have irresistible facts on their side. The doctor sees that the woman is being killed by her monstrous breakfasts: the husband knows, as everybody knows, that as good work can be done, and as long lives lived, on the diet of the saints and the cranks as on that of the men about town. Probably he reads my articles, and finds them as vigorous as those of my carnivorous colleagues. The sensible solution is obvious enough. It is the doctor's business to go to the patient and say, "My good lady: do you wish to remain a vegetarian or not? If you do, I must cut you down from your present allowance of forage enough at every meal to feed six dragoons and their horses for a day, to something that you can manage and relish. If not, I can settle the difficulty at once by simply sending you back to cutlets, in which your experience will prevent you from overeating yourself." But alas! doctors seldom do know their business. This particular doctor and his client do not get beyond the Pickwickian position: " 'Crumpets is wholesome, sir,' says the patient. 'Crumpets is *not* wholesome, sir,' says the doctor, wery fierce." When the dramatist takes sides in such a wrangle he is lost. His drama, beginning in excellent realistic comedy, and making fair way with the audience on that plane, ends in bathos and folly. The doctor, to rescue the lady from her cucumber pie, proposes an elopement. She consents. The husband comes back just in time to save her from ruin and disgrace. But he brings back with him hominy porridge, surfeit, and death. Feeling the delicacy of the situation, he considerately drops dead there and then. The doctor, wrong to the last, diagnoses heart disease; but the audience quite understands that he perishes simply because there must be a happy ending to all plays, even anti-vegetarian ones.

There is some unintentional comedy in the casting of the piece as well as in the drama itself. The fanatic has a female accomplice who is also a Spartan abstainer, and who should therefore, if the doctor's views are to be made good, be on the verge of starvation. This lady is impersonated by Miss Kate Phillips. Now Miss Phillips stands out in this inept generation as an exceptionally accomplished and expert actress; but the one thing she cannot do is to look as if she were dying of starvation. Her plump contours do not curve that way, and her inspiring vital energy irresistibly suggests that her diet, whatever it is, is probably the right diet for persons in quest of stamina. She gives the dramatist's didactic position away with every line of her figure and every point in her speeches, presenting Matilda Maudsley as a good platform speaker and capable agitator; getting what comedy there is to be got out of the part; and altogether declining to give the audience the mean satisfaction of seeing a clever woman made uncomely and ridiculous. The doctor, on the other hand, is presented by Mr J. G. Grahame as a well-meaning, well-dressed creature with a sympathetic "bedside manner" and a cheerfully common brain, in whose wake one can see rows of graves smelling of all the drugs in the pharmacopœia. Miss Fordyce cannot make the wife otherwise than silly, her part being written that way. One would unhesitatingly back her fanatical husband's opinion against hers, in spite of the elaborately pasty complexion with which Mr Gurney endows him. On the whole, Mr Day, without quite intending it, has given better parts to the fanatics than to the orthodox cutlet-eaters; and as Mr Gurney and Miss Phillips make the most of them, the total effect produced is against both the bowl and the butcher.

The only other persons of any importance in the piece are the fanatic's backsliding son, pleasantly played by Mr Charles Troode, and a sympathetic secretary of the Taffy order, as whom Mr Nye Chart, notwithstanding a weakness for imitating some of the comedy methods of Mr John Drew, makes something of a not too interesting part.

I approach the subject of the St James's play with much reluctance. Mr Carton's plays are so extremely goodnatured that they disarm criticism. But there is a point at which goodnature rouses malice; and that point is reached and overstepped in The Tree of Knowledge. It is to me an unbearable play. Its staleness is not to be described: the situations are expected and inevitable to such a degree of obviousness that even when Mr Alexander remonstrates with Miss Julia Neilson in the manner of Bill Sikes with Nancy, and all but strangles her in full view of the audience, the effect is that of a platitude. Not for a moment is it possible to see anybody in the figures on the stage but Mr Alexander, Mr Vernon, Mr Terry, Mr Esmond, Miss Fay Davis, Miss Neilson, and Miss Addison. There are five mortal acts; and there is not a moment of illusion in them. All that can be said in its favor is that Mr H. B. Irving, fresh from the unnatural occupation of tearing the romantic trappings off his father's favorite heroes in the magazines, did contrive, in a cynical part of the old Byron-Montague type, to throw a glamor of the genuine ante-Shakespearean-Irving kind over a few of his scenes, and scored the only personal success of the evening; and that Mr George Shelton, as the bad character of the village, also left us with some sense of having made a new acquaintance. But the rest was nothing but a new jug of hot water on very old tea leaves. Acting under such circumstances is not possible. Mr Esmond went back to the old business, brought in by Mr Hare in the sixties, of the young man made up as an old one. The make-up seemed to me as unreal as the part; and I venture to suggest to Mr Esmond that if he keeps on doing this sort of thing he will find, some day, that the pretence has become a reality, and will regret that he wasted his prime on sham caducity when there were young parts going. Mr Alexander, having a great deal to do and no discoverable scrap of character in his part, desperately burlesqued his own mannerisms: a policy in which he was outdone by Miss Julia Neilson, who, as a second Mrs Tanqueray—a sort of person whom Mr Carton understands less, if possible, than Mr Pinero, and whom Miss Neilson does not understand at all—gave us an assortment of all the best known passages in modern acting, not excepting her own, and including, for the first time, Miss Achurch's frozen stare from the last act of A Doll's House. I do not blame either Mr Alexander or Miss

Neilson: they had to fill in their parts somehow; but the spectacle was an extremely trying one for all parties. Mr Fred Terry was more fortunate. After struggling manfully for many years with the family propensity to act, he has of late succumbed to it, and now bears up against Mr Carton almost as cheerfully as Miss Ellen Terry bears up against Shakespear. Miss Fay Davis, Mr Vernon, and Miss Carlotta Addison, having nothing to do but illustrate the author's amiability, did it with all possible amenity and expertness: indeed, but for the soothing effect of Miss Davis's charm, I should have gone out at the end of the fourth act and publicly slain myself as a protest against so insufferable an entertainment.

I should perhaps state my objections to The Tree of Knowledge more clearly and precisely; but how can I, with my mind unhinged by sitting out those five acts? My feeling towards Mr Carton's plays is generally almost reprehensibly indulgent; for his humor is excellent; his imagination is genial and of the true storytelling brand; he is apt and clear as a man of letters; and his sympathies are kindly and free from all affectation and snobbery. But he seems to have no dramatic conscience, no respect for the realities of life, and, except in his humor, no originality whatever. The quantity of very bad early Dickens, of the Cheeryble-Linkinwater sort, which he pours out, is beyond endurance. One should begin where Dickens left off, not where he started. All this throwing back to Pickwick, and to the theatre of Byron and Robertson, for some sort of fanciful decoration for a hackneyed plot, is bad enough when there is at least some quaint pretence of character, like that of the old bookseller in Liberty Hall. But when there is no such pretence; when the thing is spun out to five acts; and when the fifth act consists largely of the novice's blunder of making one of the characters describe what passed in the fourth, then even the most patient critic cannot repress a groan.

By the way, if Mr Alexander is going to make a speciality of plays lasting from three to four hours, may I suggest that he should get his upholstery and curtains dyed green, or some more restful color than the present crimson? I believe my irresistible impulse to rush at The Tree of Knowledge and gore and trample it is chiefly due to the effect of all that red drapery on me.

CHIN CHON CHINO

THE CAT AND THE CHERUB. By Chester Bailey Fernald. Lyric Theatre, 30 October 1897.

THE FIRST BORN. By Francis Powers. Globe Theatre, 1 November 1897.

A RETROSPECT OF THE STAGE FESTIVALS OF 1876. By Richard Wagner. Translated by W. Ashton Ellis. In Richard Wagner's Prose Works, Vol. VI, Part 2. London: Kegan Paul. 1897.

[6 *November* 1897]

THE latest attempt to escape from hackneydom and cockneydom is the Chinatown play, imported, of course, from America. There is no reason, however, why it should not be manufactured in England. I beg respectfully to inform managers and syndicates that I am prepared to supply "Chinese plays," music and all, on reasonable terms, at the shortest notice. A form of art which makes a merit of crudity need never lack practitioners in this country. The Chinese music, which we are spared at the Lyric, is unmitigated humbug. At the Globe it is simply very bad American music, with marrowbones and cleaver, teatray and cat-call, *ad lib*. And the play is nothing but Wilkie Collins fiction disguised in pigtail and petticoats.

The result is worth analysing. The dramatic art of our day has come to such a pass of open artificiality and stale romantic convention that the sudden repudiation of all art produces for the moment almost as refreshing a sensation as its revival would. In The First Born the death of the little boy at the end of the first scene, and the murder of the man whose corpse is propped up against the doorpost by his murderer and made to counterfeit life whilst the policeman passes, might be improvised in a schoolroom: yet they induce a thrill which all the resources of the St James's Theatre, strained during five long acts to their utmost, cannot attain to for the briefest instant. Truly the secret of wisdom is to become as a little child again. But our art-loving authors will not learn the lesson. They cannot understand that when a great genius lays hands on a form of art and fascinates all who understand its language with it, he makes it say all that it can say, and leaves it exhausted. When Bach has got the last word out of the fugue, Mozart out of the opera, Beethoven out of the symphony, Wagner out of the symphonic drama, their enraptured admirers exclaim: "Our masters have shewn us the way: let us compose some more fugues, operas, symphonies, and Bayreuth dramas." Through just the same error the men who have turned dramatists on the frivolous ground of their love for the theatre have plagued a weary world with Shakespearean dramas in five acts and in blank verse, with artificial comedies after Congreve and Sheridan, and with the romantic goody-goody fiction which was squeezed dry by a hundred strong hands in the first half of this century. It is only when we are dissatisfied with existing masterpieces that we create new ones: if we merely worship them, we only try to repeat the exploit of their creator by picking out the titbits and stringing them together, in some feeble fashion of our own, into a "new and original" botching of what our master left a good and finished job. We are encouraged in our folly by the need of the multitude for intermediaries between its childishness and the maturity of the mighty men of art, and also by the fact that art fecundated by itself gains a certain lapdog refinement, very acceptable to lovers of lapdogs. The Incas of Peru cultivated their royal race in this way, each Inca marrying his sister. The result was that an average Inca was worth about as much as an average fashionable drama bred carefully from the last pair of fashionable dramas, themselves bred in the same way, with perhaps a cross of novel. But vital art work comes always from a cross between art and life: art being of one sex only, and quite sterile by itself. Such a cross is always possible; for though the artist may not have the capacity to bring his art into contact with the higher life of his time, fermenting in its religion, its philosophy, its science, and its statesmanship (perhaps, indeed, there may not be any statesmanship going), he can at least bring it into contact with the obvious life and common passions of the streets. This is what has happened in the case of the Chinatown play. The dramatist, compelled by the nature of his enterprise to turn his back on the fashionable models for "brilliantly" cast plays, and to go in search of documents and facts in order to put a slice of Californian life on the stage with crude realism, instantly wakes the theatre up with a piece which has some reality in it, though its mother is the cheapest and most conventional of the daughters of art, and its father the lowest and darkest stratum of Americanized yellow civilization. The phenomenon is a very old one. When art becomes effete, it is realism that comes to the rescue. In the same way, when ladies and gentlemen become effete, prostitutes become prime ministers; mobs make revolutions; and matters are readjusted by men who do not know their own grandfathers.

This moral of the advent of the Chinatown play is brought out strikingly by the contrast between the rival versions at the Lyric and at the Globe. The Lyric version, entitled The Cat and the Cherub, and claiming to be the original (a claim which is apparently not contradicted), is much the more academic of the two. It is a formal play, with comparatively pretentious acting parts, and the local color blended into the dramatic business in the most approved literary manner: the whole ending with a complicated death struggle, in which the victim is strangled with his own pigtail, and performs an elaborate stage fall. In the Globe version there is comparatively no art at all: we see the affair as we see a street row, with all the incidents of the Chinatown slum going on independently—vulgar, busy, incongruous, irrelevant, indifferent, just as we see them in a London slum whilst the policeman is adjusting some tragedy at the corner. Placed between an academic play and a vulgar play, the high-class London critic cannot hesitate. He waves the Globe aside with scorn and takes the Lyric to his bosom. It seems to me that the popular verdict must go the other way. It is of course eminently possible that people may not care to pay West End theatre prices for a very short entertainment which, at best, would make an excellent side show at Earl's Court. But if they choose either way, they will probably like the crude, coarse, curious, vivid and once or twice even thrilling hotch-potch at the Globe, better than the more sedate and academic drama at the Lyric. A good deal will depend on which they see first. Nine-tenths of the charm of Chinatown lies in its novelty; and a comparison of the opinions of those who saw the two plays in the order of their production, and those who, like myself, saw the Globe play first, will prove, I think, that the first experience very heavily discounts the second.

I am not sure that there is not more initiative for art in commercial speculations like these sham Chinese plays than in academic-revolutionary bodies like the New Century Theatre, the Independent Theatre, or the Bayreuth Festival Playhouse. These enterprises, indifferent to public demand, can do no more than create a taste for the already achieved works of the artists who seem to them at the moment of their foundation to be the most advanced of their time. It is no doubt heroic of the Independent Theatre to send out a mission to accustom the demoralized and recalcitrant provincial playgoer to Ibsen's plays and mine. It is at least prudent, if not glorious, for the New Century Theatre to promote the spread of the New Drama by sitting tightly on its copyrights and neither performing its Echegaray and Ibsen plays itself nor allowing anyone else to do so. Bayreuth no doubt makes the most of its opportunities by steadily exploiting the reputation of its dead founder, and keeping Parsifal as a luxury for tourists. But what did the great founder of Bayreuth say to it himself? We can now learn that in his own words; for Mr Ashton Ellis's translation of Wagner's writings has now passed safely through the pregnant but labored essays of the master's middle age, and has arrived at the clear, humorous, wise journalism of his Bayreuth time, when he cast back to his early ways as a musical critic in Paris, and anticipated the most entertaining features of modern Saturday Reviewing. His style does not lose in the hands of Mr Ashton Ellis: nobody but Carlyle has ever before made English German so fascinating. The irony of Ein Rückblick auf die Bühnenfestspiele des Jahres 1876 is brought out with a vengeance. Wagner's description of his triumphant achievement of the building of the great Festspielhaus, and the first Bayreuth festival in 1876, is one of the most amusing and thrilling documents in the history of art. There he tells of his gallery of kings, every one of whom complimented him on his indomitable pluck, and confessed that they had never believed it possible for him to pull it through, exactly as if he were Sir Augustus Harris: not one of them having the faintest sense of what he was really driving at. Then he goes on, with an intense relish for the joke against himself, to tell how the thing was really done—how the little congregations of worshippers who had been formed throughout Germany to provide the festival with an audience of true worshippers, and exclude all the fashionable heathen, were really speculators who joined to get the seats and sell them again to the aforesaid heathen, the result being as worldly and unprepared an audience as one could desire at the private view of the Royal Academy. The account of the collection of the funds by an energetic lady, who was wonderfully successful with people who did not know who Wagner was, and actually levied her largest tributes on the Sultan and the Khedive of Egypt, is the climax of the irony, though perhaps the climax of the fun is the story of the ordering of the dragon from a famous English firm, which, after our commercial manner, delivered it in instalments at the last moment, and finally sent the neck irrecoverably to the wrong address. It would carry me too far to draw the moral, but it certainly does not point to the founding of societies and the building of theatres as being any better a device in art than the founding of orders and the building of cathedrals has proved in religion. Not that these things are not worth doing, since they lead to so many incidental improvements, especially in architecture. But it is certain that they never do what the Master Builder meant them to do.

Up to a late hour on Monday night I persuaded myself that I would hasten from the Globe to Her Majesty's, and do my stern duty by Katharine and Petruchio. But when it came to the point I sacrificed duty to personal considerations. The Taming of the Shrew is a remarkable example of Shakespear's repeated attempts to make the public accept realistic comedy. Petruchio is worth fifty Orlandos as a human study. The preliminary scenes in which he shews his character by pricking up his ears at the news that there is a fortune to be got by any man who will take an ugly and ill-tempered woman off her father's hands, and hurrying off to strike the bargain before somebody else picks it up, are not romantic; but they give an honest and masterly picture of a real man, whose like we have all met. The actual taming of the woman by the methods used in taming wild beasts belongs to his determination to make himself rich and comfortable, and his perfect freedom from all delicacy in using his strength and opportunities for that purpose. The process is quite bearable, because the selfishness of the man is healthily goodhumored and untainted by wanton cruelty, and it is good for the shrew to encounter a force like that and be brought to her senses. Unfortunately, Shakespear's own immaturity, as well as the immaturity of the art he was experimenting in, made it impossible for him to keep the play on the realistic plane to the end; and the last scene is altogether disgusting to modern sensibility. No man with any decency of feeling can sit it out in the company of a woman without being extremely ashamed of the lord-of-creation moral implied in the wager and the speech put into the woman's own mouth. Therefore the play, though still worthy of a complete and efficient representation, would need, even at that, some apology. But the Garrick version of it, as a farcical afterpiece!—thank you: no.

Mr Louis Parker's Vagabond King has now come to the Court Theatre from Camberwell, where it has been succeeded by a comic opera, which, like it, is an original product of Mr Mulholland's suburban enterprise, and not a West End piece at second hand. The West End will no doubt presently borrow the comic opera, too, from Camberwell.

SHAKESPEAR AND MR BARRIE

THE TEMPEST. Performance by the Elizabethan Stage Society at the Mansion House, 5 November 1897.

THE LITTLE MINISTER. A play in four acts. By J. M. Barrie, founded on his novel of that name. Haymarket Theatre, 6 November 1897. [13 *November* 1897]

IT was a curious experience to see The Tempest one night and The Little Minister the next. I should like to have taken Shakespear to the Haymarket play. How well he would have recognized it! For he also once had to take a popular novel; make a shallow, unnatural, indulgent, pleasant, popular drama of it; and hand it to the theatre with no hint of his feelings except the significant title As You Like It. And we have not even the wit to feel the snub, but go on complacently talking of the manufacture of Rosalinds and Orlandos (a sort of thing that ought really to be done in a jam factory) as "delineation of character" and the like. One feels Shakespear's position most strongly in the plays written after he had outgrown his interest in the art of acting and given up the idea of educating the public. In Hamlet he is quite enthusiastic about naturalness in the business of the stage, and makes Hamlet hold forth about it quite Wagnerianly: in Cymbeline and The Tempest he troubles himself so little about it that he actually writes down the exasperating clownish interruptions he once denounced; brings on the god in the car; and, having indulged the public in matters which he no longer set any store by, took it out of them in poetry.

The poetry of The Tempest is so magical that it would make the scenery of a modern theatre ridiculous. The methods of the Elizabethan Stage Society (I do not commit myself to their identity with those of the Elizabethan stage) leave to the poet the work of conjuring up the isle "full of noises, sounds and sweet airs." And I do not see how this plan can be beaten. If Sir Henry Irving were to put the play on at the Lyceum next season (why not, by the way?), what could he do but multiply the expenditure

enormously, and spoil the illusion? He would give us the screaming violin instead of the harmonious viol; "characteristic" music
scored for wood-wind and percussion by Mr German instead of
Mr Dolmetsch's pipe and tabor; an expensive and absurd stage
ship; and some windless, airless, changeless, soundless, electric-
lit, wooden-floored mockeries of the haunts of Ariel. They would
cost more; but would they be an improvement on the Mansion
House arrangement? Mr Poel says frankly, "See that singers'
gallery up there! Well, lets pretend that it's the ship." We agree;
and the thing is done. But how could we agree to such a pretence
with a stage ship? Before it we should say, "Take that thing away:
if our imagination is to create a ship, it must not be contradicted
by something that apes a ship so vilely as to fill us with denial and
repudiation of its imposture." The singing gallery makes no attempt to impose on us: it disarms criticism by unaffected submis-
sion to the facts of the case, and throws itself honestly on our
fancy, with instant success. In the same way a rag doll is fondly
nursed by a child who can only stare at a waxen simulacrum of
infancy. A superstitious person left to himself will see a ghost in
every ray of moonlight on the wall and every old coat hanging on
a nail; but make up a really careful, elaborate, plausible, picturesque, bloodcurdling ghost for him, and his cunning grin will
proclaim that he sees through it at a glance. The reason is, not
that a man can *always* imagine things more vividly than art can
present them to him, but that it takes an altogether extraordinary
degree of art to compete with the pictures which the imagination
makes when it is stimulated by such potent forces as the maternal
instinct, superstitious awe, or the poetry of Shakespear. The
dialogue between Gonzalo and that "bawling, blasphemous, in-
charitable dog" the boatswain, would turn the House of Lords
into a ship: in less than ten words—"What care these roarers for
the name of king?"—you see the white horses and the billowing
green mountains playing football with crown and purple. But the
Elizabethan method would not do for a play like The White
Heather, excellent as it is of its kind. If Mr Poel, on the strength of
the Drury Lane dialogue, were to leave us to imagine the singers'

gallery to be the bicycling ring in Battersea Park, or Boulter's Lock, we should flatly decline to imagine anything at all. It requires the nicest judgment to know exactly how much help the imagination wants. There is no general rule, not even for any particular author. You can do best without scenery in The Tempest and A Midsummer Night's Dream, because the best scenery you can get will only destroy the illusion created by the poetry; but it does not at all follow that scenery will not improve a representation of Othello. Maeterlinck's plays, requiring a mystical inscenation in the style of Fernand Knopf, would be nearly as much spoiled by Elizabethan treatment as by Drury Lane treatment. Modern melodrama is so dependent on the most realistic scenery that a representation would suffer far less by the omission of the scenery than of the dialogue. This is why the manager who stages every play in the same way is a bad manager, even when he is an adept at his one way. A great deal of the distinction of the Lyceum productions is due to the fact that Sir Henry Irving, when the work in hand is at all within the limits of his sympathies, knows exactly how far to go in the matter of scenery. When he makes mistakes, they are almost always mistakes in stage management, by which he sacrifices the effect of some unappreciated passage of dialogue of which the charm has escaped him.

Though I was sufficiently close to the stage at The Tempest to hear, or imagine I heard, every word of the dialogue, yet it was plain that the actors were not eminent after-dinner speakers, and had consequently never received in that room the customary warning to speak to the second pillar on the right of the door, on pain of not being heard. Though they all spoke creditably, and some of them remarkably well, they took matters rather too easily, with the result that the quieter passages were inaudible to a considerable number of the spectators. I mention the matter because the Elizabethan Stage Society is hardly yet alive to the acoustic difficulties raised by the lofty halls it performs in. They are mostly troublesome places for a speaker; for if he shouts, his vowels make such a roaring din that his consonants are indistinguishable; and if he does not, his voice does not travel far enough.

They are too resonant for noisy speakers and too vast for gentle ones. A clean, athletic articulation, kept up without any sentimental or indolent relaxations, is indispensable as a primary physical accomplishment for the Elizabethan actor who "takes to the halls."

The performance went without a hitch. Mr Dolmetsch looked after the music; and the costumes were worthy of the reputation which the Society has made for itself in this particular. Ariel, armless and winged in his first incarnation, was not exactly a tricksy sprite; for as the wing arrangement acted as a strait waistcoat, he had to be content with the effect he made as a living picture. This disability on his part was characteristic of the whole performance, which had to be taken in a somewhat low key and slow tempo, with a minimum of movement. If any attempt had been made at the impetuosity and liveliness for which the English experts of the sixteenth century were famous throughout Europe, it would have not only failed, but prevented the performers from attaining what they did attain, very creditably, by a more modest ambition.

To our host the Lord Mayor I take off my hat. When I think of the guzzling horrors I have seen in that room, and the insufferable oratory that has passed through my head from ear to ear on its way to the second pillar on the right of the door (which has the advantage of being stone deaf), I hail with sincere gratitude the first tenant of the Mansion House who has bidden me to an entertainment worthy of the first magistrate of a great city, instead of handing me over to an army of waiters to be dealt with as one "whose god is his belly."

The Little Minister is a much happier play than The Tempest. Mr Barrie has no impulse to throw his adaptation of a popular novel at the public head with a sarcastic title, because he has written the novel himself, and thoroughly enjoys it. Mr Barrie is a born storyteller; and he sees no further than his stories—conceives any discrepancy between them and the world as a shortcoming on the world's part, and is only too happy to be able to rearrange matters in a pleasanter way. The popular stage, which was a prison to Shakespear's genius, is a playground to Mr

Barrie's. At all events he does the thing as if he liked it, and does it very well. He has apparently no eye for human character; but he has a keen sense of human qualities, and he produces highly popular assortments of them. He cheerfully assumes, as the public wish him to assume, that one endearing quality implies all endearing qualities, and one repulsive quality all repulsive qualities: the exceptions being comic characters, who are permitted to have "weaknesses," or stern and terrible souls who are at once understood to be saving up some enormous sentimentality for the end of the last act but one. Now if there is one lesson that real life teaches us more insistently than another, it is that we must not infer one quality from another, or even rely on the constancy of ascertained qualities under all circumstances. It is not only that a brave and good-humored man may be vain and fond of money; a lovable woman greedy, sensual, and mendacious; a saint vindictive; and a thief kindly; but these very terms are made untrustworthy by the facts that the man who is brave enough to venture on personal combat with a prizefighter or a tiger may be abjectly afraid of ghosts, mice, women, a dentist's forceps, public opinion, cholera epidemics, and a dozen other things that many timorous mortals face resignedly enough; the man who is stingy to miserliness with coin, and is the despair of waiters and cabmen, gives thousands (by cheque) to public institutions; the man who eats oysters by the hundred and legs of mutton by the dozen for wagers, is in many matters temperate, moderate, and even abstemious; and men and women alike, though they behave with the strictest conventional propriety when tempted by advances from people whom they do not happen to like, are by no means so austere with people whom they do like. In romance, all these "inconsistencies" are corrected by replacing human nature by conventional assortments of qualities. When Shakespear objected to this regulation, and wrote All's Well in defiance of it, his play was not acted. When he succumbed, and gave us the required assortment "as we like it," he was enormously successful. Mr Barrie has no scruples about complying. He is one with the public in the matter, and makes a pretty character as a milliner makes a pretty bonnet, by "matching" the materials. And why not, if everybody is pleased?

To that question I reply by indignantly refusing, as a contemporary of Master-Builder Solness, to be done out of my allowance of "salutary self-torture." People dont go to the theatre to be pleased: there are a hundred cheaper, less troublesome, more effective pleasures than an uncomfortable gallery can offer. We are led there by our appetite for drama, which is no more to be satisfied by sweetmeats than our appetite for dinner is to be satisfied with meringues and raspberry vinegar. One likes something solid; and that, I suppose, is why heroes and heroines with assorted qualities are only endurable when the author has sufficient tact and comic force to keep up an affectionate undercurrent of fun at their expense and his own. That was how Shakespear pulled his amiable fictions through; that is how Mr Carton does it; that is how Mr Barrie does it. Dickens, with his fundamental seriousness and social conscience always at war with his romantic instincts and idealism, and even with his unconquerable sense of humor, made desperate efforts to take his assorted heroines quite seriously by resolutely turning off the fun, with a result—Agnes Wickfield, Esther Summerson, and so forth—so utterly unbearable that they stand as a warning to all authors that it is dangerous to be serious unless you have something real to be serious about, even when you are a great genius. Happily, Mr Barrie is not serious about his little minister and his little minister's Babby. At most he is affectionate, which is quite a different thing. The twain are nine-tenths fun and the other tenth sentiment, which makes a very toothsome combination.

I should explain, however, that I took care not to read the novel before seeing the play; and I have not had time to read it since. But it is now clear to me that Mr Barrie has depended on the novel to make his hero and heroine known to the playgoer. Their parts consist of a string of amusing and sometimes touching trivialities; but it is easy to divine that the young minister's influence over his elders, and perhaps Babby's attraction for him, are more fully accounted for in the book. I should hope also that Rob Dow and the chief elder, who in the play are machine-made after a worn-out pattern, are more original and natural in the novel. Otherwise, I found the work self-sufficing.

As a success for the Haymarket Theatre the play has fulfilled and exceeded all expectation. It has every prospect of running into the next century. It is the first play produced under Mr Cyril Maude's own management that has given him a chance as an actor. It is quite characteristic of the idiotic topsyturviness of our stage that Mr Maude, who has a remarkable charm of quaintly naïve youthfulness, should have been immediately pitched upon—nay, have pitched on himself—as a born impersonator of old men. All he asked from the author was a snuff-box, a set of grease paints, and a part not younger than sixty-five to make him perfectly happy. There was Mr Grundy's Sowing the Wind, for instance: Mr Maude was never more pleased with himself than when, after spending the afternoon in pencilling impossible wrinkles all over his face, he was crustily taking snuff as the old man in that play. The spectacle used to exasperate me to such a degree that nothing restrained me from hurling the nearest opera-glass at those wrinkles but the fear that, as I am unfortunately an incorrigibly bad shot, I might lay Miss Emery low, or maim Mr Brandon Thomas for life. I do declare that of all the infuriating absurdities that human perversity has evolved, this painted-on "character-acting" is the only one that entirely justifies manslaughter. It was not that Mr Cyril Maude did it badly; on the contrary, he did it very cleverly indeed: it was that he ought to have been doing something else. The plague of the stage at present is the intolerable stereotyping of the lover: he is always the same sort of young man, with the same cast of features, the same crease down his new trousers, the same careful manners, the same air of behaving and dressing like a gentleman for the first time in his life and being overcome with the novelty and importance of it. Mr Maude was just the man to break this oppressive fashion; and instead of doing it, he amused himself with snuff, and crustiness, and wrinkles as aforesaid, perhaps for the

247

sake of the novelty which gentility could not offer him. As the little minister he at last plays without disguise, and with complete success. He is naturally shy at shewing himself to the public for the first time; but the shyness becomes him in the part; and I dare say he will run Mr Forbes Robertson hard for the rest of the season as a much-admired man. Miss Winifred Emery, as Babby, has a rare time of it. She plays with the part like a child, and amuses herself and the audience unboundedly. Her sudden assumption of Red-Robe dignity for a few minutes in the fourth act constitutes what I think may be described safely as the worst bit of acting the world has yet seen from a performer of equal reputation, considering that it is supposed to represent the conduct of a girl just out of the schoolroom; but she soon relapses into an abandonment to fun compared to which Miss Rehan's most reckless attacks of that nature are sedate. Mr Kinghorne is, I think, the best of the elders; but Mr Brandon Thomas and Mrs Brooke are in great force. There was a good deal of curiosity among the women in the audience to see Mr Barrie, because of his evident belief that he was shewing a deep insight into feminine character by representing Babby as a woman whose deepest instinct was to find a man for her master. At the end, when her husband announced his intention of caning her if she deserved it, she flung her arms round his neck and exclaimed ecstatically that he was the man for her. The inference that, with such an experience of the sex, Mr Barrie's personality must be little short of godlike, led to a vociferous call for him when the curtain fell. In response, Mr Harrison appeared, and got as far as "Mr Barrie is far too modest a man—" when he was interrupted by a wild shriek of laughter. I do not doubt that many amiable ladies may from time to time be afflicted with the fancy that there is something voluptuous in getting thrashed by a man. In the classes where the majority of married women get that fancy gratified with excessive liberality, it is not so persistent as Mr Barrie might think. I seriously suggest to him that the samples of his notion of "womanliness" given by Babby are nothing but silly travesties of that desire to find an entirely trustworthy leader which is common to men and women.

Sir A. C. Mackenzie's overture was drowned by the conversation, which was energetically led by the composer and Sir George Lewis. But I caught some scraps of refreshingly workmanlike polyphony; and the *mélodrame* at the beginning of the garden scene was charming.

ON PLEASURE BENT

[20 *November* 1897]

UP to a certain point, I have never flinched from martyrdom. By far the heaviest demand ever made upon me by the public weal is that which nearly three years ago devoted my nights to the theatres and my days to writing about them. If I had known how exceedingly trying the experience would be, I am not sure that I should not have seen the public weal further before making this supreme sacrifice to it. But I had been so seldom to the theatre in the previous years that I did not realize its horrors. I firmly believe that the trials upon which I then entered have injured my brain. At all events matters reached a crisis after the critical activities of last week. I felt that I must have a real experience of some kind, under conditions, especially as regards fresh air, as unlike those of the stalls as possible. After some consideration it occurred to me that if I went into the country, selected a dangerous hill, and rode down it on a bicycle at full speed in the darkest part of the night, some novel and convincing piece of realism might result. It did.

Probably no man has ever misunderstood another so completely as the doctor misunderstood me when he apologized for the sensation produced by the point of his needle as he corrected the excessive openness of my countenance after the adventure. To him who has endured points made by actors for nearly three years, the point of a surgeon's darning needle comes as a delicious relief. I did not like to ask him to put in a few more stitches merely to amuse me, as I had already, through pure self-indulgence, cut into his Sunday rest to an extent of which his kindness made me ashamed; but I doubt if I shall ever see a play again without longing for the comparative luxury of that quiet country surgery, with the stillness without broken only by the distant song and throbbing drumbeat of some remote Salvation Army corps, and the needle, with its delicate realism, touching my sensibilities, stitch, stitch, stitch, with absolute sincerity in the hands of an artist who had actually learned his business and knew how to do it.

To complete the comparison it would be necessary to go into the economics of it by measuring the doctor's fee against the price of a stall in a West End theatre. But here I am baffled by the fact that the highest art revolts from an equation between its infinite value and a finite pile of coin. It so happened that my voice, which is an Irish voice, won for me the sympathy of the doctor. This circumstance must appear amazing almost beyond credibility in the light of the fact that he was himself an Irishman; but so it was. He rightly felt that sympathy is beyond price, and declined to make it the subject of a commercial transaction. Thereby he made it impossible for me to mention his name without black ingratitude; for I know no more effectual way of ruining a man in this country than by making public the smallest propensity on his part to adopt a benevolent attitude towards necessitous strangers. Here the West End manager will perhaps whisper reproachfully, "Well; and do *I* ever make you pay for your stall?" To which I cannot but reply, "Is that also due to the sympathy my voice awakens in you when it is raised every Saturday?" I trust I am not ungrateful for my invitations; but to expect me to feel towards the manager who lacerates my nerves, enfeebles my mind, and destroys my character, as I did towards the physician who healed my body, refreshed my soul, and flattered my vocal accomplishments when I was no more to him than an untimely stranger with an unheard-of black eye, is to dethrone justice and repudiate salvation. Besides, he said it was a mercy I was not killed. Would any manager have been of that opinion?

Perhaps the most delightful thing about this village was that its sense of the relative importance of things was so rightly adjusted that it had no theatrical gossip; for this doctor actually did not know who I was. With a cynicism for which his charity afterwards made me blush, I sought to reassure him as to the pecuniary competence of his muddy, torn, ensanguined and facially spoiled visitor by saying "My name is G. B. S.," as who should say "My name is Cecil Rhodes, or Henry Irving, or William of Germany." Without turning a hair, he sweetly humored my egotistic garrulity by replying, in perfect lightness of heart, "Mine's F——: *what are you?*" Breathing at last an atmosphere in which it mattered so little who and what G. B. S. was, that nobody knew either one or the other, I almost sobbed with relief whilst he threaded his needle with a nice white horsehair, tactfully pretending to listen to my evasive murmur that I was a "sort of writer," an explanation meant to convey to him that I earned a blameless living by inscribing names in letters of gold over shop windows and on perforated wire blinds. To have brought the taint of my factitious little vogue into the unperverted consciousness of his benevolent and sensible life would have been the act of a serpent.

On the whole, the success of my experiment left nothing to be desired; and I recommend it confidently for imitation. My nerves completely recovered their tone and my temper its natural sweetness. I have been peaceful, happy, and affectionate ever since, to a degree which amazes my associates. It is true that my appearance leaves something to be desired; but I believe that when my eye becomes again visible, the softness of its expression will more than compensate for the surrounding devastation.

However, a man is something more than an omelette; and no extremity of battery can tame my spirit to the point of submitting to the sophistry by which Mr Beerbohm Tree has attempted to shift the guilt of Katharine and Petruchio from his shoulders and Garrick's to those of Shakespear. I have never hesitated to give our immortal William as much of what he deserves as is possible considering how far his enormities transcend my powers of invective; but even William is entitled to fair play. Mr Tree contends that as Shakespear wrote the scenes which Garrick tore away from their context, they form a genuine Shakespearean play; and he outdares even this audacity by further contending that since the play was performed for the entertainment of Christopher Sly the tinker, the more it is debauched the more appropriate it is. This line of argument is so breath-bereaving that I can but gasp out an inquiry as to what Mr Tree understands by the one really eloquent and heartfelt line uttered by Sly: "Tis a very excellent piece of work: would twere done!"

This stroke, to which the whole Sly interlude is but as the handle to the dagger, appears to me to reduce Mr Tree's identification of the tastes of his audiences at Her Majesty's with those of a drunken tinker to a condition distinctly inferior to that of my left eye at present. The other argument is more seriously meant, and may even impose upon the simplicity of the Cockney playgoer. Let us test its principle by varying its application. Certain anti-Christian propagandists, both here and in America, have extracted from the Bible all those passages which are unsuited for family reading, and have presented a string of them to the public as a representative sample of Holy Writ. Some of our orthodox writers, though intensely indignant at this controversial ruse, have nevertheless not scrupled to do virtually the same thing with the Koran. Will Mr Tree claim for these collections the full authority, dignity, and inspiration of the authors from whom they are culled? If not, how does he distinguish Garrick's procedure from theirs? Garrick took from a play of Shakespear's all the passages which served his baser purpose, and suppressed the rest. Had his object been to discredit Shakespear in the honest belief that Shakespearolatry was a damnable error, we might have respected Katharine and Petruchio even whilst deploring it. But he had no such conviction: in fact, he was a professed Shakespearolater, and no doubt a sincere one, as far as his wretched powers of appreciation went. He debased The Taming of the Shrew solely to make money out of the vulgarity of the taste of his time. Such a transaction can be defended on commercial grounds: to defend it on any other seems to me to be either an artistic misdemeanor or a profession of Philistinism. If Mr Tree were to declare boldly that he thinks Katharine and Petruchio a better play than The Taming of the Shrew, and that Garrick, as an actor-manager, knew his business better than a mere poet, he would be within his rights. He would not even strain our credulity; for a long dynasty of actor-managers, from Cibber to Sir Henry Irving, have been unquestionably sincere in preferring their own acting versions to the unmutilated master-pieces of the genius on whom they have lavished lip-honor. But Mr Tree pretends to no such preference: on the contrary, he openly stigmatizes the Garrick version as tinker's fare, and throws the responsibility on Shakespear because the materials were stolen from him.

I do not wish to pose academically at Mr Tree. My object is a practical one: I want to intimidate him into a thorough mistrust of his own judgment where Shakespear is concerned. He is about to produce one of Shakespear's great plays, Julius Cæsar; and he is just as likely as not to cut it to ribbons. The man who would revive Katharine and Petruchio at this time of day would do anything un-Shakespearean. I do not blame him for this: it is a perfectly natural consequence of the fact that, like most actors and managers, he does not like Shakespear and does not know him, although he conforms without conscious insincerity to the convention as to the Swan's greatness. I am far from setting up my own Shakespearean partialities and intimacies, acquired in my childhood, as in any way superior to Mr Tree's mature distaste or indifference. But I may reasonably assume—though I admit that the assumption is unusual and indeed unprecedented—that Shakespear's plays are produced for the satisfaction of those who like Shakespear, and not as a tedious rite to celebrate the reputation of the author and enhance that of the actor. Therefore I hope Mr Tree, in such cutting of Julius Cæsar as the limits of time may force upon him, will carefully retain all the passages which he dislikes and cut out those which seem to him sufficiently popular to meet the views of Christopher Sly. He will not, in any case, produce an acting version as good as Mr Forbes

Robertson's Hamlet, because Mr Forbes Robertson seems to have liked Hamlet; nor as good as Mr George Alexander's As You Like It, because Mr Alexander apparently considers Shakespear as good a judge of a play as himself; but we shall at least escape a positively anti-Shakespearean Julius Cæsar. If Mr Tree had suffered as much as I have from seeing Shakespear butchered to make a Cockney's holiday, he would sympathize with my nervousness on the subject.

As I write—or rather as I dictate—comes the remarkable news that the London managers have presented the Vice-Chamberlain with 500 ounces of silver. One cannot but be refreshed by the frank publicity of the proceeding. When the builders in my parish proffer ounces of silver to the sanitary inspector, they do so by stealth, and blush to find it fame. But the Vice-Chamberlain, it appears, may take presents from those over whom he is set as an inspector and judge without a breath of scandal. It seems to me, however, that the transaction involves a grave injustice to Mr Redford. Why is he to have nothing? A well-known Irish landlord once replied to a threatening letter by saying, "If you expect to intimidate me by shooting my agent, you will be disappointed." One can imagine Mr Redford saying to the managers in a similar spirit, "If you expect to bribe me by presenting 500 ounces of silver to my vice-principal, you will be disappointed." I do not suppose that Sir Spencer Ponsonby-Fane has dreamt of giving any serious thought to this aspect of what I shall permit myself to describe as a ludicrously improper proceeding; for the Censorial functions of his department will not bear serious thought. His action is certainly according to precedent. Sir Henry Herbert, who, as Master of the Revels to Charles I, did much to establish the traditions of the Censorship, has left us his grateful testimony to the civility of a contemporary actor-manager who tactfully presented his wife with a handsome pair of gloves. Still, that actor-manager did not invite the Press to report the speech he made on the occasion, nor did he bring a large public deputation of his brother managers with him. I suggest that his example in this respect should be followed in future rather than that of Tuesday last. I shall be told, no doubt, that Sir Spencer Ponsonby-Fane has nothing to do with the licensing of plays. And I shall immediately retort, "What then have the London managers to do with Sir Spencer Ponsonby-Fane?"

THE BOARD SCHOOL

[*27 November* 1897]

THE electioneering farce on which the curtain fell at nine o'clock the day before yesterday, must not pass without a word of dramatic criticism. Its bearing on the theatre needs no renewed explanation in this column. I have pointed out, only too often, how the theatre has stooped to meet the rising flood of popular literateness. Hitherto I have not complained; for it is better that the theatre should stoop to raise the millions above sing-songs and cock-fights, than soar for the benefit of a handful of experts above the level of Shakespear and Molière.

But behind this magnanimous preference for the interests of the many there has always lurked in me an implacable contempt for the process of literation, commonly and most erroneously called education, conducted in the popular school. I make no distinction between Board school and Voluntary school, or, for the matter of that, between the workhouse school and Harrow or Eton. They all turn out barbarians. I grant that the taste of the barbarian is the opportunity of the dauber in all the arts; but I understand the importance of the artist's function in society far too well to accept this result with complacency. We all quote the gentleman who professed the most complete indifference as to who made the laws of his country so long as he was allowed to write its songs; yet how many of us, I wonder, feel any real force in that epigram, even in England, the nation of all others most governed by artists? We are so susceptible to artistic fiction, rhetoric, and oratory, that we will not receive them as art, but rather as clear matter of fact or divinely revealed truth. Let me explain myself gently, coming to my dangerous point by degrees.

Some twenty years or so ago I found myself in the Isle of

Wight, lodging in the house of an intelligent London & South-Western railway guard, who placed his library at my disposal. Its principal attraction happened to be Robinson Crusoe, which I then read through for the first time since my childhood. My host's wife, noticing this, informed me that it was her husband's favorite book. Thereupon I made some conventional remark about it. The conventional remark unhappily implied that I regarded Robinson as a creature of Defoe's invention. She at once begged me not to betray any such scepticism in her husband's presence, he being absolutely convinced, on the internal evidence of the narrative, that it was no vain product of a romancer's fancy, but a veracious record of a seaman's experience. She confessed that she herself leaned towards my view of the matter; but she thought it best, for the sake of her home and her affections, to conform to her husband's faith. He was, she explained, a man of a prosaic turn, hating idle stories, and loving gravity and verity in all things: in short, precisely the sort of man to be fiction-ridden all his life without suspecting it. Now please observe that to read Robinson Crusoe and believe it literally, is to become the dupe of an imposture and the champion of a lie. On the other hand, to read it as a work of art—that is, to surrender oneself voluntarily to the illusion it creates, without for a moment compromising the integrity of our relations with the real world —is to learn a good deal from it, both of life and art, to say nothing of our enjoyment of the story.

Let us now suppose, merely to amuse ourselves, that my friend the railway guard were a member of the Isle of Wight School Board, if such a body exists. He would no doubt propose Robinson Crusoe as a standard reading-book for the school curriculum; and so excellent a proposal could hardly be rejected on its merits. But somebody would be sure to question his view that it should be presented to the children as history, not as parable. If he found any considerable support on the Board, or among the ratepayers, the result would probably be a compromise. Robinson Crusoe would be read; but the children would be left to draw their own conclusions, or to consult their parents or other advisers out of school.

The pious will now perceive the cloven hoof. The School Board election this week turned on a compromise concerning, not merely a book, but actually a whole literature; though, to be sure, the average English citizen thinks it a book, because it is all bound into one cover, and because he never reads it, not being literary in his tastes. If he does not actually regard it as an amulet, and believe that if a soldier carries it into battle it will magically attract and stop the Lee-Metford bullet, he may be regarded as an exceptionally enlightened person. But, numerically strong as he is, the very existence of the nation depends on the force of character with which those who know better overrule, in the public work of education, a superstition which would have horrified the Fathers of the Church, and which arose a few hundred years ago as an ephemeral effect of early Protestantism on minds not yet strong enough for so heroic a doctrine. In other departments of Government it may be expedient to fool your democratic voter to the top of his bent; but when he clamors to be allowed to perpetuate his folly by forcing educated people to teach what they do not believe, then it is for those educated people to refuse to do anything of the sort; to support one another resolutely in that refusal; and to invite the average North Sea Islander to do without them if he can.

Like all highly developed literatures, the Bible contains a great deal of sensational fiction, imagined with intense vividness, appealing to the most susceptible passions, and narrated with a force which the ordinary man is no more able to resist than my friend the railway guard was able to resist the force of Defoe. Perhaps only an expert can thoroughly appreciate the power with which a story well told, or an assertion well made, takes possession of a mind not specially trained to criticize it. Try to imagine all that is most powerful in English literature bound into one volume, and offered to a comparatively barbarous race as an instrument of civilization invested with supernatural authority! Indeed, let us leave what we call barbarous races out of the question, and suppose it offered to the English nation on the same assumptions as to its nature and authority which the children in our popular schools are led to make today concerning the Bible under the School Board compromise! How much resistance would there be to the illusion created by the art of our great storytellers? Who would dare to affirm that the men and women created by Chaucer, Shakespear, Bunyan, Fielding, Goldsmith, Scott, and Dickens had never existed? Who could resist the force of conviction carried by the tremendous assertive power of Cobbett, the gorgeous special-pleading of Ruskin, or the cogency of Sir Thomas More, or even Matthew Arnold? Above all, who could stand up against the inspiration and moral grandeur of our prophets and poets, from Langland to Blake and Shelley? The power of Scripture has not waned with the ages. We have no right to trick a child's instinctive sense of revelation and inspiration by such a surpassingly blasphemous pessimistic lie as that both have become extinct, and that the wretched world, like its dead moon, is living out its old age on a scanty remnant of spiritual energy, hoarded from thousands of years ago. And yet the whole question at stake in the School Board election was whether this lie should be told as a black lie or a white one. The stupid part of the business is that it is quite unnecessary to tell any lies at all. Why not teach children the realities of inspiration and revelation as they work daily through scribes and lawgivers? It would, at all events, make better journalists and parish councillors of them.

Until some such conception of the dignity and importance of art as the sole possible method of revelation for the forecasts of the spirit reaches our Board School population, the theatre will remain pretty much at its present level, in spite of such superficial improvements as the ordinary march of progress involves. In the meantime, however, man will not submit to spiritual starvation. I have over and over again pointed out that whilst the theatre has done hardly anything to adapt itself to modern demands, the Church has been waking up in all directions to its opportunities. I believe that many of the playgoers who are sufficiently conscious of the social importance of art to care to read these columns, never dream of going to church, and have no idea that they would find anything there but boredom, hypocrisy, and superstition. Let me beg them to try the experiment. Let them spend a fortnight in going to the best London churches, and a fortnight in going to the best London theatres. If they find one-tenth as much boredom, hypocrisy, superstition, humbug, snobbery, stupidity, vulgarity, foul air, bad music, draughts, late hours, stuffy smells, and unhappy and disagreeable people in the auditorium, not to mention professional incompetence on the part of the performers, in the churches as they will in the theatres, I will eat this number of the Saturday Review unbuttered.

I am rebuked by Messrs J. Avery & Co., window blind manufacturers, of 81 Great Portland Street, for having thoughtlessly mentioned "perforated wire-blinds" in my last article, in the teeth of the obvious fact that perforated blinds are not wire, and wire blinds not perforated. Let me, in return, give Messrs Avery a piece of advice. Never waste sarcasm on an inaccurate person: *correct* him. They have, in their severity, forgotten to teach me what a perforated blind is made of. I surmise zinc, but must not risk a second blunder by committing myself to that material.

A BREATH FROM THE SPANISH MAIN

A MAN'S SHADOW. Adapted from the French play Roger la Honte by Robert Buchanan. Revival. Her Majesty's Theatre, 27 November 1897.

ADMIRAL GUINEA. A play in four acts. By R. L. Stevenson and W. E. Henley. HONESTY: A COTTAGE FLOWER. In one act. By Margaret Young. The New Century Theatre, Avenue Theatre, 29 November 1897.   [4 *December* 1897]

IT is not in human nature to regard Her Majesty's Theatre as the proper place for such a police-court drama as A Man's Shadow. Still, it is not a bad bit of work of its kind; and it would be a good deal better if it were played as it ought to be with two actors instead of one in the parts of Lucien Laroque and Luversan. Of course Mr Tree, following the precedent of The Lyons Mail, doubles the twain. Equally of course, this expedient completely destroys the illusion, which requires that two different men should resemble one another so strongly as to be practically indistinguishable except on tolerably close scrutiny; whilst Mr Tree's reputation as a master of the art of disguising himself requires that he shall astonish the audience by the extravagant dissimilarity of the two figures he alternately presents. No human being could, under any conceivable circumstances, mistake his Laroque for his Luversan; and I have no doubt that Mr Tree will take this as the highest compliment I could possibly pay him for this class of work. Nevertheless, I have no hesitation in saying that if the real difficulty—one compared to which mere disguise is child's play—were faced and vanquished, the interest of the play would be trebled. That difficulty, I need hardly explain, is the presentation to the spectators of a single figure which shall yet be known to them as the work of two distinct actors. As it is, instead of two men in one, we have one man in two, which makes the play incredible as well as impossible.

However, as I have said, the play serves its turn. The one act into which the doubling business enters for a moment only (a very disastrous moment, by the way) is thoroughly effective, and gives Mr Tree an opportunity for a remarkable display of his peculiar talent as an imaginative actor. Indeed, he plays so well as the prisoner in the dock that all the applause goes to the bad playing of the advocate who saves himself from the unpleasantness of defending his friend at the expense of his wife's reputation by the trite expedient of dropping down dead. I dare say this will seem a wanton disparagement of a stage effect which was unquestionably highly successful, and to which Mr Waller led up by such forcible and sincere acting that his going wrong at the last moment was all the more aggravating. But if to let the broken-hearted Raymond de Noirville suddenly change into Serjeant Buzfuz at the very climax of his anguish was to go wrong, then it seems to me that Mr Lewis Waller certainly did go wrong. When he turned to the jury and apostrophized them as GENTLE-

MEN, in a roll of elocutionary thunder, Raymond de Noirville was done for; and it was really Lucien Laroque who held the scene together. The gallery responded promptly enough to Mr Waller, as the jury always does respond to Serjeant Buzfuz; but I venture to hope that the very noisiness of the applause has by this time convinced him that he ought not to have provoked it.

By the way, since Mr Tree is fortunate enough to have his band made so much of as it is by Mr Raymond Roze, he would, I think, find it economical to lavish a few "extra gentlemen" (or ladies) on the orchestra, even if they had to be deducted from his stage crowd. Two or three additional strings would make all the difference in such works as Mendelssohn's Ruy Blas over-ture.

Considering the lustre of the blazing galaxy of intellect which has undertaken the administration of the New Century Theatre, I really think the *matinées* of that institution might be better tempered to the endurance of the public. It is true that one has the vindictive satisfaction of seeing the committee men sharing the fatigue of the subscribers, and striving to outface their righteous punishment with feeble grins at their own involuntary yawns. But this is not precisely the sort of fun the New Century Theatre promised us. I ask Mr Archer, Mr Massingham, Mr Sutro, and Miss Robins, what the— I beg Miss Robins's pardon—what on earth they mean by putting on a long first piece in front of an important four-act play for no other purpose, apparently, than to damage the effect of that play, and overdrive a willing audience by keeping it in the theatre from half-past two until a quarter to six. If the first piece had been one of surpassing excellence, or in any way specially germane to the purposes of the New Century Theatre, I should still say that it had better have been reserved for another occasion. But as it only needed a little obvious trim-ming to be perfectly eligible for the evening bill at any of our ordinary commercial theatres, its inclusion must be condemned as the very wantonness of bad management, unless there was some munificent subscriber to be propitiated by it. Or was Miss Kate Rorke's appearance as the lodging-house slavey the attraction? If so, Miss Rorke and the committee have to share between them the responsibility of a stupendous error of judgment. Miss Rorke is congenitally incapable of reproducing in her own person any single touch, national or idiosyncratic, of Clorindar Ann. She can industriously pronounce face as fice, mile as mawl, and no as nah-oo; but she cannot do it in a London voice; nor is her imaginative, idealistic, fastidious sentiment even distantly related to the businesslike passions of the Cockney kitchen. Whatever parts she may have been miscast for before she won her proper place on the stage, she had better now refer applicants for that sort of work to Miss Louie Freear or Miss Cicely Richards. It would give me great pleasure to see Miss Rorke again as Helena in A Midsummer Night's Dream; but I think I had almost rather be boiled alive than go a second time to see Honesty, which, on this occasion, was most decidedly not the best policy for the New Century Theatre.

Hardly anything gives a livelier sense of the deadness of the English stage in the eighties than the failure of Stevenson and Mr Henley to effect a lodgment on it. To plead that they were no genuine dramatists is not to the point: pray what were some of the illiterate bunglers and ignoramuses whose work was preferred to theirs? Ask any playgoer whether he remembers any of the fashionable successes of that period as vividly as he remembers Deacon Brodie! If he says yes, you will find that he is either a simple liar, or else no true playgoer, but merely a critic, a fireman, a policeman, or some other functionary who has to be paid to induce him to enter a theatre. Far be it from me to pretend that Henley and Stevenson, in their Boy Buccaneer phase, took the stage seriously—unless it were the stage of pasteboard scenes and characters, and tin lamps and slides. But even that stage was in the eighties so much more artistic than the real stage—so much more sanctified by the childish fancies and dreams in which real dramatic art begins, that it was just by writing for it, and not for the West End houses, that Henley and Stevenson contrived to get ahead of their time. Admiral Guinea is perhaps their most frankly boyish compound of piracy and pasteboard, coming occasionally very close to poetry and pasteboard, and written with prodigious literary virtuosity. Indeed, both of them had a literary power to which maturity could add nothing except prudence, which in this style is the mother of dullness. Their boyishness comes out in their barbarous humor, their revelling in blood and broadswords, crime, dark lanterns, and delirious supernatural terrors: above all, in their recklessly irreligious love of adventure for its own sake. We see it too in the unnatural drawing of the girl Arethusa, though the womanliness aimed at is not altogether ill divined in the abstract. The Admiral himself is rank pasteboard; but the cleverness with which he is cut out and colored, and his unforgettable story of his last voyage and his wife's death, force us to overlook the impossibilities in his anatomy, and to pretend, for the heightening of our own enjoyment, that he not only moves on the authors' slides, and speaks with their voices, but lives. Pew is more convincing; for his qualities are those that a man might have; only, if a real man had them, he would end, not as a blind beggar, but as ruler of the Queen's Navee. This does not trouble the ordinary playgoer, who, simple creature! accepts Pew's villainy as a sufficient cause for his exceeding downness on his luck. Students of real life will not be so easily satisfied: they will see in him the tact, ability, force of character, and boldness which have been associated with abominable vices in many eminently successful men, but which no vicious tramp, however impudent, reckless, greedy and ferocious, ever had, or ever will have.

The juvenility of the piece is very apparent indeed in the contrast between the clumsy conduct of the action, and the positive inspiration of some of the stage effects. The blind robber, disturbed by the strangely tranquil footsteps of the sleepwalker, and believing himself to be hidden by the night until, groping his way to the door, he burns his hand in the candle and infers that he must be visible to the silent presence, is a masterstroke of stage effect; but it is not better in its way than the quieter point made when the Admiral opens his famous treasure chest and shews that it contains an old chain, an old ring, an old wedding dress, and nothing more. These triumphs are the fruit of the authors' genius. When we come to the product of their ordinary intelligence, our admiration changes to exasperation. Anything more ludicrously inept than the far-fetching of Kit French into the Admiral's house by Pew in the third act, will not soon be seen again, even on the English stage. The fact is, Kit French should be cut out of the play altogether; for though it is hard to leave Arethewsa without her Sweet Willyum, it is still harder to have a work of art which in all other respects hits its mark, reduced to absurdity by him. One burglary is enough; and three acts are enough. On reflection, I relent so far that I think that Kit might be allowed to live for the purpose of drawing out of Admiral Guinea and Arethusa their very fine scene at the beginning of the third act, and officiating as Pew's executioner; but the rest of his exploits, like the House of Lords, are useless, dangerous, and ought to be abolished.

The performance was a remarkably good one. The stage manager should not have so far neglected the ancient counsel to "jine his flats" as to leave a large gap in the roof of the Admiral's house; but there was nothing else to complain of. Mr Sidney Valentine had a rare chance as Pew. He proved unable to bear the extraordinary strain put by the authors on his capacity for rum, and frankly stopped after the first gallon or two; but in no other respect was he found wanting. Mr Mollison played the Admiral very carefully and methodically. The part was not seen by flashes of lightning; but none of it was lost. What man could do with the impossible Kit French Mr Loraine did; and Miss Dolores Drummond was well within her means as the landlady of the Benbow Inn. The part of Arethusa, pretty as it is, is so romantically literary that Miss Cissie Loftus could shew us nothing about herself in it except what we already know: namely, that she is like nobody else on the stage or off it, and that her vocation is beyond all doubt.

THE HAPPY LIFE

THE HAPPY LIFE. A new and original comedy in four acts. By
  Louis N. Parker. Duke of York's Theatre, 7 December 1897.
THE TRIPLE ALLIANCE. A new and original farcical polygamous
  comedy in three acts. By W. S. Beadle. Strand Theatre,
  6 December 1897. [11 *December* 1897]

THE Happy Life has driven me reluctantly to the conclusion that
Mr Louis N. Parker is at present our most disastrous dramatic
author. By his artistic culture, his fun, and a very pretty gift of
fancy, he has succeeded in getting the case for an advance in the
seriousness of the theatre staked on his plays, although the
Family Herald would revolt at the old-maidishness of his sentimental plots, and Messrs Hamilton and Raleigh, in their most
unscrupulous Drury Lane confections, would not venture on
anything so stale as his romantic conventionalities. If The Happy
Life were a satire on Bostonian culture—if the American gentleman who thinks he is in the very middle of the highest art when
he is snugly curtained into his chambers in the Temple, with
memories of Goldsmith in the atmosphere, Horace on the shelf,
and FitzGerald's mock-Persian drivel open on his knee, and who
feels bound as a gentleman to marry a strange young woman
because she has been compelled by an accident to spend the night
in his easy chair, were offered up, as he deserves, to feed the
comic spirit and be devoured as Molière or Cervantes would
have devoured him, then The Happy Life might end as well as
it begins. But when it becomes apparent that Mr Parker is going
to endorse his hero's drafts on our sympathy, and invent spurious
happy consequences for his fatuity—a point reached at the end
of the second act—the intellectual and poetic interest of the piece
vanishes, because we foresee that Mr Parker must spend the remaining two acts in doing vapidly what Mr Carton would have
done effectively. The secret of Mr Parker's inferiority to Mr
Carton at this sort of work is not very recondite. Mr Carton,
blessed with a scatter-brained spontaneity of romantic invention,

presents agreeable images to our fancy with the same delightful freedom from the conditions of real life that Don Quixote's favorite knights-errant enjoyed from paying for their beds and breakfasts. Mr Parker, intellectually more coherent, allows his ultra-Cartonic sentiment and fancy to be hampered by scruples proper only to dramatists who strive to hold the mirror up to nature, and feel that a single touch of romance would leave their problem shirked and their work worthless. That Mr Parker can conceive such scruples as having any application to flimsy romantic trash like the misunderstanding between the Bostonian and Evelyn, or the sentimental outrage practised on her father, is no doubt part of the general indeterminateness which disables him from complete maturity as a dramatist at present. I wish he would either discard the scruples, and give us romance in all its irresponsible luxuriance, or else draw his materials from the real life to which conscientious scruples are appropriate. At present he is like a musician writing fashionable waltzes without venturing to break the rules of fifteenth century unaccompanied vocal counterpoint.

So far, it is in his realism and not in his romance that he is successful. No author could desire a heartier reception for his play than he enjoyed up to the end of the second act. The party in the Temple, and the Pettigrew-Smith household on Christmas Day, come off convincingly, with all the characters distinct and idiosyncratic. We were not meeting Mr Beauchamp, Mr Sidney Brough, Mr Fred Kerr, and the rest for the hundred-and-fiftieth time: we were making the acquaintance of Charteris the First, Jimmy Pastor, Charteris the Second, and so on. Even Mrs Pettigrew-Smith, a rather poor caricature, unworthily descended from the immortal Mrs Wilfer, was credible with the help of the goodwill created by the others. We were all handsomely entertained; we swallowed the bit of poetry about the figure at the door ravenously; and though two terrible mistakes had been made in casting the play, they did it no harm: it was, on the realistic plane, actor-proof. Then the realist suddenly changed into the old maid (a masculine euphemism for the young bachelor);

and its credibility and interest began to wane. The Bostonian and the compromised lady, fast married, had to adore one another secretly, each believing that the other had been dragged reluctantly to the altar by Mrs Grundy, and to stave off the inevitable enlightenment by mere shyness (which is not a thrillingly dramatic quality) until the last two minutes. The foreign prince, without the faintest prospect of success or complication of any threatening kind, had to make love to the wife for the sake of gravely proposing the customary stage duel, which the husband as gravely accepted. Jimmy Pastor ceased to exist and left in his place Mr Sidney Brough struggling with his old task of comic relief. The Pettigrew-Smith brother, borrowed very frankly, actor and all, from The Benefit of the Doubt, had to commit a quite irrelevant forgery to keep things going. Worst of all, the unfortunate old father, the literary hack for whom some genuine sympathy had been gained in the second act, was made the dupe of a hoax so cruel that I really cannot imagine how Mr Parker managed to persuade himself that it was an act of kindness. The Bostonian pays a publisher to "accept" one of the old man's books, and buys up the edition, leaving him under the impression that he has had a genuine success. Stage philanthropy is, I admit, often enough based on the very ignorant notion that people have an unlimited right to gratify their benevolent instincts at the expense of others; but so utterly heartless a liberty as this, presented, if you please, as a fine trait in the hero, is a little beyond even the customary stage beyonds. I hoped up to the last moment that the old man, when the disclosure came, would give his son-in-law's monstrous sentimental officiousness and thoughtlessness the snubbing it deserved; but of course he only dissolved in gratitude: indeed Mr Hermann Vezin, with the dexterity of an old hand, dissolved so cunningly that he brought down the house, though his part gave him no adequate cue for so powerful a stroke.

As to the husband and wife, if their parts had been cast with any sort of common sense, they might not only have pulled through themselves, but pulled the play with them when it began to flag. During the latter half of the play Evelyn and Cyril have to depend for the sympathy of the audience, not on anything particular that they say or do, but on their mute emotion. Now if there is an actor in London whose emotional condition is always completely reassuring, it is Mr Fred Kerr. His robust sanity is the point from which his comedy starts—comedy so excellent that it is intolerable that he should be condemned to ape the snivelling "interestingness" of the sentimental leading man. There is, however, one person on the stage compared to whom even Mr Kerr is sentimental; and that is Miss Dorothea Baird. There is something terrifying to an ignorant and old-fashioned man like myself in Miss Baird's combination of the efficiency, knowledge, and self-possession of the educated modern woman with bewitching prettiness and an artistic calling. Nothing can be more businesslike than the way in which she whitens her face and gets up all the pathetic business of Evelyn's part as if she were doing it for a scholarship. And one cannot deny her the full complement of marks; for she gives the accepted answer without "fluff," and is prompt, reliable, cool, and clear-headed. Like all successful examinees, she knows what is required of her, and supplies it, but takes no responsibility for its validity. Being well trained physically and intellectually, she is not easily affected: to really move her with fictitious matter you must either put it in a form which appeals to her artistic sense (the only sense in which she has deliberately cultivated susceptibility), or else it must be no mere commonplace from the penny serials, but something that an intellectually practised person can feel concerned about. The emotional hyperesthesia which enables many actresses to be touched and to touch others in feeble and silly passages is happily not among Miss Baird's qualifications for the stage. It is evident that the ordinary sentimental leading part will, in nine cases out of ten, touch her neither as an artist nor as a woman. It is equally evident that instead of letting this hinder her from grappling with it, she will attack it resolutely in the examinee attitude, and pass her examination on the first night letter-perfect, gesture-perfect, paint-perfect, dress-perfect, beauty-perfect, and imitation-pathos-perfect. Only, if the play depends on the part being lived from the inside instead of put on as a shepherd putteth on his garment, then it will fail, though Miss Baird may seem to succeed. Mind: I do not complain of this: the more such failures we have, the better. It is the business of the dramatist to make an exceptionally subtle and powerful appeal to the feelings and interests of the actress, not hers to make good his deficiencies by an abnormal and unhealthy susceptibility to every worthless and incoherent suggestion of conventional pathos. Evelyn in The Happy Life is not a woman at all: she is merely the vehicle of a trumpery sentimentality of Mr Parker's; and I do not want to see a clever and highly trained woman like Miss Baird the dupe of that sentimentality. But I confess that neither do I want to see her elbowing her way through it dry-eyed; for though the destructive effect is beneficial to the drama in the long run, and will effectually warn Mr Parker that if he wants her to do for him what she has done very creditably for Du Maurier and Shakespear, he must give her equally interesting material, yet the process is not congenial to the spectator. On the whole, Mr Kerr, as the more experienced performer, made much more of his misfit than Miss Baird did of hers; but the best they could do between them did not for a moment succeed in producing the effect which must suffuse the last two acts from end to end if the play is ever to realize the author's conception.

What effect these untoward circumstances may have on the commercial fortunes of this particular piece remains to be seen; but its fortunes cannot greatly affect Mr Parker's position as a dramatist, which may now be taken as consolidated. The fresh flavoring which he manages to give to themes by no means fresh is evidently relished by the public; and since his dramas are so far no more really advanced than Flotow's Martha is an advanced opera, and appeal to a taste which the London playgoer is rapidly acquiring, they will soon bring him all the success his manager can desire.

There was a great reunion of the Thorne family at the Strand Theatre on Monday afternoon. Their welcome was warm for the sake of old times. I left the theatre at the end of the second act, as the play did not interest me.

HAMLET REVISITED

[18 *December* 1897]

PUBLIC feeling has been much harrowed this week by the accounts from America of the 144 hours' bicycle race; but what are the horrors of such an exhibition compared to those of the hundred-nights run of Hamlet! On Monday last I went, in my private capacity, to witness the last lap but five of the Lyceum trial of endurance. The performers had passed through the stage of acute mania, and were for the most part sleep-walking in a sort of dazed blank-verse dream. Mr Barnes raved of some New England maiden named Affection Poo; the subtle distinctions made by Mrs Patrick Campbell between madness and sanity had blurred off into a placid idiocy turned to favor and to prettiness; Mr Forbes Robertson, his lightness of heart all gone, wandered into another play at the words "Sleep? No more!" which he delivered as, "Sleep no more." Fortunately, before he could add "Macbeth does murder sleep," he relapsed into Hamlet and saved the situation. And yet some of the company seemed all the better for their unnatural exercise. The King was in uproarious spirits; and the Ghost, always comfortable, was now positively pampered, his indifference to the inconveniences of purgatory having developed into a bean-fed enjoyment of them. Fortinbras, as I judged, had sought consolation in religion: he was anxious concerning Hamlet's eternal welfare; but his general health seemed excellent. As Mr Gould did not play on the occasion of my first visit, I could not compare him with his former self; but his condition was sufficiently grave. His attitude was that of a castaway mariner who has no longer hope enough to scan the horizon for a sail; yet even in this extremity his unconquerable generosity of temperament had not deserted him. When his cue came, he would jump up and lend a hand with all his old alacrity and resolution. Naturally the players of the shorter parts had suffered least:

Rosencrantz and Guildenstern were only beginning to enjoy themselves; and Bernardo (or was it Marcellus?) was still eagerly working up his part to concert pitch. But there could be no mistake as to the general effect. Mr Forbes Robertson's exhausting part had been growing longer and heavier on his hands; whilst the support of the others had been falling off; so that he was keeping up the charm of the representation almost single-handed just when the torturing fatigue and monotony of nightly repetition had made the task most difficult. To the public, no doubt, the justification of the effort is its success. There was no act which did not contain at least one scene finely and movingly played; indeed some of the troubled passages gained in verisimilitude by the tormented condition of the actor. But Hamlet is a very long play; and it only seems a short one when the high-mettled comedy with which it is interpenetrated from beginning to end leaps out with all the lightness and spring of its wonderful loftiness of temper. This was the secret of the delighted surprise with which the public, when the run began, found that Hamlet, far from being a funereally classical bore, was full of a celestial gaiety and fascination. It is this rare vein that gives out first when the exigencies of theatrical commerce force an actor to abuse it. A sentimental Hamlet can go on for two years, or ten for the matter of that, without much essential depreciation of the performance; but the actor who sounds Hamlet from the lowest note to the top of his compass very soon finds that compass contracting at the top. On Monday night the first act, the third act, and the fifth act from the entrance of Laertes onward, had lost little more than they had gained as far as Mr Forbes Robertson was concerned; but the second act, and the colloquy with the grave-digger, which were the triumphs of the representation in its fresher stages, were pathetically dulled, with the result that it could no longer be said that the length of the play was forgotten.

The worst of the application of the long-run system to heroic plays is that, instead of killing the actor, it drives him to limit himself to such effects as he can repeat to infinity without committing suicide. The opposite system, in its extreme form of the old stock company playing two or three different pieces every night, led to the same evasion in a more offensive form. The recent correspondence in the Morning Post on The Stage as a Profession, to which I have myself luminously contributed, has produced the usual fallacious eulogies of the old stock company as a school of acting. You can no more prevent contributors to public correspondences falling into this twenty-times-exploded error than from declaring that duelling was a school of good manners, that the lash suppressed garotting, or any other of the gratuitous ignorances of the amateur sociologist. The truth is, it is just as impossible for a human being to study and perform a new part of any magnitude every day as to play Hamlet for a hundred consecutive nights. Nevertheless, if an actor is required to do these things, he will find some way out of the difficulty without refusing. The stock actor solved the problem by adopting a "line": for example, if his "line" was old age, he acquired a trick of doddering and speaking in a cracked voice: if juvenility, he swaggered and effervesced. With these accomplishments, eked out by a few rules of thumb as to wigs and face-painting, one deplorable step dance, and one still more deplorable "combat," he "swallowed" every part given to him in a couple of hours, and regurgitated it in the evening over the footlights, always in the same manner, however finely the dramatist might have individualized it. His infamous incompetence at last swept him from the reputable theatres into the barns and booths; and it was then that he became canonized, in the imagination of a posterity that had never suffered from him, as the incarnation of the one quality in which he was quite damnably deficient: to wit, versatility. His great contribution to dramatic art was the knack of earning a living for fifty years on the stage without ever really acting, or either knowing or caring for the difference between the Comedy of Errors and Box and Cox.

A moment's consideration will shew that the results of the long-run system at its worst are more bearable than the horrors of the past. Also, that even in point of giving the actor some chance of varying his work, the long-run system is superior, since the modern actor may at all events exhaust the possibilities of his part before it exhausts him, whereas the stock actor, having barely time to apply his bag of tricks to his daily task, never varies his treatment by a hair's breadth from one half century to another. The best system, of course, lies between these extremes. Take the case of the great Italian actors who have visited us, and whose acting is of an excellence apparently quite beyond the reach of our best English performers. We find them extremely chary of playing every night. They have a repertory containing plays which count as resting places for them. For example, Duse relieves Magda with Mirandolina just as our own Shakespearean star actors used to relieve Richard the Third and Othello with Charles Surface and Don Felix. But even with this mitigation no actor can possibly play leading parts of the first order six nights a week all the year round unless he underplays them, or routines them mechanically in the old stock manner, or faces a terrible risk of disablement by paralysis, or, finally, resorts to alcohol or morphia, with the usual penalties. What we want in order to get the best work is a repertory theatre with alternative casts. If, for instance, we could have Hamlet running at the Lyceum with Sir Henry Irving and Miss Ellen Terry on Thursdays and Saturdays, Mr Forbes Robertson and Mrs Patrick Campbell on Wednesdays and Fridays, and the other two days devoted to comedies in which all four could occasionally appear, with such comedians as Mr Charles Wyndham, Mr Weedon Grossmith, Mr Bourchier, Mr Cyril Maude, and Mr Hawtrey, then we should have a theatre which we could invite serious people to attend without positively insulting them. I am aware that the precise combination which I have named is not altogether a probable one at present; but there is no reason why we should not at least turn our faces in that direction. The actor-manager system, which has hitherto meant the star system carried to its utmost possible extreme, has made the theatre so insufferable that, now that its monopoly has been broken up by the rise of the suburban theatres, there is a distinct weakening of the jealous and shameless individualism of the last twenty years, and a movement towards combination and co-operation.

By the way, is it quite prudent to start a public correspondence on the Stage as a Profession? Suppose someone were to tell the truth about it!

ON THE LIVING AND THE DEAD

[25 *December* 1897]

QUITE the best comedy of the season is the indignant protest which has broken out on all sides against Mr Clement Scott's now famous Great Thoughts interview. Mr Raymond Blathwayt, on behalf of that journal, called on Mr Scott, to ask him, as a critic of thirty-seven years' standing and of eminent influence, "Does the theatre make for good?" In such inquiries English public opinion looks to its favorites to tell lies. Mr Scott was not equal to the occasion. He did not tell the whole truth (or perhaps he did, and Great Thoughts was afraid to publish it); but he told the truth and nothing but the truth, from his point of view, which is precisely that unctuously taken on all public occasions by our actors and managers. He said that he was the worse for his thirty-seven years of playgoing; that actresses are not, as a rule, ladies, nor "pure," and that their prospects frequently depend on the nature and extent of their compliances; that the theatrical profession "induces the vain and egotistical that is in all of us to a degree that would be scarcely credited by the outsider"; that whilst the pit and gallery retain the old faith, the men who write and criticize are freethinkers; that Ibsen is an atheist; and that whilst Cardinal Manning at one end of the religious scale hated the theatre, and the Puritan, Wesleyan, or Baptist minister detests it at the other, the philosophic man of the world, with an equal knowledge of human nature, stands between them, and says that they are each right.

To this it is replied, virtually, that the man who makes such statements is no gentleman. That is no doubt the case. I have never been able to see how the duties of a critic, which consist largely in making painful remarks in public about the most sensitive of his fellow-creatures, can be reconciled with the manners of a gentleman. But, gentleman or no gentleman, a critic is most certainly not in the position of a co-respondent in a divorce case: he is in no way bound to perjure himself to shield the reputation of the profession he criticizes. Far from being the instigator of its crimes and the partner of its guilty joys, he is the policeman of dramatic art; and it is his express business to denounce its delinquencies. On the whole, I think more wisdom has been shewn by those who have made fun of Mr Scott, since they thereby evade their obligations, as fellow-critics, to stand by him, without committing themselves on the other hand to a flustered and ridiculous denial of what everybody knows to be perfectly true.

For my part, I do not see how Mr Scott, holding the opinions he does, could honestly have said less. He might, I repeat, have said a great deal more on the same side, and yet been well within the mark. He might, for example, have said that no member of the theatrical profession ever dreams of believing any statement made by any other member of it; that a tradesman will give credit to any professional man more confidently than to an actor of equal standing; that disloyalty, often operating as what a trade-unionist would call shameless blacklegging, excites neither surprise nor disapprobation in the green-room; that theatrical agreements are perhaps the riskiest securities in the world; and that the extent to which modern industrial developments are daily throwing masses of money into idle, irresponsible, ignorant, and immature hands, has made the stage probably more corrupt at present than it has ever been in the history of the world before. In short, Mr Scott has erred, as he always errs, on the side of good nature.

But whilst I exhort the theatre to revise its standard of conduct in the light of Mr Scott's criticism, I wish I could persuade Mr Scott to revise his standards of judgment in the light of modern thought. If those standards involve the conclusion that Ibsen's plays are "nasty, dirty, impure, clever if you like, but foul to the last degree," the inevitable consequence is that the ablest modern women will be perfectly content to seem nasty, dirty, impure, clever, and foul to Mr Scott. And the really nasty people, who thoroughly deserve censure, will easily escape it by simply hiding behind the petticoats of the Ibsenists. I submit to Mr Scott that he has given away the whole force of his attack by allowing Mr Blathwayt to lead him on from the practical morality of the theatrical profession to the theoretical tendency of the modern drama. At the moment of victory he has suddenly abandoned his position to call on the pit and gallery, as believers in God and Robertson, to follow him against the free-thinking stalls as believers in no God and Ibsen. Such a digression hopelessly compromises the authority of his opening utterances. Anyone can drive a coach and six backwards and forwards through everything he said after the fatal term "problem-play" passed Mr Blathwayt's lips. "The old-fashioned denizens of pit and gallery, who still believe that there *is* a God," howled down Mr Henry James's Guy Domville, mainly because its last act could only interest those who were susceptible to religious sentiment. Mr Scott, in one of his best criticisms, tried to rally the pit and gallery to its support; and the pit and gallery turned their backs on him at once. The fact is, Mr Blathwayt, with diabolical ingenuity, steered Mr Scott imperceptibly from category to category at that interview until he landed him up to his neck in confusion. Mr Scott cannot have meant to imply that The Pilgrim's Progress and The Sign of the Cross are more religious than Ibsen's Brand, or that what makes a play religious is the introduction of the Lord's Prayer (he might have cited the burial service in a recent Adelphi melodrama) or the representation of a scene from Scripture as at Ober Ammergau. But Mr Blathwayt has given him an air of doing so; and the enemy will be able to retreat in good order in consequence.

As far as any real defence can be made to the practical side of Mr Scott's attack, it must take the form of a frank repudiation of his morality. If an actress has commanding talent, and is indispensable on the stage, she can be what she likes. Sarah Bernhardt and Réjane can be, and are, what they like: Madame Mary

Anderson de Navarro and Mrs Kendal can be, and are, what *they* like. The prospects of such stars do not depend, as Mr Scott puts it, "on the nature and extent of their compliance," though those of their humbler colleagues generally do. But it is quite certain that the range of an actress's experience and the development of her sympathies depend on a latitude in her social relations which, though perfectly consistent with a much higher degree of self-respect than is at all common among ordinary respectable ladies, involves a good deal of knowledge which is forbidden to "pure" women. Any actress who denies this is rightly classed by public opinion as a hypocrite. Further, an actress is essentially a work-woman and not a lady. If she is ashamed of this, she deserves all the mortification her shame may bring her. I therefore do not think that Mr Scott has considered deeply enough when using such question-begging terms as "lady," "pure," and so on. I very much doubt whether he, as a lover of humanity and art, would tolerate the conventional limitations of ladyhood and "innocence" either on the stage or off. Certainly, posterity will not gather from his criticisms that his most affectionate admiration and respect are reserved for those actresses whose withers—good heavens, what metaphors Shakespear leads us into!—whose lives will stand the moral tests applied by Mr Clement Scott under the artful leading questions of Mr Blathwayt.

It is a pity that so interesting a figure as William Terriss should receive such scant justice from the obituarists. Now that the first shock of his assassination is over, it is easy to see that our civilization might have had in store for him many "natural" deaths far worse than the fate of Cæsar. That being so, I need not inflict a fresh paraphrase of the "Breezy Bill" conception of him on a surfeited public. The part a man plays to perfection before the world is never his real self; and the success with which Terriss impersonated "Breezy Bill" is the best proof that they were as different as I am from G. B. S. The instructive thing about Terriss, as I knew him, was that he made everybody like him by not caring a rap for anybody. Instead of counting one man (or woman) as a hundred, in the affectional manner, he counted them all twelve to the dozen, and so got right with them to an extent that would have implied enormous tact in a more emotional man. He did not believe that you could get anything for nothing; and it was that rare piece of soundheadedness rather than any desire for artistic perfection that nerved him to take such trouble to do his work well at the Adelphi, and made him, within certain limits, the most efficient actor in London. For art as art he cared nothing, and made no secret of it: for efficiency he cared a good deal. I am not sure that he cared as much for money as he pretended, though his sense of its power was shewn by the pains he took to make people believe that its acquisition was his main object in life, and that if you wanted to interest him you must tell him about some licensed house that was for sale, and not about a five-act tragedy. When he asked me once to write a play for him, he wasted very little time indeed in flattering me: instead, he shewed me a bank-book containing a record of the author's fees on a very popular melodrama then running at the Adelphi. I believe he had no idea that he was an unrivalled executive instrument for my purposes as a dramatist, and that I accordingly had a strong artistic incentive to write for him; on the contrary, he had a confused idea that I was an extremely learned man, and that the only chance of inducing me to condescend to the Adelphi was by an appeal to my pocket, which he rightly regarded as a vital organ even in the most superior constitutions. He at first proposed a collaboration and produced a scenario. I explained to him why the scenario would not do; and he immediately put it into the fire with the most imperturbable phlegm. I wrote the play for him; but when it was finished, there was no immediate occasion for it; and since plays did not interest him as works of art, I found it absolutely impossible to induce him to apply his mind seriously to it, in spite of a quite pathetic effort on his part to pay me that compliment. He was like a child in church, longing to be at anything else.

I sincerely wish we had more actors like him. His positiveness of character, his freedom from illusions in serious business, the self-sufficiency and self-centralization which made him a man certain never to become a burden on anyone, were as far as possible removed from the maudlin amiabilities which we (or obliging interviewers speaking in our names) have been heaping on his memory; but they were the secret of his undeniable attraction—of what we are driving at when we talk of his virility.

PEACE AND GOODWILL TO MANAGERS

THE BABES IN THE WOOD. The Children's Grand Pantomime. By Arthur Sturgess and Arthur Collins. Music by J. M. Glover. Theatre Royal, Drury Lane, 27 December 1897.

[1 *January* 1898]

I AM sorry to have to introduce the subject of Christmas in these articles. It is an indecent subject; a cruel, gluttonous subject; a drunken, disorderly subject; a wasteful, disastrous subject; a wicked, cadging, lying, filthy, blasphemous, and demoralizing subject. Christmas is forced on a reluctant and disgusted nation by the shopkeepers and the press: on its own merits it would wither and shrivel in the fiery breath of universal hatred; and anyone who looked back to it would be turned into a pillar of greasy sausages. Yet, though it is over now for a year, and I can go out without positively elbowing my way through groves of carcases, I am dragged back to it, with my soul full of loathing, by the pantomime.

The pantomime ought to be a redeeming feature of Christmas, since it professedly aims at developing the artistic possibilities of our Saturnalia. But its professions are like all the other Christmas professions: what the pantomime actually does is to abuse the Christmas toleration of dullness, senselessness, vulgarity, and extravagance to a degree utterly incredible by people who have never been inside a theatre. The manager spends five hundred pounds to produce two penn'orth of effect. As a shilling's worth is needed to fill the gallery, he has to spend three thousand pounds for the "gods," seven thousand five hundred for the pit, and so on in proportion, except that when it comes to the stalls and boxes he caters for the children alone, depending on their credulity to pass off his twopence as a five-shilling piece. And yet even this is not done systematically and intelligently. The wildest superfluity and extravagance in one direction is wasted by the most sordid niggardliness in another. The rough rule is to spend money recklessly on whatever can be seen and heard and recognized as costly, and to economize on invention, fancy, dramatic faculty—in short, on brains. It is only when the brains get thrown in gratuitously through the accident of some of the contracting parties happening to possess them—a contingency which managerial care cannot always avert—that the entertainment acquires sufficient form or purpose to make it humanly apprehensible. To the mind's eye and ear the modern pantomime, as purveyed by the late Sir Augustus Harris, is neither visible nor audible. It is a glittering, noisy void, horribly wearisome and enervating, like all performances which worry the physical senses without any recreative appeal to the emotions and through them to the intellect.

I grieve to say that these remarks have lost nothing of their force by the succession of Mr Arthur Collins to Sir Augustus Harris. In Drury Lane drama Mr Collins made a decided advance on his predecessor. In pantomime he has, I think, also shewn superior connoisseurship in selecting pretty dummies for the display of his lavishly expensive wardrobe; but the only other respect in which he has outdone his late chief is the cynicism with which he has disregarded, I will not say the poetry of the nursery tale, because poetry is unthinkable in such a connection, but the bare coherence and common sense of the presentation of its incidents. The spectacular scenes exhibit Mr Collins as a manager to whom a thousand pounds is as five shillings. The dramatic scenes exhibit him as one to whom a crown-piece is as a million. If Mr Dan Leno had asked for a hundred-guinea tunic to wear during a single walk across the stage, no doubt he would have got it, with a fifty-guinea hat and sword-belt to boot. If he had asked for ten guineas' worth of the time of a competent dramatic humorist to provide him with at least one line that might not have been pirated from the nearest Cheap Jack, he would, I suspect, have been asked whether he wished to make Drury Lane bankrupt for the benefit of dramatic authors. I hope I may never again have to endure anything more dismally futile than the efforts of Mr Leno and Mr Herbert Campbell to start a passable joke in the course of their stumblings and wanderings through barren acres of gag on Boxing-night. Their attempt at a travesty of Hamlet reached a pitch of abject resourcelessness which could not have been surpassed if they really had been a couple of school children called on for a prize-day Shakespearean recitation without any previous warning. An imitation of Mr Forbes Robertson and Mrs Patrick Campbell would have been cheap and obvious enough; but even this they were unequal to. Mr Leno, fortunately for himself, was inspired at the beginning of the business to call Hamlet "Ham." Several of the easily amused laughed at this; and thereafter, whenever the travesty became so frightfully insolvent in ideas as to make it almost impossible to proceed, Mr Leno said "Ham," and saved the situation. What will happen now is that Mr Leno will hit on a new point of the "Ham" order at, say, every second performance. As there are two performances a day, he will have accumulated thirty "wheezes," as he calls them, by the end of next month, besides being cut down to strict limits of time. In February, then, his part will be quite bearable—probably even very droll—and Mr Collins will thereby be confirmed in his belief that if you engage an eccentric comedian of recognized gagging powers you need not take the trouble to write a part for him. But would it not be wiser, under these circumstances, to invite the critics on the last night of the pantomime instead of on the first? Mr Collins will probably reply that by doing so he would lose the benefit of the press notices, which, as a matter of Christmas custom, are not criticisms, but simply gratuitous advertisements given as a Christmas-box by the newspaper to the manager who advertises all the year round. And I am sorry to say he will be quite right.

It is piteous to see the wealth of artistic effort which is annually swamped in the morass of purposeless wastefulness that constitutes a pantomime. At Drury Lane many of the costumes are extremely pretty, and some of them, notably those borrowed for the flower ballet from one of Mr Crane's best-known series of designs, rise above mere theatrical prettiness to the highest class of decorative art available for fantastic stage purposes. Unhappily, every stroke that is at all delicate, or rare, or precious is multiplied, and repeated, and obtruded, usually on the limbs of some desolatingly incompetent young woman, until its value is heavily discounted. Still, some of the scenes are worth looking at for five minutes, though not for twenty. The orchestral score is very far above the general artistic level of the pantomime. The instrumental resources placed at the disposal of Mr Glover— quite ungrudgingly as far as they consist of brass—would suffice for a combined Bach festival and Bayreuth Götterdämmerung performance. To hear a whole battery of Bach trumpets, supported by a park of trombones, blasting the welkin with the exordium of Wagner's Kaisermarsch, is an ear-splitting ecstasy not to be readily forgotten; but these mechanical effects are really cheaper than the daintiness and wit of the vocal accompaniments, in which Mr Glover shews a genuine individual and original style in addition to his imposing practical knowledge of band business.

If I were Mr Collins I should reduce the first four scenes to one short one, and get some person with a little imagination, some acquaintance with the story of the Babes in the Wood, and at least a rudimentary faculty for amusing people, to write the dialogue for it. I should get Messrs Leno and Campbell to double the parts of the robbers with those of the babes, and so make the panorama scene tolerable. I should reduce the second part to the race-course scene, which is fairly funny, with just one front scene, in which full scope might be allowed for Mr Leno's inspiration, and the final transformation. I should either cut the harlequinade out, or, at the expense of the firms it advertises, pay the audience for looking at it; or else I should take as much trouble with it as Mr Tree took with Chand d'Habits at Her Majesty's. And I should fill up the evening with some comparatively amusing play by Ibsen or Browning.

Finally, may I ask our magistrates on what ground they permit the legislation against the employment of very young children as money makers for their families to be practically annulled in favor of the pantomimes? If the experience, repeated twice a day for three months, is good for the children, I suggest that there need be no difficulty in filling their places with volunteers from among the children of middle and upper-class parents anxious to secure such a delightful and refining piece of education for their offspring. If it is not good for them, why do the magistrates deliberately license it? I venture to warn our managers that their present monstrous abuse of magistrates' licences can only end in a cast-iron clause in the next Factory Act unconditionally forbidding the employment of children under thirteen on any pretext whatever.

I have to congratulate Mrs Bernard Beere on the warm welcome she received last week at the Comedy Theatre, when she played Anne Carew in A Sheep in Wolf's Clothing, an obsolete play, though still fresher in parts than many modern novelties.

PETER THE BLACKGUARD

[8 *January* 1898]

WHEN Mr Laurence Irving's Peter the Great came into my hands some time ago, I found it so interesting that I became impatient for the Lyceum production to set me free to comment on it publicly. It is quite the biggest piece of work the rising generation has given us. It needs some critical nicety to analyse it, because, whilst its version of the historical facts is, in skeleton, almost as conventionally romantic as Meyerbeer's L'Étoile du Nord, its handling—above all, its characterization—is essentially modern and realistic.

First, let us dispose of its divergences from history. In the play, Catherine is represented as the friend in need of Peter's discarded wife, Eudoxia, and the generous intercessor for the Tsarevitch Alexis, her own infant son's rival in the heirship to the Tsardom. The real Catherine treated Eudoxia worse than

Peter did. No sooner was the breath out of her husband's body than she dragged her ruined and harmless rival out of her convent prison, and threw her into a dungeon, where she would probably have literally rotted to death if Catherine had not taken a shorter method with herself by the almost continuous orgy of debauchery and brandy with which, when her tyrant and dupe was gone, she killed herself in sixteen months. Her one act of interference on behalf of the Tsarevitch is doubtful. According to one account, when she saw that Peter's daily amusement of torturing his son was making him delirious with cruelty, she stopped it, much as she used to stop his drinking bouts when they were going too far, by sending down her surgeon to bleed Alexis to death. Nevertheless, the appearance of Catherine as the good angel of Peter's victims, and her frank and modest deference, as a humble woman of the people, in the presence of the nobly-born royal consort, is no mere fabrication of Mr Irving's. Catherine was a consummate actress, with a natural talent for getting round people. The frank-modest-deferential business, which Mr Irving represents her as playing off on Eudoxia, was actually her way of inducing civilized queens at foreign courts to make friends with her in spite of her humble birth, and her notorious drunkenness and prostitution. She interceded for mercy systematically and industriously, because it was her main source of income. Peter's personal stinginess was almost as remarkable as his personal poltroonery; and it was only when it became the established practice of condemned criminals to bribe the Tsarina to beg them off that Catherine's pecuniary circumstances became at all easy.

As far as the Tsarevitch himself is concerned, I think Mr Irving's dramatic portrait of him might have something to say for itself as a representation of Alexis unalcoholized and undebauched. There are glimpses of potential grace in such records as we possess of the poor creature's necessarily foul life. But as to Peter himself, it is impossible to make an authentic moral hero of him. It was, of course, a sufficiently extraordinary accident that a seventeenth-century Russian, with the vitality of a man of genius, and a gigantic childishness that saw civilization as an imaginative boy sees a box of toys, should have been born as free from medieval scruples and superstitions as a nineteenth-century American millionaire; and there is no denying that the childishness offered a rare opportunity to literary and courtly idolizers after his death. Thanks to it, nothing is easier than to represent Peter's angry dread that Alexis would burn his toy fleet and let his toy capital sink into its native swamps, as the concern of a great social savior for the permanence of the golden age he is inaugurating. But how are we to get over the fact that Peter took no steps whatever to secure the succession of the ideas which are attributed to him, or that he, with his boon scoundrels, Menschikoff, Tolstoi, and Company, made up a knouting party, and returned again and again to the torture chamber to glut themselves with the Tsarevitch's convulsions until they had knouted him to death, exactly as a squad of soldiers will return again and again to the public-house until they have spent their last farthing? Peter was as festive after the event as Squire Western might have been after his favorite terrier had killed a hundred rats inside two minutes; and the only mercy he shewed was in not countermanding Alexis's customary unlimited allowance of brandy during the sport. Mr Irving, in making him cry, "Oh, Absalom, my son, my son!" has thrown reality overboard. But reality has a way of avenging itself; and I doubt whether this highly Lyceum-like sentimental ending will carry conviction. I have repeatedly had to point out, from actual theatrical experience, that it does not do to mix romance and reality in the same play. Mr Irving has undervalued this lesson. He has so far planked himself on reality that his characterization, which is the really remarkable, and, as regards his own gift as a dramatist, the conclusive part of the play, is altogether realistic. Further, it is to be noted that it is essentially comedic: that is to say, it is historically right. Peter, like the whole string of theatrical blackguards, from Gustavus Adolphus to Napoleon, who devastated Europe after the Renaissance, was essentially a hero of comedy, or rather of a frightful harlequinade raised to the dignity of comedy by its effects on human destiny, and by the irony with which its clowns were doomed, like Mephistopheles, to produce good by devising mischief. Take a single instance in the case of Peter. The seclusion of Russian women in the Terem was one of the sacred institutions of his country. Like most sacred institutions, it was perhaps the most deadly obstacle to social progress. There is not the smallest reason to suppose that Peter had any perception of this; but it was his hobby to imitate countries where women played the chief part in fashionable Society; and it was his personal taste to have women to get drunk with, to pour brandy down their throats by force, and to use their presence to heighten the zest of the indescribable indecencies which, next to drunkenness, were the staple of his festivities. Therefore he burst open the doors of the Terem and dragged the women out of it by main force. When the conservatism of Moscow withstood his threats of the knout, he provided, in St Petersburg, a new capital in which the tradition of womanly conduct was, from the first, not only free but scandalously licentious. Here, again, it is perfectly easy for our foolish hero-worshipping and hero-manufacturing idealists to discover in Peter the enlightenment of the author of A Doll's House. The real dramatic irony and historical interest of the situation lie in the fact that Peter's iconoclastic blackguardism, violence, and folly, indulged with the asinine naïveté which distinguishes him from such dashing rascals as Charles XII, broke down the prison walls against which Ibsen, had he been Tsar, would probably have written and argued in vain. It is the same with all Peter's great reforms: what he worked away at so titanically was the demolition of old Russia and the rebuilding of it according to his own personal tastes and habits, which, in so far as they were active, simple, wilful, utilitarian, open-air tastes and habits, were healthy and hopeful in comparison with those of old Russia, just as the tastes and habits of tramps and tinkers are healthy in comparison with those of scholarly bookworms and recluses. There is plenty of comedy in the possibility that a despotic bushranger might do a great deal of good where a despotic John Henry Newman might do a great deal of harm, though the personal ferocity and obscenity of the bushranger

286

might make the incidents of the comedy too hideous for enjoyment or laughter. But any attempt to make the bushranger tragic is out of the question.

The extent to which Mr Irving's instinct has outstripped his intellectual consciousness in divining this is shewn by the way in which he has dramatized Peter. His play is a comedy, grave only when it is too brutal to be laughed at. His Peter belongs to the family of Petruchio, not of Coriolanus, or even Richard III. The only mistake he makes in the invention of characteristic incident is in representing the Tsar as caring nothing about the running over of the child by his artillery; for Peter, regarding children as future cannon-fodder, was as terribly severe on infanticide as he was infinitely indulgent to illegitimacy. This, it will be admitted, is a tolerably venial slip. The scenes are written with immense vivacity and courage in frank, contemporary, vernacular English, exactly as a young dramatist with the right stuff in him would be sure to write it. The first act shews an altogether exceptional power and resource: you do not have to look at your play-bill to find out who is who. The incident of Tolstoi stirring all Peter's most sympathetic emotions by striking him is drama of the first order. Unfortunately no living English actor has yet proved himself capable of scoring such points. The second act is decidedly immature, though its most boyish passages have plenty of fun in them, and the grip of character remains perfectly sure throughout. Eudoxia is rather an innocent fiction; but it is astonishing how little Peter suffers, as a dramatic character, by the approach of the piously spurious ending. The resemblance of Catherine to Madame Sans-Gêne is only an unlucky accident. For stage purposes the two are one and the same character; and there is more historical warrant for the Catherine incidents (always barring the sentimental magnanimity to Eudoxia) in Mr Irving's play than for the Sans-Gêne incidents in M. Sardou's.

What the representation at the Lyceum is like, Heaven and my fellow-critics know: I do not. Sir Henry Irving has not invited me to witness it; and, under the circumstances, this is something more than an omission: it is an appeal to me to stay away. As there is certainly no need for any such modesty on Mr Laurence Irving's account, I take it that Sir Henry Irving is modest on his own. However, as he may be doing himself an injustice, I shall perhaps later on claim my right as a private individual to pay the Lyceum a visit without inflicting my criticism publicly on the manager.

THE COMEDY OF CALF-LOVE

A BACHELOR'S ROMANCE. A new comedy in four acts. By Miss Martha Morton. Globe Theatre, 8 January 1898.

[15 *January* 1898]

THE bitterest of prayers is the prayer that our prayers may not be granted; but it has been prayed ever since we discovered that the meanest trick our gods can play us is to take us at our word. This is not altogether because we so seldom know what is good for us: it just as often comes from our not liking what is good for us when we get it. My own case at present is worse even than this. I have unselfishly prayed for something that is good for the theatre; and now that the theatre has got it, it makes life bitter to me. My prayer was that contemporary drama might be brought up to the level of contemporary fiction. I pointed out that even the romances written by governesses and read by parlormaids were more literate, more decent, more fanciful than the coarse pleasantries and maudlin sentimentalities concocted by obsolete Bohemians for festive undergraduates. Now that the substitution has been effected, I am more than justified; for the change is not only a very manifest improvement, but is much appreciated by the public; yet to say that I enjoy it would be to say the thing that is not. It is not in man's nature to be grateful for negative mercies. When you have the toothache, the one happiness you desire is not to have it: when it is gone, you never dream of including its absence in your assets. Now that the pot-house drama no longer obtrudes its obscene existence on me, I find myself grumbling as much as ever at the deficiencies of the ladylike plays which have supplanted it.

My consolation is that ladylike drama, though it worries me as a critic, reassures me as a human being. The truth is, I am no longer what is invidiously called a young man. Like Mr Pinero and his Princess, I have turned forty, and am somewhat worn by industry and eld. Yet I find, by the unanimous testimony of the women who, as purveyors of the newest new drama, are breaking down the male monopoly of dramatic authorship in all directions, that the older I get, and the more I wrinkle, and the faster my grey hairs multiply, and the more flabbily my feet shuffle and my ideas footle, the more I shall be adored by their sex. I used to think that calf-love—the only love that deserves all the beautiful things the story-books say about the tender passion—was peculiar to the human male, and was, indeed, a mark of his superiority. But I now learn, from the latest fashion in plays, that the modern woman's dream is to be an old man's darling. In Sweet Nancy, revived last week at the Avenue, there was still one drop of bitterness left for me, since the hero, though fifty, was military. But in A Bachelor's Romance, at the Globe, the hero is not only an old fogey, but a literary man, with fads not altogether unlike my own. And the author is no unwomanly Ibsenite, but that womanliest of all women, the American woman. She was born in New York city; she received her education in a public school; and as a girl she contributed poetry and short stories to many magazines. Can anything be more womanly? If A Bachelor's Romance were her first play, I might misdoubt me that it was no more than the sowing of her wild oats. But it is not so: Miss Martha Morton has produced at least six plays, all apparently successful, since her Refugee's Daughter appeared eight years ago. Therefore I take the Globe play to be the expression of a mature, deliberate, experienced conviction that the most fascinating person in the world is a nice old literary gentleman between forty and sixty. Later on I may perhaps plead for an extension of these limits, encouraged by the fact that Mr Gladstone was never positively adored until he turned seventy; but for the present I am content to be just such an old dear as Mr Hare is now impersonating with a success that Don Juan has never attained. And, depend on it, this new dramatic theme will not be confined to one sex. It is in the air. There is a play called Candida, lately performed in the provinces by the Independent Theatre, in which the hero is under eighteen and the heroine a matron who confesses to "over thirty." Calf-love is the sentiment of the hour.

Miss Morton's success as a playwright is, of course, founded on a clear gift of telling stories and conjuring up imaginary people. But her easy conquest of managerial favor is due to the aptitude with which she sketches congenial and easily acted parts for good actors to fill up, and to that sympathy-catching disposition to be goodnatured at all costs, which is so very agreeable to the public just at present. I fancy if Mr Hare had to choose between playing for nothing in three extra performances of A Bachelor's Romance and carrying his portmanteau from Somerset House to the Globe Theatre, he would unhesitatingly submit to the three performances. Yes, easy as his task is, he gets as much applause as if the author were taxing his powers as severely as Ibsen. Mr Frederick Kerr, too, achieves an impersonation which, to the very coloring of his face and the thinning on the top of his wig, is masterly, at a cost to himself comparable to the lifting of an egg by Sandow. Miss May Harvey, one of the cleverest actresses we have, is almost dangerously underparted, like a heavy charge in a light gun; and Miss Susie Vaughan would be all the better for a little more stuff in her part to steady her. I confess I grudge four such players to a work so far inside their capacity: I had rather see them all groaning under grievous burthens. And yet I do not see how this flimsy, pretty, amusing, rather tender sort of play is to be worked up to concert pitch without better acting than it is artistically worth. Its commercial value, when fine talents are liberally wasted on it, is beyond question, but as it is not my business to judge plays by the standards of the board-room and box-office, I need not deny that there were moments during A Bachelor's Romance when the cheapness and spuriousness of the sentiment provoked a spasm of critical indignation in me. For instance, since Mr Hare has dealt so handsomely with Miss Morton's play, she might surely have provided him with some more subtle, or at least more sensible means of securing the sympathy of the audience than handing sovereigns about to needy people like a Jack Tar in a Surrey-side nautical melodrama. When Miss Susie Vaughan has to shew that the crusty old maid, Miss Clementina, has what London beggars call a feeling heart, she must be somewhat incommoded by having no more plausible statement to make on the subject than that when she wakes up in the morning she hears Sylvia singing under her window, and cannot tell which is the girl in the garden and which the lark in the heavens. This, I submit, is not poetry: it is gammon; and it destroys the verisimilitude of an otherwise passable character sketch. The play, in short, needs here and there just a little more sincerity to bring it up at all points even to its own impenitently romantic scale of illusion.

The second rank of the company is nearly as good as an ordinary West End front rank. Mr Gilbert Hare amuses himself cleverly but nonsensically by playing a very old man, a sort of folly in which his father wasted too much of his prime. I challenge Mr Gilbert Hare to look at himself in the glass whilst he is doing that dance—"one, two, three: one, two, three"—in the third act, and to say whether any extremity of white wig and painted wrinkles could turn the quicksilver in his legs into chalkstones.

Will Miss Morton and other American authors please note that the art of writing plays without explanatory asides has been brought to perfection here, and that the English high-critical nose is apt to turn up at dramatists who have not mastered it. And will Mr Hare remonstrate seriously with his musical director for inflicting on an audience which never injured him a so-called "overture" entitled The Globe, consisting of an irritating string of national anthems, and finally dragging the audience out of their seats with God save the Queen. It did not inconvenience me personally, because even if I were the most loyal of subjects I should not stand up on my hind legs like a poodle for every person who waved a stick and played a tune at me; but the more compliant people can hardly enjoy being disturbed except on special occasions.

Sweet Nancy seemed to me a little stale at the Avenue: Miss Hughes, with all her cleverness, played it on the first night as if she had had enough of it. Miss Thornhill, the lessee, plays Mrs Huntly, presumably for practice. Miss Lena Ashwell is now the Barbara Gray. In the first act she does one of her wonderful exits, which almost bring the house after her with a rush; but the part is quite beneath her; and I deliberately came away at the end of the second act because I knew she would get round me in the pathetic bit in the third if I waited.

CHURCH AND STAGE

THE CONVERSION OF ENGLAND. An ecclesiastical drama in two scenes. By the Rev. Henry Cresswell. Performed in the Great Hall of the Church House, Westminster, 13 January 1898.

[22 *January* 1898]

IT has come at last. Again and again in these columns I have warned the managers—or rather the syndicates: a manager nowadays is only the man in possession—that they would be supplanted by the parsons if they did not take their business a little more seriously. I meant no more by this than that the modern Church, with its attractive musical services carefully advertised in the hall of the local hotel side by side with the pantomimes, would finally be discovered by the playgoer as a much pleasanter, cheaper, wholesomer, restfuller, more recreative place to spend a couple of hours in than a theatre. But now the parson has carried the war into the enemy's country. He has dramatized the lessons of the Church, and is acting them with scenery, costumes, lime-light, music, processions, and everything complete in Church House great halls which hold £200 easily. Not that he charges for admission: such worldliness is as far from him as from the Independent Theatre when it performs Ibsen's Ghosts. But just as the Independent Theatre encourages the New Drama by inviting those who subscribe to it to witness Ghosts; so the charitable persons who subscribe to the Waifs and Strays Society, to the building of St Peter's Church, South Tottenham, or the parish of St

Ann, South Lambeth, receive, to their surprise and delight, a reserved seat or seats for the performance of The Conversion of England, in positions which, by a remarkable coincidence, are spectatorially favorable in proportion to the number of half-sovereigns, crowns, or half-crowns contained in the subscription. And the view is not obstructed by *matinée* hats; for before the performance a clergyman, clad with the whole authority of the Church of England, steps before the curtain and orders those hats to come off. What is more, they actually do come off, except in those desperate cases in which the hat and the hair, all in one piece, are equally foreign to the wearer. There is no band to play the overture to Mireille and Mr German's Lyceum dances for the 735th time: instead, the choir sings a hymn, and the audience may stand up and join in it if it likes. Further, the scenery consists of pictures, with all the capacity of pictures for beauty and poetry. Unroll one painted cloth and you are in Rome: unroll another and you are in Britain. This may seem a small matter to people who have no eye for pictures, and who love nothing better than a built-in stage drawing room full of unquestionable carpets and curtains and furniture from Hampton's and Maple's, not to mention a Swan & Edgar windowful of costumes. But if these worthy people only knew how much of the dullness and monotony of modern fashionable drama is produced by the fact that on the stage nowadays "three removes are as bad as a fire," and how much livelier the old adventurous plays, with a change of scene every ten minutes, were than the modern drama chained for forty-five minutes at a time to the impedimenta of Jack Hinton's Rooms in Whitehall Court and the like, they would understand what a formidable rival the miracle play in ten short scenes may prove to fixture plays in three long ones by any but the ablest hands.

There is another point on which, in the present excited state of public feeling on the question of actors' morals, I touch with trembling. To say that the clergymen who enact the miracle plays speak better than actors is nothing; for at present all the professions and most of the trades can make the same boast. But the difference is something more than a technical one. The tone of a man's voice is the tone of his life. The average clergyman's utterance betrays his ignorance, his conceit, his class narrowness, his snobbery, and his conception of religion as an official authorization of all these offences so unmistakeably that in a lawless community he would be shot at sound as a mad dog is shot at sight. But the clergymen who are coming into the field against the managers are not average clergymen. The Conversion of England on their playbills means something more than the title of an entertainment; and that something is not the conversion of England's follies and vices into box-office returns. At the Westminster performance last Saturday the actors spoke as men speak in the presence of greater matters than their own personal success. You may go to the theatre for months without hearing that particular dramatic effect. The men who can make it will finally play the men who cannot make it off the stage, in spite of the hankering of the public after the vulgarities which keep its own worst qualities in countenance. I should add, by the way, that the applause which our actors declare they cannot do without was excommunicated in the Church House like the hats, and that the effect on the performance was highly beneficial.

As to Mr Cresswell's drama, I cannot speak with any confidence. I came to it from a round of duties which included such works as Never Again at the Vaudeville; so that the mere force of contrast made it perfectly enthralling to me. When the British Bishop, objecting to the Roman missionaries, exclaimed "The whole world is heretic! There is no knowledge of the truth anywhere except at Bangor," I shrieked with laughter. No doubt it was not a first-class joke; but after the dreary equivoques of the farcical comedians it was as manna in the wilderness. Indeed, I suspect Mr Cresswell of being more of a humorist than he pretends. I dare not flatly assert that his sketch of Bertha, the Christian Queen of Kent, is a lively caricature of some Mrs Proudie who oppressed him in his early curacies; but I will quote a sample of the lady and leave my readers to draw their own conclusions. Sebba, the priest of Woden ("pagan, I regret to say," as Mr Pecksniff observed), tells the pious princess that the gods have declared a certain fact by an oracle. Here is her reply, to be delivered, according to the stage directions, with an incredulous smile. "Ah!—*your* gods, Sebba! They must be very clever gods to be able to tell you what they do not know themselves. [*Aside*] I scarcely dare to interfere. These people are so attached to their superstitions. Poor souls, they know no better!"

The Conversion of England evades censorship by not taking money at the doors. Otherwise the Lord Chamberlain would probably suppress it, unless Mr Cresswell consented to cut out the religious passages, and assimilate the rest to Gentleman Joe and Dandy Dan.

The controversy about the morality of the stage has been stabbed stone dead by an epigram. Mr Buchanan's "Thousands of virtuous women on the stage, but only six actresses!" is so irresistible that it is exceedingly difficult to say anything more without anti-climax. Nevertheless there are one or two points that had better be clearly understood. First, that there has been no genuine moral discussion. In England there never is. Our habit of flooding the newspapers with prurient paragraphs about women, whether actresses or duchesses matters not a rap, is not a habit of threshing out moral questions. But even on this trivial ground Mr Clement Scott's position remains entirely unshaken. He made his charge in terms of the perfectly well-understood marriage morality on which, to cite a leading case, Parnell was driven out of public life and a great political combination wrecked. The theatrical profession may profess that morality or it may repudiate it. When Ibsen, following the footsteps of the great hierarchy of illustrious teachers who have made war on it, attacked it with intense bitterness in Ghosts, those who supported him were vilified in terms compared to which Mr Clement Scott's strictures are enthusiastic eulogies. The issue between natural human morality and the mechanical character tests of Mr Stead was then vehemently raised in the theatrical world by Mr Scott himself. Its leaders, I am sorry to say, ranged themselves on the side of Mr Stead with sanctimonious promptitude. The rod they helped to pickle then, and which they laid so zealously on Ibsen's back, has now been laid on their own; and I should be more than human if I did not chuckle at their shrieks of splendid silence. Mr Buchanan, whilst chivalrously refusing to join in the cowardly rush which has been made at Mr Scott under the very mistaken impression that he is down, declares that a profession that can boast such names as those of—he mentions six leading actors and actresses—should surely disdain to defend itself against Mr Scott's charges. As to that, I beg to point out remorselessly that at least three out of the six are artists whose characters on the point at issue must notoriously stand or fall with that of Parnell, and that these very three are the most admired, the most respected, the most unshamed and un-ashamed, the most publicly and privately honored members of their profession. What should we think of them if they were to burst into frenzied accusations of falsehood and calumny against Mr Scott, and exculpatory asserverations of their own perfect con-formity to Mr Stead's ideal? They would at once put themselves in the wrong, not only from the point of view of Mr Stead and of a devout Roman Catholic critic bound by his Church to regard even the marriage of divorced persons as a deadly sin, but from any point of view that discountenances flagrant and cowardly hypocrisy. The gentlemen who are just now so busily claiming Mr Stead's certificate of "purity" for our most esteemed English actresses had better ask those ladies first whether they would accept it if it were offered to them.

Do not let it be supposed, however, that the hypocrisy is all on one side. I have before me a pile of press cuttings from such papers as Great Thoughts, the Christian Commonwealth, the Christian Million, and the British Weekly, from which I learn that I am held to have testified, with Mr Clement Scott, that the theatre is so evil a place and its professors so evil a people, that "so long as women are exposed to such temptations and perils as Mr Clement Scott describes, no man who reverences woman as Christ rever-enced her can possibly support the stage." These are the words of Mr Hugh Price Hughes. I am sorry we have led Mr Hughes to deceive himself in this matter. The only authority I have at hand as to Christ's view of the subject is the Bible; and I do not find there that in his reverence for humanity he drew Mr Stead's line at publicans or sinners, or accepted the marriage laws of his time as having any moral authority. Indeed, I gather that his object was to discredit legal tests of conduct, and that he would not have objected to go to the theatre on Sunday with Mary Magdalene if Jerusalem had been Paris. However, I will not rest my case on these pious claptraps. Mr Price Hughes knows as well as I do that women are employed in the manufacture of sacred books on terms which make the prostitution of a certain percentage of them virtually compulsory. He knows that no actress is trampled into the gin-sodden degradation of the wretched laundresses who provide the whited walls of starched shirt that make his congregation look so respectable on Sunday. He knows that many a church and chapel in this country would fall into ruin without the conscience money of traders who pay girls from five to seven shillings a week to exhaust in their shops and factories the strength nourished on the contributions of their sweethearts. And he ought to know that the stage, of which neither I nor Mr Clement Scott has said the worst, is nevertheless, from the point of view of the consideration shewn to women on it, and the wages paid to them, much more worthy of his support than any other commercially supported English institution whatsoever, the Methodist churches not excepted. And so, reverend gentlemen, do not give sceptical persons like myself occasion to scoff by an outburst of Pharisaism. Never mind the mote in the actor's eye: you will find plenty of beams behind the spectacles of your own congregations.

TAPPERTIT ON CÆSAR

JULIUS CÆSAR. Her Majesty's Theatre, 22 January 1898.

[29 *January* 1898]

THE truce with Shakespear is over. It was only possible whilst Hamlet was on the stage. Hamlet is the tragedy of private life—nay, of individual bachelor-poet life. It belongs to a detached residence, a select library, an exclusive circle, to no occupation, to fathomless boredom, to impenitent mugwumpism, to the illusion that the futility of these things is the futility of existence, and its contemplation philosophy: in short, to the dream-fed gentleman-ism of the age which Shakespear inaugurated in English litera-ture: the age, that is, of the rising middle class bringing into power the ideas taught it by its servants in the kitchen, and its fathers in the shop—ideas now happily passing away as the on-slaught of modern democracy offers to the kitchen-taught and home-bred the alternative of achieving a real superiority or going ignominiously under in the class conflict.

It is when we turn to Julius Cæsar, the most splendidly written political melodrama we possess, that we realize the apparently im-mortal author of Hamlet as a man, not for all time, but for an age only, and that, too, in all solidly wise and heroic aspects, the most despicable of all the ages in our history. It is impossible for even the most judicially minded critic to look without a revulsion of indignant contempt at this travestying of a great man as a silly braggart, whilst the pitiful gang of mischief-makers who de-stroyed him are lauded as statesmen and patriots. There is not a single sentence uttered by Shakespear's Julius Cæsar that is, I will not say worthy of him, but even worthy of an average Tam-many boss. Brutus is nothing but a familiar type of English sub-urban preacher: politically he would hardly impress the Thames Conservancy Board. Cassius is a vehemently assertive nonentity. It is only when we come to Antony, unctuous voluptuary and self-seeking sentimental demagogue, that we find Shakespear in his depth; and in his depth, of course, he is superlative. Regarded as a crafty stage job, the play is a triumph: rhetoric, claptrap, effec-tive gushes of emotion, all the devices of the popular playwright, are employed with a profusion of power that almost breaks their backs. No doubt there are slips and slovenliness of the kind that careful revisers eliminate; but they count for so little in the mass of accomplishment that it is safe to say that the dramatist's art can be carried no further on that plane. If Goethe, who under-stood Cæsar and the significance of his death—"the most sense-less of deeds" he called it—had treated the subject, his conception of it would have been as superior to Shakespear's as St John's

Gospel is to the Police News; but his treatment could not have been more magnificently successful. As far as sonority, imagery, wit, humor, energy of imagination, power over language, and a whimsically keen eye for idiosyncrasies can make a dramatist, Shakespear was the king of dramatists. Unfortunately, a man may have them all, and yet conceive high affairs of state exactly as Simon Tappertit did. In one of the scenes in Julius Cæsar a conceited poet bursts into the tent of Brutus and Cassius, and exhorts them not to quarrel with one another. If Shakespear had been able to present his play to the ghost of the great Julius, he would probably have had much the same reception. He certainly would have deserved it.

When it was announced that Mr Tree had resolved to give special prominence to the character of Cæsar in his acting version, the critics winked, and concluded simply that the actor-manager was going to play Antony and not Brutus. Therefore I had better say that Mr Tree must stand acquitted of any belittlement of the parts which compete so strongly with his own. Before going to Her Majesty's I was curious enough to block out for myself a division of the play into three acts; and I found that Mr Tree's division corresponded exactly with mine. Mr Waller's opportunities as Brutus, and Mr McLeay's as Cassius, are limited only by their own ability to take advantage of them; and Mr Louis Calvert figures as boldly in the public eye as he did in his own production of Antony and Cleopatra last year at Manchester. Indeed, Mr Calvert is the only member of the company who achieves an unequivocal success. The preference expressed in the play by Cæsar for fat men may, perhaps, excuse Mr Calvert for having again permitted himself to expand after his triumphant reduction of his girth for his last appearance in London. However, he acted none the worse: in fact, nobody else acted so skilfully or originally. The others, more heavily burdened, did their best, quite in the spirit of the man who had never played the fiddle, but had no doubt he could if he tried. Without oratory, without style, without specialized vocal training, without any practice worth mentioning, they assaulted the play with cheerful self-sufficiency, and gained great glory by the extent to which, as a masterpiece of the playwright's trade, it played itself. Some small successes were not lacking. Cæsar's nose was good: Calpurnia's bust was worthy of her: in such parts Garrick and Siddons could have achieved no more. Miss Evelyn Millard's Roman matron in the style of Richardson—Cato's daughter as Clarissa —was an unlooked-for novelty; but it cost a good deal of valuable time to get in the eighteenth century between the lines of the first B.C. By operatic convention—the least appropriate of all conventions—the boy Lucius was played by Mrs Tree, who sang Sullivan's ultra-nineteenth-century Orpheus with his Lute, modulations and all, to a pizzicato accompaniment supposed to be played on a lyre with eight open and unstoppable strings, a feat complexly and absurdly impossible. Mr Waller, as Brutus, failed in the first half of the play. His intention clearly was to represent Brutus as a man superior to fate and circumstance; but the effect he produced was one of insensibility. Nothing could have been more unfortunate; for it is through the sensibility of Brutus that the audience have to learn what they cannot learn from the phlegmatic pluck of Casca or the narrow vindictiveness of Cassius: that is, the terrible momentousness, the harrowing anxiety and dread, of the impending catastrophe. Mr Waller left that function to the thunderstorm. From the death of Cæsar onward he was better; and his appearance throughout was effective; but at best his sketch was a water-color one. Mr Franklyn McLeay carried off the honors of the evening by his deliberate staginess and imposing assumptiveness: that is, by as much of the grand style as our playgoers now understand; but in the last act he was monotonously violent, and died the death of an incorrigible poseur, not of a noble Roman. Mr Tree's memory failed him as usual; and a good deal of the technical part of his work was botched and haphazard, like all Shakespearean work nowadays; nevertheless, like Mr Calvert, he made the audience believe in the reality of the character before them. But it is impossible to praise his performance in detail. I cannot recall any single passage in the scene after the murder that was well done: in fact, he only secured an effective curtain by bringing Calpurnia on the stage to attitudinize over Cæsar's body. To say that the demagogic oration in the Forum produced its effect is nothing; for its effect is inevitable, and Mr Tree neither made the most of it nor handled it with any pretence of mastery or certainty. But he was not stupid, nor inane, nor Bard-of-Avon ridden; and he contrived to interest the audience in Antony instead of trading on their ready-made interest in Mr Beerbohm Tree. And for that many sins may be forgiven him nowadays, when the playgoer, on first nights at all events, goes to see the cast rather than the play.

What is missing in the performance, for want of the specific Shakespearean skill, is the Shakespearean music. When we come to those unrivalled grandiose passages in which Shakespear turns on the full organ, we want to hear the sixteen-foot pipes booming, or, failing them (as we often must, since so few actors are naturally equipped with them), the ennobled tone, and the tempo suddenly steadied with the majesty of deeper purpose. You have, too, those moments when the verse, instead of opening up the depths of sound, rises to its most brilliant clangor, and the lines ring like a thousand trumpets. If we cannot have these effects, or if we can only have genteel drawing room arrangements of them, we cannot have Shakespear; and that is what is mainly the matter at Her Majesty's: there are neither trumpets nor pedal pipes there. The conversation is metrical and emphatic in an elocutionary sort of way; but it makes no distinction between the arid prairies of blank verse which remind one of Henry VI at its crudest, and the places where the morass suddenly piles itself into a mighty mountain. Cassius in the first act has a twaddling forty-line speech, base in its matter and mean in its measure, followed immediately by the magnificent torrent of rhetoric, the first burst of true Shakespearean music in the play, beginning—

Why, man, he doth bestride the narrow world
Like a Colossus, and we petty men
Walk under his huge legs and peep about
To find ourselves dishonorable graves.

301

I failed to catch the slightest change of elevation or reinforcement of feeling when Mr McLeay passed from one to the other. His tone throughout was dry; and it never varied. By dint of energetic, incisive articulation, he drove his utterances harder home than the others; but the best lines seemed to him no more than the worst: there were no heights and depths, no contrast of black thunder-cloud and flaming lightning flash, no stirs and surprises. Yet he was not inferior in oratory to the rest. Mr Waller certainly cannot be reproached with dryness of tone; and his delivery of the speech in the Forum was perhaps the best piece of formal elocution we got; but he also kept at much the same level throughout, and did not at any moment attain to anything that could be called grandeur. Mr Tree, except for a conscientiously desperate effort to cry havoc and let slip the dogs of war in the robustious manner, with no better result than to all but extinguish his voice, very sensibly left oratory out of the question, and tried conversational sincerity, which answered so well that his delivery of "This was the noblest Roman of them all" came off excellently.

The real hero of the revival is Mr Alma Tadema. The scenery and stage coloring deserve everything that has been said of them. But the illusion is wasted by want of discipline and want of thought behind the scenes. Every carpenter seems to make it a point of honor to set the cloths swinging in a way that makes Rome reel and the audience positively seasick. In Brutus's house the door is on the spectators' left: the knocks on it come from the right. The Roman soldiers take the field each man with his two javelins neatly packed up like a fishing-rod. After a battle, in which they are supposed to have made the famous Roman charge, hurling these javelins in and following them up sword in hand, they come back carrying the javelins still undisturbed in their rug-straps, in perfect trim for a walk-out with the nursery-maids of Philippi.

The same want of vigilance appears in the acting version. For example, though the tribunes Flavius and Marullus are replaced by two of the senators, the lines referring to them by name are not altered. But the oddest oversight is the retention in the tent scene of the obvious confusion of the original version of the play, in which the death of Portia was announced to Brutus by Messala, with the second version, into which the quarrel scene was written to strengthen the fourth act. In this version Brutus, already in possession of the news, reveals it to Cassius. The play has come down to us with the two alternative scenes strung together; so that Brutus's reception of Messala's news, following his own revelation of it to Cassius, is turned into a satire on Roman fortitude, the suggestion being that the secret of the calm with which a noble Roman received the most terrible tidings in public was that it had been carefully imparted to him in private beforehand. Mr Tree has not noticed this; and the two scenes are gravely played one after the other at Her Majesty's. This does not matter much to our playgoers, who never venture to use their common sense when Shakespear is in question; but it wastes time. Mr Tree may without hesitation cut out Pindarus and Messala, and go straight on from the bowl of wine to Brutus's question about Philippi.

The music, composed for the occasion by Mr Raymond Roze, made me glad that I had already taken care to acknowledge the value of Mr Roze's services to Mr Tree; for this time he has missed the Roman vein rather badly. To be a Frenchman was once no disqualification for the antique, because French musicians used to be brought up on Gluck as English ones were brought up on Handel. But Mr Roze composes as if Gluck had been supplanted wholly in his curriculum by Gounod and Bizet. If that prelude to the third act were an attempt to emulate the overtures to Alceste or Iphigenia I could have forgiven it. But to give us the soldiers' chorus from Faust, crotchet for crotchet and triplet for triplet, with nothing changed but the notes, was really too bad.

I am sorry I must postpone until next week all consideration of Mr Pinero's Trelawny of the Wells. The tragic circumstances under which I do are as follows. The manager of the Court Theatre, Mr Arthur Chudleigh, did not honor the Saturday Review with the customary invitation to the first performance.

When a journal is thus slighted, it has no resource but to go to its telephone and frantically offer any terms to the box-offices for a seat for the first night. But on fashionable occasions the manager is always master of the situation: there are never any seats to be had except from himself. It was so on this occasion; and the Saturday Review was finally brought to its knees at the feet of the Sloane Square telephone. In response to a humble appeal, the instrument scornfully replied that "three lines of adverse criticism were of no use to it." Naturally my curiosity was excited to an extraordinary degree by the fact that the Court Theatre telephone, which knew all about Mr Pinero's comedy, should have such a low opinion of it as to be absolutely certain that it would deserve an unprecedentedly contemptuous treatment at my hands. I instantly purchased a place for the fourth performance, Charlotte Corday and Julius Cæsar occupying my time on the second and third nights; and I am now in a position to assure that telephone that its misgivings were strangely unwarranted, and that, if it will excuse my saying so, it does not know a good comedietta when it sees one. Reserving my reasons for next week, I offer Mr Pinero my apologies for a delay which is not my own fault. (Will the Mining Journal please copy, as Mr Pinero reads no other paper during the current fortnight?)

I find this article has already run to such a length that I must postpone consideration of Charlotte Corday also, merely remarking for the present that I wish the play was as attractive as the heroine.

MR PINERO'S PAST

CHARLOTTE CORDAY. A drama in four acts. Anonymous. Adelphi
  Theatre, 21 January 1898.
TRELAWNY OF THE WELLS. An original comedietta in four acts.
  By Arthur W. Pinero. Court Theatre, 20 January 1898.

[5 *February* 1898]

MR PINERO has not got over it yet. That fatal turning-point in life, the fortieth birthday, still oppresses him. In The Princess and the Butterfly he unbosomed himself frankly, making his soul's trouble the open theme of his play. But this was taken in such extremely bad part by myself and others (gnawed by the same sorrow) that he became shy on the subject, and, I take it, began to cast about for some indirect means of returning to it. It seems to have occurred to him at last that by simply shewing on the stage the fashions of forty years ago, the crinoline, the flounced skirt, the garibaldi, the turban hat, the chenille net, the horse-hair sofa, the peg-top trouser, and the "weeper" whisker, the chord of memory could be mutely struck without wounding my vanity. The delicacy of this mood inspires the whole play, which has touched me more than anything else Mr Pinero has ever written.

But first let me get these old fashions—or rather these middle-aged fashions: after all, one is not Methuselah—off my mind. It is significant of the difference between my temperament and Mr Pinero's, that when he, as a little boy, first heard Ever of thee I'm fondly dreaming, he wept; whereas, at the same tender age, I simply noted with scorn the obvious plagiarism from Cheer, Boys, Cheer.

To me the sixties waft ballads by Virginia Gabriel and airs from Il Trovatore; but Mr Pinero's selection is none the less right; for Virginia Gabriel belonged to Cavendish Square and not to Bagnigge Wells; and Il Trovatore is still alive, biding its time to break out again when M. Jean de Reszke also takes to fondly dreaming.

The costumes at the Court Theatre are a mixture of caricature and realism. Miss Hilda Spong, whose good looks attain most happily to the 1860 ideal (Miss Ellen Terry had not then been invented), is dressed exactly after Leech's broadest caricatures of crinolined English maidenhood; whereas Miss Irene Vanbrugh clings to the finer authority of Millais' masterly illustrations to Trollope. None of the men are properly dressed: the "lounge coat" which we all wear unblushingly today as a jacket, with its corners sloped away in front, and its length behind involving no friction with the seats of our chairs, then clung nervously to the traditions of the full coat, and was longer, straighter, rectangular

—cornerder and franker as to the shoulders than Mr Pinero has been able to persuade the tailors of the Court Theatre to make it today. I imagine, too, that Cockney dialect has changed a good deal since then. Somewhere in the eighties, Mr Andrew Tuer pointed out in the Pall Mall Gazette that the conventional representations in fiction of London pronunciation had ceased to bear any recognizable relation to the actual speech of the coster and the flower-girl; and Mr Anstey, in Punch, was the first author to give general literary currency to Mr Tuer's new phonetics. The lingo of Sam Weller had by that time passed away from London, though suggestions of it may be heard even today no further off than Hounslow. Sir Henry Irving can no longer be ridiculed, as he was in the seventies, for substituting pure vowel sounds for the customary colloquial diphthongs; for the man in the street, without at all aiming at the virtuosity of our chief actor, has himself independently introduced a novel series of pure vowels. Thus *i* has become *aw*, and *ow ah*. In spite of Sir Henry, *o* has not been turned into a true vowel; but it has become a very marked *ow*, whilst the English *a* is changed to a flagrant *i*. There is, somewhere in the old files of All the Year Round a Dickensian description of an illiterate lady giving a reading. Had she been represented as saying, "The scene tikes plice dahn in the Mawl En' Rowd" (takes place down in the Mile End Road) Dickens would apparently not have understood the sentence, which no Londoner with ears can now mistake. On these grounds, I challenge the pronunciation of Avonia Bunn, in the person of Miss Pattie Browne, as an anachronism. I feel sure that if Avonia had made *so* rhyme to *thou* in the sixties, she would have been understood to have alluded to the feminine pig. On this point, however, my personal authority is not conclusive, as I did not reach London until the middle of the seventies. In England everything is twenty years out of date before it gets printed; and it may be that the change had been in operation long before it was accurately observed. It has also to be considered that the old literary school never dreamt of using its eyes or ears, and would invent descriptions of sights and sounds with an academic self-sufficiency which led later on to its death from acute and incurable imposture. Its ghost still walks in our resurrectionary reviewing enterprises, with precipitous effects on the circulation.

It is not in the nature of things possible that Mr Pinero's first variation on the theme of The Princess should be successfully acted by a modern London company. If he had scoured the provinces and America for elderly actors, thirty years out of date, and, after raising their wildest hopes by a London engagement, met them at rehearsal with the brutal announcement that they were only wanted to burlesque themselves, the thing might doubtless have been done. But every line of the play proclaims the author incapable of such heartlessness. There are only two members of the "theatrical-folk" section of the cast who carry much conviction; and these are the two Robertsonians, to whom success comes only with the then new order. Miss Irene Vanbrugh is quite the woman who was then the New Woman; and Mr Paul Arthur, a contemporary American, only needs to seize the distinction made by the Atlantic between "comedy" and "cawmedy" to hit off the historical moment of the author of Caste to perfection. And Miss Spong's fairness, fortunately, is universal enough to fit all the centuries and all the decades. But when we come to Ferdinand Gadd, the leading juvenile of The Wells, we find Mr Gerald Du Maurier in a difficulty. At his age his only chance of doing anything with the part is to suggest Sir Henry Irving in embryo. But Mr Pinero has not written it that way: he has left Ferdinand Gadd in the old groove as completely as Mr Crummles was. The result is that the part falls between two stools. The Telfers also miss the mark. Mr Athol Forde, the English creator of Kroll in Rosmersholm, is cut off from the sixties by a mighty gulf. Mrs Telfer's criticism of stage queens as being "considered merely as parts, not worth a tinker's oath," is not founded on the real experience of Mrs Saker, whose career has run on lighter lines. My own age in the sixties was so tender that I cannot pretend to know with any nicety what the "principal boy" of the pantomime was like in her petticoats as a private person at that period; but I have a strong suspicion that she tended to be older and occasionally stouter than the very latest thing in that line; and it is the ultra-latest thing that Miss Pattie Browne has studied for Avonia Bunn. On the whole I doubt whether the Court company knows a scrap more about the professional atmosphere of the old "Wells" than the audience.

The "non-theatrical folk" came off better, with one exception. I know that Mr Dion Boucicault as Sir William Gower can claim a long-established stage convention in favor of his method of portraying crusty senility. But I have grown out of all endurance of that convention. It is no more like a real old man than a worn-out billiard table is like a meadow; and it wastes and worries and perverts the talent of an actor perfectly capable of making a sincere study of the part. We would all, I believe, willingly push the stage old man into the grave upon whose brink he has been cackling and doddering as long as we can remember him. If my vengeance could pursue him beyond the tomb, it should not stop there. But so far, at least, he shall go if my malice can prevail against him. Miss Isabel Bateman is almost charming as Sir William's ancient sister, and would be quite so if she also were not touched by the tradition that old age, in comedy, should always be made ridiculous. Mr James Erskine is generally understood to be a Lordling, and, as such, a feeble amateur actor. I am bound to say, in defence of a trampled aristocracy, that he rose superior to the accident of birth, and acted his part as well as it could be acted. This, I observe, is explained away on the ground that he has only to be himself on the stage. I can only reply that the accomplishment of a feat so extremely difficult entitles him to count the explanation as a very high compliment. Mr Sam Sothern gives us a momentary glimpse of Lord Dundreary: I wonder what the younger generation thinks of it? Miss Irene Vanbrugh, in the title part, which is not, to tell the truth, a difficult one in the hands of the right person, vanquishes it easily and successfully, getting quite outside those comic relief lines within which her lot has been so often cast.

As to the play itself, its charm, as I have already hinted, lies in a certain delicacy which makes me loth to lay my critical fingers on it. The life that it reproduces had been already portrayed in the real sixties by Dickens in his sketch of the Crummles company, and by Anthony Trollope in his chronicles of Barsetshire. I cannot pretend to think that Mr Pinero, in reverting to that period, has really had to turn back the clock as far as his own sympathies and ideals are concerned. It seems to me that the world is to him still the world of Johnny Eames and Lily Dale, Vincent Crummles and Newman Noggs: his Paula Tanquerays and Mrs Ebbsmiths appearing as pure aberrations whose external differences he is able to observe as far as they can be observed without the inner clue, but whose point of view he has never found. That is why Mr Pinero, as a critic of the advanced guard in modern life, is unendurable to me. When I meet a musician of the old school, and talk Rossini and Bellini and Donizetti, Spohr and Mendelssohn and Meyerbeer with him, we get on excellently together; for the music that is so empty and wooden and vapid and mechanical to the young lions of Bayreuth, is full of sentiment, imagination, and dramatic force to us. But when he begins to deplore the "passing craze" for Wagner, and to explain the horrors and errors of the Bayreuth school: its lack of melody, its perpetual "recitative," its tearing discords, its noisy orchestration overwhelming and ruining the human voice, I get up and flee. The unsympathetic discourse about Wagner may be wittier than the sympathetic discourse about Donizetti; but that does not make it any the more tolerable to me, the speaker having passed from a subject he understands to one that has virtually no existence for him. It is just so with Mr Pinero. When he plays me the tunes of 1860, I appreciate and sympathize. Every stroke touches me: I dwell on the dainty workmanship shewn in the third and fourth acts: I rejoice in being old enough to know the world of his dreams. But when he comes to 1890, then I thank my stars that he does not read the Saturday Review. Please remember that it is the spirit and not the letter of the date that I insist on. The Benefit of the Doubt is dressed in the fashions of today; but it might have been written by Trollope. Trelawny of the Wells confessedly belongs to the days of Lily Dale. And whenever Lily Dale and not Mrs Ebbsmith is in question, Mr Pinero may face with complete equanimity the risk of picking up the Saturday Review in mistake for the Mining Journal.

Very different are my sentiments towards the author of Charlotte Corday at the Adelphi, whoever he may be. He has missed a rare chance of giving our playgoers a lesson they richly deserve. Jean Paul Marat, "people's friend" and altruist *par excellence*, was a man just after their own hearts—a man whose virtue consisted in burning indignation at the sufferings of others and an intense desire to see them balanced by an exemplary retaliation. That is to say, his morality was the morality of the melodrama, and of the gallery which applauds frantically when the hero knocks the villain down. It is only by coarsely falsifying Marat's character that he has been made into an Adelphi villain—nay, prevented from bringing down the house as an Adelphi hero, as he certainly would if the audience could be shewn the horrors that provoked him and the personal disinterestedness and sincerity with which he threw himself into a war of extermination against tyranny. Ibsen may have earned the right to prove by the example of such men as Marat that these virtues were the making of a scoundrel more mischievous than the most openly vicious aristocrat for whose head he clamored; but the common run of our playgoers will have none of Ibsen's morality, and as much of Marat's as our romantic dramatists can stuff them with. Charlotte Corday herself was simply a female Marat. She, too, hated tyranny and idealized her passionate instinct for bloody retaliation. There is the true tragic irony in Marat's death at her hand: it was not really murder: it was suicide—Marat slain by the spirit of Marat. No bad theme for a playwright capable of handling it!

What the Adelphi play must seem to anyone who understands this situation, I need not say. On its own conventional stage lines, it appears as a page of romantic history, exciting as the police intelligence is exciting, but not dramatic. Mr Kyrle Bellew's Marat is a made-up business, extremely disfiguring to himself, which could be done as well or better by any other actor in the very competent company. Mrs Brown Potter is everything that can be desired from the pictorial point of view (school of Delaroche); and her cleverness and diligence carry her successfully through all the theatrical business of the part. Miss Mabel Hackney and Mr Vibart gain some ground by their playing: the older hands do not lose any. But the play is of no real importance.

MANCHESTER STILL EXPIATING

[12 *February* 1898]

MR WILLIAM ARCHER, speaking at the Royal Institute of British Architects on Monday last, said that the endowed theatre was in the air. That, I may remark, is precisely where it has been for a long time. The problem is to get it on the ground. It appears that Manchester is about to lead the way. It is noteworthy that Manchester always does lead the way in such matters. Its artistic activity, highly abnormal in England, is a reaction from starvation. Manchester is an ugly place—a quite infernally ugly place. It is a brutally noisy place; for its ponderous traffic can only be borne by the roughest stone pavements. It is a demoralized place; because the development of the cotton industry there enabled the founders of its prosperity (meaning the aforesaid ugliness and noisiness) to amass huge fortunes by the diligent exercise of their moral deficiencies. Its great inventors were mere tinkers: I have gone through a first-rate modern cotton mill without any other feeling than one of astonishment that the human race, centuries after it had achieved such a comparative masterpiece of ingenuity as the common kitchen clock, should have so far degenerated as to take about a hundred years to perfect the trite and obvious arrangements which were exhibited to me as the triumphs of modern yarn-spinning mechanism. For Manchester is hugely proud of itself, vanity being the most constant symptom of a shameful life. But Man, always scheming to degrade himself, struggles in vain against the destiny of his spirit. The artistic institutions which only exist in London as accidents of the fashion, wealth, and cosmopolitanism of the capital of the world, were founded in Manchester by design. Manchester has had for forty years one of the first classical orchestras in the world. Manchester summoned the greatest English dramatic painter of the nineteenth century to do his best on the walls of its town hall when London could see in him only a butt for the most foolish of her witlings. It was worth a manager's while to produce, and produce superbly, such works as Byron's Sardanapalus in Manchester whilst the West End of London declared that even Shakespear spelt ruin. For any sort of London parallel to the parts played in Manchester by Hallé, Ford Madox Brown, and Charles Calvert, we have to turn to the work of August Manns at the Crystal Palace, and of Phelps at Sadler's Wells, there being no parallel at all in the case of the great painter. Even in these suburban triumphs of individual persistence and devotion, London, as a whole, can claim no such share as Manchester can in the work of its artistic heroes. Manchester, too, has had of late years its Independent Theatre and its experiments in Ibsen. And now it appears that to such notorious plotters for an endowed theatre as Judge Parry and Mr Charles Hughes, the Lord Mayor of Manchester has said, "Will you walk into my parlor?"

A cheerful feature of this project is the use it has found for the reputation of Shakespear. The bait held out to Manchester is perpetual Bard. No wonder Mr Archer was provoked to point out that man does not live by Shakespear alone. But he also pointed out, very pertinently, that the reason a theatre is so much more difficult to endow than a museum, library, or picture gallery, is that the theatre is a live thing whose future behavior must be guaranteed. Given a collection of pictures, books, or specimens, all you have to do is to provide a building, a catalogue, a turnstile, an umbrella-stand, and a custodian; and there you are, an ascertained quantity for all posterity to profit by. The statues by Phidias in the British Museum cannot be turned into waxwork murderers, nor the Mazarin Bible into a lewd novel, any more than the National Gallery can be turned into a Wiertz Museum. But a theatre can be transformed in this way with a vengeance, since it is at bottom nothing but the conduct of the

312

manager, the author, and the company. You may endow it in order that great dramatists may help your fellow-citizens to a purifying consciousness of the deepest struggles of the human soul with itself. You may visit it a year after and find these very fellow-citizens hanging breathless on the issue of a stage horse race or prize fight. Hence the need for a guarantee of good conduct. And what more convincing guarantee could be given than the name of Shakespear as exclusive author to the establishment? No name stands higher in England than his; because the average Englishman never reads his works, and of the small percentage who do, some drop off to sleep at the second page; some find, not what they read, but only the nebulous greatness hypnotically suggested to them by our William's reputation; whilst the few real disciples soon find out the Bard's very serious shortcomings, and are regarded as reduced to absurdity by their own monstrous discovery. Take my own case—a most deserving one—for example. A fortnight ago I ventured to point out in these columns that Julius Cæsar in Shakespear's play says nothing worthy, or even nearly worthy, of Julius Cæsar. The number of humbugs who have pretended to be shocked by this absolutely incontrovertible remark has lowered my opinion of the human race. There are only two dignified courses open to those who disagree with me. One is to suffer in silence. The other, obviously, is to quote the passage which, in the opinion of the objectors, *is* worthy of Julius Cæsar. The latter course, however, would involve reading the play; and they would almost as soon think of reading the Bible. Besides, it would be waste of time; for since Shakespear is accepted as the standard of first-rate excellence, an adverse criticism of him need only be quoted to be accepted as damning evidence against itself. I do not mention this by way of complaint: if these gentlemen saw eye to eye with me they would all be G. B. S.'s; and a press written entirely in my style would be, like an exclusively Shakespearean municipal theatre, a little too much of a good thing. I merely wish to shew how the difficulty about guaranteeing the future good conduct of an endowed theatre can always be got over by simply mentioning our

William's name. Assure the public that you will play Shakespear and that you will not play Ibsen, and your endowment fund will be second in respectability only to the restoration fund of a cathedral.

With regard to Ibsen, Mr Archer judiciously renounced him wholly as an endowed theatre author; and insisted on our growing our own higher drama. His point was that with a public theatre in the field, not only would those write who never wrote before, but those who write today will write the more. Mr Sachs, in his lecture, had mentioned the instructive fact that the late Mr Phipps used to take pains to make his theatres look as common as possible lest he should be suspected of being "an Art architect" and lose all his clients. This deliberate debasement of work to suit the ignorance of the customer is a necessary rule of competitive business. Mr Archer, when he came to speak of our leading dramatists, shewed that they were precisely in the Phipps position, and could only raise the standard of their work at the cost of their livelihood. Here, however, certain stirs of scepticism were felt. Suppose the Waterloo block to the west of Trafalgar Square had been cleared away, and placed, with unlimited funds, at the disposal of Phipps, to do his utter best in the erection of a national theatre there! Would he have proved himself a Wren, compelled by circumstances up to that time to be a nobody? Not altogether, I think. He would no doubt have surpassed himself sufficiently to surprise us, as he did in the case of Her Majesty's Theatre; but the difference would have been the difference between a hundred pounds and a thousand rather than between a great artist-builder and a commercial architect. What happens under our system is that the tradesman supersedes the artist. The tradesman adapts himself to the market: he offers you a third-class article for a third-class price, and a second-class article for a second-class price, preferring the third-class contract if, as often happens, it is the more profitable. First-class work he cannot do at all; and the man who can do it, the artist, cannot do anything else. When second- or third-class work is demanded, he may, and very often does, try to do it for the sake of the money, a man with a wife and family being, as Talleyrand said, capable of any-thing; but he inevitably botches it, and only confirms his em-ployer's prejudice against artists and in favor of tradesmen. A Bovril or Condensed Milk poster by Sir Edward Burne-Jones will probably be worth no more than Wagner's Philadelphia Centennial march.

But the world is not quite so clear-cut as this description of it. The distinction between artist and tradesman is not a distinction between one man and another, but between two sides of the same man. The number of persons who, being unquestionably eminent artists, have yet been so absolutely uncommercial as to be uninfluenced by their market, is very small indeed; and of these some, like Giotto, have found their market so entirely sympathetic that in doing as they pleased they simply sailed before the wind; whilst others, like Shelley, Goethe, or Landor, were independent of it in point of both money and social stand-ing. Beethoven, Wagner, and Ibsen, though dependent on their art for both money and position, certainly did eventually take Europe by the scruff of the neck and say, "You shall take what I like and not what you want"; but in comparison with Bunyan and Blake they were keen men of business. I know of no dramatist dependent on his profession who has not been very seriously influenced by his market. Shakespear's case, the leading one for England, is beyond a doubt. He would have starved if he had followed his bent towards a genuine science of life and character. His instinct for reality had to be surreptitiously gratified under the mask of comedy. Dr Johnson pointed out long ago that it was only in comedy that our immortal stalking-horse for bogus criticism was really happy. To this day such splendid melo-dramas as Othello, with its noble savage, its villain, its funny man, its carefully assorted pathetic and heavy feminine interest, its smothering and suicide, its police-court morality and common-place thought; or As You Like It, with its Adelphi hero, its prize-fight, its coquet in tights, its good father and wicked uncle, represent the greatness of Shakespear to nine-tenths of his adorers, who mostly, when you mention Helena, or the Countess of

Rousillon, or Isabella, or Cressida, or Ulysses, or Bertram, stare at you, and think you are talking about Calderon and Homer. We admire Shakespear solely for his popular plays; and our habit of extolling to the skies what pleases us in them is only our way of flattering our own tastes. The moment we are taken outside Hamlet and the half-dozen big popular melodramas which the Bard has sublimified by his tempests of grandiose verse, we are compelled to confess that we prefer Sherlock Holmes for private reading.

If the theatre for which Shakespear wrote had been of the rank of the Athenian theatre of the Periclean age, I believe on the evidence of his unpopular and practically unknown plays that he would have done much higher work. And what is true of Shakespear is no doubt true also, as Mr Archer suggested (without mentioning names), of Mr Henry Arthur Jones and Mr Pinero. What I do not believe is that a public theatre could get so far above the level of its age as to encourage either gentleman to go much further than he has already done. The public theatre will be independent of the greed of syndicates, and will have moral, as distinguished from purely capitalistic aims; but if it has to start with an assurance from Mr Archer himself that its attitude towards Ibsen will be practically that of the Lyceum Theatre, it is evident that the very wide difference between Sir Henry Irving's opinion of Ibsen and Mr William Archer's is not expected to find expression in a municipal theatre. I do not demur to the scheme on this ground. A public theatre will take us a step in advance; but I do not think that step will take the drama beyond the point reached 300 years ago in the most popular plays of Shakespear. In all higher developments, I believe the theatre will follow the dramatic poet, and not the dramatic poet the theatre. Even this next step, which is not to take us as far as Ibsen, is only felt to be necessary because Ibsen has raised our standards and made us ashamed of ourselves. Before 1889, who, except Matthew Arnold, asked for anything more than Sir Henry Irving, Sir Squire Bancroft, and Mr Hare could give us? Since then, who has been content with that prospect? And what happened in 1889 to begin such a revolution? A Doll's House, of course.

BEAUMONT AND FLETCHER

THE COXCOMB. By Beaumont and Fletcher. Acted by the Elizabethan Stage Society in the Hall of the Inner Temple, 10 February 1898.

THE DOVE-COT (JALOUSE). From the French of MM. Bisson and Leclerq. The Duke of York's Theatre, 12 February 1898.

[19 *February* 1898]

I CONFESS to a condescending tolerance for Beaumont and Fletcher. It was, to be sure, no merit of theirs that they were born late enough to come into the field enthusiastically conscious of their art in the full development to which Shakespear had brought it, instead of blundering upon its discovery like the earlier men. Still, merit or no merit, they were saved from the clumsy horse-play and butcherly rant of Marlowe as models of wit and eloquence, and from the resourceless tum-tum of his "mighty line" as a standard for their verse. When one thinks of the donnish insolence and perpetual thick-skinned swagger of Chapman over his unique achievements in sublime balderdash, and the opacity that prevented Webster, the Tussaud laureate, from appreciating his own stupidity—when one thinks of the whole rabble of de-humanized specialists in elementary blank verse posing as the choice and master-spirits of an art that had produced the stories of Chaucer and the old mystery plays, and was even then pregnant with The Pilgrim's Progress, it is hard to keep one's critical blood cold enough to discriminate in favor of any Elizabethan whatever. Nothing short of a statue at Deptford to the benefactor of the human species who exterminated Marlowe, and the condemnation of Mr Swinburne to spend the rest of his life in selling photographs of it to American tourists, would meet the poetic justice of the case. We are not all, happily, victims of the literary aberration that led Charles Lamb to revive Elizabethanism as a modern cult. We forgive him his addiction to it as we forgive him his addiction to gin.

317

Unfortunately, Shakespear dropped into the middle of these ruffianly pedants; and since there was no other shop than theirs to serve his apprenticeship in, he had perforce to become an Elizabethan too. In such a school of falsehood, bloody-mindedness, bombast, and intellectual cheapness, his natural standard was inevitably dragged down, as we know to our cost; but the degree to which he dragged their standard up has saved them from oblivion. It makes one giddy to compare the execrable rottenness of the Jew of Malta with the humanity and poetry of the Merchant of Venice. Hamlet, Othello, and Iago are masterpieces beside Faustus, Bussy d'Amboise, and Bosola. After Shakespear, the dramatists were in the position of Spohr after Mozart. A ravishing secular art had been opened up to them, and was refining their senses and ennobling their romantic illusions and enthusiasms instead of merely stirring up their basest passions. Cultivated lovers of the beauties of Shakespear's art—true amateurs, in fact—took the place of the Marlovian crew. Such amateurs, let loose in a field newly reaped by a great master, have always been able to glean some dropped ears, and even to raise a brief aftermath. In this way the world has gained many charming and fanciful, though not really original, works of art—blank verse dramas after Shakespear, rhetorical frescoes after Raphael, fugues after Bach, operas after Mozart, symphonies after Beethoven, and so on. This, I take it, is the distinction between Marlowe and Company and the firm of Beaumont and Fletcher. The pair wrote a good deal that was pretty disgraceful; but at all events they had been educated out of the possibility of writing Titus Andronicus. They had no depth, no conviction, no religious or philosophic basis, no real power or seriousness—Shakespear himself was a poor master in such matters—but they were dainty romantic poets, and really humorous character-sketchers in Shakespear's popular style: that is, they neither knew nor cared anything about human psychology, but they could mimic the tricks and manners of their neighbors, especially the vulgarer ones, in a highly entertaining way.

The Coxcomb is not a bad sample of their art. Mr Poel has had to bowdlerize it in deference to the modesty of the barristers of the Inner Temple. For instance, Mercury's relations with Maria stop short of exacting her husband's crowning sacrifice to friendship; and when the three merry gentlemen make Riccardo too drunk to keep his appointment to elope with Viola, the purpose with which the four roysterers sally out into the street, much insisted on by Beaumont and Fletcher, is discreetly left to the guilty imagination of the more sophisticated spectators. With these exceptions the play was presented as fairly as could be expected.

The performance was one of the best the Elizabethan Stage Society has achieved. I confess that I anticipated failure in the part of Riccardo, who is not a human being, but an embodiment of the most delicate literary passion of Elizabethan romantic poetry. Miss Rehan, one felt, might have done something with it on the lines of her Viola in Twelfth Night; but then Miss Rehan was not available. The lady who was available did not allow her name to appear in the bill; and I have no idea who she is. But she certainly hit that part off to perfection, having, by a happy temperamental accident, the musical root of the poetic passion in her. Her performance was apparently quite original. There was no evidence in it of her ever having seen Miss Rehan act: if she suggested anybody, it was Calvé. Mr Sherbrooke's Mercury also was an excellent performance. The vivacity of his pantomime, and a trick of pronouncing his *d*'s and *t*'s foreign fashion, with the tongue against the teeth, raised some doubt as to whether he was quite as English as his name; but his performance was none the worse. In delivering his asides he convinced me more than any of the rest that he had divined the method and style of the Elizabethan stage. I should like to say a special word about every one of the performers, but the program reminds me that there are no less than twenty-four of them; so I can only add hastily that Mr Poel himself played the Coxcomb; that Mr Paget Bowman spoke the prologue and played Valerio; that the Justice was impersonated by Mr J. H. Brewer, and not, as some supposed, by Sir Peter Edlin; that Miss Imogen Surrey played Viola and

Miss Hepworth Valerio's mother; and that these and all the other parts, especially the tinker and his trull, and not forgetting Mr Leonard Howard's Alexander, come out quite vividly and intelligibly. I have no doubt some of the audience were bored; but the explanation of that is simple: they were the people who have no taste for Elizabethan drama. After all, you cannot plunge into these things absolutely without connoisseurship.

The most remarkable point in the adaptation of Jalouse at the Duke of York's Theatre is its recognition of the fact, often insisted on in these columns, that no English audience, however frivolous, can bear three acts of farcical comedy without weariness and demoralization. The Dove-cot is saved by the sentimentality of its second act. It almost invariably happens, when a play is altered to meet the views of the management, that nobody in the theatre is sharp enough to detect the contingent alterations which the main one involves. The Dove-cot is no exception to this rule. The adaptation is a jumble; but it serves its turn. It is very well acted. Miss Ellis Jeffreys, who captured the leading position for this sort of work during Mr Alexander's recent supplementary season at the Royalty, holds that position firmly. It is a kind of work in which manners make the actress: vulgarly played, it is detestable; elegantly played, it is delightful. Miss Jeffreys plays it elegantly. Miss Leonora Braham, no longer a Savoy prima donna, is the flamboyant Carlist. Mr Seymour Hicks, Mr James Welch, Mr William Wyes, Mr Sugden, and Miss Carlotta Addison are also in the cast, which is unusually strong and well chosen.

SHAKESPEAR'S MERRY GENTLEMEN

Much Ado About Nothing. St James's Theatre, 16 February 1898.   [26 *February* 1898]

Much Ado is perhaps the most dangerous actor-manager trap in the whole Shakespearean repertory. It is not a safe play like The Merchant of Venice or As You Like It, nor a serious play like Hamlet. Its success depends on the way it is handled in performance; and that, again, depends on the actor-manager being enough of a critic to discriminate ruthlessly between the pretension of the author and his achievement.

The main pretension in Much Ado is that Benedick and Beatrice are exquisitely witty and amusing persons. They are, of course, nothing of the sort. Benedick's pleasantries might pass at a sing-song in a public-house parlor; but a gentleman rash enough to venture on them in even the very mildest £52-a-year suburban imitation of polite society today would assuredly never be invited again. From his first joke, "Were you in doubt, sir, that you asked her?" to his last, "There is no staff more reverend than one tipped with horn," he is not a wit, but a blackguard. He is not Shakespear's only failure in that genre. It took the Bard a long time to grow out of the provincial conceit that made him so fond of exhibiting his accomplishments as a master of gallant badinage. The very thought of Biron, Mercutio, Gratiano, and Benedick must, I hope, have covered him with shame in his later years. Even Hamlet's airy compliments to Ophelia before the court would make a cabman blush. But at least Shakespear did not value himself on Hamlet's indecent jests as he evidently did on those of the four merry gentlemen of the earlier plays. When he at last got conviction of sin, and saw this sort of levity in its proper light, he made masterly amends by presenting the blackguard *as* a blackguard in the person of Lucio in Measure for Measure. Lucio, as a character study, is worth forty Benedicks and Birons. His obscenity is not only inoffensive, but irresistibly entertaining, because it is drawn with perfect skill, offered at its true value, and given its proper interest, without any complicity of the author in its lewdness. Lucio is much more of a gentleman than Benedick, because he keeps his coarse sallies for coarse people. Meeting one woman, he says humbly, "Gentle and fair: your brother kindly greets you. Not to be weary with you, he's in prison." Meeting another, he hails her sparkingly with "How now? which of your hips has the more profound sciatica?" The one woman is a lay sister, the other a prostitute. Benedick or Mercutio would have cracked their low jokes on the lay sister, and been held up as gentlemen of rare wit and excellent discourse for it. Whenever they approach a woman or an old man, you shiver with apprehension as to what brutality they will come out with.

Precisely the same thing, in the tenderer degree of her sex, is true of Beatrice. In her character of professed wit she has only one subject, and that is the subject which a really witty woman never jests about, because it is too serious a matter to a woman to be made light of without indelicacy. Beatrice jests about it for the sake of the indelicacy. There is only one thing worse than the Elizabethan "merry gentleman," and that is the Elizabethan "merry lady."

Why is it then that we still want to see Benedick and Beatrice, and that our most eminent actors and actresses still want to play them? Before I answer that very simple question let me ask another. Why is it that Da Ponte's "dramma giocosa," entitled Don Giovanni, a loathsome story of a coarse, witless, worthless libertine, who kills an old man in a duel and is finally dragged down through a trapdoor to hell by his twaddling ghost, is still, after more than a century, as "immortal" as Much Ado? Simply because Mozart clothed it with wonderful music, which turned the worthless words and thoughts of Da Ponte into a magical human drama of moods and transitions of feeling. That is what happened in a smaller way with Much Ado. Shakespear shews himself in it a commonplace librettist working on a stolen plot, but a great musician. No matter how poor, coarse, cheap, and obvious the thought may be, the mood is charming, and the music of the words expresses the mood. Paraphrase the encounters of Benedick and Beatrice in the style of a bluebook, carefully preserving every idea they present, and it will become apparent to the most infatuated Shakespearean that they contain at best nothing out of the common in thought or wit, and at worst a good deal of vulgar naughtiness. Paraphrase Goethe, Wagner, or Ibsen in the same way, and you will find original observation, subtle thought, wide comprehension, far-reaching intuition, and serious psychological study in them. Give Shakespear a fairer chance in the comparison by paraphrasing even his best and maturest work, and you will still get nothing more than the platitudes of proverbial philosophy, with a very occasional curiosity in the shape of a rudiment of some modern idea, not followed up. Not until the Shakespearean music is added by replacing the paraphrase with the original lines does the enchantment begin. Then you are in another world at once. When a flower-girl tells a coster to hold his jaw, for nobody is listening to him, and he retorts, "Oh, youre there, are you, you beauty?" they reproduce the wit of Beatrice and Benedick exactly. But put it this way. "I wonder that you will still be talking, Signior Benedick: nobody marks you." "What! my dear Lady Disdain, are you yet living?" You are miles away from costerland at once. When I tell you that Benedick and the coster are equally poor in thought, Beatrice and the flower-girl equally vulgar in repartee, you reply that I might as well tell you that a nightingale's love is no higher than a cat's. Which is exactly what I do tell you, though the nightingale is the better musician. You will admit, perhaps, that the love of the worst human singer in the world is accompanied by a higher degree of intellectual consciousness than that of the most ravishingly melodious nightingale. Well, in just the same way, there are plenty of quite second-rate writers who are abler thinkers and wits than William, though they are unable to weave his magic into the expression of their thoughts.

It is not easy to knock this into the public head, because comparatively few of Shakespear's admirers are at all conscious that they are listening to music as they hear his phrases turn and his lines fall so fascinatingly and memorably; whilst we all, no matter how stupid we are, can understand his jokes and platitudes, and are flattered when we are told of the subtlety of the wit we have relished, and the profundity of the thought we have fathomed. Englishmen are specially susceptible to this sort of flattery, because intellectual subtlety is not their strong point. In dealing with them you must make them believe that you are appealing to their brains when you are really appealing to their senses and feelings. With Frenchmen the case is reversed: you must make them believe that you are appealing to their senses and feelings when you are really appealing to their brains. The Englishman, slave to every sentimental ideal and dupe of every sensuous art, will have it that his great national poet is a thinker. The Frenchman, enslaved and duped only by systems and calculations, insists on his hero being a sentimentalist and artist. That is why Shakespear is esteemed a master-mind in England, and wondered at as a clumsy barbarian in France.

However indiscriminate the public may be in its Shakespear worship, the actor and actress who are to make a success of Much Ado must know better. Let them once make the popular mistake of supposing that what they have to do is to bring out the wit of Benedick and Beatrice, and they are lost. Their business in the "merry" passages is to cover poverty of thought and coarseness of innuendo by making the most of the grace and dignity of the diction. The sincere, genuinely dramatic passages will then take care of themselves. Alas! Mr Alexander and Miss Julia Neilson have made the plunge without waiting for my advice. Miss Neilson, throwing away all her grace and all her music, strives to play the merry lady by dint of conscientious gambolling. Instead of uttering her speeches as exquisitely as possible, she rattles through them, laying an impossible load of archness on every insignificant conjunction, and clipping all the important words until there is no measure or melody left in them. Not even the wedding scene can stop her: after an indignant attitude or two she redoubles her former skittishness. I can only implore her to give up all her deep-laid Beatricisms, to discard the movements of Miss Ellen Terry, the voice of Mrs Patrick Campbell, and the gaiety of Miss Kitty Loftus, and try the effect of Julia Neilson in all her grave grace taken quite seriously. Mr Alexander makes the same mistake, though, being more judicious than Miss Neilson, he does not carry it out so disastrously. His merry gentleman is patently a dutiful assumption from beginning to end. He smiles, rackets, and bounds up and down stairs like a quiet man who has just been rated by his wife for habitual dullness before company. It is all hopeless: the charm of Benedick cannot be realized by the spryness of the actor's legs, the flashing of his teeth, or the rattle of his laugh: nothing but the music of the words—above all, not their meaning—can save the part. I wish I could persuade Mr Alexander that if he were to play the part exactly as he played Guy Domville, it would at once become ten times more fascinating. He should at least take the revelation of Beatrice's supposed love for him with perfect seriousness. The more remorsefully sympathetic Benedick is when she comes to bid him to dinner after he has been gulled into believing she loves him, the more exquisitely ridiculous the scene becomes. It is the audience's turn to laugh then, not Benedick's.

Of all Sir Henry Irving's manifold treasons against Shakespear, the most audacious was his virtually cutting Dogberry out of Much Ado. Mr Alexander does not go so far; but he omits the fifth scene of the third act, upon which the whole effect of the later scenes depends, since it is from it that the audience really gets Dogberry's measure. Dogberry is a capital study of parochial character. Sincerely played, he always comes out as a very real and highly entertaining person. At the St James's, I grieve to say, he does not carry a moment's conviction: he is a mere mouthpiece for malapropisms, all of which he shouts at the gallery with intense consciousness of their absurdity, and with open anxiety lest they should pass unnoticed. Surely it is clear, if anything histrionic is clear, that Dogberry's first qualification must be a complete unconsciousness of himself as he appears to others.

Verges, even more dependent than Dogberry on that cut-out scene with Leonato, is almost annihilated by its excision; and it was hardly worth wasting Mr Esmond on the remainder.

When I have said that neither Benedick nor Beatrice have seen sufficiently through the weakness of Shakespear's merriments to concentrate themselves on the purely artistic qualities of their parts, and that Dogberry is nothing but an excuse for a few laughs, I have made a somewhat heavy deduction from my praises of the revival. But these matters are hardly beyond remedy; and the rest is excellent. Miss Fay Davis's perfect originality contrasts strongly with Miss Neilson's incorrigible imitativeness. Her physical grace is very remarkable; and she creates her part between its few lines, as Hero must if she is to fill up her due place in the drama. Mr Fred Terry is a most engaging Don Pedro; and Mr H. B. Irving is a striking Don John, though he is becoming too accomplished an actor to make shift with that single smile which is as well known at the St James's by this time as the one wig of Mr Pinero's hero was at "The Wells." Mr Vernon and Mr Beveridge are, of course, easily within their powers as Leonato and Antonio; and all the rest come off with credit—even Mr Loraine, who has not a trace of Claudio in him. The dresses are superb, and the scenery very handsome, though Italy contains so many palaces and chapels that are better than handsome that I liked the opening scenes best. If Mr Alexander will only make up his mind that the piece is irresistible as poetry, and hopeless as epigrammatic comedy, he need not fear for its success. But if he and Miss Neilson persist in depending on its attempts at wit and gallantry, then it remains to be seen whether the public's sense of duty or its boredom will get the upper hand.

I had intended to deal here with the O.U.D.S. and its performance of Romeo and Juliet; but Much Ado has carried me too far; so I must postpone Oxford until next week.

ELIZABETHAN ATHLETICS AT OXFORD

Romeo and Juliet. Oxford University Dramatic Society, New Theatre, Oxford, 16–22 February 1898.

The White Knight. An original comedy in three acts. By G. Stuart Ogilvie. Terry's Theatre, 26 February 1898.

[5 *March* 1898]

The unaccountable thing about Mr Ogilvie's play at Terry's Theatre is its ghastly background of white lead manufacture. The very mention of white lead brought me to the theatre expecting a drama of frightful power and reality, with Mr Terry as the White Knight coming to the rescue of the wretched women who, for a couple of shillings a day, devote themselves to disfigurement, agony, and final destruction by lead poisoning. Imagine my feelings on finding him bent wholly on increasing the dividend by a new process, without the faintest reference to the callously villainous traffic in human life for which his trade is infamous. Why did Mr Ogilvie choose so deadly an industry for the whitening of his knight, who might just as easily have been a miller inventing the latest patent bread? Was the explanation cut out in deference to Mammon in the stalls, and to the intense repugnance of our theatre to any of the real joys and sorrows of life? However that may be, the play, as performed at Terry's, does not contain a line that could bring a blush to the cheek of the most unscrupulous shareholder or the most complaisant Home Secretary. The chivalry of the white knight, like his inventive genius, is assumed without any credible evidence. Mr Edward Pennyquick, like Tom Pinch, gains everybody's good word because he is such a nincompoop that nobody could possibly envy him, and because we are all so guiltily conscious, more or less, of stupidity and clumsiness that we like to see an association set up between them and goodness of heart. These plays about good-hearted elderly duffers no doubt please duffing playgoers; but since they take comedians like Mr Hare and Mr Edward Terry to all intents and purposes out of their profession of acting to make mere entertainers of them, they do a good deal of harm to dramatic art. Mr Terry has created characters in his time, and memorable characters too. In the White Knight he is merely submitting to the exploitation of his own popularity.

This time the sacrifice is shared, unfortunately, by the author. Mr Ogilvie is no mere twaddling novelettist: his fault hitherto has been an ambitious addiction to the heroics of the operatic-historical school. His exploits in that line suggested that if he would only once come to terms with real life, his imagination, wit, and literary aptitude might produce something solid. Now that the hoped-for occasion has arrived, it has been spoiled by the commercial necessity for producing a safe part for Mr Terry, written down to the ignorance and lazy indulgence of the simpler sort of Strand playgoer. Furthermore, Mr Ogilvie is by no means cured as yet of his Quixotism. The business in the last act, where Pennyquick tells a senseless and mischievous lie, and sacrifices himself and several other persons in order to shield a thief, is about as glaring an example of false pathos, not to say perverse immorality, as one would find in a fortnight's theatre-going. Need I add that the thief is a woman?

A great deal of the incidental business of the drama is good, and involves some excellent touches of character. There are one or two no-thoroughfares in it which suggest careless cutting: at least that was how I accounted to myself for the failure of the office-boy's machinations to produce any results, as well as for the extreme gratuitousness of the assumptions as to Penny-quick's chivalry. But on the whole there is a good deal that is amusing and fairly believable in the picture. The acting could not be bettered to any purpose. Miss Mary Rorke is charming as the old lady: Miss Kate Rorke does more for the young one than she altogether deserves. Mr Abingdon plays the city sharper as if he loved him; and Miss Esmé Beringer, very artistic and competent as usual, makes Guillietta (*sic*) Guaraschino, *alias* Tibby, absurdly like Mr Forbes Robertson.

It is characteristic of the authorities at Oxford that they should consider a month too little for the preparation of a boat-race, and grudge three weeks to the rehearsals of one of Shakespear's plays. The performance of Romeo and Juliet by the Oxford University Dramatic Society naturally did not, under these circumstances, approach the level of skill attained on the Thames. The one advantage that amateurs have over professionals—and it is such an overwhelming advantage when exhaustively used that the best amateur performances are more instructive than the most elaborate professional ones—is the possibility of unlimited rehearsal. An amateur company prepared to rehearse Romeo and Juliet for six months would in some respects easily beat an ordinary London company. But there is a still better way within the reach of amateurs. Everyone who has seen the annual performances of Latin plays at Westminster School must have been struck by the absence of that feebleness and futility of utterance which makes the ordinary amateur so obnoxious. Yet the Westminster plays get no such extraordinary measure of rehearsals. Again, if we watch the amateur performances of Elizabethan drama with which Mr William Poel does such good work, we find that those performers who are members of the Shakespear Reading Society, or of the little private circles formed by inveterate Elizabethan readers, acquit themselves much better, in point of delivery, than average professional actors. This gives us the secret of the Westminster play. The schoolboy is well practised in the utterance of Latin, not colloquially as he utters English, but as a task in the nature of a performance to be submitted to the approval of his master, just as the Elizamaniac utters Shakespearean verse every week at least for the delectation of his circle. Here, surely, is the clue to the right course for the O.U.D.S. Let the members devote two nights a week all the year round to reading Elizabethan plays, and let it be a rule that no member shall be allotted a principal part without a very high average of attendances. A tradition of skill and practice in what is one of the finest of physical accomplishments will soon be established; and the O.U.D.S. will in course of time become popular as a club of artistic athletes instead of being ridiculed, as I fear it is to some extent at present, as a set of unrepresentative æsthetes. To play Shakespear without considerable technical skill and vocal power is, frankly, to make an ass of oneself; and the contempt of the average undergraduate for such exhibitions is by no means mere Philistinism. If the boat-race were rowed by men who never took an oar in their hands until the middle of February, and only did so then because they were vain enough to want to figure in some footling imitation of the Olympian games, the University would not care two straws about the boat-race. I am bound to say that it has had much the same reason for not concerning itself about the late performance of Romeo and Juliet. If the performers had been able to handle their vowels and consonants as bats and balls and sculls are handled at Oxford in the racket-courts and cricket-fields and on the river, then, whether they were able to act or not, the performance would have been full of technical interest; the gallery would have seethed with youthful hero-worship; and the performers, doing something that every undergraduate would like to do if he could, would now be holding their heads high even among the athletes. On no other lines is there the smallest chance of a dramatic club becoming a really vital organ of an English University, or forcing the authorities, by sheer weight of public opinion, to build a University theatre as an indispensable part of their educational equipment.

The amateur company which performed Romeo and Juliet was under-trained and under-rehearsed to a degree of which, I think, it had itself no suspicion. Consequently, though its intentions were excellent, it had very little power of carrying them out: ideas and taste were not lacking; but executive power was at a huge premium. Romeo had cultivated a pretty *mezza voce*, which carried him in a sentimentally lyrical way through a performance which certainly maintained a distinctly artistic character and style all through, though it was deficient in variety and power. Mercutio, when illustrating Tybalt's accomplishments as a fencer, fell and put his knee out. He rose, with his knee-cap visibly in that excruciating condition, and continued his performance with undiminished dash. He did not faint; but I should certainly have done so if the dislocation had not fortunately reduced itself in the slow course of about two minutes. I protest against these exhibitions of fortitude: the Spartans may have considered them good manners; but a really considerate modern should frankly yell when he is hurt, and thereby give the sympathetic spectators an opportunity to relieve their feelings with equal demonstrativeness. Except for his hypocrisy in this matter, Mercutio deserved well of the Club. The part is a puzzling one; and his notion of handling it was by no means an unhappy one. Juliet was a convincing illustration of the advantages of practice. The balcony scene and the phial scene—that is to say, the two scenes which she had probably often recited—were quite presentable. The rest, got up merely for the occasion, was uncertain and helpless. Friar Laurence got on tolerably well; and the effect of playing the last scene in its entirety was decidedly good. But I desire to dwell on the weak parts in the performance rather than on the passable ones. It was not worth doing for its own immediate sake; and as the candid friend of the O.U.D.S., I advise them to drop Shakespear unless they are prepared to work continuously at the Elizabethan drama all the year round, in the way I have suggested. They have not yet qualified themselves to split the ears of the groundlings, which they should all be able to do, in the style of the apprentice in The Knight of the Burning Pestle, to begin with. Later on they can keep within the modesty of nature; but it is the business of youth "to fetch up a couraging part" valiantly, and master all the technical difficulties and audacities of art, just as the pianist, at eighteen, dazzles us with transcendent execution, though he cannot play a Mozart sonata. The secret of art's humanity will come later, when the university has been exchanged for the real world.

The anniversary performance of La Poupée has almost converted me to a resolution to forswear first nights, and only attend when the piece has run for a year. This La Poupée is a very different business from Gentleman Joe and its successors. It is a delightful little opera; and Miss Jessie Huddlestone, Mr Courtice Pounds, Mr Norman Salmond, and Mr Edouin make a memorable quartet. I confess myself astonished. I thought the secret of that art had been lost, and that Mr Lowenfeld had turned his back on it for ever. My best apologies!

THE NATURAL AND THE STAGE VILLAIN

THE SEA FLOWER. A play in four acts. By Arthur Law. Comedy Theatre, 5 March 1898.

THE KING'S SWEETHEART. A comic opera. By Arthur Sturgess and J. M. Glover. Théâtre Métropole, Camberwell, 7 March 1898. [12 *March* 1898]

IF the world had no more ideas than the theatre has, how long would society hold together? I know no spectacle more pitiable

than the average literary or artistic person driven from his handi-
craft of description and imitation to ethics and sociology. I can
almost hear the yell of peevish protest these two terrible words
will wring from the ordinary theatre fancier; but I can assure him
that the only plays which can dispense with ethics are those photo-
graphically realistic ones which he most abhors, and which, in
his abysmal ignorance, he supposes to be nothing if not didactic.
The popular play must have doctrine in it, and reasoned doctrine
too. We have lately had our respected William Shakespear intemperately scolded by his disciples for making Don John in
Much Ado a stage villain. Now if ever there was a villain who
was not a stage villain it is Don John. What is a stage villain?
Clearly, not a real villain, but a mere machine impelled by some
interested motive to keep the plot of a play in action. He wants to
succeed to a property; or he must have twenty thousand pounds
instantly to save him from ruin; or he is in love with some woman
who wants to marry the hero. Shakespear, with all his superficiality, knew that villainy is something simpler and deeper than
a mere means to an end. Don John is a true natural villain: that is
to say, a malevolent person. Only, he is un-English, because he
is quite conscious of his villainy, and disguises it neither from
himself nor his accomplices. Iago is also a true villain; but he is
English to the backbone. That is why English commentators are
so careful to expatiate on his Italianateness. Having no motive
in the world except sheer love of evil, he is for ever explaining
that Othello has probably made love to his wife; that Cassio is
lowering the standard of practical soldiership by arithmetic pedantry; that Roderigo is a fool who deserves to lose his money,
and the like transparently flimsy pretexts. Further, he has a steady
eye to the main chance, and tries to combine money-gain and
promotion with the luxury of mischief. Thus he is English in the
mode of his villainy. It is so effective a mode that it is rather fortunate for humanity that the English as a nation are not particularly villainous: villainy for villainy's sake attracts them as
little as art for art's sake. All one can say, therefore, is that if an
Englishman were a villain he would talk like Iago, not like Don

John. Being what he is, he usually stops doing mischief when there is nothing more to be got by it, and has even a distinct preference for virtue when it costs nothing. In short, he has, properly speaking, no moral character at all: he is in the first place a utilitarian and in the second a pious romanticist; and this, I take it, is the reason why the villains and heroes of the everyday English theatre are all stage villains and heroes, not real ones. Also, why on the appearance of a real villain like Don John, he is unanimously denounced in England as an unnatural and impossible stage convention.

In the piece by Mr Arthur Law, just produced at the Comedy Theatre, there is a hero. And such a hero! What the English public demands in that line is the sort of person whose hand rough men, husky with emotion, can grasp with a resounding slap as they exclaim: "I declare, Sir, you are the noblest man I ever met!" and on whose knuckles women, with bending knees, can imprint reverent kisses. To this no reasonable person can take any exception: it is a capital thing to know quite clearly and satisfactorily exactly what you want. The only difficulty is to invent the strokes of virtuous conduct that will entitle your hero to such ovations. The English dramatist in the throes of such invention is, as I began by saying, a lamentable spectacle. The one point to which he holds steadily is that the noble deed on which his drama is to turn must be what he calls a sacrifice, causing the most widespread disaster possible to all the deserving persons in the play, and profiting only the undeserving ones. This principle has rarely been carried out with such thoroughness as by Mr Arthur Law. In fact, in his determination to make his hero disastrous he has quite forgotten to make him virtuous as well; and I greatly fear that even the British public will see nothing but a mischievous fool where he intended them to see one of nature's noblemen. This gentleman tells us in the last act that he owes his excellence to the golden rule imparted to him by his father—"Always ride straight." Unfortunately, paternal wisdom was in vain. Were he to ride straight in the first act there would be no play. So inveterately does he ride crooked that a happy ending is only secured by an accidental discovery of the truth concerning the most important event in his career.

The exact state of affairs is as follows. Captain Sherwood is in command of a force with orders to hold a certain dangerous position on the Indian frontier. He is smitten with fever, and acquires a habit of raving, which clings to him, more or less, during the subsequent four acts of his life. Next in command to him is Lieutenant Trafford, who, on ascertaining that the defence of the position means death to every man in it, is dastard enough to feel depressed by that glorious prospect. When his Captain falls ill he orders a retreat, and alleges that he acted by the orders of the Captain. The Captain is court-martialled. He has a perfect answer to the charge, for not only was he too ill to be responsible for his actions, but a convenient corporal has overheard everything, and can prove that the alleged order was never given. Alas! that gallant Captain loves the wife of that wicked Lieutenant. He straitly enjoins the convenient corporal to hold his peace. The corporal instantly becomes husky; takes his officer's hand with a mighty slap; declares that he is the noblest man on earth; pledges himself to prove his humble friendship by conniving at the Captain's ruin as requested; and retires, stifled with tears, but consoled by the plaudits of all the donkeys in the house. The Captain then declines to make any defence before the court-martial, and is in due course expelled with ignominy from the service. And the whole play rests on the assumption that this dishonorable course, adopted from purely personal motives, is an act of heroism. By it the Captain disgraces himself, basely sells the friends who have pledged themselves for his honor, leaves a traitor in the mess of his regiment in war time, places an unmerited stigma on his own wife and child, and leaves the woman for whose sake he has steeped himself in all this rascality cruelly deluded as to the characters of the husband who has lost her esteem and the friend who has gained it.

The exasperating part of the business is that this masterpiece of false morality and senseless pathos damns not only its unworthy self but a good deal of very different work. The fisherman's household, with the courtship of Joan Roper and Corporal Nancarrow, is so entertaining that it is easy to see why Miss Gladys Homfrey, who plays Joan, believed so strongly in the merits of the play. If all the characters were as good as Joan, The Sea Flower would be a very safe play indeed. Unfortunately they are mostly mere satellites of that central absurdity, Captain Sherwood. I strongly recommend Mr Law to boldly cut out the Captain's heroism, and make him the unwilling victim of circumstances instead of the criminally stupid self-manufactured martyr he is at present. Otherwise I can hardly believe that even the London playgoer will be able to stand much of him.

A comedy cast without Mr Hawtrey or Mrs Calvert is rather heavily handicapped; but the author cannot complain of the wealth of talent placed at his disposal. Mr Beauchamp, too sane an actor for such an idiotically emotional part as Sherwood, steered it clear of positive ridicule, which was a considerable feat under the circumstances. Mr Cosmo Stuart is rather a heavy juvenile for so airy-fairy a partner as Miss Eva Moore. Miss Lena Ashwell has only one real opportunity: a scene in the first act which she plays very finely—indeed exquisitely. If Miss Ashwell is not careful she will play herself off the stage: it is dangerous to act too well under existing conditions. Mr Playfair and Mr Groves are capital as the corporal and the fisherman; but the parts are not difficult enough to make this much of a compliment. Mr Lovell, as the wicked lieutenant, was good enough to be quite disagreeable; and Miss Homfrey made the hit of the evening as Joan.

The King's Sweetheart at the Métropole is a comic opera perverted in the second act into a variety entertainment by the interpolation of coon songs, topical songs, and the like. This is supposed to be a concession to the vulgarity of certain persons described generally as the British public. The result proves that this mysterious body, to whose demands the self-respect of the rest of the world is habitually sacrificed, has no existence. The moment the dreary variety business began, the gallery, for whose sake it was dragged in, sank into lassitude—"got the hump," as it would have said itself. It woke up delightedly when Mr Glover's pretty mock madrigal brought the entertainment back to the level of the first act. There is not a single argument for introducing a coon song in a comic opera that would not apply equally to making a lively knockabout turn of the battle of Philippi at Her Majesty's. Mr Glover's score is very clever and dainty. His command of the orchestra, and the wit and ingenuity with which the accompaniments are figured and embroidered, enable him to present the simplest and most obvious tunes with distinction. The principal singers in the company, Miss Elise Cooke, Miss Aynsley Cook, and Mr Charles Angelo, acquit themselves very pleasantly and do much to relieve the gloom spread by the low comedians and by the four beauteous ladies who, though apparently competent dancers, persist in punctuating their evolutions with graceless high kicks which finally get on one's nerves—not, I may add, the particular nerves to which they are addressed.

ARCHER'S ANNUAL

THE THEATRICAL WORLD OF 1897. By William Archer. London: Walter Scott. [19 *March* 1898]

THIS time Mr Archer has amused himself by reckoning up the British Drama of the last five years in an "epilogue statistical." Among the authors, Mr Henry Arthur Jones, estimated by the total number of weeks his plays have held the stage, romps in an easy winner, beating the immortal William by ten weeks. Mr Pinero is third, Mr Grundy fourth, and Mr Carton fifth. But surely the worthlessness of this method of calculation must have struck Mr Archer when he observed—if he did observe—that it placed *me* at the bottom of the list. Yet if I had produced forty failures with an average run of three nights each, I should have come out above Mr Jones, and left Shakespear nowhere. Clearly the number of weeks must be divided by the number of plays in order to get the average length of run, which is the true criterion of popularity. On this system the tables are completely turned. I come out, with an average of eleven weeks, ahead of Mr Henry

Arthur Jones with ten and seven-tenths: a narrow but decisive advantage. Besides, Mr Jones has had to write ten plays to secure his place, whereas I have secured mine with one. And Shakespear is at the bottom of the list.

However, as I am not now electioneering, I may as well admit that the change in the method of calculation affects all the other authors as well as the three eminent ones just mentioned. It sends Mr Barrie to the top with an average of over seventeen weeks per play. Mr Pinero is second with fifteen weeks, and Mr Oscar Wilde third with over fourteen weeks. Shakespear, with an average of about six and a half, takes the wooden spoon among British dramatists, though he has the consolation of beating Ibsen, whose average is only a trifle over a fortnight.

But here, again, the figures collapse on examination. The plays of our modern writers are given, verbally at least, as the author writes them; and they are run as long as people will come to them, and often considerably longer. Our unfortunate William, on the other hand, has his text altered and mutilated by most managers; and his plays are frequently produced for a limited number of performances as part of a star's repertory. If, in justice to him, we strike out of Mr Archer's list all those occasional performances which vitiate the comparison with the fully run plays of the modern men, we jump the Bard up instantly to the first flight, immediately behind Messrs Barrie, Pinero, Wilde, and Carton. If we go a step further and fairer, and eliminate the productions of Sir Henry Irving and Mr Augustin Daly and Mr Tree (Julius Cæsar does not come into the period dealt with) as entertainments for which, however meritorious and interesting they may or may not be, Shakespear can hardly be held responsible, and count only those productions by Mr Forbes Robertson and Mr Alexander which were designed to give as much Shakespear as possible, the illustrious author passes Mr Carton and all but ties Mr Wilde and Mr Pinero. Mr Barrie still maintains himself far ahead; but as his figures include twenty-seven weeks of Walker, London, in a very small theatre, whereas William has had to fill the Lyceum and St James's, it may be fairly claimed that he holds his own against the most popular dramatists of the day. A similar scrutiny of Mr Jones's list shews that the accidental week of The Middleman and the strange adventure of Michael and his Lost Angel should be excluded, raising his average by three weeks.

A further scrutiny shews that a table should be compiled allotting the runs, not by authors, but by managements and actors. For instance, it is quite clear from Mr Archer's table that Mr Wyndham's acting, and the size of his theatre, are potent factors in run-making, and that Mr Alexander is a pre-eminently capable manager. The furore created by Mrs Patrick Campbell in 1893 must have contributed largely to the staying powers of The Second Mrs Tanqueray: still, a selection of those Pinero plays which clearly succeeded altogether on their own merits, brings out an excellent average, though not quite so good a one as that of Mr Oscar Wilde, who seems to carry off the palm as an "actor-proof" author. A good many of these cross lights on the figures are so interesting, that I suggest to Mr Archer, being too lazy to do it myself, that he should, in a magazine article, supplement his epilogue by working out the statistics for theatres (classified according to capacity), managers, leading ladies, leading men, and so on.

The most interesting and significant table given is that of failures and successes. Mr Archer estimates that only sixty-five West End plays, out of the 235 produced within the five years (pantomimes, operas, and plays performed in foreign languages are not included), have been successes. Fifty-four he puts down as doubtful, and the remaining 117 as failures. Since theatrical accounts are not published, and nobody connected with a theatre has ever, within the memory of mortal man, been known to tell the truth about the box-office, these figures are admittedly guessed at; but they are pretty sure to overestimate the success and underestimate the failure; for the bluffing that goes on is so heroic, that the real figures of theatrical enterprise are incredible and unthinkable even by seasoned sceptics. Probably if Mr Archer were to classify the plays, and then compare the financial result in the different classes, it would be found that the ultra-popular plays were the most disastrous, and Ibsen's the safest.

Mr Archer lays a good deal of stress on two features of the five years. "Whatever its value," he says, "a new literary movement set in with the production of The Second Mrs Tanqueray, in 1893; and it was about the same time, or a little earlier, that the all-conquering musical farce began its triumphal progress." Now the only "literary movement" I have observed—and a most significant one it is—is the sudden conquest of the stage by the novelists. With this Mr Pinero has clearly nothing to do, for he is distinctly a playwright. The Second Mrs Tanqueray is not only a stage play in the most technical sense, but even a noticeably old-fashioned one in its sentiment and stage mechanism. Mr Archer cannot mean that its success in any way helped to prepare the triumphs of Trilby, The Prisoner of Zenda, and Under the Red Robe, nor to secure tolerance for the prettiness of such drama-tized novelettes as One Summer's Day and A Bachelor's Rom-ance. Of such plays it would have been unhesitatingly said five years ago that they were not "du théâtre." Mr Charringon's des-perate attempt to bring the novelists to the rescue of the stage seemed at that time a mere blunder, though he hit on some of the very men who are now ousting the playwrights proper. But The Second Mrs Tanqueray might have been produced ten years ago, and been all the more modish for the backwardation. I take it therefore that Mr Archer is thinking of something else when he uses the term "literary movement." I suggest that this something else requires more careful definition. I cannot for the life of me see that any new impulse came to our dramatic literature between 1889, when "the potent and sundering word" of Ibsen first reached us, and the irruption of the novelists, headed by Du Maurier and Mr Anthony Hope, in 1895 and 1896. The irruption occurred exactly at the moment when the attempt made by Mr Jones and Mr Pinero to bring our fashionable drama up to the Norwegian standard of seriousness had been practically defeated by the rather sulky reception of The Triumph of the Philistines, Michael and his Lost Angel, The Notorious Mrs Ebbsmith, and

The Benefit of the Doubt, not to mention the fact, by that time pretty well established, that a play by Ibsen himself meant a fortnight's business and no more. What the novelists proved was that the playgoing public, formerly illiterate, had now become a novel-reading public, and could catch aptly enough those bookish touches of humor, strains of sentimentality, and gentle strokes of character, which were once too flimsy to be of any use on the stage. Nay, we are actually shewing a most alarming incapacity for taking in any stronger style of work. Our old dramatic hands, therefore, find that their liberty to deal in the delicacies of the novelist, to indulge in his wilful excursiveness, and to hang a good deal of elegant trifling on trivially fantastic themes, is enormously enlarged: hence we have The Princess and the Butterfly, and Trelawny of the Wells, plays which would not have been tolerated in the eighties, although, as I have said, Mrs Tanqueray would have been quite at home there. The earlier instances of Mr Jones's Case of Rebellious Susan and The Masqueraders, though their significance was obscured at the time by the strong melodramatic element in the latter, reveal the same tendency now quite plainly in the light of subsequent events; and as for The Liars, it might quite conceivably have been written by Mr W. D. Howells, if he had had Mr Jones's technical training. On the whole, the gain has been considerable; but the attempt at greater poetic depth and philosophic seriousness on the long-run plane has been decisively defeated.

As to the musical farce movement, it was only a new fashion of catering for that impulse to go on the spree which still overtakes highly respectable members of the community from time to time. But, though negligible artistically, it may have had some economic significance; for the success of Morocco Bound seems to have brought the practice of forming syndicates to finance theatrical productions into fashion in the City. That is to say, Capital, which used to back the manager, especially the actor-manager, now backs the play, and hires its manager and company for the occasion just as it hires its carpenters. It is quite possible that in course of time the City may begin to deal in serious artistic plays as well as in pornographic entertainments, and that our authors will lease their dramatic rights to City firms instead of dealing directly with the managers. It is even possible that there may be no managers at all in the present sense of the word. In truth, there are already more managers in London than the public supposes, who are no more masters in their own theatres than the L. and N.W. stationmaster is the owner of Rugby junction.

I note with alarm an appalling doubt expressed by Mr Archer as to the continuance of his annual register. I can only say that if there is the remotest prospect of the disappearance of what has become an indispensable work of reference as well as a unique critical history of the English stage, its publishers must be asleep, or else their market, huge as it is, is the wrong market for the enterprise. The demand of the public libraries alone ought to make The Theatrical World as safe as the Encyclopædia Britannica.

ENGLAND'S DELICATE COMPLIMENT TO IBSEN

[26 *March* 1898]

THE English theatre distinguished itself last week. The occasion was Ibsen's seventieth birthday. On the Continent it was celebrated by special representations of his works. The English theatre took not the smallest notice of Ibsen, but gave an enthusiastic and unprecedented benefit to Miss Nellie Farren. This is quite as it should be. It expresses the real condition of dramatic art in this country with just the characteristic British touch of caricature. Sir Henry Irving and the other leaders of his profession probably feel proud of it. Mr Beerbohm Tree, who ventured to contribute three guineas towards the purchase of a drinking-cup for Ibsen (all Norwegians are assumed to be mighty drinkers), must feel rather like a man in morning dress at a smart dinner-party; for no other manager compromised himself by meddling in the business. And the managers were quite right. They are not in Ibsen's line; and Ibsen is not in theirs. He has seated himself over their heads without the slightest assistance from them, or the faintest comprehension on their part why or how he was establishing himself on high without their having voice or part in the matter.

I must offer the drinking-cup committee a mild remonstrance as to their rather maladroit handling of our little celebration. Ibsen will receive two impressions from it: first, that his admirers in England consist of an insignificant clique of fifty persons, of whom only four could be persuaded to contribute more than a guinea; and second, that these fifty are such gross ignoramuses and Philistines as to believe that the art of making beautiful drinking-vessels for State occasions reached its highest point in the reign of George II. Now the truth is that all the guinea subscriptions of which I have any knowledge were limited to that snobbish minimum at the suggestion of the committee, and were accompanied by an intimation that a higher subscription would be equally agreeable to the subscriber. When the published list revealed the fact that three or four gentlemen had been allowed to break through the arrangement and give double or treble subscriptions, the rest were naturally furious. Had such a result been proposed or contemplated, some of the subscriptions would have amounted to perhaps double the total amount collected. More aggravating still, it now appears that so far from any serious effort having been made to bring the subscription under the notice of all those who would obviously have supported it—not to mention the great body of undistinguished and unknown disciples— the call had been whispered so timidly that the effect produced was that of a deliberate attempt to make the affair the private property of a clique. Now that the mistake is apparent, the apology made is that Ibsen's seventieth birthday was rushed on an unprepared world with such precipitation that there was no time to communicate with more than the few nearest Ibsenites. The excuse is a bold one, considering how outrageously impossible and incredible it is. Plenty of people who are just as accessible and eligible as I was heard nothing of the affair. It is quite clear to me that the whole business must have presented itself to the organizing secretary as a private tribute from a few friends and admirers of the Master, acting together in the matter as a sectional group wishing, as such, to individualize its share in the birthday offerings. But in that case, what right had he to spring its little present on the press and public as England's tribute to Ibsen? When you meddle with a big man you must do it in a big way. Through overlooking this the group has landed itself in sending Ibsen a paltry present and filling his disciples with rage and shame, which of course found expression promptly in the press. Fortunately it will not matter much to a man so deeply skilled as Ibsen in parochialism. He will quite understand that I and the other signatories of the address represent merely one of a dozen little sets, each of which regards some great man as its own private discovery and exclusive property. And he will write us a nice letter in which he will gravely pretend to believe that we are the people of England. Then, presumably, he will refresh himself with a glance at the accounts of the circulation of his works rendered by his English publishers, and wink.

To Mr Archer, also, I have a remonstrance to address. He has dropped into poetry, to the extent of a column and a half in the Chronicle, over the same matter. And he has actually dragged in Shakespear! Is it kind to Shakespear? Is it polite to Ibsen? I notice how very guardedly it is done: a careful scrutiny will shew that Mr Archer has committed himself to nothing more controversial than the statement that Ibsen will go the way that Shakespear went, which may mean no more than the way of all flesh. But I am greatly afraid that Ibsen will infer, at the first glance, that he is expected to feel complimented at being compared to Shakespear, in which case he will certainly be so unspeakably enraged that no subsequent explanations will ever restore the good understanding existing between him and his translator. It reminds one of the painful occasion when, at a musical celebration, a wreath was solemnly awarded to Gounod and Wagner as representing jointly all that was great in modern music, with the result, of course, of throwing both masters into a frenzy. Considering that the literary side of the mission of Ibsen here has been the rescue

343

of this unhappy country from its centuries of slavery to Shake-spear, it does seem a little strong to inform the creator of the Master-builder and Hedda Gabler that he is going the way of the creator of Prospero and the Queen in Hamlet. There is nothing that requires more discretion than the paying of com-pliments to great men. When an American journalist describes Sir Edward Burne-Jones as "the English Gustave Doré," or declares Madox Brown to have been "as a realist, second only to Frith," he means well; and possibly the victims of his good in-tentions give him credit for them. But I do most earnestly beg the inhabitants of this island to be extremely careful how they compare any foreigner to Shakespear. The foreigner can know nothing of Shakespear's power over language. He can only judge him by his intellectual force and dramatic insight, quite apart from his beauty of expression. From such a test Ibsen comes out with a double first-class: Shakespear comes out hardly anywhere. Our English deficiency in analytic power makes it extremely hard for us to understand how a man who is great in any respect can be insignificant in any other respect; and perhaps the average foreigner is not much cleverer. But when the foreigner has the particular respect in which our man is great cut off from him artificially by the change of language, as a screen of colored glass will shut off certain rays from a camera, then the deficiency which is concealed even from our experts by the splendor of Shake-spear's literary gift, may be obvious to quite commonplace people who know him only through translations. In any language of the world Brand, Peer Gynt, and Emperor or Galilean prove their author a thinker of extraordinary penetration, and a moralist of international influence. Turn from them to To be or not to be, or The seven ages of man, and imagine, if you can, anybody more critical than a village schoolmaster being imposed on by such platitudinous fudge. The comparison does not honor Ibsen: it makes Shakespear ridiculous: and for both their sakes it should not be drawn. If we cannot for once let the poor Bard alone, let us humbly apologize to Ibsen for our foolish worship of a foolish collection of shallow proverbs in blank verse. Let us plead that if we compare, not the absolute Shakespear with the absolute Ibsen, but the advance from the old stage zany Hamblet to our William's Hamlet with the advance from Faust to Peer Gynt, Hamlet was really a great achievement, and might stand as an isolated feat against Peer Gynt as an isolated feat. But as it led to nothing, whereas Peer Gynt led to so much that it now ranks only as part of Ibsen's romantic wild oats—above all, as Ibsen's message nerved him to fight all Europe in the teeth of starvation, whereas Shakespear's was not proof even against the ignorance and vulgarity of the London playgoer, it only needs another turn of the discussion to shew that a comparison of the two popular masterpieces is like a comparison of the Eiffel Tower to one of the peaks in an Alpine chain. It is quite useless to attempt to flatter the great men of the nineteenth century by comparing them to the men of the decadent sixteenth. It shews a want of respect for them and for ourselves. If Ibsen had got no further than "the path that Shakespear trod," he would never have been heard of outside Norway; and as it is quite possible that he may be perfectly aware of this, I implore Mr Archer never to mention Stratford-on-Avon to him, especially as he has already conferred the Order of the Swan on Maeterlinck. Ibsen may be as little disposed to share honors with "the Belgian Shakespear" as Wagner was with Gounod.

MR HEINEMANN AND THE CENSOR

SUMMER MOTHS. A play in four acts. By William Heinemann. London: Lane. 1898.   [2 *April* 1898]

I WONDER whether Mr William Heinemann is the coming dramatist. He tells us that he submitted Summer Moths to a critic "peerless among those who sit to judge." This gentleman expressed astonishment at the relentless morality of the play, and assured Mr Heinemann that it "fulfilled unquestionably the Aristotelean $\kappa \acute{a} \theta a \rho \sigma \iota \varsigma$." On the evidence of this opinion I make bold to denounce this peerless person, however illustrious, as a polite humbug. There is no relentless morality whatever about Summer

Moths; and the tenderest soul may take it in without experiencing any cathartic effects. Furthermore, it is a play which confesses to a quite exceptional lack of specific talent. It is not adroitly constructed; it is not witty; it shews no mastery of language—not even ordinary fluency; and it deals with common sorts of common men and women without venturing on a single stroke of rare individual personality. This is why the peerless one was driven into pompous evasion and Greek literation in his obvious effort to spare the author's feelings.

So much, and no less, any artist-critic must say for the relief of his starving soul after a meal of Summer Moths. But he does not thereby dispose of the play in the least; on the contrary, he only lays bare the secret of its importance. If Mr Heinemann were an artist of brilliant and facile specific theatrical talent, he would do what our popular dramatists do: that is, pour another kettle-full of water on the exhausted tea-leaves of romance and idealism, and make the pale decoction palatable by all sorts of innutritious sweets and spices and effervescents and stimulants. Luckily, he is as incapable of doing this as Millet was of painting like Bouguereau or Fortuny. Under these circumstances one may ask, Why write plays at all? As the elder Dumas said, it is so easy not to write them. But this position, carefully considered, will be found to apply just as forcibly to Dumas himself, or to Shakespear, or Ibsen, as to Mr Heinemann. All art is gratuitous; and the will to produce it, like the will to live, must be held to justify itself. When that will is associated with brilliant specific talent for the established forms and attractions of fine art, no advance is made, because the artist can distinguish and satisfy himself by novel, witty, and touching rehandlings of the old themes. If Wagner had possessed the astonishing specific talent of Mozart, or Mr George Meredith that of Dickens, they would not have been forced to make a revolution in their art by lifting it to a plane on which it developed new and extraordinary specific talents in themselves, and revealed the old specific talents to them as mere hindrances. A critic who has not learned this from the nineteenth century has learned nothing. Such a one, on discovering that a writer is deficient in all the current specific talents, at once condemns him without benefit of clergy. But for my part, when I find the characteristic devotion of the born artist accompanied by a hopeless deficiency in all the fashionable specific talents—and this appears to be Mr Heinemann's case—I immediately give him my most respectful attention, and am particularly careful to indulge in none of those prophecies of extinction which were so confidently launched at Wagner, Ibsen, and Meredith.

Let me put the thing in a practical way. Mr Heinemann has now published two dramas: The First Step and Summer Moths. I ask anybody who has read these plays whether Mr Heinemann will ever write like Mr Pinero? The answer can only be an emphatic Never—never to his dying day. Will he ever handle a pen and play with an idea as Mr Max Beerbohm and Mr Oscar Wilde can? Clearly never—not even if we were to wrap him in blotting-paper and boil him in ink for a week to make his literary faculty supple and tender.

But then we do not want another Pinero: indeed it is Mr Pinero's confounded aptitude for doing what other people have done before that makes him a reactionary force in English dramatic literature, and helps to keep the stage bound to the follies of the eighteen-sixties. Now nobody will accuse Mr Heinemann of having the smallest aptitude for doing anything that any dramatist has done before him. That would not prevent him from trying to do it—vainly and hopelessly trying—if he were the mere foolish, incapable, amateur sort of person whose manuscripts he himself has to reject by the dozen in the way of his business. I conclude from the fact that he does not try, that he is not that sort of person. There is no trace of any sort of literary ambition in his dramas. Whether he has been driven back from conventional literary professionalism after taking the opinion of peerless judges on a deskful of blank verse tragedies and fashionable comedies, or whether he accepted his natural disabilities straight off, I do not know, and do not care. For in either case he has done the right thing in giving up literature and the specific talents, and beginning to drive as hard as he can at real life. Out of that anything may come. So far the output has not been very wonderful, although the fact of a man going to work in that way in England today *is* rather wonderful. It is true that when Maupassant's vogue was at its height, Mr Heinemann's method would not have surprised anybody in France. But since England is not France, and since Mr Heinemann does not in the least imitate Maupassant, though he does what Maupassant did, he must be allowed to be that very rare phenomenon, an original writer. And there, for the present, criticism had better leave him. It is waste of time to talk about a man's second play if he is really breaking new ground. Mr Heinemann has given us, in a rather hampered and anything but charming way, two somewhat squalid and limited bits of life which we cannot deny to be true, and which are at all events large enough to raise formidable problems and create tragic conflicts pending their solution. If he will now kindly hurry along to, say, his Opus 6, then I shall begin to get interested.

It appears from the preface to Summer Moths that Mr Heinemann has once more got into trouble with the Censorship. He tells us that the Queen's reader of plays, "requiring, with lady-like niceness, a good character for the frail heroine, not only deprived the play of its purpose, but rendered it, if not positively *im*moral, *un*moral, to say the least." But why on earth should an official be reviled for doing exactly what he is appointed to do? The serious drama is perhaps the most formidable social weapon that a modern reformer can wield. When the English governing classes discovered this on the occasion of Fielding's threat to attack parliamentary corruption from the stage, they deliberately resolved that the weapon should be so blunted by a court official as to make it useless for the purposes of the reformer. Mr Redford is not appointed to make the theatre moral, but solely to prevent its having any effect on public opinion: in other words, to make it, as Mr Heinemann rightly says, *un*moral. That is what he is there for; and why should he not do his official duty? Nay, even if he were free to do exactly as he liked in the matter, he could not recommend the Lord Chamberlain to license a serious play without thereby accepting some degree of responsibility for the author's opinions. And—if Mr Redford will excuse my saying so—what dramatist of any serious pretension could level his conceptions of the destiny of society to the little set of social prejudices which constitute the "views" of a gentleman appointed without examination to a post in the palace household with a salary of £320 a year? Why, the Astronomer Royal, with an infinitely less important, responsible, and difficult office, gets £1000 a year. A County Court judge, whose functions are a joke in comparison, gets £1500 a year. Neither the Astronomer Royal nor a County Court judge can procure his appointment without having his qualifications pretty severely tested. But it is the essence of an effective Censorship that its officials should have no qualifications at all. If Mr Redford knew the difference between a good play and a bad one, the temptation to license the good plays and veto the bad ones would be overwhelming; and the stage would instantly become a social and political power—the very thing his post was instituted to prevent. Even as it is, he knows too much to be a good Censor. He has already licensed plays, including some of my own, which were meant to influence public opinion, and which have created public discussion.

But the Censorship has lately taken a new departure. Formerly, when it objected to a play, it specified the passage it objected to. It expurgated your play for you, and licensed it "with the exception of all words and passages which are specified by the examiner in the endorsement of this licence." In this way the oppressed author or manager at least knew that when he had paid his two guineas he had no further extortion to fear. But now the practice has changed. Mr Buchanan, it seems, has been one of the first victims; but I am not sure that I was not beforehand with him. The other day I was forced to submit a play for licence in order to protect myself from the possibly very heavy loss from forfeiture of stage right which its publication without a preliminary performance might inflict on me. The result was so far a foregone conclusion that the play, though not yet published, was already printed with a preface announcing the refusal of the Censor to license it. Consequently, when I sent in my play and my two guineas to Mr Redford, I could not help feeling rather anxious lest in a careless moment he should license my play, and so put me to the heavy expense of cancelling, rewriting, and reprinting my preface. I had even marked his copy conspicuously as a play with a serious purpose, in order to rouse his worst suspicions. But he behaved nobly, and did exactly what I had said he would do. I then applied for the usual indication of the objectionable passages, in order that I might still secure my copyright by performing that part of the play which had no meaning, objectionable or otherwise, apart from such passages. The Censor promptly replied, in the teeth of the very terms of his printed form of licence, that it was not his business to expurgate my play, and that if I would send in a licensable play he would license it without reference to any previous play submitted to him. I confess that I then began to respect the business capacity of the Lord Chamberlain's department for the first time. I found myself forced not only to debauch my own play with my own hands, so that I could not afterwards turn round, like Mr Heinemann, and accuse the Censorship of having done it, but to disgorge another two guineas. And if I had shewn the slightest reluctance or want of thoroughness in obliterating every syllable which gave moral purpose to my play and redeemed it from being a mere sensational brutality, Mr Redford could have continued refusing and demanding a new version at the rate of two guineas per refusal until he had driven me to the point at which it would have been cheaper to dispense with him altogether by a method which need not here be described. So I "expurgated" that play until it was as gratuitous an offence against good manners as any dramatist was ever guilty of, in which condition Mr Redford was as much bound to license it as he had been not to license it when it meant something and might have done some good. It was then duly sanctioned by the Lord Chamberlain and performed; and presently the original version will be published without the omission of a single comma. And for the life of me, absurd and extor-

tionate and obscurantist and indecent and hypocritical and purposely tyrannical and evil as the whole institution of the Censorship is, I do not see what else Mr Redford could have done, or
why he should expurgate any play when he has the power to
make the author do it himself, in addition to paying twice over
for having it done by somebody else. If his post could be a useful
one in the hands of a good man I should say nothing against it.
But if the Angel Gabriel could be induced to take it, it would
only become a greater nuisance, if possible, than it is at present.

THE DRAMA IN HOXTON

[9 *April* 1898]

OF late, I am happy to say, the theatres have been so uneventful
that I should have fallen quite out of the habit of my profession
but for a certain vigorously democratic clergyman, who seized
me and bore me off to the last night of the pantomime at "the
Brit." The Britannia Theatre is in Hoxton, not far from Shoreditch Church, a neighborhood in which the Saturday Review is
comparatively little read. The manager, a lady, is the most
famous of all London managers. Sir Henry Irving, compared to
her, is a mushroom, just as his theatre, compared to hers, is a back
drawing room. Over 4000 people pay nightly at her doors; and
the spectacle of these thousands, serried in the vast pit and em-
pyrean gallery, is so fascinating that the stranger who first beholds
it can hardly turn away to look at the stage. Forty years ago Mrs
Sara Lane built this theatre; and she has managed it ever since. It
may be no such great matter to handle a single playhouse—your
Irvings, Trees, Alexanders, Wyndhams, and other upstarts of
yesterday can do that; but Mrs Lane is said to own the whole
ward in which her theatre stands. Madame Sarah Bernhardt's
diamonds fill a jewel-box: Mrs Lane's are reputed to fill sacks.
When I had the honor of being presented to Mrs Lane, I thought
of the occasion when the late Sir Augustus Harris, her only
serious rival in managerial fame, had the honor of being presented to me. The inferiority of the man to the woman was mani-

fest. Sir Augustus was, in comparison, an hysterical creature. Enterprise was with him a frenzy which killed him when it reached a climax of success. Mrs Lane thrives on enterprise and success, and is capable, self-contained, practical, vigilant, every-thing that a good general should be. A West End star is to her a person to whom she once gave so many pounds or shillings a week, and who is now, in glittering and splendid anxiety, begging for engagements, desperately wooing syndicates and potential backers, and living on Alnaschar dreams and old press notices which were unanimously favorable (if you excluded those which were obviously malignant personal attacks). Mrs Lane, well furnished with realities, has no use for dreams; and she knows syndicates and capitalists only as suspicious characters who want her money, not as courted deities with powers of life and death in their hands. The fortune of her productions means little to her: if the piece succeeds, so much the better: if not, the pantomime pays for all.

The clergyman's box, which was about as large as an average Metropolitan railway station, was approached from the stage itself; so that I had opportunities of criticizing both from before the curtain and behind it. I was struck by the absence of the worthless, heartless, incompetent people who seem to get em-ployed with such facility—nay, sometimes apparently by pre-ference—in West End theatres. The West End calculation for musical farce and pantomime appears to be that there is "a silver mine" to be made by paying several pounds a week to people who are worth nothing, provided you engage enough of them. This is not Mrs Lane's plan. Mr Bigwood, the stage-manager, is a real stage-manager, to whom one can talk on unembarrassed human terms as one capable man to another, and not by any means an erratic art failure from Bedford Park and the Slade School, or one of those beachcombers of our metropolitan civilization who drift to the West End stage because its fringe of short-lived ventures provide congenital liars and impostors with unique opportunities of drawing a few months' or weeks' salary before their preoccupied and worried employers have leisure to realize that they have made a bad bargain. I had not the pleasure of making the prompter's acquaintance; but I should have been surprised to find him the only person in the theatre who could not read, though in the West I should have expected to find that his principal qualification. I made my way under the stage to look at the working of the star-trap by which Mr Lupino was flung up through the boards like a stone from a volcano; and there, though I found eight men wasting their strength by overcoming a counterweight which, in an up-to-date French *théâtre de féerie*, is raised by one man with the help of a pulley, the carpenter-machinist in command was at once recognizable as a well-selected man. On the stage the results of the same instinctive sort of judgment were equally apparent. The display of beauty was sufficiently voluptuous; but there were no good-for-nothings: it was a company of men and women, recognizable as fellow-creatures, and not as accidentally pretty cretinous freaks. Even the low comedians were not blackguards, though they were certainly not fastidious, Hoxton being somewhat Rabelaisian in its ideas of broad humor. One scene, in which the horrors of sea-sickness were exploited with great freedom, made the four thousand sons and daughters of Shoreditch scream with laughter. At the climax, when four voyagers were struggling violently for a single bucket, I looked stealthily round the box, in which the Church, the Peerage, and the Higher Criticism were represented. All three were in convulsions. Compare this with our West End musical farces, in which the performers strive to make some inane scene "go" by trying to suggest to the starving audience that there is something exquisitely loose and vicious beneath the dreary fatuity of the surface. Who would not rather look at and laugh at four men pretending to be sea-sick in a wildly comic way than see a row of young women singing a chorus about being "Gaiety Girls" with the deliberate intention of conveying to the audience that a Gaiety chorister's profession—their own pro-fession—is only a mask for the sort of life which is represented in Piccadilly Circus and Leicester Square after midnight? I quite agree with my friend the clergyman that decent ladies and gentlemen who have given up West End musical farce in disgust will find themselves much happier at the Britannia pantomime.

I shall not venture on any searching artistic criticism of Will o' the Wisp, as the pantomime was called. If it were a West End piece, I should pitch into it without the slightest regard to the prestige and apparent opulence of the manager, not because I am incorruptible, but because I am not afraid of the mere shadow of success. I treat its substance, in the person of Mrs Lane, with careful respect. Shew me real capacity; and I bow lower to it than anybody. All I dare suggest to the Hoxtonians is that when they insist on an entertainment lasting from seven to close upon midnight, they have themselves to thank if the actors occasionally have to use all their ingenuity to spin out scenes of which a judicious playgoer would desire to have at least ten minutes less.

The enthusiasm of the pit on the last night, with no stalls to cut it off from the performers, was frantic. There was a great throwing of flowers and confectionery on the stage; and it would happen occasionally that an artist would overlook one of these tributes, and walk off, leaving it unnoticed on the boards. Then a shriek of tearing anxiety would arise, as if the performer were wandering blindfold into a furnace or over a precipice. Every factory girl in the house would lacerate the air with a mad scream of "Pick it up, Topsy!" "Pick it up, Voylit!" followed by a gasp of relief, several thousand strong, when Miss Topsy Sinden or Miss Violet Durkin would return and annex the offering. I was agreeably astonished by Miss Topsy Sinden's dancing. Thitherto it had been my miserable fate to see her come on, late in the second act of some unspeakably dreary inanity at the West End, to interpolate a "skirt dance," and spin out the unendurable by the intolerable. On such occasions I have looked on her with cold hatred, wondering why the "varieties" of a musical farce should not include a few items from the conventional "assault-at-arms," culminating in some stalwart sergeant, after the usual slicing of lemons, leaden bars, and silk handkerchiefs, cutting a skirt-dancer in two at one stroke. At the Britannia Miss Sinden really danced, acted, and turned out quite a charming person. I was not surprised; for the atmosphere was altogether more bracing than at the other end of the town. These poor playgoers, to whom the expenditure of half a guinea for a front seat at a theatre is as outrageously and extravagantly impossible as the purchase of a deer forest in Mars is to a millionaire, have at least one excellent quality in the theatre. They are jealous *for* the dignity of the artist, not derisively covetous of his (or her) degradation. When a white statue which had stood for thirteen minutes in the middle of the stage turned out to be Mr Lupino, who forthwith put on a classic plasticity, and in a series of rapid poses claimed popular respect for "the antique," it was eagerly accorded; and his demon conflict with the powers of evil, involving a desperate broadsword combat, and the most prodigious plunges into the earth and projections therefrom by volcanic traps as aforesaid, was conducted with all the tragic dignity of Richard III and received in the true Aristotelean spirit by the audience. The fairy queen, a comely prima donna who scorned all frivolity, was treated with entire respect and seriousness. Altogether, I seriously recommend those of my readers who find a pantomime once a year good for them, to go next year to the Britannia, and leave the West End to its boredoms and all the otherdoms that make it so expensively dreary.

Oh, these sentimental, second-sighted Scotchmen! Reader: would you like to see me idealized by a master hand? If you would, buy the Sunday Special of the 3rd instant, and study Mr Robert Buchanan's open letter to me. There you will find the ideal G. B. S. in "the daring shamelessness of a powerful and fearless nudity." This is the sort of thing that flatters a timid, sedentary literary man. Besides, it protects him: other people believe it all, and are afraid to hit the poor paper Titan. Far be it from me to say a word against so effective an advertisement; though when I consider its generosity I cannot but blush for having taken in so magnanimous an idealizer. Yet a great deal of it is very true: Mr Buchanan is altogether right, it seems to me, in identifying my views with his father's Owenism; only I claim that Comte's law of the three stages has been operating busily since

Owen's time, and that modern Fabianism represents the positive stage of Owenism. I shall not plead against the highly complimentary charge of impudence in its proper sense of shamelessness. Shame is to the man who fights with his head what cowardice is to the man who fights with his hands: I have the same opinion of it as Bunyan put into the mouth of Faithful in the Valley of Humiliation. But I do not commit myself to Mr Buchanan's account of my notions of practical reform. It is true that when I protest against our marriage laws, and Mr Buchanan seizes the occasion to observe that "the idea of marriage, spiritually speaking, is absolutely beautiful and ennobling," I feel very much as if a Chinese mandarin had met my humanitarian objection to starving criminals to death or cutting them into a thousand pieces, by blandly remarking that "the idea of evil-doing leading to suffering is, spiritually speaking, absolutely beautiful and ennobling." If Mr Buchanan is content to be forbidden to spiritually ennoble himself except under legal conditions so monstrous and immoral that no disinterestedly prudent and self-respecting person would accept them when free from amorous infatuation, then I am not. Mr Buchanan's notion that I assume that "marriage is essentially and absolutely an immoral bargain between the sexes in so far as it conflicts with the aberrations and caprices of the human appetite," is a wildly bad shot. What on earth has marriage to do with the aberrations and caprices of human appetite? People marry for companionship, not for debauchery. Why that wholesome companionship should be a means of making amiable and honest people the helpless prey of drunkards, criminals, pestiferous invalids, bullies, viragoes, lunatics, or even persons with whom, through no fault on either side, they find it impossible to live happily, I cannot for the life of me see; and if Mr Buchanan can, I invite him to give his reasons. Can any sane person deny that a contract "for better, for worse" destroys all moral responsibility? And is it not a revolting and indecent thing that any indispensable social contract should compulsorily involve a clause, abhorrent to both parties if they have a scrap of honor in them, by which the persons of the parties are placed at each other's disposal by legal force? These abominations may not belong to "the idea of marriage, spiritually speaking"; but they belong to the fact of marriage, practically speaking; and it is with this fact that I, as a Realist (Mr Buchanan's own quite correct expression), am concerned. If I were to get married myself, I should resort to some country where the marriage law is somewhat less than five centuries out of date; and as this seems to me as unreasonable a condition for the ordinary man as a trip to Bayreuth is to the ordinary gallery opera-goer, I do what I can to relieve him of it, and make married people as responsible for their good behavior to one another as business partners are. Hereupon Mr Buchanan discourses in the following terms:— "The Naked Man [me!] posing as a realist, cries, 'away with sanctions! let us have no more of them'; but the man who is clothed and in his right mind knows that they are inevitable and accepts them." Did anyone ever hear such nonsense? Do the Americans accept them? Do the French accept them? Would we accept them but for our national preference for hypocrisy eked out with collusive divorce cases? I have no objection to Mr Buchanan idealizing me; but when he takes to idealizing the English law at its stupidest, he oversteps my drawn line. I am none the less obliged to him for giving me an excuse for another assault on these patent beautifiers and ennoblers without which, it is assumed, we should all fall to universal rapine, though the danger of licence is plainly all the other way. I verily believe that if the percentage of happy marriages ever rises to, say, twenty-five, the existence of the human intellect will be threatened by the very excesses against which our marriage law is supposed to protect us.

MR CHARLES FROHMAN'S MISSION

THE SPANISH GIPSY. By Middleton and Rowley. The Elizabethan Stage Society, St George's Hall, 5 April 1898.

JULIA. A new and original play in three acts. By Arthur Sturgess. Royalty Theatre, 7 April 1898.

THE HEART OF MARYLAND. A drama in four acts. By David
Belasco. Adelphi Theatre, 9 April 1898.

THE COUSIN FROM AUSTRALIA. A new and original farcical
comedy in three acts. Opéra Comique, 11 April 1898.

[16 *April* 1898]

AFTER The Heart of Maryland, at the Adelphi, I begin to regard
Mr Charles Frohman as a manager with a great moral mission.
We have been suffering of late years in England from a wave of
blackguardism. Our population is so large that even its little
minorities of intellectual and moral dwarfs form a considerable
body, and can make an imposing noise, so long as the sensible
majority remain silent, with its clamor for war, for "empire," for
savage sports, savage punishments, flogging, duelling, prize-
fighting, 144 hours' bicycle races, national war dances to celebrate
the cautious pounding of a few thousand barbarians to death with
machine projectiles, followed by the advance of a whole British
brigade on the wretched survivors under "a withering fire"
which kills twenty-three men, and national newspaper paragraphs
in which British heroes of the rank and file, who will be flung
starving on our streets in a year or two at the expiration of their
short service, proudly describe the sport of village-burning, remarking, with a touch of humorous Cockney reflectiveness, on
the amusing manner in which old Indian women get "fairly
needled" at the spectacle of their houses and crops being burnt,
and mentioning with honest pride how their officers were elated
and satisfied with the day's work. My objection to this sort of
folly is by no means purely humanitarian. I am quite prepared
to waive the humanitarian point altogether, and to accept, for
the sake of argument, the position that we must destroy or be
destroyed. But I do not believe in the destructive force of a combination of descriptive talent with delirium tremens. I do not
feel safe behind a rampart of music-hall enthusiasm: on the contrary, the mere thought of what these poor, howling, half-drunk
patriots would do if the roll of a hostile drum reached their ears,
brings out a cold sweat of pity and terror on me. Imagine going

to war, as the French did in 1870, with a stock of patriotic idealism and national enthusiasm instead of a stock of military efficiency. The Dervishes have plenty of racial idealism and enthusiasm, with religious fanaticism and personal hardihood to boot; and much good it has done them! What would have happened to them if they had been confronted by the army of the future is only conceivable because, after all, the limit of possibility is annihilation, which is conceivable enough. I picture that future army to myself dimly as consisting of half-a-dozen highly paid elderly gentlemen provided with a picnic basket and an assortment of implements of wholesale destruction. Depend upon it, its first meeting with our hordes of Continental enslaved conscripts and thriftless English "surplus population," disciplined into combining all the self-helplessness of machinery with the animal disadvantages of requiring food and being subject to panic, and commanded by the grown-up boyishness for which the other professions have no use, will be the death of military melodrama. It is quite clear, at all events, that the way out of the present militaristic madness will be found by the first nation that takes war seriously, or, as the melodramatizers of war will say, cynically. It has always been so. The fiery Rupert, charging for God and the King, got on excellently until Cromwell, having some experience as a brewer, made the trite experiment of raising the wages of the Parliamentary soldier to the market value of respectable men, and immediately went over Rupert like a steam-roller. Napoleon served out enthusiasm, carefully mixed with prospects of loot, as cold-bloodedly as a pirate captain serves out rum, and never used it as an efficient substitute for facts and cannon. Wellington, with his characteristic Irish common sense, held a steadfast opinion of the character of the average British private and the capacity of the average British officer which would wreck the Adelphi theatre if uttered there; but he fed them carefully, and carried our point with them against the enemy. At the present time, if I or anyone else were to propose that enough money should be spent on the British soldier to make him an efficient marksman, to attract respectable

and thrifty men to the service, to escape the necessity for filling
the ranks with undersized wasters and pretending to believe the
glaring lies as to their ages which the recruiting sergeant has
to suggest to them, and to abolish the military prison with its
cat-o'-nine-tails perpetually flourishing before our guardsmen in
Gibraltar "fortress orders" and the like, there would be a howl
of stingy terror from the very taxpayers who are now weeping
with national enthusiasm over the heroism of the two Dargai
pipers who, five years hence, will probably be cursing, in their
poverty, the day they ever threw away their manhood on the
British War Office.

The question for the dramatic critic is, how is it possible to
knock all this blood-and-thunder folly out of the head of the
British playgoer? Satire would be useless: sense still more out of
the question. Mr Charles Frohman seems to me to have solved
the problem. You cannot make the Britisher see that his own
bunkum is contemptible. But shew him the bunkum of any other
nation, and he sees through it promptly enough. And that is
what Mr Frohman is doing. The Heart of Maryland is an American melodrama of the Civil War. As usual, all the Southern
commanders are Northern spies, and all the Northern commanders Southern spies—at least that is the general impression
produced. It may be historically correct; for obviously such an
arrangement, when the troops once got used to it, would not
make the smallest difference; since a competition for defeat, if
earnestly carried out on both sides, would be just as sensible, just
as exciting, just as difficult, just as well calculated to call forth all
the heroic qualities, not to mention the Christian virtues, as a
competition for victory. Maryland Cawlvert (spelt Calvert) is
"a Southern woman to the last drop of her blood," and is, of
course, in love with a Northern officer, who has had the villain
drummed out of the Northern army for infamous conduct. The
villain joins the Southerns, who, in recognition no doubt of his
high character and remarkable record, at once make him a colonel,
especially as he is addicted to heavy drinking. Naturally, he is
politically impartial, and, as he says to the hysterical Northerner

(who is, of course, the hero of the piece), fights for his own hand. "But the United States!" pleads the hysterical one feebly. "Damn the United States" replies the villain. Instantly the outraged patriot assaults him furiously, shouting "Take back that. Take it back." The villain prudently takes it back; and the honor of America is vindicated. This is clearly the point at which the audience should burst into frantic applause. No doubt American audiences do. Perhaps the Adelphi audience would too if the line were altered to "Damn the United Kingdom." But we are sensible enough about other people's follies; and the incontinent schoolboyishness of the hero is received with the coolest contempt. This, then, is the moral mission of Mr Charles Frohman. He is snatching the fool's cap from the London playgoer and shewing it to him on the head of an American. Meanwhile, our foolish plays are going to America to return the compliment. In the end, perhaps, we shall get melodramas in which the heroism is not despicable, puerile, and blackguardly, nor the villainy mere mechanical criminality.

For the rest, The Heart of Maryland is not a bad specimen of the American machine-made melodrama. The actors know the gymnastics of their business, and work harder and more smartly, and stick to it better than English actors. Mrs Leslie Carter is a melodramatic heroine of no mean powers. Her dresses and graces and poses cast a glamor of American high art on Mr Belasco's romance; and her transports and tornadoes, in which she shews plenty of professional temperament and susceptibility, give intensity to the curtain situations, and secure her a flattering series of recalls. She disdains the silly and impossible sensation scene with the bell, leaving it to a lively young-lady athlete, who shews with every muscle in her body that she is swinging the bell instead of being swung by it. Mr Morgan, as the villain, is received with special favor; and Mr Malcolm Williams pretends to be a corpse in such a life-like manner that he brings down the house, already well disposed to him for his excellent acting before his decease. Nobody else has much of a chance.

The Elizabethan Stage Society has achieved a very tolerable

performance of The Spanish Gipsy—a sort of Elizabethan Morocco Bound—at St George's Hall. At the same time, it has issued a balance-sheet which is a very genuine tragedy. Since September 1893, when the now familiar model of an Elizabethan stage was first set up for the performance of Measure for Measure at the Royalty Theatre (Mr Poel then having nothing at his back but a donation of £100 from Mr Arthur Dillon and a contribution of £25 from the members of the Shakespear Reading Society), about ten productions have been undertaken, involving unprecedented expenditure, care, and research in the matter of costumes; for an equipment which looks well enough on an ordinary stage in a blaze of light, and with a painted scene behind it, is out of the question when the actor has to walk into the hall of a city company or Inn of Court, and go through his part at no greater advantage in the way of illusion than a quadrille party at a fancy ball enjoys. Here Mr Poel has unquestionably made a contribution to theatrical art. As usual, he has received little acknowledgment except for the quainter aspects of his Elizabethanism; but the truth is that nothing like the dressing of his productions has been seen by the present generation: our ordinary managers have simply been patronizing the conventional costumier's business in a very expensive way, whilst Mr Poel has achieved artistic originality, beauty, and novelty of effect, as well as the fullest attainable measure of historical conviction. Further, he has gained the assistance of Mr Dolmetsch, and so brought the most remarkable musical revival of our time to bear on his enterprise. He has of late striven valiantly to leave Shakespear to the ordinary theatres, in spite of the fact that no other Elizabethan dramatist draws. He has done extraordinary things with the amateur talent at his disposal, the last few performances shewing not only that he has at last succeeded in forming a company of very considerable promise, but that something like a tradition of Elizabethan playing is beginning to form itself in the society. The result, on the whole, is that those who have attended the performances have learnt to know the Elizabethan drama in a way that no extremity of reading the plays—or rather reading *about* the plays and then pretending to have read them—could have led them to; and this, I take it, is what Mr Poel promised our literary amateurs. Unfortunately there has been another result: to wit, a deficit of £1000, which Mr Poel has had to meet out of his own private resources. To anyone who knows the thousand impossibilities of the enterprise it will seem that Mr Poel must be an extraordinarily able man to run such a forlorn hope for less than £225 a year net loss; but he can hardly be expected to continue to endow the public at this rate in return for the enthusiast's usual tribute of misunderstanding and ridicule. It seems a pity that the society should succumb just as it is getting into shape, and beginning to understand its business thoroughly. I have learnt a good deal from it; and though I know how few people, especially among the stage-struck, have either the desire or the capacity for learning anything whatsoever of an artistic nature, I mention the fact on the chance of directing a grain or two of the public spirit of art in Mr Poel's direction.

As The Spanish Gipsy violates the first rule of the Censorship by presenting a heroine whose virginity is not intact, the Lord Chamberlain's department is no doubt in an agony of apprehension as to the consequences of the performance on English morality. But the nation will probably recover in due time. Several of the parts were very creditably played. The lady whose remarkable performance I noticed in Beaumont and Fletcher's Coxcomb gave her name this time as Miss Alice Arden, and played Cardochia with the same individuality and impetuosity. Miss Imogen Surrey steadily advances in competence by dint of her industry and sincerity; but her slow touch and monotonous style limit her too much: E flat minor is a very impressive key; but one does not want a whole sonata in it. The comic men erred, as usual, on the side of tomfoolery; but the serious parts, both young and old, were very presentable, Mr Ernest Meads as the Corregidor, Mr Sherbrook as Alvarez, Mr West as Roderigo, and one or two other gentlemen whose names and characters are confused beyond identification in my memory, letting themselves go with some success. Miss Lilian Deane was a sufficiently attractive gipsy, or, as she would have been called in the days of Balfe and Wallace, "gitana."

The piece at the Royalty admits of no fresh development for the genius of Miss Louie Freear: indeed, it is not so amusing as the comparatively idiotic Oh, Susannah! Miss Freear is an altogether extraordinary actress; and I hope we shall one day see her in a real play, not in an exhibition. Mr Sturgess has contrived the exhibition this time rather adroitly and sensibly; but the result shews that he might just as well have been as economical of his brains as the three Susannah authors were.

I am infinitely obliged to Mr Holles for inviting me to The Cousin from Australia at the Opéra Comique. It is a harmless pleasantry for very simple-minded folk; and though I slipped away and went quietly home at the end of the first act, I have no doubt that the piece has plenty of harmless fun in it for the right sort of audience.

THE DRAMA PURIFIED

THE CONQUERORS. A drama in four acts. By Paul M. Potter. St James's Theatre, 14 April 1898.
Shakespear Week at the Théâtre Métropole, Camberwell.

[23 *April* 1898]

WHEN civilization becomes effete, the only cure is an irruption of barbarians. When the London dramatist has driven everybody out of the theatre with his tailor-made romances and suburban love affairs, the bushranger and the backwoodsman become masters of the situation. These outlandish people have no grace of language or subtlety of thought. Their women are either boyishly fatuous reproductions of the beautiful, pure, ladylike, innocent, blue-eyed, golden-haired divinities they have read about in obsolete novels, or scandalous but graphic portraits of female rowdies drawn from the life. Their heroes are criminals and hard drinkers, redeemed, in an extremely unconvincing manner, by their loves for the divinities aforesaid. Their humor is irreverent and barbarous; and their emotional stock-in-trade contains nothing but the commonest passions and cupidities, with such puerile points of honor as prevail among men who are outcasts where civilization exists, and "pioneers" where it does not. All the same, these bushwhacking melodramatists have imagination, appetite, and heat of blood; and these qualities, suddenly asserting themselves in our exhausted theatre, produce the effect of a stiff tumbler of punch after the fiftieth watering of a pot of tea. Being myself a teetotaller, with a strong taste for the water of life, their punch has no charms for me; but I cordially admit its superiority to the tea-leaf infusion; and I perceive that it will wake up the native dramatist, and teach him that if he does not take the trouble to feel and to invent, and even to think and to know, he will go under, and his place be taken by competitors whose more appropriate function in literature would appear to be the production of interminable stories of adventure in weekly numbers as a bait for the pennies of School Board children.

It is quite impossible, in view of the third and fourth acts of The Conquerors, to treat it with any sort of serious respect, even as a melodrama. And yet it produced what very few plays at the St James's produce: that is, a strong illusion that we were looking at the persons and events of Mr Potter's story, and not merely at our friends Mr Alexander, Miss Neilson, and party, in their newest summer costumes. At the end of the first act, a gentleman in the audience so completely forgot Mr Alexander's identity, that he got up and indignantly remonstrated with him for the blackguardism with which he was behaving in the character of "the Babe." The incident which produced this triumph was, it is true, borrowed from Guy de Maupassant; but the realistic vigor and brutality of the expression was Mr Potter's.

The second act of the play may be taken as the reply of the Censorship to Mr Heinemann's charges of illiberality. It culminates in a long, detailed, and elaborate preparation by the hero for a rape on the person of the heroine. After a frantic scene of ineffectual efforts to escape, with prayers for mercy, screams for help, and blood-curdling hysteria, the lady faints. The gentleman then observes that he is a blackguard, and takes himself off. Now it is to be noted that if he had been represented as having effected his purpose, the Lord Chamberlain would have refused to license the play. The present arrangement entertains the public with just as much of a rape as it is possible to present on the stage at all, Censorship or no Censorship. But the scene is supposed to be "purified" by a formal disclaimer, after all that is possible in stage libertinage has been done. The subsequent developments are as follows. When the lady comes to, and finds herself alone, she concludes that the man has actually carried out his threat. Under this impression she raves through two acts in a frenzy of passion which is half murderous and half incipiently affectionate. The mere imagination of the rape has produced what I may politely call a physiological attachment on the part of the victim. So she first plunges a knife into the hero, and then, in a transport of passionate remorse, carries him off to her bedroom to nurse him back to life. When her brother—to whom she is supposed to be devoted—has to make his escape either through this bedroom or through a garden where there is a sharpshooter behind every tree waiting to kill him, she unhesitatingly sends him through the garden, lest he should discover and shoot her ravisher. Finally, she learns that the ravisher is "innocent," and has been redeemed by her love; on which edifying situation they fall into one another's arms, and make a happy ending of it.

Now I do not object to the representation of all this if the public wishes to see it represented; but I do want to know whether were we to abolish not only the Lord Chamberlain's jurisdiction, but also the ordinary legal remedies against the abuse of such freedom as the Press enjoys, any dramatist, however viciously or voluptuously disposed, could go further than Mr Potter in the direction which the Censorship is supposed to bar? The truth is, that at the point reached three minutes before the fall of the curtain on the second act of The Conquerors, the only possible way of making the play acceptable to an audience which is at all scrupulous is to allow the drunken blackguard to commit the crime, and then mercilessly work out the consequences in the sequel. The Lord Chamberlain's formula is about as effective a safeguard of morality as a deathbed repentance. However excellent its intention may be, it operates as an official passport for licentiousness. It does not prevent the exhibition at the St James's Theatre of sensational sexuality, brutality, drunkenness, and murder; but it takes care that all these things shall end happily, charmingly, respectably, prettily, lady - and - gentlemanlikely for all parties concerned. And on these conditions it relieves the public, and the managers, and the actors, and the audience, of all sense of responsibility in the matter. The relief appears cheap at two guineas, but as it unfortunately involves the prohibition of an honest treatment of the theme, and suppresses the moral influence of Ibsen and Tolstoi in the interest of Mr Potter and the authors of pieces like A Night Out and Gentleman Joe, it is perfectly clear to me that it would pay the nation very well indeed to commute the expectations of the Lord Chamberlain and Mr Redford for a lump sum, buy their office from the Queen, and abolish the whole Censorship as a pestiferous sham which makes the theatre a plague-spot in British art.

The Conquerors is not a difficult play to act; and the St James's Company has no trouble in producing an impression of brilliant ability in it, with the single exception of Miss Julia Neilson, who only compromises her dignity and throws away her charm by attempting this tearing, screaming, sensational melodramatic business. Mr Alexander, having at last got hold of a part which has some brute reality about it (until the Lord Chamberlain intervenes), plays strongly and successfully; and Mr Fred Terry creates so much interest by his appearances as the noble brother in the first two acts that the subsequent petering out of his part is highly exasperating. Miss Fay Davis, dividing the comic relief with Mr Esmond, is in the last degree fascinating; Mr Irving condescends to murder and corduroys with his usual glamor; Mr Bertram Wallis sings the Erl King; Mr Vernon is a gruff general; Mr Beveridge, a whiskered major; Mr Loraine, a nobody (a little wasteful, this); Miss Constance Collier, a handsome and vindictive Chouan woman, who could not possibly have been born and bred anywhere but in London; and Miss

Victor is brought on expressly to make her age, sex, and talent ridiculous, a vulgar outrage which the audience, to its great credit, refuses to tolerate. As usual at the St James's, the mounting is excellent, and the stage management thoroughly well carried out; but Mr Alexander, it seems to me, has not yet noticed that these barbarian melodramas, with their profusion of action and dialogue, do not require, and in fact will not bear, the long silences which are necessary in order to give a stale, scanty, London-made play an air of having something in it, even if that something has to be manufactured between the lines out of impressive listenings, posing, grimacings, and "business." If Mr Alexander will take a look at the Americans at the Adelphi, he will see that they talk straight on, losing as little time as possible. There is none of the usual English attempt to get the acting in between the lines instead of on the lines. They know better than to give the audience time to think.

Mr Mulholland has been giving Camberwell its annual Shakespear Week at the Métropole. The management at the Garrick having taken the usual steps to protect Mr Gillette against my criticism on the occasion of his appearance in Too Much Johnson, I went off to see Macbeth, and found that Mr Ben Greet had collected as much as he could get of the company of the recent Manchester revival. He had failed to capture Miss Janet Achurch, whose place was taken by Miss Eleanor Calhoun. The editor of this journal has so completely and convincingly knocked the bottom out of Macbeth as a character-study, that the incongruity of the ferocious murders and treacheries and brutalities of the legendary Thane of Fife with the humane and reflective temperament of the nervous literary gentleman whom Shakespear thrust into his galligaskins, was more than usually glaring. Mr William Mollison did his best under the circumstances, and occasionally recited a passage with a fair degree of impressiveness. Both he and Miss Calhoun were much bothered by a few unlucky accidents and hitches which occurred, and they were a very ill-matched pair artistically, Miss Calhoun being modern, brilliant, mettlesome, and striking in appearance, and Mr Mollison heavy, parental, and almost boastfully abstinent in the matter of ideas.

He was so disdainful of modern realism and so Shakespearean that, like Cassio or Tybalt, he fought Macduff "by the book of arithmetic," and counted the prearranged strokes aloud—One, Two, Three, Four, Five, Six. His scenes with Lady Macbeth, on the other hand, were obviously unrehearsed and unconcerted. After his long Manchester engagement he had no doubt become completely dependent on Miss Achurch's "business"; and Miss Calhoun, dragged one way by the necessity for giving him this business, and the other by her own view of the part, could do little more than keep up appearances, except in the scenes where she had the stage to herself, when she displayed all that exceptional training and professional competence which is, I suppose, the reason why one sees so little of her nowadays in that Duffer's Paradise, the West End stage. On the whole, the most successful scenes were those of Macduff (Mr Black), Malcolm (Mr Penny), and Lennox (Mr Pearce), where there were no stage difficulties, and the actors had their work at their fingers' end.

KATE TERRY

THE MASTER. An original comedy in three acts. By G. Stuart Ogilvie. Globe Theatre, 23 April 1898.

LORD AND LADY ALGY. An original light comedy in three acts. By R. C. Carton. Comedy Theatre, 21 April 1898.

[30 *April* 1898]

I MUST say Mr Stuart Ogilvie has an odd notion of how to write a part to suit a particular actor. Here is Mr Hare, one of the very few English actors one dare send a foreigner to see, excelling in the representation of all sorts and conditions of quick, clear, crisp, shrewd, prompt, sensible men. Enter to him Mr Ogilvie, with a part expressly designed to shew that all this is nothing but a pig-headed affectation, and that the true humanity beneath it is the customary maudlin, muzzy, brainless, hysterical sentimentality and excitability which is supposed to touch the heart of the British playgoer, and which, no doubt, does affect him to some extent when he induces in himself the necessary degree of susceptibility with a little alcohol. What a situation! And it would have been so easy to provide Mr Hare with a part shewing the worth and dignity of his own temperament! All through The Master Mr Ogilvie seems to be trying to prove to Mr Hare what a much finer and more genuine fellow he would have been if nature had made him a Charles Warner or a Henry Neville. Apart from the point being an extremely debateable one, it seems hardly quite polite to Mr Hare, who, after all, cannot help being himself. This comes of an author making no serious attempt to get to the point of view of the character he professes to have dramatized—of simply conspiring with the stupid section of the pit to make an Aunt Sally of it. Half the play might be made plausible if The Master were played as a savage, iron-jawed, madly selfish old brute, but the other half is evidently laid out for Mr Hare's refinement and humanity of style. And then there is a revolting obviousness about the operations of destiny with a view to a happy ending. The old gentleman first puts his son out of the house, then puts out his daughter, and finally puts out his wife, whereupon the servants leave of their own accord. Immediately, with a punctuality and perfect expectedness which is about as dramatic as the response of a box of vestas to a penny in the slot, comes the winning of the Victoria Cross in India by the disinherited son, the heroic rescue of a band of entombed miners by the manly young husband for whose sake the daughter defies her father, and the sacrifice by the discarded wife of her whole fortune to save her oppressor from ruin. For a man of Mr Ogilvie's calibre I call this gross. It is not the fine art of the dramatist: it is the trade of the playwright, and not even a first-class job at that. For the life of me I cannot see why Mr Ogilvie should thus aim at rank commonness in his drama any more than at the rank illiteracy of expression which usually accompanies it, and which he saves his play from absolute intolerableness by avoiding. He may reply that the public like rank commonness. That may be, when it comes from the man to whom it is natural, and who, in doing it, is doing his best. But whether the public will like it from Mr Ogilvie remains to be seen. Miss Marie

Corelli's novels may be more widely read within a month of their publication than Mr Meredith's used to be; but it does not at all follow that if Mr Meredith were deliberately to try to do Miss Corelli's work the result would be popular. The public does not like to see a man playing down; and I should insult Mr Ogilvie most fearfully if I were to assume that he was doing his best in The Master. When, after stooping to a baby, he took the final plunge with a band playing Soldiers of our Queen to a cheering crowd outside, I hid my face and heard no more.

The interest of the occasion was strongly helped out by the reappearance of Miss Kate Terry, an actress unknown, except as an assiduous playgoer, to the present generation. Miss Terry entered apologetically, frankly taking the position of an elderly lady who had come to look after her daughter, and tacitly promising to do her best not to be intrusive, nor to make any attempt at acting or anything of that sort, if the audience would only be a little indulgent with her. She sat down on a sofa, looking very nice and kindly; but the moment she had to say something to Mr Hare her old habits got the better of her, and the sentence was hardly out of her mouth before she recognized, as its cadence struck her ear, that she had acted it, and acted it uncommonly well. The shame of this discovery made her nervous; but the more nervous she was, the less she could help acting; and the less she could help acting, the more she put on the youth of the time when she had last acted—a fearful indiscretion. However, as the audience, far from taking it in bad part, evidently wanted more of it, Miss Terry, after a brief struggle, abandoned herself to her fate and went recklessly for her part. It was not much of a part; but she gave the audience no chance of finding that out. She apparently began, in point of skill and practice, just where she had left off years ago, without a trace of rust. Her first two or three speeches, though delicately distinct, had a certain privacy of pitch, I thought; but almost before I had noticed it, it vanished, as she recaptured the pitch of the theatre and the ear of the crowded audience. She has distinguished skill, infallible judgment, altogether extraordinary amenity of style, and withal a

371

quite enchanting air of being a simple-minded motherly lady, who does not mean to be clever in the least, and never was behind the scenes in a theatre in her life. I sometimes dream that I am on a concert platform with a violin in my hands and an orchestra at my back, having in some inexplicable madness undertaken to play the Brahms Concerto before a full audience without knowing my G string from my chanterelle. Whoever has not dreamt this dream does not know what humility means. Trembling and desperate, I strike Joachim's attitude, and find, to my amazement, that the instrument responds instantly to my sense of the music, and that I am playing away like anything. Miss Terry's acting reminds me of my imaginary violin-playing: she seems utterly innocent of it, and yet there it is, all happening infallibly and delightfully. But, depend on it, she must know all about it; for how else does her daughter, Miss Mabel Terry, come to be so cunningly trained? She has walked on to the stage with a knowledge of her business, and a delicacy in its execution, to which most of our younger leading ladies seem no nearer than when they first blundered on to the boards in a maze of millinery and professional ignorance. Yes: the daughter gives the apparent naïveté of the mother away: if that art were an accident of Nature it could never be taught so perfectly. Indeed, there were plenty of little revelations of this kind for sharp eyes. I have already described how Miss Kate Terry's momentary nervousness at first threw her back to the acting of thirty years ago. In that moment one saw how much of the original Kate Terry her daughter had just been reproducing for us. Then Miss Terry recovered her self-possession and her own age; and here again one saw that she was by no means going to be the maidenly Kate Terry with a matronly face and figure, but virtually a new actress of matronly parts, unsurpassed in stage accomplishment, and with a certain charm of temperament that will supply our authors with something that they get neither from the dazzling cleverness of Mrs Kendal nor the conviction and comic force of Mrs Calvert, who alone can lay claim to anything approaching her technical powers. I do not feel sure that Miss Terry could play Mrs Alving in Ghosts as Mrs Theodore Wright

372

plays it—if, indeed, she could bring herself to play it at all—but I am sure that her art will not fail her in any play, however difficult, that does not positively antagonize her sympathies.

Stage art, even of a highly cultivated and artificial kind, sits so naturally on the Terrys that I daresay we shall hear a great deal about the family charm and very little about the family skill. Even Miss Ellen Terry, whose keenness of intelligence is beyond all dissimulation, has often succeeded in making eminent critics believe that her stagecraft and nervous athleticism are mere efflorescences of her personal charm. But Miss Mabel Terry has no special enchantments to trade upon—only the inevitable charms of her age. She is not recognizably her aunt's niece. She is not majestically handsome and graceful like Miss Julia Neilson; nor voluptuously lovely like Miss Lily Hanbury; nor perilously bewitching like Mrs Patrick Campbell. But she can speak beautifully, without the slightest trick or mannerism of any sort; and no moment of nervousness can disable her: the word gets rightly touched even when she can hardly hear it herself. She never makes a grimace, nor is there a trace of consciousness or exaggeration about her gestures. She played between her mother and Mr Hare without being technically outclassed. Most of our stage young ladies would have sustained the comparison like an understudy volunteered in a desperate emergency by the nearest amateur. If we are to write this down as the family charm, let us not forget that it is a charm which includes a good deal of industriously acquired skill. It ought to be called artistic conscience.

Mr Gilbert Hare is condemned to his usual premature grey hairs. If he ever gets a chance as Romeo, I am convinced that, from mere force of habit, the first thing he will say to Juliet will be, "I have known your uncle close on fifty years. Your mother was a sweet, gentle lady, God bless her." There is only five minutes—more's the pity—of Mr Kerr. His Major Hawkwood is a younger brother of Baron Croodle, whose second coming, by the way, ought to be at hand by this time. Mr Gillmore and Mr Cherry as the two heroes, and Mr Rock as the butler, leave nothing to be desired except less obvious parts for them. Mr

Ross struck me as not quite plausible enough in his villainy for the favorite of so exacting a principal as The Master.

Lord and Lady Algy at the Comedy is an ignoble, but not unamusing, three-act farce. I should have nothing more to say about it had my eye not been caught by the astounding epithet "wholesome" applied to it. I declare that it is the most immoral play I ever saw. Lord and Lady Algy are a middle-aged pair more completely and shamelessly void of self-respect than any other couple for whom the theatre has ventured to claim sympathy. They have one resource, one taste, one amusement, one interest, one ambition, one occupation, one accomplishment, and that is betting on the turf. The "wholesomeness" consists of the woman's boast that though she flirts, she always "runs straight"—as if it mattered a straw to any human being whether she ran straight or not. A lady who is a gambler, a loafer, and a sponge, is not likely to have any motive of the smallest moral value for refraining from adultery. There are people who are beneath law-breaking as well as people who are above it, and Lord and Lady Algy are of that class. But the play is altogether too trivial and sportive to raise moral questions; and I laughed at its humors without scruple. Mr Henry Ford's jockey was the best bit of character in the performance. Mr Hawtrey, as the Duke of Marlborough at a fancy ball, harmlessly drunk, makes plenty of inoffensive fun; and he and Miss Compton have plenty of their popular and familiar business in the first and third acts. The other parts are really exasperating in view of the talent thrown away in them.

VAN AMBURGH REVIVED

THE CLUB BABY. A farce in three acts. By Edward G. Knoblauch. Avenue Theatre, 28 April 1898.

THE MEDICINE MAN. A melodramatic comedy in five acts. By H. D. Traill and Robert Hichens. Lyceum Theatre, 4 May 1898.   [7 *May* 1898]

THE Club Baby at the Avenue ought to have been called The Stage Baby's Revenge. The utter worthlessness of the sentiment

374

in which our actors and playgoers wallow is shewn by their readiness to take an unfortunate little child who ought to be in bed, and make fun of it on the stage as callously as a clown at a country fair will make fun of a sucking pig. But at the Avenue the baby turns the tables on its exploiters. The play tumbled along on the first night in an undeservingly funny way until the end of the second act, when the baby was rashly brought on the stage. Then it was all over. It was not so much that the audience looked at the baby, for audiences, in their thoughtless moments, are stupid enough to look at anything without blushing. But that baby looked at the audience; and its gaze would have reclaimed a gang of convicts. The pained wonder and unfathomable sadness with which it saw its elders, from whom its childlike trust and reverence had expected an almost godlike dignity, profanely making fools of themselves with a string of ribald jests at its expense, came upon us as the crowing of the cock came upon Peter. We went out between the acts and drank heavily as the best available substitute for weeping bitterly. If even one man had had the grace to hang himself I should still have some hopes of the British public. As it is, I merely beg the Home Secretary to ask the magistrate who is responsible for the appearance of this child on the stage on what grounds he went out of his way to permit it. We have been at the trouble of passing an Act of Parliament to forbid the commercial exploitation of children on the stage, except in cases where the enforcement of the Act would banish from the theatre some masterpiece of dramatic art written before the passing of the Act. For instance, we did not wish to make Richard III impossible by unconditionally abolishing the little Duke of York, nor to suppress A Doll's House by depriving Nora Helmer of her children. But The Club Baby is a play newly written with the deliberate intention of doing precisely what the Act was passed to prevent. It is a play without merit enough of any sort to give it a claim to the most trivial official indulgence, much less the setting aside of an Act of Parliament in its interest. And yet a magistrate licenses the employment in it, not of a boy or girl, but actually of a child in arms who is handed about the stage until eleven o'clock at night. It is useless to appeal to playgoers, managers, authors, and people of that kind in this matter. If the exhibition of a regiment of new-born babies would raise an extra laugh or draw half-a-guinea over its cost, that regiment of babies would be ordered and a play written round it with the greatest alacrity. But the Home Office is responsible for the prevention of such outrages. Sir Matthew White Ridley is at present receiving £5000 a year, partly at my expense, for looking after the administration of the laws regulating the employment of children. If a factory owner employed a child under the specified age, or kept a "young person" at work ten minutes after the specified hour, Sir Matthew would be down on him like five thousand of brick. If the factory owner were to plead that his factory was producing goods of vital utility and the rarest artistic value, the plea would not be listened to for a moment. In the name of common sense, why are speculators in Club Babies and the like to enjoy illegal and anti-social privileges which are denied to manufacturers?

I have been invited to the Strand Theatre to a play called The J.P. In the bill the following appears: "Charles Vivian, Junior. By a Baby Three Months old." What right has Mr Edouin, the manager, to invite me to witness such an outrage?

I suggest to the Home Office that a rigid rule should be made against the licensing of children for any new entertainment whatsoever. With regard to old plays, a privileged list might be made of works of the Richard III order; but the licences given under this list should be limited to specified parts: for example, the Richard III privilege should apply solely to the part of the Duke of York, and not be made an excuse for introducing a coronation scene with a procession of five-year-old infants strewing flowers. If it were once understood that applications for licences outside this list would be refused as a matter of course, the present abuses would disappear without further legislation. I would remind my critical colleagues that about six years ago a sort of epidemic of child exhibition broke out at the theatres devoted to comic opera. I was a critic of music at that time; and I remember an opera at the Lyric Theatre in which a ballet of tiny Punchinellos was danced between eleven o'clock and midnight by a troop of infants in a sort of delirium induced by the conflict between intense excitement and intense sleepiness. I vainly tried to persuade some of the most enlightened of my fellow-critics to launch the thunder of the press at this abomination. Unfortunately, having little children of their own, and having observed that a single night's private theatricals gave much innocent delight to their babes, they thought it was quite a charming thing that the poor little Punchinellos should have such fun every night for several months. Truly, as Talleyrand said, the father of a family is capable of anything. I was left to launch the little thunder I could wield myself; and the result, I am happy to say, was that the managers, including a well-known stage-manager since deceased, suffered so much anguish of mind from my criticisms, without any counterbalancing conviction that their pieces were drawing a farthing more with the children than they would have drawn without them, that they mended their ways. But of late the epidemic has shewn signs of breaking out again. I therefore think it only fair to say that I also am quite ready to break out again, and that I hope by this time my colleagues have realized that their "bless-its-little-heart" patrosentimentality is not publicism.

As to the performance of The Club Baby, all I need say is that a long string of popular comedians do their best with it, and that a Miss Clare Greet, whom I do not remember to have seen before, distinguishes herself very cleverly in the part of the country girl.

Now that Sir Henry Irving has taken to encouraging contemporary literature, it cannot be denied that he has set to work in a sufficiently original fashion. Mr H. D. Traill is an academic literary gentleman who, like Schopenhauer, conceives the world as Will and the intellectual representations by which Man strives to make himself conscious of his will; only Mr Traill conceives these things in a professional mode, the will being to him not a Will to Live, but a Will to Write Books, and the process of making us conscious of these books by intellectual representation being simply reviewing. Some time in the eighties London rose up in revolt against this view. The New Journalism was introduced. Lawless young men began to write and print the living English language of their own day instead of the prose style of one of Macaulay's characters named Addison. They split their infinitives, and wrote such phrases as "a man nobody ever heard of" instead of "a man of whom nobody had ever heard," or, more classical still, "a writer hitherto unknown." Musical critics, instead of reading books about their business and elegantly regurgitating their erudition, began to listen to music and distinguish between sounds; critics of painting began to look at pictures; critics of the drama began to look at something else besides the stage; and descriptive writers actually broke into the House of Commons, elbowing the reporters into the background, and writing about political leaders as if they were mere play-actors. The interview, the illustration and the cross-heading, hitherto looked on as American vulgarities impossible to English literary gentlemen, invaded all our papers; and, finally, as the climax and masterpiece of literary Jacobinism, the Saturday Review appeared with a signed article in it. Then Mr Traill and all his generation covered their faces with their togas and died at the base of Addison's statue, which all the while ran ink. It is true that they got up and went home when the curtain fell; but they made no truce with Jacobinism; and Mr Traill fled into the fortress of the Times, and hurled therefrom, under the defiant title of Literature, a destructive mass of reviews and publishers' advertisements which caught me one morning in a railway carriage and nearly killed me. One of the Jacobins was Mr Hichens. He paid me the compliment of following up the assault on Academicism on my old lines—those of musical criticism. He was well received by a revolutionary and licentious generation; but whatever circulation his novels and articles might achieve, it was not to be expected that Mr Traill would ever consent to be seen speaking to him in the street. And yet Sir Henry Irving, in the calmest manner, seems to have ordered a play from the twain jointly. What is more, he has got it. I hardly know how to describe the result. I trace the theme of the piece to a story, well known to Mr Traill's generation, of the lion-tamer Van Amburgh, who professed to quell the most ferocious animals, whether human or not, by the power of his eye alone. Challenged to prove this power on the person of a very rough-looking laborer, he approached the man and fixed a soul-searching gaze on him. The laborer soon evinced the greatest disquietude, became very red and self-conscious, and finally knocked Van Amburgh down, accompanying the blow with a highly garnished demand as to who he was staring at. In The Medicine Man we have Van Amburgh with the period of quelling contemplation extended to five acts, and including not only the laborer, Bill Burge, but also a beauteous maiden named Sylvia. One can understand the humorous insanity of such a story fascinating Mr Hichens, and Mr Traill chuckling secretly at having planted it on the young Jacobin as a new idea. I find myself totally unable to take it seriously: it sends me into a paroxysm of laughter whenever I think of it. I wonder which of the two authors gave the muscular victim of Van Amburgh Tregenna the name of a very eminent contemporary pugilist, known affectionately to the fancy as the Coffee Cooler. If Mr Burge should take the suggested portrait at all amiss, and should seek personal redress at the hands of the authors or the manager, one shudders at the possible consequences to literature and the stage.

There was infinite comedy in the first night of the play at the Lyceum. It lasted from eight to past eleven, and contained just matter enough for a half-hour pantomimic sketch by Mr Martinetti. Sir Henry Irving, pleased by the lion-taming notion, was perfectly delighted with his part, and would evidently have willingly gone on impressing and mesmerizing his devoted company for three hours longer. Miss Ellen Terry, on the other hand, was quite aware of the appalling gratuitousness of his satisfaction. To save the situation she put forth all her enchantments, and so beglamored the play act by act that she forced the audience to accept Sylvia as a witching and pathetically lovely creation of high literary drama. The very anguish the effort caused her heightened the effect. When, after some transcendently idiotic speech that not even her art could give any sort of plausibility to, she looked desperately at us all with an expression that meant

"Dont blame me: *I* didnt write it," we only recognized a touch of nature without interpreting it, and were ravished. Hand-in-hand with the innocently happy Sir Henry, she endured the curtain calls with a proud reticence which said to us plainly enough, "I will play this part for you unworthy people, since you have no better use to make of me; but I will not pretend to like it," which was really hardly fair; for we were, as I have said, in a state of enchantment, and thought it all adorable. Mr Mackintosh as Bill Burge is laboriously impossible. His Hogarthian make-up is not like anything now discoverable at the docks; his dialect has no touch of the East End in it; he is as incapable of walking out of a room naturally as a real dock laborer is of "doing an exit." However, it does not matter much; the whole business is such utter nonsense that a stagy dock laborer is quite in keeping with the freakish humors of Mr Hichens, to whom the life of the poor is a tragi-comic phantasmagoria with a good deal of poker and black eye in it. Only at a West End theatre could such a picture pass muster. Some of it—the humors of Mrs Burge, for instance —is an outrage on humanity. But Mr Hichens will retrieve The Medicine Man easily enough, for he has by no means mistaken his vocation in writing for the stage, though he had better avoid collaboration with the chartered dullness of academic history and the solemn frivolity of academic literature. It would take ten years' hard descriptive reporting for the Star or Daily Mail to teach Mr Traill to observe life and to write seriously. The first tinker he meets will tell him a better ghost story than the vague figment, despicable to his own common sense, which he has thought good enough to make a theme for the most exacting of all the forms of literary art. That is your literary man all over—any old theme for a great occasion, provided only nobody can suspect you of believing in it.

G. B. S. VIVISECTED

[14 *May* 1898]

EUREKA! I have found it out at last. I now understand the British drama and the British actor. It has come about in this way.

A few weeks ago one of my feet, which had borne me without complaining for forty years, struck work. The spectacle of a dramatic critic hopping about the metropolis might have softened a heart of stone; but the managers, I regret to say, seized the opportunity to disable me by crowding a succession of first nights on me. After The Medicine Man at the Lyceum, the foot got into such a condition that it literally had to be looked into. I had no curiosity in the matter myself; but the administration of an anæsthetic made my views of no importance. It is to the anæsthetic that I owe the discovery which elicits my cry of Eureka!

The beginning of the anæsthesia threw no new light on the theatre. I was extinguished by the gas familiar to dentists' patients, and subsequently kept in a state of annihilation with ether. My last recollection is a sort of chuckle at being wideawake enough to know when the operator lifted my eyelid and tapped my eyeball to convince himself that he had made an end of me. It was not until I was allowed to recover that the process became publicly interesting. For then a very strange thing happened. *My character did not come back all at once.* Its artistic and sentimental side came first: its morality, its positive elements, its common sense, its incorrigible Protestant respectability, did not return for a long time after. For the first time in my life I tasted the bliss of having no morals to restrain me from lying, and no sense of reality to restrain me from romancing. I overflowed with what people call "heart." I acted and lied in the most touchingly sympathetic fashion; I felt prepared to receive unlimited kindness from everybody with the deepest, tenderest gratitude; and I was totally incapable of even conceiving the notion of rendering anyone a service myself. If only I could have stood up and talked distinctly as a man in perfect health and self-possession, I should have won the hearts of everybody present until they found me out later on. Even as it was, I was perfectly conscious of the value of my prostrate and half-delirious condition as a bait for sympathy; and I deliberately played for it in a manner which now makes me blush. I carefully composed effective little ravings, and repeated them, and then started again and let my voice die away, without an atom of shame. I called everybody by their Christian names, except one gentleman whose Christian name I did not know, and I called him "dear old So-and-so." Artistically, I was an immense success: morally, I simply had no existence.

At last they quietly extinguished the lights, and stole out of the chamber of the sweet invalid who was now sleeping like a child, but who, noticing that the last person to leave the room was a lady, softly breathed that lady's name in his dreams. Then the effect of the anæsthetic passed away more and more; and in less than an hour I was an honest taxpayer again, with my heart perfectly well in hand. And now comes the great question, Was that a gain or a loss? The problem comes home to me with special force at this moment, because I have just seriously distracted public attention from the American war by publishing my plays; and I have been overwhelmed as usual by complaints of my want of heart, my unnaturally clear intellectual consciousness, my cynicism, and all the rest of it. One of my female characters, who drinks whisky, and smokes cigars, and reads detective stories, and regards the fine arts, especially music, as an insufferable and unintelligible waste of time, has been declared by my friend Mr William Archer to be an exact and authentic portrait of myself, on no other grounds in the world except that she is a woman of business and not a creature of romantic impulse. In this "nation of shopkeepers," the critics no sooner meet a character on the stage with the smallest trace of business sagacity, or an author who makes the least allowance for the provident love of money and property as a guarantee of security, comfort, and independence, which is so powerful a factor in English society, than they immediately declare such a character totally inhuman and unnatural, and such an author a cynical crank. If I am the unfortunate author, they dispose of the character at once as a mere dramatization of my own personal eccentricities.

This, regarded as one of the humors of natural self-unconsciousness, is so farcically paradoxical and preposterous that I have always felt it to be too coarse for the exquisite high comedy of real life. And I have been right. The protests come only from what we call the artistic class, by which contemptuous expression (for such it is in England) we mean the men and women who love books and pictures, histories and operas, and shrink from business and public affairs so persistently that in the end their consciousness becomes absolutely fictitious, in which condition reality seems unreal to them, and the most commonplace characteristics of English life, when dramatized, produce on them the effect of a mere bizarrerie. When this effect is strong enough to give a serious jar to their artistic habits, they generally mistake the disagreeable sensation for a shock to their moral sense, it being one of their artistic conventions that it is possible to shirk real life, and yet possess moral sense.

Often as I have had to point this out, I had, until yesterday, yet to realize fully the difference between observing it in other people and experiencing it oneself. At last I can speak of it at first hand; and now I understand it as I never understood it before. No longer shall I look at my sentimental, fiction-loving friends as Bismarck might look at a rather engaging South Sea chief; for I have actually changed personalities with them. What is more, I know how to reproduce the miracle at will as certainly as if I possessed the wishing-cap of Siegfried. My wishing-cap is a bag of ether. With that, I can first plunge into the darkness that existed before my birth and be simply nothing. Then I can come to life as an artist and a man of feeling—as everything that I have been reproached so bitterly for not being. I can prolong that condition indefinitely by taking a whiff or two of ether whenever I feel the chill of a moral or intellectual impulse. I can write plays in it; I can act in it; I can gush in it; I can borrow money to set myself up as an actor-manager in it; I can be pious and patriotic in it; I can melt touchingly over disease and death and murder and hunger and cold and poverty in it, turning all the woes of the world into artistic capital for myself; and finally I can come back to full consciousness and criticize myself as I was in it. The parable of Dr Jekyll and Mr Hyde will be fulfilled in me, with this difference, that it is Hyde who will be popular and petted, and Jekyll who will be rebuked for his callous, heartless cynicism. I have already ordered a set of cards inscribed "G. B. S. . . . At Home . . . Tuesdays and Fridays under ether for sentimental, theatrical, and artistic purposes . . . Mondays and Saturdays normal for business engagements and public affairs."

Here I must summarily break off. My doctor's investigation of my interior has disclosed the fact that for many years I have been converting the entire stock of energy extractable from my food (which I regret to say he disparages) into pure genius. Expecting to find bone and tissue, he has been almost wholly disappointed, and a pale, volatile moisture has hardly blurred the scalpel in the course of its excursions through my veins. He has therefore put it bluntly to me that I am already almost an angel, and that it rests with myself to complete the process summarily by writing any more articles before I have recovered from the effects of the operation and been renovated in the matter of bone and muscle. I have therefore pledged myself to send only the briefest line explaining why my article cannot appear this week. It is also essential, in order to keep up the sympathy which rages at my bedside, to make the very worst of my exhausted condition. Sad to say, there is enough of the ether clinging round me still to keep me doing this with a very perceptible zest.

I can no more.

VALEDICTORY

[21 *May* 1898]

As I lie here, helpless and disabled, or, at best, nailed by one foot to the floor like a doomed Strasburg goose, a sense of injury grows on me. For nearly four years—to be precise, since New Year 1895—I have been the slave of the theatre. It has tethered me to the mile radius of foul and sooty air which has its centre in the Strand, as a goat is tethered in the little circle of cropped and trampled grass that makes the meadow ashamed. Every week it clamors for its tale of written words; so that I am like a man fighting a windmill: I have hardly time to stagger to my feet from the knock-down blow of one sail, when the next strikes me down.

Now I ask, is it reasonable to expect me to spend my life in this way? For just consider my position. Do I receive any spontaneous recognition for the prodigies of skill and industry I lavish on an unworthy institution and a stupid public? Not a bit of it: half my time is spent in telling people what a clever man I am. It is no use merely doing clever things in England. The English do not know what to think until they are coached, laboriously and insistently for years, in the proper and becoming opinion. For ten years past, with an unprecedented pertinacity and obstination, I have been dinning into the public head that I am an extraordinarily witty, brilliant, and clever man. That is now part of the public opinion of England; and no power in heaven or on earth will ever change it. I may dodder and dote; I may potboil and platitudinize; I may become the butt and chopping-block of all the bright, original spirits of the rising generation; but my reputation shall not suffer: it is built up fast and solid, like Shakespear's, on an impregnable basis of dogmatic reiteration.

Unfortunately, the building process has been a most painful one to me, because I am congenitally an extremely modest man. Shyness is the form my vanity and self-consciousness take by nature. It is humiliating, too, after making the most dazzling displays of professional ability, to have to tell people how capital it all is. Besides, they get so tired of it, that finally, without dreaming of disputing the alleged brilliancy, they begin to detest it. I sometimes get quite frantic letters from people who feel that they cannot stand me any longer.

Then there are the managers. Are *they* grateful? No: they are simply forbearing. Instead of looking up to me as their guide, philosopher, and friend, they regard me merely as the author of a series of weekly outrages on their profession and their privacy. Worse than the managers are the Shakespeareans. When I began to write, William was a divinity and a bore. Now he is a fellow-creature; and his plays have reached an unprecedented pitch of popularity. And yet his worshippers overwhelm my name with insult.

These circumstances will not bear thinking of. I have never

had time to think of them before; but now I have nothing else to do. When a man of normal habits is ill, everyone hastens to assure him that he is going to recover. When a vegetarian is ill (which fortunately very seldom happens), everyone assures him that he is going to die, and that they told him so, and that it serves him right. They implore him to take at least a little gravy, so as to give himself a chance of lasting out the night. They tell him awful stories of cases just like his own which ended fatally after indescribable torments; and when he tremblingly inquires whether the victims were not hardened meat-eaters, they tell him he must not talk, as it is not good for him. Ten times a day I am compelled to reflect on my past life, and on the limited prospect of three weeks or so of lingering moribundity which is held up to me as my probable future, with the intensity of a drowning man. And I can never justify to myself the spending of four years on dramatic criticism. I have sworn an oath to endure no more of it. Never again will I cross the threshold of a theatre. The subject is exhausted; and so am I.

Still, the gaiety of nations must not be eclipsed. The long string of beautiful ladies who are at present in the square without, awaiting, under the supervision of two gallant policemen, their turn at my bedside, must be reassured when they protest, as they will, that the light of their life will go out if my dramatic articles cease. To each of them I will present the flower left by her predecessor, and assure her that there are as good fish in the sea as ever came out of it. The younger generation is knocking at the door; and as I open it there steps spritely in the incomparable Max.

For the rest, let Max speak for himself. I am off duty for ever, and am going to sleep.

INDEX

Abingdon, W. L., iii. 41, 140, 328

Abnormal people, i. 84

Achurch, Janet, i. 19, 146, 183; iii. 139, 144, 145, 146, 149, 185, 368, 369; plays in A Doll's House, ii. 148; iii. 132, 133, 233; Antony and Cleopatra, iii. 34, 77-83; Little Eyolf, ii. 240, 260, 261, 263, 271-8; The New Magdalen, i. 232-7

ACIS AND GALATEA, ii. 171

Acting—is it a real profession? ii. 126-8; the art of, i. 91, 146, 147, 151, 152, 269-75; ii. 113-14, 145, 191; iii. 58, 59, 145-7; has been prostituted into the art of pleasing, ii. 283, 284; see also Emotion; French acting; Tragic acting

Actor-manager system, iii. 273

Actors and actresses — drinking amongst, i. 220; morality of, iii. 274, 277, 295-7; snobbery amongst, iii. 223; social position of, i. 32; iii. 6-7, 39, 274; the accomplishments of the trained and the amateur, i. 211-213; the great actress, i. 147; the stage actress, iii. 197; the preponderance of the brainless-susceptible type of actress, ii. 112-14; the trained actor squeezed out by the society-struck actor, iii. 223; training, salaries, and standard of ability, iii. 112; their characters and reactions, i. 113; their stupidity, iii. 180; what is an actor nowadays? i. 270; why are skill and good sense so fatal to an actor or actress? iii. 59; see also Amateur actor; Character actor; Classical actor; Leading men; Pathetic actor; Stock-company system

Actress-manageresses, i. 92

Addison, Carlotta, iii. 233, 234, 320

ADMIRAL GUINEA, iii. 98, 259, 262-4

Advertisements, i. 186

Age, iii. 91-2, 289

Ainsworth, Harrison, iii. 135

ALADDIN, iii. 21-7

Albert-Mayer, M., ii. 254

Alexander, Sir George, i. 70; ii. 237; iii. 197; as a producer and manager, i. 176, 193-5, 274; ii. 232, 266; iii. 33, 99, 200, 254, 337, 338, 368; plays in As You Like It, ii. 270, 271; Guy Domville, i. 7, 8, 9; Liberty Hall, i. 250; Much Ado About Nothing, iii. 324-6; The Conquerors, iii. 365, 367; The Divided Way, i. 262; The Importance of Being Earnest, i. 43; The Misogynist, i. 262; The Princess and the Butterfly, iii. 96, 97; The Prisoner of Zenda, ii. 10, 11, 42-3, 232; The Second Mrs Tanqueray, i. 168; The Tree of Knowledge, iii. 233-4; The Triumph of the Philistines, i. 124

ALEXANDRA, i. 70; iii, 139

Alexis, Tsarevitch, iii. 283-5

ALL ALIVE, OH! iii. 170, 176

ALL THAT GLITTERS IS NOT GOLD, iii. 1, 6, 167

Allen, Grant, i. 52, 113; ii. 257; iii. 154

ALL'S WELL THAT ENDS WELL, i.
24, 27-30; iii. 2, 245
Alma-Tadema, Sir Lawrence, iii.
302
Alvary, Max, ii. 154
Amateur actor, i. 131, 210, 269;
iii. 328
Ambient, Mark, iii. 207, 214
American methods in farcical
comedy, iii. 216-18
AMI DES FEMMES, i. 242
Anæsthesia, iii. 381-4
Ancona, Mario, ii. 176
Anderson, Mary (Madame de Na-
varro), i. 72, 241, 282; ii. 85-91;
iii. 276-7
Angelo, Charles, iii. 336
Anson, Mr, i. 107; ii. 156, 194
Anstey, Mr, iii. 306
ANTONY AND CLEOPATRA, i. 145;
iii. 2, 76-83, 144, 147
Applause in the theatre, ii. 119,
199; iii. 69
Appleby, Arthur, iii. 121
Appleton, G. W., ii. 202, 208
Archer, Charles, ii. 248
——, William, i. 31, 54, 87-92,
148, 250; ii. 53, 55, 57, 72, 74,
75, 76, 139, 140, 144, 160, 161,
162, 177, 213, 238, 248, 278;
iii. 28, 80, 100, 102, 103, 122,
123, 151, 153, 155, 157, 261,
311-16, 336-41, 343, 345, 382
Arden, Alice, iii. 363
Armbruster, Herr, ii. 21, 142
ARMS AND THE MAN, i. 42, 165;
ii. 60
Army, the, iii. 359; as represented
on the stage, i. 95, 117-18,
285-7; ii. 2
Arnold, Edward, ii. 30
——, Matthew, ii. 214; iii. 316
Art—and life, iii. 236; and religion, ii. 23-8; and the law, i.

82; art culture in England, i.
13; iii. 84; fashionable art, ii.
152; art is gratuitous, iii. 346;
love of art, i. 90; see also
Pictures
Arthur, Julia, ii. 291; iii. 9, 40
—— Paul, iii. 307
Artificiality of dramatic art, iii.
235
Artist, the—his distaste for work,
i. 9; superseded by the tradesman, iii. 314; the artist's soul,
i. 81; artists' biographies, i. 100
Artistic class, iii. 383
Artistic execution in stage-work,
i. 76
Artistic sense, the, i. 211-13; ii. 145
Artois, Armand d', iii. 170, 176
AS YOU LIKE IT, ii. 114, 116, 264,
266-71; iii. 200, 207-10, 241,
254, 315, 320
Ashwell, Lena, plays in Carmen,
ii. 289; Her Advocate, i. 209;
King Arthur, ii. 289; Richard
III, ii. 289, 292; Sweet Nancy,
iii. 292; The Fool of the Family,
ii. 35, 40; The Matchmaker, ii.
137; The Prude's Progress, i.
140; The Sea Flower, iii. 335;
The Vagabond King, iii. 226
Assassinations, stage, i. 134
Atherton, Alice, ii. 173
Atwood, A., iii. 207, 214
Auclaire, Suzanne, ii. 254; iii. 139
Audiences, see Applause; First
night audiences; Gallery
rowdyism; Hooting; Laughter;
Morality of audiences
Augier, Emile, iii. 164, 168
Authorship, dramatic, ii. 203
Autographs, iii. 199
Aynesworth, Allan, i. 43, 261;
iii. 218
Ayres, Mrs Arthur, i. 230

BABES IN THE WOOD, iii. 279
Bach, Johann Sebastian, ii. 25, 244
BACHELOR'S ROMANCE, iii. 288-91, 339
Backers, i. 53
Baird, Dorothea, i. 241; ii. 114, 270; iii. 268
Balfour, Jabez, ii. 192; iii. 116
Balzac, Honoré de, ii. 31; iii. 189
Bancroft, Lady, i. 139; iii. 188
——, George, iii. 63
——, Sir Squire, i. 139, 276; ii. 278-85; iii. 122, 165, 166, 316
BARABBAS, iii. 45
Barbieri, Madame, ii. 255
Barnard, Mr, ii. 144
Barnes, J. H., plays in Four Little Girls, iii. 197; Hamlet, iii. 206, 270; Her Advocate, i. 209; Lost, Stolen or Strayed, iii. 121; The Rise of Dick Halward, i. 227
Barrett, Oscar, his plays, iii. 21-26, 32, 196
Barrett, Wilson, ii. 22, 23, 26, 71, 111; iii. 46, 66, 114, 185; his plays, ii. 7, 12, 13, 33; iii. 41-6, 53; dramatises The Manxman, i. 251; ii. 264, 265; plays in Othello, iii. 148, 149, 150; The Daughters of Babylon, iii. 45, 46; The Manxman, ii. 264
Barrie, Sir James M., iii. 241, 244-6, 337
Barry, James, ii. 85
Barton, Dora, iii. 129
Bassetto, Corno di, ii. 161, 162
Bateman, Miss, iii. 228
——, Isabel, iii. 308
——, Jessie, ii. 220
Bayreuth, Stage Festival Playhouse, ii. 67, 68, 71; iii. 102, 238, 239
Beadle, W. S., iii. 265

Beauchamp, John, iii. 151, 214, 266; plays in Jedbury Junior, ii. 50; The Ladies' Idol, i. 106; The Sea Flower, iii. 335; The Strange Adventures of Miss Brown, i. 169; The Wanderer from Venus, ii. 156
Beaugarde, Miss, i. 22
Beaumont and Fletcher, i. 131; ii. 183; iii. 317-20
Beerbohm, Max, iii. 95, 347
Beere, Mrs Bernard, iii. 283
Beet, Miss, i. 224
Beethoven, ii. 25, 170, 185, 186; iii. 23, 28, 29, 315; his Nine Symphonies, ii. 242-7; iii. 190
BEHIND THE SCENES, ii. 181
Belasco, David, his plays, i. 92, 96; iii. 358, 361
Bell, Mr, iii. 169
——, Mrs Hugh, ii. 73
——, Patty, iii. 97
BELLE BELAIR, iii. 144, 151
Bellew, Mr, iii. 213
——, Kyrle, iii. 310
Bellini, Giovanni, i. 174
——, Vincenzo, ii. 26
BENEFIT OF THE DOUBT, i. 217-21, 268; ii. 55, 56; iii. 132, 137, 309, 340
Benson, Mr, iii. 185
Beringer, Esmé, i. 106, 169, 221; ii. 98; iii. 41, 214, 328
——, Mrs Oscar, her plays, i. 66-9; iii. 1, 8, 48, 55, 214
——, Vera, ii. 156
Berlioz, Hector, iii. 173
Bernage, George, ii. 194; iii. 47
Bernhardt, Sarah, i. 91, 147-54, 181, 196; ii. 39, 55, 261; iii. 187, 188, 209, 210, 276, 351; plays in Gismonda, i. 137-9; Home (Magda), i. 149, 152-4, 162; ii. 146, 147; La Princesse

Lointaine, i. 158-62; Lorenzaccio, iii. 174-6
Berton, Paul M., iii. 14, 20
Besant, Mrs, i. 62
BETSY, iii. 1, 7
Beveridge, J. D., iii. 326, 367
BIARRITZ, ii. 98, 102-4, 172, 220
Bible, The, i. 63, 83; iii. 35, 88, 252, 257, 258
Bicycling, iii. 249
Bigwood, Mr, iii. 352
Bishop, Alfred, i. 123, 244; iii. 96
Bismarck, ii. 223; iii. 383
Bispham, David, ii. 242
Bisson, A., his plays, i. 210; iii. 170, 317
BIT OF OLD CHELSEA, iii. 48, 55
Bizet, Georges, i. 235; ii. 95, 155
Black, Mr, iii. 369
——, George F., iii. 82
——, William, ii 274
BLACK-EY'D SUSAN, iii. 1, 6, 7
Blackguardism, iii. 358
Blake, William, iii. 315
Blakeley, W., i. 215; ii. 123; iii. 54, 197
Blanche, Ada, iii. 24
Blank verse, i. 27; ii. 61, 62, 115, 181, 186, 269
Blathwayt, Raymond, iii. 274, 276
BLEAK HOUSE, ii. 132, 134-6
Blum, Ernest, i. 262, 269
Blushing, i. 154
Boïto, Arrigo, ii. 27
Bond, Acton, ii. 73
Bonney, Mr, i. 22
Booth, Hope, i. 71
——, Junius Brutus, ii 160
BOOTS AT THE HOLLY TREE INN, iii. 8
Bottomley, Master, iii. 219
Boucicault, Mrs, i. 2; ii. 32, 33
——, Aubrey, iii. 54

Boucicault, Dion, ii. 28, 31-3; iii. 169, 308
——, Nina, ii. 59, 220, 265
Boughton, Mr, ii. 91
Bourchier, Arthur, i. 5, 210, 274; ii. 118; iii. 81, 120, 177; plays in Donna Diana, ii. 238; The Chili Widow, i. 215; ii. 122; The Liar, ii. 190; The New Baby, ii. 122; The Queen's Proctor, ii. 151; iii. 120, 121
Bourne, Florence, i. 132
Bouval, Jules, iii. 129
Bowman, Paget, iii. 319
Boyd, Maud, ii. 173
Boyne, Leonard, i. 220
Boys of fourteen, ii. 223
Bradlaugh, Charles, ii. 22
Braham, Leonora, iii. 320
BRAND, i. 264; ii. 72; iii. 14, 15, 276, 344
Brandon, Olga, ii. 12, 187, 232
Brema, Marie, iii. 79
Brewer, J. H., iii. 319
Britannia Theatre, Hoxton, iii. 351
British public, see Public
Brock, Mr, iii. 172
Brontë, Charlotte, iii. 137
Brooke, Mrs, ii. 221; iii. 248
——, Sarah, ii. 20, 65, 149, 172, 188
Brookfield, Charles, ii. 1, 217, 220; iii. 120, 214; plays in A White Elephant, ii. 265; A Woman's Reason, ii. 6, 7; An Ideal Husband, i. 12; On the March, ii. 173; The Home Secretary, i. 122, 230
Brough, Fanny, i. 11, 140, 223; ii. 54, 97; iii. 7, 220
——, Lionel, i. 169; ii. 131, 186, 187; iii. 120, 192
——, Sidney, i. 72; ii. 51, 58, 109,

187; iii. 54; plays in The Happy Life, iii. 266, 267; The Home Secretary, i. 123, 196, 230; The Rivals, i. 254; The Rogue's Comedy, ii. 106

Broughton, Phyllis, ii. 103; iii. 228

——, Rhoda, iii. 48, 54, 55

Brown, Ford Madox, iii. 70-74, 194, 312, 344

——, Graham, ii. 194

Brown-Potter, Mrs, iii. 213, 311

Browne, Pattie, ii. 122; iii. 306, 308

Browning, Robert, i. 53, 189; iii. 123

Bruckman, W. L., iii. 97, 104

Brueys, Admiral, iii. 51

Buchanan, Robert, iii. 295, 296, 355-7; his plays, i. 163, 169; ii. 53, 58, 59, 152, 156, 157; iii. 48, 55, 70, 75, 259, 349

Bucklaw, Mr, ii. 82

Buckley, Rawson, ii. 116

Buckstone, John, i. 138

Buist, Scott, ii. 149, 194

Bulow, Cosima von, i. 258

——, Hans von, i. 258

Bunning, Herbert, ii. 104

Bunyan, John, iii. 1-5, 90, 315

Burbage, Richard, i. 190, 191

Burnand, F. C., his plays, i. 167, 262, 268; iii. 1, 70

Burne-Jones, Sir Edward, i. 13, 14, 16, 18, 32, 174; ii. 141; iii. 193, 344

Burnett, J. P., ii. 132-6

Burney, Estelle, iii. 158, 163-4

Burns, John, i. 160

Business sagacity, iii. 382

Butt, Dame Clara, iii. 120

BYGONES, i. 113, 119-20

Byron, H. J., i. 42; iii. 121, 156, 169

——, Lord, i. 119, 156, 164; ii. 184, 257; iii. 170, 312

Caine, Sir Hall, i. 251-4; ii. 264, 265

Caldwell, Miss, ii. 147; iii. 129

Calf love, iii. 289, 290

Calhoun, Eleanor, i. 5; ii. 54; iii. 144, 368, 369

Calvé, Emma, i. 91, 138, 235, 279; ii. 154-5, 177

Calvert, Charles, iii. 81, 312

——, Mrs Charles, iii. 185, 372; plays in A White Elephant, ii. 265, 266; One Summer's Day, iii. 219; Saucy Sally, iii. 76

——, Louis, iii. 76, 80-81, 299

Campbell, Herbert, iii. 24, 281, 282

——, Nellie, ii. 158

——, Mrs Patrick, i. 101, 223; ii. 19, 39; iii. 34, 185, 281, 338, 373; plays in Fedora, i. 134-6, 138-9; For the Crown, ii. 59, 60, 65, 66, 119, 146; Hamlet, iii. 205, 270; Little Eyolf, ii. 240, 262, 271-8; Magda (Home), ii. 146-9, 275; Nelson's Enchantress, iii. 53-4; Romeo and Juliet, i. 198-99, 202-3; The Notorious Mrs Ebbsmith, i. 61, 64, 127-9, 192; The School for Scandal, ii. 171, 172; The Second Mrs Tanqueray, i. 47, 60

CANDIDA, iii. 290

Canterbury, Archbishop of, ii. 212

Carlyle, Thomas, i. 84; iii. 88, 170, 179, 238

CARMEN, ii. 95, 152-6

Carne, Mr, i. 40

Carpaccio, Vittore, i. 174

Carpenter, Alfred, iii. 8

Carr, F. Osmond, ii. 98, 104

——, J. Comyns, i. 12-18, 36, 92, 97, 164, 168, 174; ii. 7, 53, 55, 141; iii. 105, 110

Carracci, Ludovico, i. 131

Carré, M., i. 210

Carson, Murray, ii. 132; iii. 120, 228

Carte, D'Oyly, iii. 117

Carter, Mrs Leslie, iii. 361

Carton, R. C., his plays, i. 121-3, 193, 195, 230, 232, 238, 242, 243; ii. 264, 265, 266; iii. 229, 232-4, 246, 265, 336, 337, 369

Cartwright, Charles, i. 209, 210, 265; ii. 35, 36, 100, 101

CASE OF REBELLIOUS SUSAN, i. 165, 193; iii. 340

CASHEL BYRON'S PROFESSION, i. 144

CASTE, i. 277; ii. 167; iii. 164-9

CAT AND THE CHERUB, iii. 235-8

Catharine II, iii. 283-4

Cautley, Lawrence, ii. 11, 206

Cavaleria, Lina, ii. 176

Cavendish, Ada, i. 231-6

Cecil, Arthur, i. 107, 108, 110

Cecil Hotel, iii. 116

Celeste, Madame, i. 138

CENCI, THE, i. 53

Censorship of plays, i. 22, 36-9, 48-55, 56-7, 65; ii. 96; iii. 295, 348, 363, 365-7

Cervantes Saavedra, Miguel de, i. 109, 115, 120, 155; ii. 182; iii. 265

Chambers, Haddon, i. 176

'CHAND D'HABITS, iii. 129, 135, 282

Change in men and manners, ii. 166-8

Chapel goers, i. 107

Chapman, George, ii. 182; iii. 317

CHAPTER FROM DON QUIXOTE, i. 113, 115, 120

Character, ideas and, ii. 192

——, the interpretation of, i. 46-7; iii. 110

Character actor, i. 60, 119

Charity and the hospitals and the drama, ii. 280-83

CHARLEY'S AUNT, ii. 210

CHARLOTTE CORDAY, iii. 304, 310

Charm, physical and moral, i. 152

Charrington, Charles, as a producer and manager, i. 19, 164, 165; iii. 34, 101, 102, 124, 129, 139, 140, 179, 339; plays in A Doll's House, iii. 131, 133; The Wild Duck, iii. 139-41

Chart, Nye, iii. 232

Chaucer, Geoffrey, i. 174; iii. 317

CHEER, BOYS, CHEER, i. 204-7

Cheesman, Mr, ii. 221

Cherry, Mr, iii. 373

Children on the stage, iii. 283, 375-7

CHILI WIDOW, i. 210, 214-16; ii. 122, 123

Chinese plays, iii. 235-8

Christian, Herr, iii. 188

Christmas, iii. 279

CHRISTMAS CAROL, ii. 278-80, 281

Chudleigh, Arthur, iii. 303

Church, the, and the theatre, i. 264; iii. 258, 292

—— ritual, its representation on the stage, ii. 21

Cibber, Colley, ii. 287, 288, 290; iii. 253

Cinquevalli, Mr, iii. 25

CLANCARTY, i. 164

Clare, Cyril, ii. 202, 203

Claretie, Jules, ii. 54

Clark, Holman, ii. 131, 226

Clark, Mr, ii. 120

——, Furtado, i. 250

——, George, i. 175, 181

——, Hamilton, iii. 207

Classical actor, iii. 201

CLEVER ALICE, iii. 102

Cleverness, iii. 385

Cliffe, Cooper, iii, 9, 206
Clifford, Dr., iii. 180
———, Mrs, ii. 73
Clifton, Miss, ii. 33
Climax, the dramatic, i. 160
Cloak-and-sword dramas, iii. 137
CLUB BABY, iii. 374-7
Cockburn, Mr, i. 253; ii. 33; iii. 41
Code-morality, ii. 219, 220
Coghlan, Mr, i. 200, 204; ii. 2, 3, 5, 220
Coleman, Fanny, i. 111, 230
———, John, ii. 131, 203, 205, 206, 266
COLLEEN BAWN, ii. 28-33
Collette, Charles, iii. 41
Collier, Constance, iii. 367
Collingham, G. G., iii. 1, 5
Collins, Arthur, iii. 220, 279, 280-82
———, Beaumont, ii. 32
———, Lottie, i. 197
———, Wilkie, i. 230-37
Comedians, iii. 219
Comédie Française, i. 76, 157
Comedy, iii. 33, 83-8; see also Farcical comedy
COMEDY OF ERRORS, i. 189, 269, 275
Commercialization of the theatre, i. 27
Common, Thomas, ii. 92
Commonplaces, iii. 166
Common sense, iii. 84-6
Compton, Miss, ii. 265; iii. 374
Comte, Auguste, iii. 355
Conduct, ii. 143
Conductors, musical, iii. 13
Connell, Norreys, iii. 183
CONQUERORS, THE, iii. 364-7
Conventions, the Englishman and, ii. 18

CONVERSION OF ENGLAND, iii. 292-6
Cook, Aynsley, iii. 336
———, Furneaux, ii. 221
Cooke, Elise, iii. 336
Cooper, Frank, ii. 290; iii. 40
Coote, William Alexander, i. 79-86; ii. 41
Coppée, François, ii. 60-62
Copyright laws, i. 148
Coquelin, Benoît, i. 142, 144, 212; ii. 108; iii. 174; plays in Les Surprises de Divorce, i. 280, 281
Corbin, John, i. 222
Cordova, Rudolph de, ii. 118
Corelli, Marie, iii. 14-21, 42, 44, 53, 371
CO-RESPONDENT, THE, ii. 202, 208
CORIOLANUS, i. 272, 273
Corneille, Pierre, ii. 62
Correspondence, iii. 199
Cosham, Ernest, ii. 188
COUNT CENCI, i. 102
COUNTESS GUCKI, ii. 188-90; iii. 184
COUNTRY GIRL, ii. 187
Country theatres, iii. 115
Country, the, compared with the theatre, iii. 111
COURT OF HONOR, iii. 143
COUSIN FROM AUSTRALIA, iii 358, 364
Coutts, Compton, iii. 176
Covent Garden Opera, ii. 173-8
Cowen, Miss, iii. 55
COXCOMB, THE, iii. 317-20
Craig, Ailsa, i. 120
———, Edith, ii. 292; iii. 40
———, Gordon, i. 175; ii. 200, 290, 292
Crane, Walter, ii. 41; iii. 282
Craven, Walter Stokes, iii. 196
Creedy, Rev., i. 113

Cresswell, Henry, iii. 292-6
CRICKET ON THE HEARTH, ii. 221
Criminals, i. 226; iii. 67
Critics and criticism: critics should educate the public, i. 7; the critic's failure to secure in stage-work the higher qualities of artistic execution, i. 76, 77; most of our criticism is born stale because our newspapers do not want good criticism and will not pay for it, i. 87; the allegation that critics do not know enough about acting to distinguish between good and bad work, i. 148; the London critic should not let artistes gain reputations too cheaply, i. 161; criticism and politics, i. 184-7; all really fruitful criticism of the drama must bring a wide and practical knowledge of real life to bear on the stage, i. 187-8; unlike the musical critic, the dramatic critic does not devote himself sufficiently to the criticism of technical execution, i. 187; the case for the critic-dramatist, i. 245-51; in criticizing actresses the critic is an open and shameless voluptuary, i. 248; the critical instinct, i. 247; the work of Clement Scott, ii. 139-45; personal feeling and criticism, ii. 140; the critic's labour is akin to that of Sisyphus, ii. 159; the actor who desires enduring fame must seek it at the hands of the critic, and not of the casual playgoer, ii. 160; the work of George Lewes, ii. 161; the cardinal faculty of the critic, ii. 161; the silencing of critics,

ii. 174; critics should pay for their seats, ii. 233-5; critics and masterpieces, iii. 8; the criticism of musical farce, iii. 8; a critic assaulted by a manager, iii. 113; the critic's salary and work, iii. 114; the French dramatic critic, iii. 152-5; English criticism, though so deficient in technical connoisseurship, is never indifferent to what it calls "the moral tendency" of the drama, iii. 152; can a critic successfully deal with both drama and music? iii. 155; why the critic finds it easier to praise than to dispraise, iii. 184; the heavy lot of the dramatic critic, iii. 198, 249, 250, 384-5; it is the business of the critic to denounce the delinquencies of the drama, iii. 275; can the critic be a gentleman? iii. 275
Cromwell, Oliver, iii. 359
CRUSADERS, THE, i. 278
Culture, lack of, in the theatre, i. 36
Cutler, Kate, i. 59
CYMBELINE, ii. 183, 195-202; iii. 2, 241

Dairolles, Adrienne, iii. 162, 195
D'Alroy, George, iii. 168
Dalton, Mr, ii. 66
Daly, Augustin, i. 26, 163-76, 177-84, 199; ii. 188-90; iii. 56, 117, 188, 208, 210, 216, 337
Dam, H. J. W., ii. 216, 220
DAME AUX CAMELLIAS, i. 152, 154
Dana, Mr, i. 210, 288; ii. 37
Dancing, iii. 9-13
Dando, Mr, i. 81

DANGEROUS RUFFIAN, i. 262
Da Ponte, iii. 322
Date, plays that, ii. 167-8
DAUGHTERS OF BABYLON, iii. 41-8, 66
Davenport, Miss, iii. 214
David, ii. 168
Davidson, John, ii. 60-62
Davies, Hill, ii. 52
Davis, Fay, i. 244; ii. 270; iii. 96, 217, 233, 234, 326, 367
Dawson, Stewart, ii. 6, 263, 276; iii. 8, 40
Day, George D., ii. 181
——, John T., iii. 229-32
DEACON BRODIE, iii. 262
Deane, Lilian, iii. 363
Decorative play, the, iii. 194
Dee, Ellas, iii. 89
Defoe, Daniel, iii. 256, 257
Delacroix, iii. 173
De Lange, H., i. 123; plays in Lost, Stolen or Strayed, iii. 121; Love in Idleness, ii. 231; The Eider Down Quilt, iii. 7; The Squire of Dames, i. 244; The White Heather, iii. 221
Delaroche, Paul, ii. 85, 99, 100
DELIA HARDING, i. 92, 97-9, 165, 192, 194
Delsarte, iii. 13
Dene, Dorothy, i. 241; ii. 111, 114; iii. 183
Dennis, Mr, i. 40
——, Will, ii. 187
Deportment on the stage, ii. 191
Dervishes, iii. 359
Despres, Suzanne, i. 77-8
Desvallières, Maurice, his plays, ii. 118, 121
Deval, M., ii. 254
Devil, the, iii. 14
Dickens, Charles, i. 52, 107, 114, 124; ii. 91, 132-6, 160, 215, 278,

279, 280; iii. 1, 60, 93, 167, 211, 212, 246, 306, 346
Dickinson, Charles, iii. 143
Diction, i. 26-7, 136, 181; ii. 38-40; iii. 106-7, 293-4, 301, 306, 329; see also Intoning; Ranting
Dietrichstein, Leo, ii. 53
Dillon, Arthur, iii. 362
DIPLOMACY, i. 164; ii. 167
Disease, the conquest of, ii. 125
Disreputable people, iii. 188
DIVIDED WAY, i. 255-62; iii. 33
DIVORÇONS, ii. 145, 149
DOCTOR FAUSTUS, ii. 181, 184
Doctors, ii. 124-5; iii. 250
Dolaro, Selina, ii. 154
Doles, iii. 165
DOLLARS AND CENTS, i. 165; iii. 184
DOLL'S HOUSE, i. 27, 164, 165, 192, 252; iii. 31, 98, 101, 129-133, 139, 317, 375
Dolmetsch, Arnold, i. 173, 191, 275; ii. 210, 239; iii. 163, 243, 244, 362
——, Helen, i. 191; iii. 163
Domenichino, i. 174
DOMINION OF DARKNESS, i. 52
DON GIOVANNI, ii. 104; iii. 30, 322
DON QUIXOTE, i. 109
Donisthorpe, Wordsworth, ii. 192
Donizetti, Gaetano, i. 279
DONNA DIANA, ii. 235-9
Donnay, Maurice, iii. 188
Doré, Gustave, iii. 172, 344
Douglas, Kenneth, iii. 219
DOULOUREUSE, LA, iii. 183, 188
DOVE-COT (JALOUSE), iii. 317, 320
Doyle, Sir A. Conan, i. 113, 115-119; ii. 222
DR BILL, iii. 196, 197
Drama and charity, ii. 281, 282
Dramatic art, artificiality of, iii. 235

Dramatic authorship, ii. 203

Dramatic climax, the, i. 160

DRAMATIC ESSAYS, ii. 159-62

Dramatists, the fashionable and the durable, ii. 167, 168

Drawing room on the stage, i. 108, 109, 277-9; iii. 57

Dress on the stage, i. 198-9; ii. 41-47, 54; iii. 75

Drew, John, i. 164, 166, 167; iii. 209, 232

Dreyfus, Captain, i. 283-6

Drinking amongst actors, i. 219-220

Drummond, Dolores, i. 201; iii. 264

Drury Lane Opera, ii. 177

DUCHESS OF BAYSWATER, ii. 213

DUCHESS OF COOLGARDIE, ii. 202-6

Dumas, Alexandre, ii. 8, 215; iii. 158-62, 189-92, 198, 346

——, Alexandre, *fils*, i. 140, 238, 244; iii. 158-60, 207, 213

Du Maurier, George, i. 238-42; iii. 339

——, Sir Gerald, iii. 120, 307

Durkin, Violet, iii. 354

Duse, Eleonora, i. 138, 145-52, 161-2, 212, 233; ii. 39, 55, 108, 111, 127, 254, 261, 283; iii. 180, 181, 186-8, 209, 210, 273; plays in Cavalleria Rusticana, i. 91; Home (Magda), i. 149, 153, 161, 162, 183, 193-4; ii. 146, 147, 275; La Femme de Claude, i. 144

Dyall, Frank, iii. 206

Eames, Emma, ii. 177

Eastlake, Miss, ii. 120

Echegaray, José, i. 99-106; ii. 241, 277; iii. 34, 56-63, 238

Edgcumbe, Rodney, ii. 158

Edlin, Sir Peter, ii. 212

Edouin, Mr, iii. 331, 376

——, May, iii. 14

Edwardes, George, i. 283, 286, 288

EIDER DOWN QUILT, iii. 1, 7

EL DESDEN CON EL DESDEN, ii. 235

Election of 1895, i. 184, 187

"Electric Christianity," iii. 15, 19

Eliot, George, i. 195, 239, 259; ii. 61, 162, 194

Elizabethan dramatists, i. 130-31; ii. 181-4; iii. 317-19

Elizabethan Stage Society, i. 184, 188, 191, 269, 275; ii. 181, 184, 186, 197, 284; iii. 158, 163, 241, 243, 244, 319, 361-3

Elliot, Mr, iii. 238

——, Maxine, i. 176

Elliot, W. G., ii. 123, 151

Ellis, W. Ashton, iii. 235, 238

Elocution, *see* Diction

Elocutionists, i. 26

Elwood, Mr, iii. 214

Emery, Winifred, ii. 7, 222, 278; iii. 182, 247; plays in A Marriage of Convenience, iii. 160-162; For the Crown, ii. 62, 64, 66; Sowing the Wind, i. 72; The Benefit of the Doubt, i. 220-21; ii. 64; iii. 132; The Little Minister, iii. 248; Under the Red Robe, ii. 227

Emmett, Robert, i. 247

Emotion, i. 138, 219, 220; iii. 146

EMPEROR, i. 165, 263; iii. 344

Endings of plays—happy endings, i. 68; ii. 219; iii. 178; the tragic ending, ii. 219

Endowed theatre, iii. 311-16

ENEMY OF THE PEOPLE, ii. 283; iii. 33

ENGLISH STAGE, THE, iii. 151-6

Englishmen—and cleverness, iii. 385; and common sense, iii.

84-6; and institutions and conventions, ii. 18; are unable to play with wit and philosophy, i. 9; seriousness of, i. 10; the typical Englishman and Englishwoman, iii. 154; values success more than fine art, iii. 84; intellectual subtlety is not their strong point, iii. 323

Enjoyment, ii. 229

Erskine, James, iii. 308

Esmond, H. V., i. 8; iii. 97, 367; his plays, i. 255-62; iii. 215, 218-20; plays in As You Like It, ii. 270; Much Ado About Nothing, iii. 325; The Rise of Dick Halward, i. 227, 229; The Second Mrs Tanqueray, i. 169; The Tree of Knowledge, iii. 233; The Triumph of the Philistines, i. 126

Evans, Marion, ii. 132

Everitt, Herbert, i. 30

Execution (performance), critics and, i. 90, 91, 187-8

Faber, Miss, iii. 55

Failures, theatrical, iii. 338

Fairbrother, Miss, ii. 208; iii. 197

Fame, the actor and, ii. 160

FANATIC, THE, iii. 229-32

Farce, the, i. 68

Farcical comedy, i. 43; ii. 120, 121, 229-31; iii. 196, 216, 217

Farquhar, Gilbert, ii. 50; iii. 228

Farquharson, Mr, iii. 151

Farr, Florence, i. 19; iii. 34, 102, 103, 139; plays in Little Eyolf, ii. 276; Rosmersholm, i. 75, 76; ii. 276

Farren, Nellie, iii. 341

——, W. (junior), ii. 292

Farren, William, i. 255; ii. 51, 171; iii. 59

Fashionable dramatists, ii. 167

Fashions, the change in, ii. 167

FAUST, i. 114; ii. 26; iii. 18, 171

Fauvet, Maria, iii. 82

Feathers in hats, ii. 74

Featherstone, Vane, i. 11, 287; iii. 134

FEDORA, i. 133-6, 138-9; ii. 187

Feeling, ii. 142

FEMME DE CLAUDE, i. 140, 144

Fenton, Frank, i. 244

Fernald, Chester Bailey, iii. 235

Fernandez, James, i. 253; ii. 149, 270

Ferrar, Beatrice, i. 244; ii. 137; iii. 55

Ferrers, Helen, iii. 55

Feydeau, Georges, ii. 118, 229

Fiction, see Novels

Field, Julian, i. 9

Fielding, Henry, i. 52; ii. 236; iii. 348

Filippi, Gigia, iii. 192, 195

——, Rosina, i. 241; iii. 192

Filon, Augustin, iii. 151-6

Financing the theatre, i. 53; iii. 340

FIRST BORN, THE, iii. 235

FIRST NIGHT, THE, ii. 181, 188

First-night audiences, i. 94, 98, 269; ii. 199; iii. 64-9

FIRST STEP, i. 19, 22-4; iii. 347

Fischer, H. F., ii. 118

Fitch, Clyde, ii. 53

Fitzgerald, Aubrey, i. 221

——, Percy, i. 31

FLAMBOYANTE, LA, iii. 70

Flemming, Herbert, i. 69-71

Flotow, Friedrich, iii. 269

FLYING DUTCHMAN, iii. 17

FOOL OF THE FAMILY, ii. 34-41

Foote, Samuel, ii. 188, 190
FOR THE CROWN, ii. 60-66, 101, 119, 146
FOR THE HONOUR OF THE FAMILY, iii. 164
Forbes, Norman, ii. 200, 292; iii. 40
Forbes-Robertson, Sir Johnston, i. 70, 198, 276; iii. 185, 200, 201, 224, 248, 281; as a producer and manager, i. 198, 199-200, 204, 274; ii. 34, 44; iii. 66, 99, 200, 205, 223, 254, 337; plays in For the Crown, ii. 60, 61, 65, 66; Hamlet, iii. 202-4, 206, 207, 270, 271; Home (Magda), ii. 149; King Arthur, i. 17; Michael and his Lost Angel, ii. 19, 20; Nelson's Enchantress, iii. 53; Romeo and Juliet, i. 201; The Notorious Mrs Ebbsmith, i. 65, 128; The School for Scandal, ii. 171
Ford, Henry, iii. 374
Forde, Athol, iii. 307
Fordyce, Miss, iii. 232
Foreign plays, i. 156
FORGET-ME-NOT, i. 164
Forrest, Edwin, ii. 160
Forster, John, ii. 159-61
Forsyth, Miss, i. 11
Foss, Mr, iii. 134
Fouquier, M., ii. 255
FOUR LITTLE GIRLS, iii. 196
FRANCILLON, iii. 207, 213
Fraser, Winifred, i. 22, 69, 232; iii. 142
FREE PARDON, iii. 34
Free seats, ii. 233-5
Free trade in theatres, i. 53
Freear, Louie, iii. 214, 224, 262, 364
FREEDOM IN FETTERS, i. 22
FREISCHÜTZ, DER, iii. 22

French acting, iii. 174, 176
French verse, i. 155-6
Frenchmen and intellectual subtlety, iii. 324
Fresh air, in country houses, i. 208; plays want plenty of, ii. 101
Frith, Walter, his plays, i. 204, 207-210, 232
——, William Powell, iii. 344
Frohman, Charles, iii. 216, 217, 224, 357, 358, 360, 361
Froissart, i. 99
FROM THE BELLS TO KING ARTHUR, ii. 139
Froude, James Anthony, iii. 88
Fryers, Austin, i. 106, 112, 258
Fulda, Ludwig, iii. 99
Fulton, Charles, iii. 6, 7, 134
Furnivall, Dr, iii. 123
Fyles, Franklin, i. 92, 96

Gabriel, Virginia, iii. 305
GALILEAN, i. 165, 263; iii. 344
Gallery rowdyism, i. 98-9; ii. 33, 208; iii. 14, 64-9
Ganthony, Nellie, iii. 197
Garden-party play, ii. 237
Garnier, Jules, i. 83
Garrick, David, i. 32, 190; ii. 236; iii. 201, 251-3
Gatti, Mr, i. 168
Gattie, A. W., ii. 188, 191, 192, 193
Gay, Madame, i. 77
GEISHA, THE, iii. 188
Genest, Mr, iii. 157
Genius, iii. 128
GENTLEMAN JOE, i. 55-9; ii. 28
Gentlemen, i. 277; ii. 166; iii. 74-5
Gerard, Florence, iii. 41
German, Edward, ii. 271; iii. 242
Gérome, Léon, ii. 99
GHOSTS, i. 52, 66, 102, 103, 267;

ii. 142, 143; iii. 177-83, 198, 295

Giddens, Mr, i. 111; ii. 121

Gilbert, Mrs, i. 164, 166, 223; ii. 190; iii. 209

——, Sir William S., i. 42, 222, 223; ii. 230

Gillette, William, iii. 143, 368

Gillmore, Frank, ii. 130, 149; iii. 373

Giotto di Bondone, i. 82; iii. 315

GIRL I LEFT BEHIND ME, i. 92-97

GISMONDA, i. 133, 137-8

Gladstone, William Ewart, i. 31, 37; ii. 88, 192; iii. 108, 289

Glenney, Charles, ii. 204, 206

Glover, J. M., i. 206; iii. 279, 282, 331, 336

Goddard, Arabella, ii. 242

Godfrey, G. W., his plays, i. 106-110, 255, 262

Goethe, Johann Wolfgang, i. 15, 114; ii. 26, 96, 196; iii. 171, 181, 298, 315, 322

Goldsmith, Oliver, ii. 167; iii. 35

Good taste, iii. 120

Goodman, Edward J., ii. 229

Goodwin, J. Cheever, iii. 115

Gordon, J. B., iii. 169

——, Stuart, ii. 79, 80, 84, 85

Gore, Holmes, see Holmes-Gore

GOSSIP, ii. 53

Gottschalk, Ferdinand, iii. 215

Gould, Bernard (Bernard Partridge), i. 288; ii. 39, 44, 144, 228; iii. 205; plays in As You Like It, ii. 116, 117; Hamlet, iii. 270; The Squire of Dames, i. 243, 244; Thyrza Fleming, i. 21

——, Nutcombe, ii. 158; iii. 53, 134, 135

Gounod, Charles François, ii. 142; iii. 18, 26, 189, 343, 345

Graham, James, i. 99-102; iii. 56

Grahame, Cissy, ii. 172

——, J. G., iii. 232

Grand, Sarah, i. 21; ii. 170, 258; iii. 49, 50, 137

GRANDE DUCHESSE, ii. 165

Grant, George, ii. 264, 266

——, James, iii. 135

Granville, Charlotte, i. 110, 244; iii. 21, 204

Graves, Clo, her plays, ii. 92, 96, 132

——, Laura, ii. 82, 83

Gray, Dr Ker, ii. 178

Great men, ii. 267; iii. 53

GREATEST OF THESE——, ii. 152, 158, 170; iii. 132, 184

Greene, Robert, i. 131; ii. 183

Greet, Ben, ii. 116; iii. 54, 135, 368

——, Clare, iii. 377

Grein, J. T., i. 19, 20, 52, 66, 67, 69, 79; iii. 102, 103, 140

Griffiths, Fred, iii. 25

Grigolati, Madame, iii. 25

Grossmith, George, iii. 146, 228

——, Weedon, i. 114; ii. 59; iii. 151; plays in His Little Dodge, ii. 230; Poor Mr Potton, i. 222, 224; The Ladies' Idol, i. 106; The Mac Haggis, iii. 63

Grove, Sir George, ii. 242-7

Groves, Mr, iii. 142, 335

Grundy, Sydney, his plays, i. 1-5, 71, 72, 133, 192, 195, 278; ii. 1, 7, 14, 15, 107, 152, 158, 167; iii. 99, 158, 159, 161, 182, 189, 336; on G. B. S., ii. 56, 57

Guido, i. 131

Guilbert, Yvette, i. 58

GUINEA STAMP, ii. 98

Guitry, M., i. 158

Gurney, Mr, iii. 168, 232

GUY DOMVILLE, i. 6-9, 194; iii. 33, 276

Hackney, Mabel, ii. 10, 12; iii. 63, 311

Haggard, Sir Henry Rider, i. 6

Hallé, Sir Charles, i. 32, 35; ii. 242; iii. 312

Hallward, Cyril, ii. 98

Hamilton, Lady, iii. 48, 51

——, Henry, his plays, i. 204; ii. 152; iii. 215, 265

——, Sir William, iii. 51

HAMLET, i. 222, 271-2; ii. 16, 115, 236; iii. 129, 134, 145, 198, 200-207, 241, 254, 270, 297, 316, 320, 321, 345

Hamlyn, Clarence, i. 217, 222

Hammersmith Socialist Society, ii. 213

Hanbury, Lily, iii. 373; plays in Hamlet, iii. 135, 205; The Daughters of Babylon, iii. 47; The Benefit of the Doubt, i. 220; The Prisoner of Zenda, ii. 12

Handel, George Frederick, ii. 25, 170

Hann, Walter, ii. 66; iii. 46

Happy endings, i. 68; ii. 219; iii. 180

HAPPY LIFE, iii. 265-70

Hare, Gilbert, i. 5; iii. 142, 290, 291, 373

——, Sir John, i. 33, 210; ii. 39, 107, 108, 124, 138; iii. 59, 136, 185, 233, 316, 327; as a producer and manager, i. 19, 67, 142, 274-9; iii. 66, 99, 117; his stage-craft, i. 279-82; plays in A Bachelor's Romance, iii. 289-291; Caste, iii. 165, 168; Les Surprises de Divorce, i. 280; Slaves of the Ring, i. 3-5; The Master, iii. 369; The Notorious Mrs Ebbsmith, i. 65, 127-9, 192

Harford, William, i. 199

Harker, Joseph, i. 199

Harlequinade, iii. 27

HARMONY, i. 214

Harris, Sir Augustus, i. 32, 83, 168, 175, 204; ii. 26, 80, 120, 133, 134, 136, 173-80, 205, 234; iii. 21, 22, 85, 103, 220, 239, 280, 351, 352

Harrison, Frederick, ii. 222; iii. 99, 186, 248

Harte, Bret, ii. 197

Harvey, Sir John Martin, iii. 40, 55, 58, 63, 151; plays in Hamlet, iii. 206; John Gabriel Borkman, iii. 128

——, May, i. 41; iii. 142, 290

Harwood, Robb, i. 169; iii. 121

Hasse, Johann Adolph, ii. 235

Hats, women's, ii. 73, 74

Hawtrey, Sir Charles, ii. 120; produces his own play, Mr Martin, ii. 216-20; plays in A White Elephant, ii. 265; An Ideal Husband, i. 11; Lord and Lady Algy, iii. 374; Mr Martin, ii. 218, 220; Mrs Ponderbury's Past, i. 269; One Summer's Day, iii. 219; Saucy Sally, iii. 76; The Notorious Mrs Ebbsmith, i. 127

Hawtrey, George P., ii. 181

——, W. F., i. 269

——, William, ii. 220

Haydn, Joseph, ii. 245

Haydon, Miss, i. 224; ii. 164

Hazlitt, William, i. 148; ii. 160, 161, 291

Headlam, Rev. Stewart, i. 232

Healy, Timothy, i. 37, 38

HEART OF MARYLAND, iii. 358-361

Heath, Richard, iii. 4

HEAVENLY TWINS, i. 20, 52, 108; ii. 170; iii. 49

INDEX

HEDDA GABLER, i. 69; iii. 154
HEIMAT, *see* HOME (MAGDA)
Heine, Heinrich, i. 263
Heinekey, Lena, i. 29
Heinemann, William, his plays, i. 19, 22-4; iii. 345-51
HELD BY THE ENEMY, ii. 4; iii. 143
Helseth, Madame, i. 75
Hendrie, Ernest, ii. 151, 190; iii. 76
Henley, William Ernest, his plays, i. 19, 114, 140-44; iii. 98, 99, 259, 262
Hennequin, Maurice, ii. 229
HENRY IV, *see* KING HENRY IV
Hepworth, Miss, iii. 320
HER ADVOCATE, i. 204, 207-10, 263, 267
Her Majesty's Theatre, iii. 115-21
Herbert, Sir Henry, iii. 254
Herford, Beatrice, ii. 53, 73
Heroes, iii. 333-5
Hervé, M., ii. 159
Hewitt, Agnes, ii. 33
Hichens, Mr, ii. 180
——, Robert, iii. 374, 378-80
Hicks, Seymour, i. 283, 286; ii. 122; iii. 97, 320
Hill, Annie, ii. 59
HIS LITTLE DODGE, ii. 229, 230
HOBBY HORSE, i. 282; iii. 136-7, 142
Hogarth, William, ii. 35
Holiday, Henry, ii. 41
Holles, Mr, iii. 364
HOLLY TREE INN, iii. 1
Holmes-Gore, Mr, i. 210; iii. 120
Holt, Clarence, i. 70
Home, Risden, iii. 48, 52, 53, 66
HOME (MAGDA), i. 149, 153, 161, 193; ii. 145-9; iii. 33
Home, the old notion of the, iii. 36

HOME SECRETARY, i. 121-3, 193, 195, 230
Homer, ii. 195
Homfrey, Gladys, i. 106, 169, 222, 223; iii. 335
Honesty, i. 245-7
HONESTY: A COTTAGE FLOWER, iii. 259, 262
HONORABLE MEMBER, ii. 188, 191-194
Hood, Basil, i. 55, 58
——, Tom, i. 234
Hooting in the theatre, iii. 67, 68
Hope, Anthony, ii. 7, 8; iii. 339
Horner, Fred, iii. 111
Hospitals, ii. 280-81
HOW TO LIVE ON SIXPENCE A DAY, i. 101
Howard, Leonard, iii. 320
——, Sidney, iii. 14
Howells, W. D., i. 262, 268; iii. 340
Huddlestone, Jessie, iii. 331
Hudson, Charles, ii. 33, 34; iii. 47
Hughes, Annie, i. 116-18, 120, 227, 229; iii. 55, 292
——, Charles, iii. 312
——, Hugh Price, iii. 296, 297
Hugo, Victor, iii. 173
Huline, clown, iii. 27
Human drama, iii. 225
HUMAN SPORT, i. 106, 112
Humanity, the sense of, ii. 93, 145
Humanization, iii. 167
Hume, Fergus, ii. 34, 35
Hunt, Leigh, i. 148
Hunter, Harrison, iii. 206
Husbands, jealous, iii. 61
Huxley, Thomas, i. 195
Hylton, Millie, ii. 103
Hypnotic suggestion, i. 55
Hypocrisy, iii. 120

Ibsen, Henrik, his plays, i. 17, 44, 52, 54, 69, 72-9, 94, 102-3, 108, 145, 164, 165, 191, 192, 195, 204, 226, 258, 263, 267, 268, 273, 279, 282; ii. 33, 72, 84, 90, 94, 142, 171, 196, 239-41, 248-64, 271-8, 284; iii. 2, 6, 14, 28-34, 49, 61, 74, 88, 98, 99, 100, 101, 103, 122-34, 138-42, 154, 170, 173, 177-83, 194, 199, 238, 274, 275, 276, 286, 295, 310, 314, 315, 316, 322, 339, 340, 341-5, 347

IDEAL HUSBAND, i. 6, 9-12, 229

Ideas and character, ii. 192

IDLER, THE, i. 176

Illusion in the theatre, i. 91, 189, 275; ii. 204, 236-7, 267; iii. 139, 242-3

Imagination, iii. 242

Impersonation, the first condition of an, iii. 58

IMPORTANCE OF BEING EARNEST, i. 41-4

IMPRESSIONS OF THEOPHRASTUS SUCH, ii. 162

Incas of Peru, iii. 236

Inconsistencies, iii. 245

Indecency, i. 79

Independent Theatre, The, i. 19, 20, 66-9, 165; ii. 192, 277; iii. 98-103, 144, 199, 238, 292

Ingres, Jean, iii. 71

Institutions, the Englishman and, ii. 18

Intellect, ii. 94; its place in the drama, i. 6

Intellectual subtley of the Englishman and Frenchman, iii. 323-4

Interest of the play, ii. 203-4

Intoning, i. 162; iii. 175

INTRUSE, L', i. 72

Ireland, Samuel, i. 273

Ireland and the Irish of romance, ii. 28-31

IRISH GENTLEMAN, iii. 164, 169

Irish have a keen sense of indelicacy, ii. 96

Irish names, pronunciation of, i. 216

IRONMASTER, THE, i. 165

Irving, H. B., plays in A Leader of Men, i. 40; As You Like It, ii. 270; Hamlet, ii. 115-16; Mariana, iii. 62, 63; Much Ado About Nothing, iii. 326; The Conquerors, iii. 367; The Fool of the Family, ii. 37, 38, 40; The Princess and the Butterfly, iii. 97; The Prisoner of Zenda, ii. 232; The Tree of Knowledge, iii. 233

———, Sir Henry, i. 202, 246; ii. 124, 144, 162, 183, 202, 261, 267; iii. 9, 31, 32, 38, 59, 74, 103, 124, 145, 146, 149, 154, 180, 182, 200, 203, 287, 288, 316, 341; and a knighthood, i. 31-3; and the municipal theatre, i. 17; as a producer and manager, i. 12-13, 19, 120, 130, 134, 228, 277; iii. 99, 185, 223, 241, 243, 337, 377, 378; his diction, i. 136; ii. 39; iii. 47, 108, 306; his impish buffoonery, i. 113-15; his lectures at the Royal Institution, i. 30-36; his interpretation of character, ii. 198; his Shakespearean parts, i. 272-3; mutilates Shakespear, i. 15; ii. 197-8; iii. 253, 325; the acquirement of his art, i. 271-4; plays in A Story of Waterloo, i. 115-19, 241; Cymbeline, ii. 199; Hamlet, i. 272; King Arthur, i. 15, 16, 18; iii. 193; Madame Sans-Gêne, iii. 110; Olivia, iii.

38-40; Richard III, ii. 286-92; The Lady of Lyons, i. 145; The Medicine Man, iii. 379; The Merchant of Venice, i. 272; ii. 198, 199

Irving, Laurence, iii. 140, 283-8

Irving Dramatic Club, i. 28, 29

Isaiah, iii. 41

Ivor, Frances, iii. 150

J.P., THE, iii. 376

Jacquinet, M., iii. 89

Jaeger, Dr, ii. 47

JALOUSE, iii. 317, 320

James, David, ii. 59

——, Henry, his plays, i. 6-9, 67, 194, 195; iii. 33, 68, 276

Jarno, J., ii. 118

JEDBURY JUNIOR, ii. 48-51

Jefferson, Joseph, i. 168, 212; ii. 108, 215; iii. 64

Jeffreys, Ellis, plays in His Little Dodge, ii. 230, 231; The Dovecot, iii. 320; The Misogynist, i. 262; The Notorious Mrs Ebbsmith, i. 65, 127, 128; ii. 232; The Prisoner of Zenda, ii. 232

Jeffries, Maud, iii. 47, 150, 217

Jenoure, Miss, i. 58, 59

Jerome, Jerome K., his plays, i. 133, 139, 225-9, 232, 263; ii. 98, 102; iii. 63, 65

——, Sadie, i. 59; ii. 103

Jerrold, Douglas, iii. 1

JEW OF MALTA, iii. 318

Jews, the, ii. 31

JO, ii. 132-6

Joachim, Joseph, i. 107; ii. 242

JOHN GABRIEL BORKMAN, iii. 17, 28, 32, 34, 45, 61, 98, 122-9

Johnson, Laura, ii. 206; iii. 64

——, Sam, ii. 266; iii. 40

——, Dr Samuel, iii. 315

Jones, Edward, i. 255; ii. 13; iii. 42

——, Henry Arthur, i. 130; ii. 65, 66; iii. 65, 156, 167; his plays, i. 41, 121, 123-6, 192, 194, 195, 214, 274, 278; ii. 14-21, 23, 27, 28, 99, 104-10, 192, 210; iii. 90-96, 181, 198, 208, 211-13, 316, 336-7, 338, 339, 340

Jonson, Ben, i. 130; ii. 183

Jopling, Louise, ii. 41

Jordan, Edith, ii. 266

Journalism, the new, iii. 378

JULIA, iii. 357

JULIUS CÆSAR, iii. 253, 254, 297-303, 313

KANGAROO GIRL, iii. 196-8

KATHARINE AND PETRUCHIO, iii. 251-3

Kaulbach, Wilhelm von, ii. 85

Kaye, Mr, iii. 54

Kean, Mrs Charles, iii. 193, 196

——, Edmund, i. 267; ii. 75, 127, 160, 291; iii. 18

Keegan, Mary, i. 69; iii. 58

Kelly, Mr, ii. 221

——, E. H., ii. 52

Kelmscott Press, iii. 114

Kemble, Henry, i. 230; ii. 7, 100, 158, 220, 265

Kendal, Dame Madge, i. 164, 278-9; ii. 54, 151, 158, 170, 232, 235; iii. 6, 136, 141, 142, 184, 277, 372; plays in The Greatest of These, ii. 157-8; iii. 132

——, William, i. 164, 278-9, 280; ii. 159

Kendrick, Mr, iii. 135

Kennett, Olive, i. 29

Kenney, Mr, ii. 33

Kenyon, Leslie, iii. 96

Kerr, Frederick, i. 169, 266, 286;

ii. 50; iii. 142, 166, 266-9, 290, 373

KING ARTHUR, i. 12-18, 174; ii. 141
KING HENRY IV, ii. 124, 128-32, 144, 145
KING LEAR, ii. 199
KING RICHARD III, i. 113; ii. 285-92; iii. 375, 376
Kinghorne, Mark, plays in All Alive, Oh! iii. 177; Donna Diana, ii. 238; Harmony, i. 215; The Chili Widow, i. 216; The Little Minister, iii. 248; The Queen's Proctor, ii. 151
KING'S SWEETHEART, iii. 331, 335
Kingsley, Miss, iii. 183
Kingston, Gertrude, i. 199; ii. 132; plays in Her Advocate, i. 209; The Fool of the Family, ii. 40; The Passport, i. 110, 111
Kipling, Rudyard, i. 131
KISS OF DELILAH, ii. 264, 266
Knight, Hamilton, i. 253
Knighthoods, actors and, i. 31-3
Knoblauch, Edward G., iii. 374
Knopf, Fernand, iii. 243
Knowles, Sheridan, ii. 24, 235
KORAN, THE, iii. 252

Labouchere, Henry, iii. 120
LADIES' IDOL, i. 99, 106
LADY FROM THE SEA, iii. 98
LADY INGER, iii. 31
LADY OF LYONS, i. 145; ii. 183; iii. 145
LADY WINDERMERE'S FAN, i. 165
Ladylike drama, iii. 289
Lago, Signor, ii. 176, 178
Lamb, Beatrice, iii. 220
——, Charles, i. 131; ii. 181; iii. 317
Lambelet, Napoleon, iii. 97
Lamoureux, M., ii. 256
Landor, Walter Savage, iii. 315

Lane, Eleanor, iii. 169
——, Mrs Sara, iii. 351-4
Langtry, Lily, ii. 54
Languages, the learning of, i. 156
Larkin, Miss, i. 215
Lart, John, iii. 143
Lassalle, Ferdinand, iii. 179
Lassus, Orlandus, i. 174
LATE MR CASTELLO, ii. 1, 7
Laughter in the theatre, i. 11, 42; ii. 118, 119, 230
Law, Arthur, his plays, i. 99, 106; iii. 331-5
Lawrence, Eweretta, ii. 48, 52
Lawyers, ii. 124, 125
Lea, Miss, i. 19
LEADER OF MEN, i. 36-41
Leading men, i. 70
LEAGUE OF YOUTH, i. 192
Leclercq, Rose, i. 43, 221; ii. 7, 98, 109, 172, 220; iii. 97
Leclerq, M., iii. 317
Lecocq, Alexandre, ii. 165
Lee, Jennie, ii. 134, 136
Leigh, Euston, ii. 202, 203
——, James, iii. 176
Leighton, Lord, i. 32, 35; iii. 70, 74
——, Alexes, ii. 155
——, Dorothy, i. 19-22; ii. 34; iii. 101
Lemaître, M., i. 141; iii. 153
Lennard, Horace, iii. 21
Leno, Dan, iii. 23-5, 214, 280-82
Lessing, Gotthold, i. 263
Lethbridge, Alice, iii. 13
Lever, Charles, i. 27
Levey, Florence, ii. 164
Lewes, George Henry, ii. 159-62, 194; iii. 155
Lewin-Mannering, Mr, i. 29
Lewis, Eric, ii. 266
——, Sir George, iii. 249

Lewis, James, i. 164, 166, 175, 176, 181; ii. 122, 190
——, John, iii. 209
LIAR, THE, ii. 188, 190, 191
LIARS, THE, iii. 208, 211-13, 340
Liberty, Lazenby, ii. 41
LIBERTY HALL, i. 250
Life, the stage representation of, i. 6, 7; iii. 19
Lind, Letty, i. 203
Lisle, James, ii. 264, 266
Liszt, Franz, i. 35; ii. 105
Literary play, the, i. 116, 142-4; iii. 222
Literature, a public department of, iii. 170
Literature and dress, ii. 43-4
Litini, Mlle, iii. 21, 88, 89
Little, Mr, i. 106
LITTLE EYOLF, i. 191; ii. 90, 240-41, 256-64, 271-8; iii. 5, 28, 29, 31
LITTLE MINISTER, iii. 241, 244-9
Living Pictures, i. 79-86; ii. 41, 47
Loftus, Cissie, i. 196; iii. 264
——, Kitty, i. 56, 59; ii. 103, 221; iii. 104
Lombroso, Cesare, i. 231
LONDON ASSURANCE, ii. 167; iii. 136
London Pavilion Music-hall, iii. 116
London season, iii. 183-6
London speech, iii. 306
Long-run system, iii. 271-3
Longvil, Miss, i. 132
Lonnen, E. J., iii. 14
Loraine, Robert, ii. 270; iii. 221, 264, 326, 367
LORD AND LADY ALGY, iii. 369, 374
LORENZACCIO, iii. 170, 173-6
LOST, STOLEN, OR STRAYED, iii. 115, 121

Love, Mabel, iii. 104
Love, i. 7; ii. 257-9; iii. 60-61, 289, 290
LOVE IN IDLENESS, ii. 229, 231-2; iii. 8
Lovell, W. T., ii. 220, 266; iii. 335
Lover, the stage, i. 276-7; iii. 247, 289
Lowe, Robert, ii. 160
Lowell, James Russell, i. 53
Lowenfeld, Mr, ii. 102; iii. 331
Lowne, Mr, ii. 206, 263, 276
Lucchesi, Signor, ii. 66
Lugné-Poë, M., i. 72, 76-8
Lumley, R. R., iii. 144
Lupino, Mr, iii. 353, 355
Luria, i. 189; iii. 123
Lussan, Zélie de, ii. 154
Lyceum Theatre, ii. 214
Lytton, Lord, ii. 38, 87

MA COUSINE, i. 170, 176
MACAIRE, i. 114, 140-44
Macaulay, Lord, i. 185; iii. 4, 191
MACBETH, i. 129-33, 272; iii. 3, 368
McCarthy, Justin Huntly, i. 185; his plays, ii. 229; iii. 48, 56
——, Lillah, i. 132, 133
McCullough, John, ii. 88
Macdonough, Glen, iii. 34
MAC HAGGIS, iii. 63, 64
McIntosh, Madge, ii. 194
Mackay, Mr, i. 111
——, J. L., iii. 214
Mackenzie, Sir Alexander, i. 32; iii. 249
Mackinder, Mr, ii. 164
——, Lionel, iii. 104
Mackintosh, Mr, i. 99; ii. 20; iii. 380
Macklin, Mr, ii. 292; iii. 40
McLean, A., ii. 216

McLeay, Franklin, iii. 46, 149, 300, 302

Macready, William, i. 173, 272, 273; ii. 160

MADAME MONGODIN, i. 262, 269

MADAME SANS-GÊNE, i. 177; iii. 105-10, 287

MADEMOISELLE DE BELLEISLE, iii. 189, 190-96

Maeterlinck, Maurice, his plays, i. 72, 76, 189; iii. 243, 345

MAGDA, see HOME

Mallet, Felicia, iii. 88

Mallon, Ada, i. 269

Maltby, Mr, i. 111; ii. 231

MAMMA, i. 280

MAM'ZELLE NITOUCHE, ii. 159, 162-5

MAN ABOUT TOWN, iii. 8-14

MAN IN THE STREET, ii. 52

Managers, theatrical, ii. 175; iii. 340

Manchester and artistic institutions, iii. 311-13

Mannering, L. D., ii. 186; iii. 228

Manners, virtuosity in, iii. 191

Manning, Cardinal, iii. 274

——, Ambrose, iii. 47, 149

Manns, August, ii. 242, 243; iii. 312

MAN'S LOVE, i. 66-71

MAN'S SHADOW, iii. 259

Mansfield, Alice, ii. 123, 131, 149, 266

——, Richard, iii. 124

MANXMAN, THE, i. 251-4, 263-5; ii. 264

Mapleson, Mr, ii. 178, 180

Marcellus, iii. 202

MARIA MARTIN, ii. 37

MARIAGE D'OLYMPE, iii. 164, 168

MARIAGE SOUS LOUIS XV, iii. 158, 189

MARIANA, i. 99, 101-5; ii. 241, 277, 278; iii. 34, 56-63, 126,

MARINERS OF ENGLAND, iii. 70, 75

Maris, John, iii. 173

Marlowe, Charles, his plays, i. 163, 169; ii. 53, 58, 152, 156; iii. 70, 75

——, Christopher, i. 131; ii. 181, 182, 184, 185; iii. 315-18

Marriage, i. 259-61; ii. 257, 258; iii. 50, 297, 356-7

MARRIAGE OF CONVENIENCE, iii. 158-63

Mars, Antony, iii. 215

Marshall, Frank, i. 246

Marston, John, ii. 183

——, Westland, ii. 235-8

Martinetti, Mr, iii. 379

Marx, Karl, iii. 179

MASQUERADERS, THE, iii. 340

Massenet, Jules, ii. 171

Massingham, H. W., ii. 35; iii. 100, 103, 123, 261

MASTER, THE, iii. 369-74

MASTER BUILDER, i. 72, 75, 77-9, 205; ii. 283; iii. 139

MATCHMAKER, THE, ii. 132, 136-7

Mathews, Charles, ii. 108; iii. 166

Maude, Cyril, i. 140, 221; ii. 98, 109, 172, 222; iii. 186; plays in A Marriage of Convenience, iii. 162; Sowing the Wind, iii. 247; The Little Minister, iii. 247; Under the Red Robe, ii. 226

Maupassant, Guy de, ii. 31; iii. 348, 365

Maurice, Mr, iii. 55

Max, M. de, i. 157

May, Henry W., iii. 97

——, Phil, i. 57

Meads, Ernest, i. 30; iii. 363

MEASURE FOR MEASURE, iii. 321, 362

MEDICINE MAN, iii. 374, 379, 380
Mee, Huan, iii. 8
Meilhac, H., his plays, i. 170, 176; ii. 159
Melba, Dame Nellie, i. 279; ii. 177
Mellish, Fuller, i. 116-18; ii. 200
Mellon, Ada, iii. 82
Mellot, Marthe, i. 74-6; iii. 139
Melnotte, Claude, iii. 145
——, Violet, ii. 208
Melodrama, i. 93, 207, 283; ii. 79, 83, 204; iii. 217
Men, change in, ii. 166
Men and women, relations between, i. 108
Mendelssohn, ii. 128, 212, 246, 247
Mendès, Catulle, iii. 129
Menter, Sophie, ii. 242
MERCHANT OF VENICE, i. 272; ii. 198; iii. 318, 320
Meredith, George, i. 53; iii. 83-8, 91, 156, 346, 347, 371
Mérimée, Prosper, i. 235, 239; ii. 152-6
Merivale, Herman, i. 133; ii. 145, 149
MERMAID, THE, iii. 214
MERRIFIELD'S GHOST, i. 245, 250
MERRY CHRISTMAS, iii. 41
Meyerbeer, Giacomo, ii. 99; iii. 173, 283
Meyrick, Leonard, iii. 34
MICHAEL AND HIS LOST ANGEL, ii. 14-21, 23, 27, 34, 40, 41, 65; iii. 338, 339
MIDDLEMAN, THE, iii. 338
Middleton, Thomas, iii. 357
MIDSUMMER NIGHT'S DREAM, i. 25, 26, 177-84; iii. 243
Millais, Sir John, i. 32
Millard, Evelyn, plays in Guy Domville, i. 8, 9; Julius Cæsar,
iii. 300; Sowing the Wind, i. 71, 168; The Divided Way, i. 261; The Importance of Being Earnest, i. 43; The Prisoner of Zenda, ii. 12, 232; The Second Mrs Tanqueray, i. 168; The Silver Key, iii. 192; Too Happy by Half, i. 9
Millaud, M., ii. 159
Millet, F. D., ii. 90
——, Maude, i. 11, 123, 230, 250; ii. 7, 50, 51, 109, 187, 272
Mills, Horace, ii. 173
Millward, Jessie, i. 97, 288; ii. 23; iii. 6, 7, 126
Milton, John, ii. 4
——, Maud, ii. 290; iii. 40
Miracle play, iii. 293
MISOGYNIST, THE, i. 255, 262
Modjeska, Helena, iii. 213
Molière, Jean B. P., i. 93; ii. 22; iii. 83, 85, 229, 230, 265
Mollison, William, ii. 130; iii. 82, 120, 264, 368
Monckton, Lady, i. 126, 169; ii. 107
MONEY SPINNER, i. 280
MONSIEUR DE PARIS, ii. 118, 123
Moodie, Louise, iii. 151
Moore, Decima, ii. 221; iii. 24, 121, 122
——, Eva, ii. 156; iii. 169, 219-20, 335
——, Mary, i. 123, 196, 230, 242, 243, 244; iii. 95
Morality, society and code-morality, ii. 219; the New Woman and, iii. 48-50
Morality of audiences, i. 53
Morality of actresses, iii. 274, 277, 295-7
Morals and the drama, iii. 18-19, 87, 152-3, 164, 168; see also Censorship

Morals, the change in, ii. 167-70
Moreau, M., iii. 105
Morell, Mr, i. 229
Moreto, ii. 235
Morgan, Mr, iii. 361
MOROCCO BOUND, iii. 340
Morris, Mrs, iii. 193
——, Felix, ii. 51, 98, 181, 188
——, Mrs Herbert, i. 30
——, William, i. 14, 16, 278; ii. 209-16; iii. 114, 179
Morse, Woolson, iii. 115, 121
Mortimer, Mr, iii. 157
Morton, Mr, i. 81
——, J. Maddison, iii. 1, 167
——, Martha, iii. 288-91
Moser, Von, ii. 48
MOTHER OF THREE, ii. 92, 96-8
Mottl, Felix, ii. 185
Mozart, Wolfgang Amadeus, i. 93, 174, 192; ii. 104, 130, 183, 244-6; iii. 23, 30, 171, 189, 322, 346
MR MARTIN, ii. 216-20
MRS LESSINGHAM, i. 276, 277; iii. 99
MRS PONDERBURY'S PAST, i. 262
MUCH ADO ABOUT NOTHING, i. 130, 189; iii. 320-26, 332
Mulholland, Mr, i. 231, 237; ii. 75, 208; iii. 197, 224, 240, 368
MUMMY, THE, ii. 181, 186
Municipal theatres, i. 17; ii. 77-9, 282; iii. 311-16
Munro, Miss, i. 132
——, Patrick, i. 30
Murder, i. 143
MURDERS IN THE RUE MORGUE, ii. 222
Murray, Alma, i. 41; iii. 183, 185
——, David Christie, iii. 164, 169
——, Thomas, ii. 172
Music—and religion, ii. 25-6; and the expression of emotion, ii.

244; the appreciation of, ii. 92-3
Musical comedy or farce, ii. 165; iii. 8-10, 340, 353-4
Musset, Alfred de, iii. 170, 173
MY FRIEND THE PRINCE, iii. 48, 54, 224
MY LADY'S ORCHARD, iii. 214
Mystery plays, iii. 317

Najac, E. de, ii. 145
Napoleon, iii. 359
National Vigilance Association, i. 79, 80, 82, 86
Natural element in the drama, ii. 236, 237, 239, 241
Neilson, Ada, i. 236
——, Julia, i. 230; ii. 171, 278; iii. 373; plays in An Ideal Husband, i. 11, 121-3; As You Like It, ii. 270; Much Ado About Nothing, iii. 324-6; The Conquerors, iii. 365, 367; The Home Secretary, i. 121-3, 196; The Princess and the Butterfly, iii. 97; The Prisoner of Zenda, ii. 232; The Tree of Knowledge, iii. 233, 234
NELSON'S ENCHANTRESS, iii. 48-54, 66, 199
Neruda, Norman, ii. 242
Nesville, Juliette, i. 126; iii. 54
Nethersole, Olga, i. 126-9; ii. 155
NEVER AGAIN, iii. 215-18
Neville, Henry, i. 206; ii. 141; iii. 370
NEW BABY, ii. 118, 120, 121, 122, 123
NEW BOY, i. 266, 269
New Century Theatre, iii. 97-103, 199, 238
New Drama, the, iii. 98, 100, 238, 338, 339
NEW MAGDALEN, i. 230-37

NEW MEN AND OLD ACRES, i. 164, 282

"New movement" in dramatic literature, i. 232

New Public, ii. 223, 226

Newman, John Henry, iii. 286

Newspapers, and criticism, i. 87; and public men, i. 248

NIBELUNG TETRALOGY, iii. 22

Nicholls, Harry, i. 288; iii. 7, 18, 128

Nietzsche, Friedrich, ii. 92-6, 142

NIGHT OUT, ii. 118, 121-2

Noel, Nancy, i. 108

Nordau, Max, i. 76, 195

Norreys, Miss, i. 227

NOTORIOUS MRS EBBSMITH, i. 59-66, 85, 126-9, 192, 195, 263; ii. 56, 99; iii. 66, 166, 339

Noufflard, M., iii. 155

Novelists and the depicting of society, iii. 211-12

Novels—contemporary fiction has maintained a higher level than contemporary drama, iii. 137, 288; great works in fiction, iii. 16; the change in novels, ii. 257; the dramatization of novels, iii. 101-2, 222, 338-41

Nudity, i. 80, 83-4, 85, 86

NUPKINS AWAKENED, ii. 212-13

Nurses, ii. 280-81

Ober Ammergau Passion Play, i. 189; ii. 27; iii. 45

OBERON, iii. 22

O'Connor, T. P., ii. 31, 162; iii. 108

Odilon, Madame, iii. 187, 188

Odysseus, ii. 168

Offenbach, Jacques, ii. 165

Ogilvie, G. Stuart, his plays, ii. 98-102; iii. 326, 327, 369-70

OH, SUSANNAH! iii. 207, 214

OLD GARDEN, ii. 52

Oldfield, Nance, i. 134

Oliffe, Geraldine, i. 269; ii. 108, 208

OLIVIA, ii. 144; iii. 34-40

Olivier, Sidney, i. 22, 23

ON 'CHANGE, ii. 48-53

ON LEAVE, iii. 111

ON THE MARCH, ii. 166, 173

ONE OF THE BEST, i. 283-8

ONE SUMMER'S DAY, iii. 215, 218-20, 339

O'Neill, Mr, iii. 62

Opéra-bouffe, ii. 165

Opera Comique, i. 44

Opera in England, ii. 175-80; iii. 156

Opp, Miss, ii. 271

Oram, Mona, ii. 52

Orders of admission, ii. 233

Orme, Aileen d', iii. 104

O'Shea, Mrs, i. 37

OTHELLO, i. 272; iii. 144, 147-50, 243, 315

Otway, Thomas, ii. 235

OUR BOYS, i. 164

Outram, Leonard, ii. 79, 80; iii. 142, 183

Owen, Robert, iii. 356

Oxford University Dramatic Society, iii. 328, 329

Pack, George, iii. 97

Paderewski, Ignace Jan, ii. 242

Page, Elliott, i. 126

Paget, Ffolliott, iii. 142

Painting, see Pictures

Palestrina, Giovanni, i. 174

Palfrey, May, i. 106, 169; ii. 59; iii. 41

Palliser, Esther, i. 21, 22

Pamphlets, dramatized, ii. 206

Pantomime, iii. 24, 25, 279-83

Paradise, the popular conception of, i. 2

Parker, Louis N., his plays, ii. 52, 132, 145, 229, 231; iii. 221, 225-228, 240, 265-70

Parnell, Charles Stewart, i. 37; iii. 295, 296

Parochialism of the English drama, iii. 156

Parry, Judge, iii. 312

PARSIFAL, ii. 27; iii. 45, 238

Partridge, Bernard, *see* Gould, Bernard

Party criticism, i. 184-7

Passion, i. 6, 74; ii. 167, 168

Passion Plays, iii. 45

PASSPORT, THE, i. 106, 110-11, 195, 210, 263

Pateman, Bella, ii. 231

Pathetic actor, iii. 219

Patriotism, ii. 205; iii. 358-9

Patti, Adelina, i. 279; iii. 187, 193

Paull, H. M., his plays, i. 217, 222, 245, 250

Paulton, Harry, iii. 41

Pauncefort, Miss, i. 114

Pearce, Mr, iii. 369

Pearson, Herbert, i. 236

PEER GYNT, ii. 248-56; iii. 15, 31, 98, 344, 345

Peile, Kinsey, i. 43

PELLÉAS ET MÉLISANDE, i. 72, 76, 189

Pemberton, T. Edgar, i. 275

Penley, William Sydney, i. 274; ii. 120; iii. 224

Pennell, Joseph, ii. 185

Penny, Mr, iii. 369

"Penny gaff," i. 141

Percyval, Wigney, iii. 149

PERIL, i. 164

Perkins, Mrs Charlotte Stetson, iii. 49

PETER THE GREAT, iii. 283-7

Peter the Hermit, i. 270

Phelps, Mrs Edmund, ii. 121, 194

——, Samuel, i. 27; iii. 312

Philips, F. C., ii. 1; iii. 34

Philistine, a, i. 124

Phillips, Kate, i. 72; plays in As You Like It, ii. 270; Henry IV, ii. 131; Slaves of the Ring, i. 2, 5; The Chili Widow, i. 215; The Fanatic, iii. 232; The Manxman, i. 253; The Wild Duck, iii. 141; True Blue, ii. 83

Phillpotts, Eden, his plays, i. 133; iii. 63

Philosophy and philosophers, ii. 92-4

Philosophy, plays must have a, ii. 96

Philp, Mr, i. 59

Phipps, Mr, iii. 118, 314

Physical charm, i. 152

PHYSICIAN, THE, iii. 90-96

Pictorial play, iii. 193-5

Pictures, ii. 209; iii. 70-75, 293; realism in, iii. 70-74; the appreciation of, ii. 92-3; the Englishman and, i. 198

PIERROT'S DREAM, iii. 21

PIERROT'S LIFE, iii. 88

Pigott. E. F. Smyth, i. 22, 23, 37-39, 48-55

PILGRIM'S PROGRESS, iii. 1-6, 276, 317

PILLARS OF SOCIETY, ii. 284; iii. 126

Pinero, Arthur W., i. 248, 270, 271; ii. 55; on G.B.S.'s criticisms, ii. 55-7; his plays, i. 41, 45-7, 59-65, 113, 119, 123, 126-9, 133, 168, 192, 195, 217-21, 268, 274; ii. 15, 99, 167; iii. 90-97, 136-7, 198, 212, 233, 304-10, 316, 336-9, 347

PINK DOMINOS, ii. 120, 121, 229

Pit-door, the struggle at the, i. 66
Plançon, Pol, ii. 177
Platform performances of plays, i. 189, 275; ii. 184; iii. 362
Playfair, Arthur, ii. 50; iii. 335
Playgoer, the, i. 107
Plays that date, ii. 167-9
Playwright's craft, ii. 203
Poë, Lugné, ii. 249-51, 254-6, 263; iii. 124, 139, 174
Poel, William, ii. 181, 185, 186, 284; iii. 163, 242, 318, 319, 329, 362, 363
Poetic drama, the staging of, i. 189
Points in acting, i. 146
Politics and criticism, i. 184-7
Polygamy, iii. 50
Ponsonby-Fane, Sir Spencer, iii. 254, 255
POOR MR POTTON, i. 217, 221, 263
Pope, Alexander, i. 174
Popular level, the supposed, ii. 36, 37
PORTER'S KNOT, ii. 221
Potter, Paul, his plays, i. 238, 240, 241; iii. 364-7
Pounds, Courtice, iii. 331
Poupée, La, iii. 331
Powers, Francis, iii. 235
Prayers, iii. 288
Preaching in the theatre, i. 263-6
Prejudices, iii. 49
PRETENDERS, THE, iii. 31
Prices of seats, ii. 49
PRINCESS AND THE BUTTERFLY, iii. 90-97, 137, 212, 304, 340
PRINCESSE LOINTAINE, i. 154-63
PRISONER OF ZENDA, ii. 7-12, 42, 43, 232; iii. 33, 222, 339
Problem play, i. 108, 265; iii. 276
PRODIGAL FATHER, iii. 34, 41
Professions, ii. 124-6

PROFLIGATE, THE, i. 60, 63; iii. 136
Programmists, musical, ii. 244, 246
Pronunciation, see Diction
Prostitution, iii. 297
Prout, Samuel, i. 173
Prozor, M. le Comte, ii. 248-50
PRUDE'S PROGRESS, i. 133, 139, 195, 229, 263
Public, the British, i. 223; iii. 335; critics should educate, i. 7; its taste and intelligence, i. 94; pleasing the public, ii. 283, 284; the danger of descending to the supposed popular level, ii. 36, 37; the New Public, ii. 223, 226
Public men and press criticism, i. 248
Punch and Judy, ii. 104, 168, 285; iii. 9, 10
Purdon, Richard, ii. 28, 31, 32
Puritan, a, i. 124-5

Qualities, endearing and repulsive, iii. 245-6
QUEEN'S PROCTOR (DIVORÇONS), ii. 145, 149-51; iii. 111, 121
QUINTESSENCE OF IBSENISM, ii. 94

Racine, Jean, ii. 62
RAILROAD OF LOVE, i. 163, 165
Raleigh, Mrs, ii. 79, 81
——, Cecil, his plays, i. 204; ii. 79, 80; iii. 97, 215, 265
Ralli-Carr, Mrs, i. 59
Ramsey, Alicia, ii. 118
——, Cecil, ii. 266
Ranting, i. 159-62
Raphael, ii. 85
Ravogli, Giulia, i. 235; ii. 154, 176, 177
——, Sofia, ii. 176
Reality in the drama and on the

stage, i. 12, 205; ii. 236, 237; iii. 194, 383

Redford, George Alexander, iii. 254, 348-51

Reed, Allan, ii. 181

——, German, i. 67

REFUGEE'S DAUGHTER, iii. 289

Rehan, Ada, i. 91, 162, 164, 196; ii. 40, 172, 289; iii. 151, 184, 185, 208-211, 248, 319; plays in A Midsummer Night's Dream, i. 181-4; As You Like It, iii. 209; Countess Gucki, ii. 189, 190; The Railroad of Love, i. 166, 167; Twelfth Night, i. 26; Two Gentlemen of Verona, i. 175

Réjane, Madame, i. 176, 177; iii. 109, 174, 183, 187-9, 209, 276

Religion and the stage, ii. 21-8; iii. 276, 292

Rembrandt, iii. 71

Renaissance, the, i. 131, 173, 175; ii. 95

Repertory theatre, ii. 74-6

Reputations, i. 161-2

Resurrectionism, ii. 132

Reszke, Edouard de, ii. 177, 180

——, Jean de, i. 201; ii. 177, 180; iii. 305

RETROSPECT OF THE STAGE FESTIVALS OF 1876, iii. 235

Reynolds, Sir Joshua, i. 32

RHEINGOLD, DAS, iii. 22

Rhetorical drama, iii. 144-6, 193

RICHARD III, see KING RICHARD III

Richards, Cicely, i. 111; iii. 41, 262

RICHELIEU, iii. 145

Richelieu, Cardinal, iii. 191

Richter, Hans, ii. 185; iii. 13

Ridley, Sir Matthew White, iii. 376

Righton, Edward, i. 140; ii. 172

Rignold, Mr, ii. 82

RISE OF DICK HALWARD, i. 225-30, 232, 263, 267

Ristori, Adelaide, i. 144, 160

RIVALS, THE, i. 251, 254

ROBBERY UNDER ARMS, i. 70

ROBERT LE DIABLE, iii. 22

ROBERT MACAIRE, see MACAIRE

Roberts, Arthur, ii. 260; iii. 104, 128; plays in Biarritz, ii. 102; Gentleman Joe, i. 55-9; The White Silk Dress, ii. 221

Robertson, Fanny, ii. 136

——, Ian, ii. 229, 232; iii. 204

——, Thomas William, his plays, i. 46, 276; ii. 142, 237; iii. 156, 164-8, 276

——, W. J., ii. 52

Robins, Elizabeth, ii. 148, 187; iii. 53, 182; as a producer and manageress, i. 19; ii. 240, 241, 255; iii. 34, 56, 100, 102, 103, 261; plays in Little Eyolf, ii. 262, 272, 273, 275, 277, 278; John Gabriel Borkman, iii. 123, 125-7; Mariana, iii. 58-63; Rosmersholm, i. 75; The Master Builder, i. 75, 78, 79

Robinson, Frederic, ii. 200

ROBINSON CRUSOE, iii. 256

Robson, Frederick, ii. 215

Rochelle, Mr, ii. 33

Rock, Mr, iii. 373

ROGER LA HONTE, iii. 259

ROGUE'S COMEDY, ii. 104-10

Romaine-Walker, Mr, iii. 118

ROMANCE OF THE SHOPWALKER, ii. 53, 58, 59

ROMANCE OF TWO WORLDS, iii. 15

Romano, Giulio, i. 82, 131

Romans, the, ii. 94

Romantic imagination, the, iii. 17

Romanticism, iii. 170-74, 225-7

ROMEO AND JULIET, i. 197-204; ii. 187; iii. 326, 328-31

Rooke, T. M., i. 173
Rorke, Kate, i. 276, 278; iii. 120, 182, 224; plays in A Midsummer Night's Dream, i. 26; Honesty, iii. 261-2; Slaves of the Ring, i. 2, 4; The Sin of St Hulda, ii. 99, 101; The Wanderer from Venus, ii. 156; The White Heather, iii. 220; The White Knight, iii. 328
Rosa, Carl, iii. 13
——, Salvator, i. 174; iii. 173
Rose, Edward, ii. 7-10, 222-8
ROSEMARY, ii. 132, 137, 138
ROSMERSHOLM, i. 72-76, 205, 258; iii. 139
Ross, Mr, iii. 374
——, Adrian, ii. 98
Rossi, M., iii. 21, 89
Rossini, Gioacchino, i. 24; ii. 181, 242, 243
Rostand, Edmond, i. 154, 155
Rowdyism, see Gallery rowdyism
Rowe, Nicholas, ii. 115
Rowley, William, iii. 357
Roze, Marie, ii. 154
——, Raymond, iii. 261, 303
Rubens, Peter Paul, i. 82
Rupert, Prince, iii. 359
Ruskin, John, i. 174, 185, 278; iii. 1, 173, 179
Ryan, Mr, i. 199; iii. 46
Ryley, Madeleine Lucette, ii. 48

Sachs, Mr, iii. 314
Sacrifice, iii. 333
St John, Florence, i. 77
Saint-Saëns, Charles, ii. 171
Saker, Mrs, i. 8; iii. 307
Salmond, Norman, iii. 331
SALVÊ, i. 66-9
Salvini, Tommaso, i. 144, 160, 161; ii. 25, 97, 127
Santley, Sir Charles, ii. 171, 242

Sarcey, M., iii. 153
SARDANAPALUS, iii. 312
Sardou, Victorien, his plays, i. 92, 97-8, 133-40, 147, 164, 165, 177, 191, 192; ii. 14, 145, 187; iii. 105, 108, 110, 287
SAUCY SALLY, iii. 70, 75
Sausages thrown at the critics, ii. 33
Scenery, see Stage scenery
Schiller, Johann, iii. 173
Schongauer, Martin, ii. 185
Schonthan, Frau von, i. 163, 167
——, Franz von, ii. 188
School Board Election, iii. 255-8
SCHOOL FOR SCANDAL, ii. 166-73
Schopenhauer, Arthur, ii. 94, 96; iii. 179, 202, 377
Schubert, Franz, i. 242; ii. 243; iii. 23
Schumann, Robert, ii. 142
Scott, Clement, i. 49-55, 65, 90, 145, 186, 250, 276; ii. 6, 139-45, 256; iii. 80, 157, 274-7, 295-7
——, Sir Walter, i. 108, 253; ii. 8, 99, 142, 195, 257, 258; iii. 36
SCRAP OF PAPER, i. 165, 276, 280
Scriptural style, to write in the, iii. 42
SEA FLOWER, iii. 331-5
Seats—critics should pay for, ii. 233-5; prices of, ii. 49
SEATS OF THE MIGHTY, iii. 115
SECOND MRS TANQUERAY, i. 41, 44-8, 60, 63, 165, 192-3; ii. 56; iii. 136, 198, 338-40
SECRET SERVICE, iii. 143
Seiffert, Henri, iii. 48
Senility, the portrayal of, iii. 308
Sensitive people, i. 84
SETTLED OUT OF COURT, iii. 158, 163

Seven Ages of Man, ii. 268

Sexes—relations between the, i. 108; ii. 169-70; the inequality of the, iii. 130

Sexual impressions, people sensitive to, i. 85-6

Shakespear, i. 52, 53, 248; ii. 91; compared with Bunyan, iii. 1-5; his appeal to the musical sense, i. 24-5, 203; iii. 76, 147, 301; Ibsen compared with, iii. 343, 344; platform versus pictorial stage effect performances, i. 189, 190, 275; players' and playgoers' appreciation of Shakespear is sheer hypocrisy, i. 25; powerful among his enemies are the commentator and the elocutionist, i. 26; the right way to declaim, iii. 76; his plays, i. 15, 24-30, 129-30, 145, 166-7, 170-74, 189-91, 197-204, 222-3, 271-3, 282; ii. 3, 61, 62, 110, 111-17, 124, 128-32, 166, 167, 182-5, 195-202, 215, 236, 237, 264-71, 284-92; iii. 31, 33, 37, 38, 76-83, 134, 144, 146-50, 163, 200-10, 239-46, 251-4, 270, 297-303, 317-18, 320-26, 328-31, 332, 336-8, 385

Shakespear Anniversary Celebration, ii. 110

Shakespear Reading Society, i. 130; iii. 329

Shaw, G. B., ii. 181

Shaw, G. Bernard, his plays, i. 42, 165, 246; ii. 60, 237; iii. 218, 238, 278, 290, 336, 349-50, 382

SHEEP IN WOLF'S CLOTHING, iii. 283

Shelley, Percy Bysshe, i. 53, 102; iii. 179, 315

Shelton, George, iii. 233

Sherbrooke, Michael, iii. 319, 363

Sheridan, Richard Brinsley, his plays, i. 251, 254; ii. 166, 167-71

Shields, Frederick, iii. 72, 73

Shine, John L., ii. 205, 206; iii. 164, 169

Shirley, Arthur, ii. 202

Shirt, the, ii. 45-7; iii. 106

Short, Hubert, iii. 55

Siddons, Mrs, i. 130; ii. 88, 235, 238

Sidney, Sir Philip, ii. 182

SIGN OF THE CROSS, ii. 7, 12-14, 33, 237; iii. 31, 46, 47, 276

Silva, Miss de, i. 120

SILVER KEY, iii. 189-96

SILVER KING, ii. 37

Sims, G. R., his plays, ii. 202, 206, 207; iii. 97, 104

SIN OF ST HULDA, ii. 98-102

Sinden, Topsy, iii. 354

Singleton, Miss, ii. 221

Sisyphus, ii. 159

Sitgreaves, Miss, iii. 58

Skill, ii. 126

Skinner, Otis, i. 166; iii. 209

SKIPPED BY THE LIGHT OF THE MOON, iii. 97, 104

Slaughter, Walter, i. 55, 59

SLAVES OF THE RING, i. 1-5, 192, 278

Smith, Aubrey, ii. 232, 271

——, W. B., iii. 143

Snobbery amongst actors, iii. 223

Social questions and the drama, i. 37, 38; iii. 165-6, 180-81, 331-2, 348-9; see also Morals and the drama

Socialism, iii. 165

Socialist League, ii. 211

Society—iii. 211, 212; and code morality, ii. 219; its representation on the stage, i. 11, 108-9; iii. 58

SODOM'S ENDE, iii. 33

Somerset, Lady Henry, i. 79
——, Mr, i. 209
Somerville, R., ii. 216
SON OF DON JUAN, i. 99, 102, 103, 105
SORROWS OF SATAN, iii. 14-21, 31
Sothern, Sam, iii. 308
SOWING THE WIND, i. 71, 72
SPANISH GIPSY, iii. 357, 362-3
Speech, see Diction
SPHINX AND THE CHIMNEY POT, iii. 97
Spies, i. 285
Spong, Hilda, ii. 204, 206, 266; iii. 305, 307
SQUIRE OF DAMES, i. 238, 242-4
Stage craft, i. 45
Stage illusion, see Illusion
Stage management, i. 279; iii. 123, 124, 139
Stage scenery, lighting, and effects, i. 172-3, 175, 205, 276-9; ii. 228; iii. 22, 26-7, 241-3, 293; see also Platform performances of plays
Stage suitability of plays, i. 141-3
Stagey drama, the, ii. 236-7, 239; iii. 222
Standard theatre, a, iii. 103
Standing, Herbert, ii. 106
Stanfield, Clarkson, i. 173
Stanley, Alma, ii. 108, 136, 188; iii. 14
——, Sir Henry M., i. 107
Stead, Mr, i. 83; iii. 295, 296
Steer, Janette, iii. 120, 164
Stephens, Yorke, i. 111; ii. 51, 52, 110; iii. 21
Stephenson, B. C., i. 106
Sternroyd, Vincent, ii. 271
Stevenson, Robert Louis, his plays, i. 19, 114, 140-43; iii. 98, 99, 259, 262
STILL WATERS RUN DEEP, i. 164

Stillman, Mrs, ii. 213; iii. 193
Stirling, Mrs, i. 223
Stock-company system, i. 270-71, 274; ii. 75-6, 91; iii. 272, 273
Storey, G. A., ii. 41
STORM, THE, ii. 229, 232
STORY OF WATERLOO, i. 113-20
STRANGE ADVENTURES OF MISS BROWN, i. 163, 169, 195, 263, 266
Street, Mr, i. 148
Struggle, the focus of the, i. 66
Stuart, Cosmo, iii. 335
Sturgess, Arthur, his plays, iii. 21, 279, 331, 357, 364
Styan, Arthur, iii. 121
Subsidized theatre, iii. 103
Suburban theatres, i. 230, 237; iii. 222-5
Suburbanity, ii. 256-7
Successes, theatrical, iii. 338
Sucher, Josef, ii. 235
Sudermann, Hermann, his plays, i. 148, 152, 161, 193-5; ii. 142, 145, 148; iii. 33, 99
Sugden, Mr, ii. 121; iii. 320
——, Mrs Charles, iii. 41
Sullivan, Sir Arthur, i. 18, 32
——, Barry, i. 182-4, 271-3; ii. 162, 288; iii. 185
Sully, Mounet, i. 77, 157; iii. 176
SUMMER MOTHS, iii. 345-8
Surgery, iii. 249-50
SURPRISES DE DIVORCE, i. 280, 281
Surrey, Imogen, iii. 319, 363
Sutro, Alfred, i. 210; iii. 100, 123, 261
Swain, Lillian, i. 178
SWEET NANCY, iii. 50, 54, 289, 292
Swinburne, Algernon, ii. 181; iii. 317
Sylvaine, A., iii. 170

Syndicates, theatrical, iii. 340
SYSTÈME RIBADIER, ii. 229

Tailor, the, and the stage, ii. 41-7
Talleyrand, iii. 315, 377
Talma, François, i. 132, 211; iii. 180
TAMING OF THE SHREW, ii. 170; iii. 201, 239, 252-3
TANNHÄUSER, iii. 155
Tapley, Mr, ii. 164
Taylor, J. G., iii. 96
——, Tom, i. 164
Telbin, Mr, i. 172, 175; iii. 46
TEMPEST, THE, iii. 158, 163, 241-4
Tempest, Marie, ii. 173
Temple Shakespear, i. 28
Tennyson, Lord, i. 32, 94; ii. 212
Terriss, Tom, i. 224-5; ii. 33
——, William, ii. 39; iii. 40, 176, 277; plays in A Marriage of Convenience, iii. 160-3; Black-Ey'd Susan, iii. 6, 7; One of the Best, i. 283, 286-8; The Girl I Left Behind Me, i. 96, 97
Terry, Edward, ii. 231; iii. 326, 327
Terry, Dame Ellen, i. 134, 137, 145, 146, 199, 282; ii. 124, 151; iii. 9, 31, 32, 60, 149, 180, 234; her stagecraft, iii. 192-5, 373; plays in Cymbeline, ii. 201-2, 215; King Arthur, i. 17; Madame Sans-Gêne, iii. 105-9; Olivia, ii. 144; iii. 37, 40; The Medicine Man, iii. 379
——, Fred, i. 30; plays in A Leader of Men, i. 40; His Little Dodge, ii. 231; Much Ado About Nothing, iii. 326; The Conquerors, iii. 367; The Home Secretary, i. 230; The School for Scandal, ii. 171;

The Tree of Knowledge, iii. 233, 234
Terry, Kate, iii. 371-2
——, Mabel, iii. 372, 373
——, Marion, i. 192; ii. 39; plays in A Leader of Men, i. 41; Guy Domville, i. 8; Michael and His Lost Angel, ii. 19, 20; The Physician, iii. 96; The Rise of Dick Halward, i. 227-9, 232
Thackeray, William Makepeace, i. 90, 238, 239, 242; ii. 4, 272; iii. 57, 211, 212, 219
Thalberg, T. B., iii. 96
Theatres—architecture and decoration of, iii. 117, 118; cost of, iii. 117; does the theatre make for good? iii. 274; enjoyment in, ii. 229-30; finance of, i. 53; iii. 340; their effect on our ideas and conduct, iii. 152-153; the function of the theatre, ii. 236; unlike the church, the theatre has done nothing to adapt itself to modern demands, iii. 258; why doesn't anybody go to the? ii. 213-15; why people go to the, i. 266; iii. 246
Théâtre de l'Œuvre, i. 72, 76, 79, 189
Theatrical management, ii. 175-7
THEATRICAL WORLD OF 1894, i. 87
THEATRICAL WORLD OF 1896, iii. 151, 157
THEATRICAL WORLD OF 1897, iii. 336
THELMA, iii. 17
Thomas, Brandon, i. 5, 72, 254; iii. 247, 248
Thorne, Fred, iii. 177
Thornhill, Miss, iii. 292
Thorpe, Courtenay, plays in A Doll's House, iii. 131; Ghosts, ii. 240; iii. 182; Hamlet, iii. 135,

204; Little Eyolf, ii. 263, 275; The Free Pardon, iii. 41; The Wild Duck, iii. 140

Thought, ii. 142

Thursby, Mr, iii. 214

THYRZA FLEMING, i. 19-22

Tietjens, Teresa, ii. 176

Titian, i. 82; ii. 85; iii. 73

Titles, actors and, i. 32-3

TITUS ANDRONICUS, iii. 318

Toche, Raoul, i. 262, 269

Tolstoi, Count, i. 52, 54

TOO HAPPY BY HALF, i. 9

Toole, John, i. 57

TOSCA, LA, i. 142

Tourneur, Cyril, i. 131; ii. 183

Towneley mysteries, ii. 211

Tracts, dramatized, ii. 206

Tragedy, iii. 33; the stage management of, iii. 124

Tragic acting, i. 151, 232-3

Tragic ending, the, ii. 219

Traill, Mr, ii. 221

——, H. D., iii. 374, 377-80

Trebel, Mr, iii. 55

Trebelli, Zelia, ii. 153, 154

Tree, Lady, iii. 120; plays in A Woman's Reason, ii. 6; Henry IV, ii. 131; John Gabriel Borkman, iii. 129; Julius Cæsar, iii. 300; The Hobby Horse, iii. 142; The Silver Key, iii. 192

——, Sir Herbert Beerbohm, i. 73, 227; iii. 120, 341; as a producer and manager, i. 20, 274; ii. 68, 69; iii. 33, 98, 99, 135, 201, 251-4, 282, 303, 337; builds Her Majesty's Theatre, iii. 115-118, 199; plays in A Man's Shadow, iii. 260; Fedora, i. 139; Henry IV, ii. 130, 131, 132, 144; Julius Cæsar, iii. 299-301, 302; The Silver Key, iii. 191; Trilby, i. 241

TREE OF KNOWLEDGE, iii. 229, 232-5

TRELAWNY OF THE "WELLS," iii. 304-10, 340

Trial-scenes, i. 208, 287

TRILBY, i. 238-42; iii. 102, 222, 339

TRIPLE ALLIANCE, iii. 265

TRISTAN AND ISOLDE, i. 1, 2; iii. 30

TRIUMPH OF THE PHILISTINES, i. 121, 123-6, 192-5; iii. 339

TROILUS AND CRESSIDA, ii. 237

TROIS MOUSQUETAIRES, ii. 222

Trollope, Anthony, iii. 212

Troode, Charles, iii. 232

TRUE BLUE, ii. 79-85

Tuer, Andrew, iii. 306

TWELFTH NIGHT, i. 25, 26, 184, 189-91; iii. 215

TWO GENTLEMEN OF VERONA, i. 170-76, 199; ii. 284

TWO LITTLE VAGABONDS, ii. 202, 206-8

TWO ROSES, iii. 145

Tyars, Mr, ii. 200

Tyler, Odette, iii. 143

Tyndall, John, i. 195

——, Kate, ii. 208

Tyree, Elizabeth, ii. 181, 187, 188

Uhde, Fritz Karl Von, ii. 27; iii. 173

UNDER THE RED ROBE, ii. 222-8, 237; iii. 137, 158, 160, 222, 339

University graduates, ii. 140

VAGABOND KING, iii. 221, 225-8, 240

Valentine, Sydney, i. 119; ii. 228; iii. 264

Valli, Lulu, iii. 41

——, Valli, iii. 8, 40

Van Amburgh, iii. 378, 379

Vanbrugh, Irene, plays in Belle Belair, iii. 151; The Chili Widow, i. 215, 216; The Importance of Being Earnest, i. 43; The Liar, ii. 191; Trelawny of the "Wells," iii. 305, 307, 308

——, Violet, plays in Donna Diana, ii. 237-9; Monsieur de Paris, ii. 123, 130; The Chili Widow, i. 215; The Queen's Proctor, ii. 151; iii. 111, 121

Vanderfeldt, Mr, ii. 204, 206

Vandyk, Ernest, ii. 180

VANITY FAIR, i. 106-10

Vaughan, Kate, iii. 13

——, Susie, iii. 290, 291

Vaun, R., iii. 207, 214

Vegetarianism, iii. 386

VENICE PRESERVED, ii. 237

Venne, Lottie, ii. 54, 120, 220; iii. 214; plays in A White Elephant, ii. 265; Madame Mongodin, i. 269; The Home Secretary, i. 230 .

Vernon, W. H., i. 19; ii. 39, 284; plays in As You Like It, ii. 270; John Gabriel Borkman, iii. 123, 124, 127; Much Ado About Nothing, iii. 326; The Conquerors, iii. 367; The Divided Way, i. 261; The Prisoner of Zenda, ii. 12, 232; The Tree of Knowledge, iii. 233, 234

Vernon-Paget, Mrs Rose, iii. 169

Veronese, Paul, i. 82

Verse, the delivery of, i. 181

Vezin, Hermann, ii. 144, 238; plays in Mariana, iii. 58-9; Olivia, iii. 37-40; The Duchess of Coolgardie, ii. 206; The Happy Life, iii. 267; The Kiss of Delilah, ii. 266; The Tempest, iii. 163, 169

Vibart, Henry, ii. 238; iii. 311

VICAR OF WAKEFIELD, ii. 144; iii. 34, 36

Vice, iii. 191

Victor, Miss, i. 169; ii. 59; iii. 197, 368

Victoria, Queen, Jubilee of, iii. 177-8

Vienna Volkstheater Company, iii. 183

Views, one of the finest, iii. 116

Vikings at Helgeland, iii. 31

Villains, i. 273, 283, 284; ii. 3, 4, 5, 219, 220; iii. 332

Vincent, Mr, i. 262; ii. 270

Violin-playing, imaginary, iii. 372

Virtue, iii. 191

Vivian, Charles, iii. 376

Vogl, Heinrich, ii. 235

Volpé, Mr, i. 106, 209; ii. 220

Vos, J. C. de, i. 66-72

Voss, Richard, i. 70; iii. 139

Vulgarity in the theatre, i. 36; iii. 24, 25

Wagner, Richard, i. 1, 2, 35, 54, 94, 145, 158, 195, 206, 258, 279; ii. 95, 96, 142, 186, 198, 212, 243, 246, 247, 258; iii. 17, 22, 23, 26, 29, 30, 40, 71, 103, 155, 172, 173, 179, 188, 190, 194, 227, 228, 235, 238, 239, 309, 315, 322, 343, 345, 346, 347

Wales, Prince of, iii. 120

Walkley, Arthur, i. 54, 250; ii. 161, 218; iii. 32, 155, 157

WALKÜRE, DIE, i. 52; iii. 17

Waller, Lewis, i. 70, 263, 266; ii. 42, 237; iii. 120; plays in A Man's Shadow, iii. 260-61; A Woman's Reason, ii. 1, 5, 6, 137; An Ideal Husband, i. 12; Henry IV, ii. 129, 131; Julius

Cæsar, iii. 299, 300, 302; Settled Out of Court, iii. 164; The Home Secretary, i. 122, 123, 196, 230; The Manxman, i. 253; The Master Builder, i. 78; The matchmaker, ii. 137; The Silver Key, iii. 191; The Sin of St Hulda, ii. 100, 101, 137; The Sorrows of Satan, iii. 20

Wallis, Bertram, iii. 367

Walpole, Sir Robert, i. 52

Walton, George, iii. 104

WANDERER FROM VENUS, ii. 152

War, iii. 359

Ward, Charles E. D., i. 36-41

——, Fannie, ii. 121

——, Geneviève, iii. 32; plays in Cymbeline, ii. 200; John Gabriel Borkman, iii. 123, 128-129; Richard III, ii. 292

Warde, Mr, i. 204

Waring, Mrs, ii. 73

——, Herbert, i. 70, 261-2; ii. 11, 232, 237; plays in A Doll's House, iii. 131; Guy Domville, i. 8; The Master Builder, i. 78; The Triumph of the Philistines, i. 125, 126; Under the Red Robe, ii. 225-7

Warner, Charles, i. 220; iii. 370

Washerwomen, iii. 106

Watson, Dr Henry, iii. 82

Watts, Dr, ii. 206

——, Mr, ii. 90

——, G. F., iii. 70, 73, 74

Webster, Ben, i. 120; ii. 200

——, John, i. 130; ii. 182; iii. 370

Weir, Charles, iii. 41

Welch, James, iii. 63, 320; plays in A Human Sport, i. 112; Four Little Girls, iii. 196-7; John Gabriel Borkman, iii. 128; Man in the Street, ii. 52; Mariana,

iii. 62; My Friend the Prince, iii. 54; On 'Change, ii. 52; The Honorable Member, ii. 193; The Wild Duck, iii. 141; Widowers' Houses, ii. 193, 194

Wellington, Duke of, iii. 359

West, Mr, iii. 363

——, Florence, i. 12, 254; ii. 5

West End theatres, iii. 222-5

Westminster School plays, iii. 329

Weyman, Stanley, ii. 222-4

Wheeler, Frank, ii. 270; iii. 121

WHITE ELEPHANT, ii. 264, 265

WHITE HEATHER, iii. 215, 220, 242

WHITE KNIGHT, iii. 326-8

WHITE SILK DRESS, ii. 216, 220

Whitechapel Road, i. 141

WIDOWERS' HOUSES, ii. 193, 194

Wieland, Clara, i. 197

WILD DUCK, i. 165, 282; iii. 33, 98, 138, 139, 198

Wilde, Oscar, his plays, i. 6, 9-12, 41-4, 109, 229; ii. 217; iii. 337, 338, 347

Wilkes, John, i. 150

Will, iii. 377

WILL O' THE WISP, iii. 354

Willard, E. S., i. 227, 229, 263, 265; ii. 37, 66; iii. 185; plays in The Rise of Dick Halward, i. 227, 229; The Rogue's Comedy, ii. 106-8

Willes, Mr, iii. 206

Williams, D. J., ii. 131

——, Ettie, i. 215

——, Malcolm, iii. 361

Wills, W. G., his plays, i. 113, 114, 120; ii. 64; iii. 6, 34, 36

Wilson, H. Schütz, i. 129

WINTER'S TALE, iii. 147

WOMAN WHO DID, i. 52; iii. 36

WOMAN'S REASON, A, ii. 1-7, 220

Women—iii. 71, 174, 177, 178,

228, 248, 276, 289; and obse-
quiousness, iii. 159; Ibsen's
portrayal of, iii. 154; polyan-
drous and monogamous, iii.
50; the relations between men
and women, i. 108; the Woman
Question, ii. 170; iii. 2, 130
Wood, Mrs John, ii. 289; iii. 151,
188, 220; plays in The Rivals,
i. 254, 255; Vanity Fair, i. 106,
107, 110
Woodall, Mr, i. 53
Woodgate, Herbert, iii. 14, 20
Wordless plays, iii. 89
Working classes, iii. 165
Worthing, Frank, i. 167, 175
Wotton, Tom S., iii. 1
Wright, Mrs Theodore, iii. 179,
180, 182; plays in For the
Honour of the Family, iii. 169;
Ghosts, iii. 372; Salvê, i. 68, 71

Wyatt, Frank, ii. 208; iii. 214
Wyes, William, ii. 121; iii. 320
Wyndham, Sir Charles, i. 33, 210;
ii. 107, 122, 123, 124; iii. 7,
197, 198, 338; as a producer
and manager, iii. 32, 59, 185;
plays in Pink Dominos, ii. 120;
Rosemary, ii. 137, 138; The
Home Secretary, i. 121-3, 196,
230; The Physician, iii. 91, 96;
The Squire of Dames, i. 242,
243

Yardley, W., i. 106
YASHMAK, THE, iii. 97, 104
Yates, Edmund, i. 89; ii. 174
Yohe, May, ii. 162-5
Yorke, Oswald, i. 210; ii. 156,
206
Young, Margaret, iii. 259
Youth and age, i. 151

THE END